State Terrorism in Latin America

State Terrorism in Latin America

Chile, Argentina, and International Human Rights

Thomas C. Wright

ROWMAN & LITTLEFIELD PUBLISHERS, INC.
Lanham • Boulder • New York • Toronto • Plymouth, UK

ROWMAN & LITTLEFIELD PUBLISHERS, INC.

Published in the United States of America
by Rowman & Littlefield Publishers, Inc.
A wholly owned subsidary of The Rowman & Littlefield Publishing Group, Inc.
4501 Forbes Boulevard, Suite 200, Lanham, Maryland 20706
www.rowmanlittlefield.com

Estover Road
Plymouth PL6 7PY
United Kingdom

British Library Cataloguing in Publication Information Available

Library of Congress Cataloging-in-Publication Data

Wright, Thomas C.
 State terrorism in Latin America : Chile, Argentina, and international human rights /
Thomas C. Wright.
    p. cm. — (Latin American silhouettes)
 Includes bibliographical references and index.
 ISBN-13: 978-0-7425-3720-0 (cloth : alk. paper)
 ISBN-10: 0-7425-3720-X (cloth : alk. paper)
 ISBN-13: 978-0-7425-3721-7 (pbk. : alk. paper)
 ISBN-10: 0-7425-3721-8 (pbk. : alk. paper)
  1. State-sponsored terrorism—Chile. 2. State-sponsored terrorism—Argentina. 3.
Human rights—Chile. 4. Human rights—Argentina. I. Title.
 HV6322.3.C5W75 2007
 982.06'4—dc22

2006027745

Printed in the United States of America

⊗™ The paper used in this publication meets the minimum requirements of American National Standard for Information Sciences—Permanence of Paper for Printed Library Materials, ANSI/NISO Z39.48-1992.

~

Contents

v

Acknowledgments

The roots of this book go back to September 1993, when a man I had recently met invited me to his Santiago home for a social gathering. As the typically lengthy Chilean dinner progressed, I became more and more intrigued with the assembled party. Except for me, all were *retornados*, former exiles forced out of Chile during the Pinochet dictatorship. My first thanks, then, go to Rody Oñate for his friendship, for introducing me in a personal way to the theme of state terrorism and human rights, and for coauthoring a book on Chilean exile.

I subsequently made the decision to write more about Latin America's human rights crisis during a 2000 visit to El Salvador, where I was deeply moved by the museum dedicated to the six Jesuits, their housekeeper, and her daughter who were brutally murdered by a death squad in 1989. That museum on the grounds of the Universidad Centroamericana José Simeón Cañas in San Salvador—so distant from my Chilean encounter with state terrorism and human rights—motivated me to delve further into the dark side of Latin America in the 1970s and 1980s. I thank my former student Kevin Baltz for the introduction to El Salvador and to the museum.

The research for this book was supported by a sabbatical leave granted by the University of Nevada, Las Vegas. I thank the university for the sabbatical and for travel funding.

This project could not have been done without important contributions by many people on three continents. I am grateful to everyone who granted my requests for interviews, all of whom are listed in the bibliography.

In Santiago, Nancy Guzmán, María Paz Vergara, Verónica Reyna, and José Zalaquett offered invaluable assistance and insights. The staffs of two important research centers, the Fundación de Documentación y Archivo de la Vicaría de la Solidaridad and the Fundación de Ayuda Social de las Iglesias Cristianas (FASIC), were extremely accommodating.

In Buenos Aires, Dr. Agustín and Graciela Colombo were my link to the world of the families of the disappeared. I thank them and my colleague Douglas Unger for introducing me to them. Patricia Valdéz selflessly shared her knowledge and her contacts. Special thanks go also to Patrick Rice, María Laura Guembe, Ilda Micucci, and Marta Vásquez. Additionally, I am deeply indebted to the staffs of the Centro de Estudios Legales y Sociales (CELS) and Memoria Abierta.

In Madrid, Carlos Slepoy, Carlos Castresana, and Marcela Prádenas were particularly helpful during the early stages of my research.

My heartfelt thanks go to Marjorie Agosín, Raquel Aldana, Alison Brysk, Joseph A. Fry, Garry Leech, Jerry L. Simich, John C. Super, Dina Titus, and John S. Wright Jr. for reading and critiquing the manuscript. Their input greatly improved the product. Series coeditors Judith Ewell and William Beezley were generous with their time and advice. Susan McEachern of Rowman & Littlefield offered guidance and support. Mary Wammack and Erin Buck provided much-needed technical assistance.

Above all, I am indebted to my wife, companion, and colleague, Dina Titus, whose acumen, critical eye, and encouragement I relied on throughout this book project.

~

Acronyms

AAA	Alianza Anticomunista Argentina (Argentine Anticommunist Alliance)
AFDD	Agrupación de Familiares de Detenidos Desaparecidos (Group of Families of Detained Disappeared) (Chile)
APDH	Asamblea Permanente por los Derechos Humanos (Permanent Assembly for Human Rights) (Argentina)
CELS	Centro de Estudios Legales y Sociales (Center for Legal and Social Studies) (Argentina)
CEMIDA	Centro de Militares para la Democracia Argentina (Center of Military Personnel for Argentine Democracy)
CNI	Central Nacional de Informaciones (National Information Center) (Chile)
CONADEP	Comisión Nacional sobre la Desaparición de Personas (National Commission on the Disappearance of Persons) (Argentina)
DINA	Dirección Nacional de Inteligencia (National Directorate of Intelligence) (Chile)
ERP	Ejército Revolucionario del Pueblo (People's Revolutionary Army) (Argentina)
FASIC	Fundación de Ayuda Social de las Iglesias Cristianas (Social Aid Foundation of the Christian Churches) (Chile)
FPMR	Frente Patriótico Manuel Rodríguez (Manuel Rodríguez Patriotic Front) (Chile)

ICC   International Criminal Court
MIR   Movimiento de Izquierda Revolucionaria (Movement of
             the Revolutionary Left) (Chile)
NGO   Nongovernmental organization
OAS   Organization of American States
PPD   Partido por la Democracia (Party for Democracy) (Chile)
RN   Renovación Nacional (National Renovation Party) (Chile)
SERPAJ   Servicio de Paz y Justicia (Peace and Justice Service) (Ar-
             gentina)
UDI   Unión Democrática Independiente (Independent Demo-
             cratic Union Party) (Chile)
UN   United Nations
UP   Unidad Popular (Popular Unity Coalition) (Chile)

~

Introduction

Army patrols attack peasant villages, massacring men, women, children, and infants. Under cover of curfew, secret police hunt down members of groups designated as enemies of the government. Prisoners are systematically tortured, brought to the edge of death, and revived to be tortured again. Kidnapped persons, following extensive torture, are thrown alive into the ocean from helicopters. Pregnant women are killed after delivering babies in secret detention centers; the babies are given to couples favored by the regime to raise as their own. Death squads patrol city streets and country roads, casually killing at will. Enemies of the regime fearfully board airplanes, leaving behind family and country, heading to unknown destinations and lives in exile. These are not scenes dreamed up by a perverse imagination, nor are they stories of Nazi atrocities or Cambodian killing fields, but glimpses of Latin America in the 1970s and 1980s.

These two decades of Latin American history were characterized by an unprecedented wave of political repression and a severe crisis of human rights. While some areas were spared the more extreme forms of repression, all experienced at least some fallout from a region-wide war against the left conducted by military and police forces and backed by right-wing politicians, substantial numbers of the countries' citizens, and, during most of the period, by the U.S. government. Some victims of the repression were targeted; many were collateral damage; all were part of the huge toll of Latin America's human rights crisis.

The period of repression came less than two decades after Latin America had reached a milestone in its quest for democracy. During the 1950s, a period that one scholar called "the twilight of the tyrants," dictators such as Argentina's Juan Perón, Peru's Manuel Odría, Venezuela's Marcos Pérez Jiménez, and Colombia's Gustavo Rojas Pinilla relinquished power, voluntarily or otherwise; by 1958, only a few dictators survived, all in small and backward countries accounting for less than 10 percent of Latin America's population.[1] Yet, by 1976, the political complexion of Latin America had changed thoroughly: Only a handful of countries and a minority of the region's population had eluded a resurgence of military rule.[2] Several of the new authoritarian governments exercised repression so severe as to make dictators of earlier periods seem benign. These were the regimes that institutionalized state terrorism.

This book examines the impact of state terrorism on human rights in Latin America in the 1970s and 1980s. It also looks at the legacies of state terrorism that continue to affect Latin America today. It focuses on civil and political rights, which are the rights central to the Western tradition and those embedded in the U.S. Constitution's Bill of Rights. But in some countries, economic and social rights of large segments of the population—the rights to work, health care, and education, in short, the right to a decent quality of life—were eviscerated through policies imposed by military rulers seeking to recast their countries' economic models by force.

Owing to the size limitations of a monograph, a country-by-country study of state terrorism and human rights would necessarily be superficial. My approach is to focus on two countries, Chile and Argentina, in order to provide an in-depth examination informed by comparative analysis. Chile was under a state terrorist regime from 1973 to 1990, Argentina from 1976 to 1983. Both countries continue to struggle with the legacies of state terrorism.

I do not claim that state terrorism and its legacies in Chile and Argentina were typical of the broader Latin American experience with state terrorism. Indeed, each country's history is unique. More people died in Guatemala, El Salvador, and Peru than in Argentina or Chile, while the state killed fewer in Brazil and Uruguay. The regimes in Chile, Argentina, Uruguay, and Brazil primarily targeted real or presumed political enemies, while in Guatemala, El Salvador, and Peru, the regimes went beyond political considerations to include class and racial targeting, directed especially at peasants (*campesinos*) and Indians. The terrorist governments of El Salvador, Peru, and Argentina faced serious insurrections, while those of Brazil, Uruguay, and Chile did not; in Guatemala, there was a long-smoldering but comparatively weak insurrection. Military governments conducted the terrorism in Chile, Argentina, Uruguay, and Brazil, while civilian administrations carried out or acquiesced in terrorism in Peru, El Salvador, and Guatemala. Finally, countries such as

Paraguay, Bolivia, Honduras, and even Mexico experienced heightened repression in the 1970s and 1980s that included torture, murder, and disappearance, but the repression there was not as widely and systematically applied as it was in several other countries.

Despite the variations from country to country, the Argentine and Chilean cases illuminate the essential elements of Latin America's human rights crisis. The military governments of these two countries constructed the most powerful and sophisticated apparatuses of repression found anywhere, yet they also engaged in the unvarnished brutality characteristic of state terrorism in Central America. They had the most ambitious agendas of any of the state terrorist regimes: the eradication of the left in their countries and, particularly in Chile, the forced introduction of a new economic model. In response to state terrorism, Chile and Argentina developed the largest, most diverse, and most vigorous and persistent human rights movements in Latin America. As a result of the latter, these two countries have undergone the most complex and prolonged period of reckoning with state terrorism and its legacies—a process that is ongoing. Finally, the experiences of both Argentina and Chile in dealing with past grave human rights violations have resonated around the world and helped to shape contemporary international human rights.

The study of state terrorism and its legacies in Latin America has progressed through several overlapping stages. The first task was to reconstruct what happened during the period of repression. Since governments controlled or censored the mass media, filmmaking, and book publishing, the standard means of studying recent history are of little value for discerning the reality of state terrorism, although they are important for understanding the official version of the history of that period. Testimonial literature by survivors of exile, prison, torture, and death camps is a valuable source of information. Memoirs and other writings by the repressors themselves provide views that justify repression and couch it in terms of patriotic duty. The publications of both international and domestic human rights organizations and the reports of truth commissions established after the dictatorships had ended are essential sources.[3]

The legacies of state terrorism have also been extensively studied. Much has been written about the politics of transitional justice: the contest between the advocates of truth and justice who sought to hold the military accountable for their terrorist acts and the military and their supporters who insisted on impunity for their role in the repression. Reckoning with crimes against human rights has been a public process, and information is readily available from all sides of the debate. Particular moments, especially the

1985 trial of the former rulers of the Argentine terrorist state and the 1998 arrest in London of former Chilean dictator Augusto C. Pinochet, focused the world's attention on the politics of transitional justice. A large body of journalistic and academic literature focuses on the period from the end of state terrorism to the present.

More recently, researchers' attention has turned to the politics of memory. This scholarship examines the struggle between two versions of truth and history: the military's account of what happened during what it considers a justified and patriotic war on Marxism and subversion, and the version put forth by victims and human rights organizations which contends that the alleged wars did not take place and that state terrorism was an unjustifiable assault on human rights. Since they controlled and shaped the truth while in power, the former repressors advocate forgetting, burying the past, and moving ahead with individual and national lives so that their truth can remain intact. The other side believes that learning all the facts that can be recovered about the period of state terrorism is essential to constructing a culture of human rights that will deter potential repressors in the future. In effect, memory politics is a struggle over how national history will be taught and understood, and thus over how future generations will think and act.[4]

This book incorporates the above approaches to Latin America's human rights crisis and its legacies. It seeks to establish what happened, and why, during the period of state terrorism in Chile and Argentina. It examines the transition from military to civilian rule, focusing on the balance between impunity and justice that kept these two societies deeply divided and prevented national reconciliation. It also examines the battles over the correct interpretation of the period of state terrorism—the creation, contestation, and preservation of memory.

In addition to the above, this book focuses on the linkages between state terrorism in Chile and Argentina, including its legacies, and international human rights. Some authors refer to the body of international human rights as the "international human rights regime." After 1973, when the Chilean military coup launched the transformation of the international human rights regime from a statement of principles into an active force on the world scene, we can also refer to the "international human rights lobby." The international human rights regime/lobby consists of international treaties, covenants, and declarations; domestic and international human rights organizations, both intergovernmental and nongovernmental (NGOs); jurisprudence; and practice. It also includes a shifting cast of actors such as foundations, unions, church and student groups, governments, and other organizations for which human rights is not the primary raison d'être, but which engage in human rights issues periodically and sometimes decisively.

I will argue that the international human rights regime and state terrorism in Argentina and Chile, including its legacies, have had a reciprocal relationship, each influencing and being influenced by the other, from 1973 to the present. When the Chilean and Argentine military dictatorships set out to eradicate the political left in their countries, domestic human rights organizations were few or nonexistent, and the international human rights regime was too weak to prevent state terrorism. Nonetheless, by gathering and disseminating information on torture, murder, and disappearance in those countries, the existing international organizations and the domestic human rights movements that developed in response to the repression caused a strong negative reaction in world opinion. This in turn led to the strengthening of international human rights from the 1970s on. As one author puts it, "The Chilean dictatorship and its counterparts in the Southern Cone, ironically, activated the dormant system of [human rights] protections with implications that extend beyond Chile's tragic human rights calamity."[5]

After the end of state terrorism in Argentina and Chile, the domestic human rights movements and international organizations lacked the power to bring human rights violators to justice for their crimes against human rights, except temporarily in Argentina. But by the late 1990s, as international human rights norms, institutions, and jurisprudence continued to evolve and domestic human rights movements remained tenaciously engaged, impunity began to crack. Early in the twenty-first century, judges in Argentina and Chile routinely investigate, try, and sentence former practitioners of state terrorism. While the international human rights regime was incapable of preventing state terrorism in Chile and Argentina, today it plays a central role in bringing to justice the human rights violators who so confidently detained, tortured, exiled, murdered, and disappeared their fellow citizens in the name of a holy crusade against Marxism and subversion.

Part I of this book examines the human rights revolution that unfolded from World War II to the present, the rise of state terrorism, and Latin America's human rights crisis of the 1970s and 1980s. Part II discusses the reasons for the establishment of state terrorist regimes in Chile and Argentina and analyzes the workings of state terrorism within the framework of "dirty wars." Part III examines transitional justice in both countries and traces the roles of domestic and international actors in the eventual breakdown of impunity for crimes against human rights. The conclusion reviews the reciprocal relationship between state terrorism and its legacies in Chile and Argentina and the international human rights regime.

Notes

1. Tad Szulc, *Twilight of the Tyrants* (New York: Holt, 1959).

2. In a few countries, notably El Salvador and Guatemala, civilian institutions remained in place but were subservient to the military.

3. Examples of these kinds of sources and those mentioned in the following two paragraphs are found throughout the book. Therefore I have not listed them here.

4. Note that the military hierarchies in Argentina and Chile have recently distanced themselves from this hard-line interpretation of the dictatorships. See chapters 5 and 6.

5. Mark Ensalaco, *Chile under Pinochet: Recovering the Truth* (Philadelphia: University of Pennsylvania Press, 2000), 68.

PART ONE

HUMAN RIGHTS, STATE TERRORISM, AND LATIN AMERICA

CHAPTER ONE

~

The Human Rights Revolution

Wars of aggression, genocide, mass rape, torture, disappearances, forced removals, and innumerable other human rights violations have occurred repeatedly in the years since Justice Robert Jackson announced that the Nuremberg trials would "do away with domestic tyranny and violence and aggression by those in power against the rights of their own people."

—Judge Richard J. Goldstone, former chief prosecutor of the international criminal tribunals for the former Yugoslavia and Rwanda[1]

Each government that confronts a subversive threat must choose, on the one hand, the path of respect for the rule of law, or, on the other hand, the descent into state terrorism.

—Inter-American Commission on Human Rights[2]

State terrorism and grave human rights violations were institutionalized in Chile and Argentina a mere quarter century after Nazi officials were convicted of war crimes and crimes against humanity at the Nuremberg trials. In reaction to the Holocaust and other wartime atrocities, efforts had begun in the aftermath of World War II to prevent repetitions of those experiences by articulating a framework of restrictions on state power over individuals. The Chilean and Argentine military dictatorships, then, were anachronisms—throwbacks to a time before the Universal Declaration of Human Rights had spelled out the civil and political rights, as well as economic, social, and cultural rights, pertaining to all humankind. These two countries, however, were far from exceptional: from the 1960s into the 1990s, regimes around the world routinely tortured and murdered their citizens, and a few even conducted campaigns of genocide reminiscent of the one that had sparked the search for a world free of crimes against humanity. Despite recent progress in Latin America and the world, institutionalized human rights violations have continued into the new millennium.

Establishing Universal Standards

Between the end of World War II in 1945 and the inauguration of the International Criminal Court in 2003, concepts and practices of human rights underwent revolutionary change. Before 1945, the term "human rights" was virtually absent from the lexicon. Few organizations existed in any country to promote and protect human rights. There were no internationally accepted standards for human rights. Today, references to human rights pervade the media. Countless books, articles, reports, dissertations, and law theses appear annually on the multifaceted topic of human rights, while specialized journals explore the theory and practice of human rights. Numerous declarations and conventions articulate internationally recognized standards for human rights, and thousands of general and specialized government entities, international agencies, and NGOs monitor governments' compliance with these standards and promote human rights in general. Courts around the world increasingly translate lofty principles of human rights into concrete, enforceable law.

The human rights revolution unfolded in three overlapping stages. First, the early post–World War II years were a time of discussion and establishment of standards for human rights that were declared to be universal. This process has continued to the present, as international bodies adopt additional declarations and individual states ratify protocols expanding the realm of human rights deemed worthy of protection.[3] Second, between the late 1950s and the 1970s, international agencies and NGOs adopted a series of mechanisms designed to monitor individual states' compliance with the standards adopted earlier and those to be ratified in the future. Additional monitoring entities have been formed in subsequent decades. Third, in the last quarter century, a number of steps have been taken toward enforcement of human rights norms as international law began to recognize a duty, not limited by national borders, to prosecute violators of human rights. The opening of the International Criminal Court in 2003 gave the world its first permanent tribunal for prosecution of crimes against human rights, culminating a half-century-long process of turning "moral issues into a legally binding framework."[4]

Prior to the post–World War II years, human rights were the business of individual states. In some countries, individual liberties were enshrined in constitutions and duly enforced. In others, human rights were not acknowledged at all. Between the extremes, many states guaranteed human rights but routinely trampled or enforced them selectively. The modern world order is premised on the notion of the sovereignty of national states; so, to cite only a few twentieth-century cases, when the Turkish government slaughtered hundreds of thousands of Armenians during World War I, the government of El Salvador massacred up to thirty thousand peasants in 1932, and Stalin's regime killed millions through forced starvation and political purges, international criticisms of these actions carried little weight.[5] Still lacking were international standards of human rights, agencies for monitoring compliance with those standards, and instruments for sanctioning governments and individuals who violated human rights.

It was only after World War II that human rights took center stage and began to enter the corpus of international law. In the view of the victorious Allies, trials for the war crimes already encoded in international conventions and treaties would be insufficient to deal with the unspeakably vile acts committed outside the framework of war. Thus, at the Nuremberg trials, Nazi leaders were prosecuted not only for war crimes but also on the novel charge of crimes against humanity, which the charter of the International Military Tribunal defined as "murder, extermination, enslavement, deportation, imprisonment, torture, rape, or other inhumane acts committed against any civilian population, or persecutions on political, racial, or religious grounds whether or not in violation of domestic law of the country where perpetrated."[6] In pursuit of a future free of holocausts, the United Nations (UN) adopted the Convention on the Prevention and Punishment of the Crime of Genocide in 1948. And in a new effort to curb the excesses inherent in warfare, the international community approved the Geneva Conventions in 1949.

The Organization of American States (OAS), founded in 1948 as the successor to the International Union of American Republics (1889) and the Pan American Union (1910), was the first international organization to articulate transnational human rights standards. Adopted in May 1948, the American Declaration of the Rights and Duties of Man asserted in its preamble that "the essential rights of man are not derived from the fact that he is a national of a certain state, but are based upon attributes of his human personality"; it continued, "the international protection of the rights of man should be the principal guide of an evolving American law." The document reflected the Western tradition of individual liberties vis-à-vis the state— rights of expression, assembly, and property; freedom of religion; freedom from arbitrary detention; and the right to a fair trial. However, it also articulated some progressive social and economic views, including the rights to work, leisure, social security, and a free education through the primary level. Its purview, of course, was the people of the OAS member states.[7]

Founded in 1945, the UN adopted a set of human rights standards for the world, the Universal Declaration of Human Rights, on December 10, 1948. While the Universal Declaration described an ideal world, far from the grim realities of colonialism, discrimination, and repression, it set a global standard for human rights for the first time in history. The Universal Declaration represented a compromise between the United States and its Western allies, on one hand, and the Soviet Union and its allies on the other, blocs of countries squaring off in the early stages of the Cold War. The Western tradition was represented in the sections on civil liberties and political rights, including the right to a democratically elected government. The values of the socialist bloc were reflected in articles guaranteeing work, social security, and the all-encompassing "standard of living adequate for . . . health and well-being . . . including food, clothing, housing and medical care and necessary social services, and the right to security in the event of unemployment, sickness, disability, widowhood, old age or other lack of livelihood" (article 25). Most of the Western democracies blinked while endorsing the social and economic provisions; nor did the leading Western countries intend to implement civil and political rights in the colonies that they still possessed. The Communist countries, on the other hand, certainly did not plan to install individual rights in states governed by the dictatorship of the proletariat. Nonetheless, the reaction against the Holocaust and war crimes was so powerful that UN member countries favored adopting a lofty albeit unwieldy and unenforceable set of principles rather than ignoring the human rights question altogether.[8]

Monitoring Human Rights

The human rights revolution proceeded slowly from the initial stage of standard setting to the second phase of monitoring compliance with those standards. The greatest obstacle to effective monitoring was the reluctance of individual states to submit to international scrutiny and jurisdiction. Doing so, many believed, would constitute a breach of national sovereignty and would subject them to pressures for change. Indeed, the UN charter specifically prohibits the institution from intervening "in matters which are essentially within the domestic jurisdiction of any state" (chapter 1, article 2.7). The OAS charter (chapter 4) contains similar language. Thus, when monitoring agencies were established, they were created with checks and balances, slow and unwieldy procedures, and confidentiality about their work. Commonly, countries under investigation for human rights violations could not be publicly named. Despite these obstacles to efficient operation, several countries have failed to ratify important international human rights treaties and covenants. The United States has ratified very few.[9]

Unencumbered by the ideological and military rivalry that polarized the UN, the OAS acted first to implement the civil and political rights articulated in its American Declaration of the Rights and Duties of Man.[10] In 1959, it established the Inter-American Commission on Human Rights, an agency charged with developing awareness of human rights, issuing relevant reports, fielding individual complaints, and conducting on-site investigations in any OAS member country. Unlike the UN's Human Rights Commission, the Inter-American Commission has a staff of professionals that operates semi-independently of the OAS General Assembly. Amendments to the Inter-American Commission on Human Rights charter, which took effect in 1970, enhanced the agency's authority. The American Convention on Human Rights, an agreement designed to flesh out the concepts of the American Declaration and bind member states to observe them, was approved in 1969 and, after obtaining sufficient ratifications, entered into force in 1978. The Inter-American Institute of Human Rights was established in 1980 to educate and train the population—in particular, judges and law enforcement agents—in human rights. The Inter-American Court of Human Rights has functioned in San José, Costa Rica, since 1980. This body is empowered to issue advisory opinions on charges brought before it and to deliver binding judgments in cases where the accused government has ratified the convention accepting its jurisdiction.[11]

Already under way at the signing of the Universal Declaration, the Cold War increasingly divided the world and set back implementation of the UN's human rights agenda. It was only in 1966 that the covenants were readied to allow willing states to endorse the Universal Declaration and bind themselves to its terms, and to establish mechanisms to monitor compliance. Reflecting Cold War reality, the provisions of the Universal Declaration were divided into two covenants: one on civil and political rights, and the other on economic, social, and cultural rights, allowing governments to embrace either the entire set of human rights standards or the one that was more compatible with their cultures. Both covenants were ratified by the requisite number of countries and went into force in 1976.[12]

The UN was also slow to establish effective human rights monitoring because each side was unwilling to give the other a propaganda weapon. It was not until 1967 that the UN's chief monitoring agency, the Human Rights Commission, received authorization to discuss violations in specific countries. In 1970, it was empowered to investigate complaints that suggested "a consistent pattern of gross and reliably attested violations of human rights and fundamental freedoms."[13] Despite the enhancement of its investigative powers, the Human Rights Commission continued to be shackled by requirements of confidentiality and procedural obstacles to timely involvement. Its effectiveness was also limited by the fact that its membership was elected by the UN General Assembly, and countries with poor human rights records often acquired seats on the Human Rights Commission in order to shield themselves from scrutiny and sanction.[14]

Despite these impediments, the UN's monitoring capacity gradually improved. By the 1970s, the Human Rights Commission was establishing working groups on specific countries and on specific classes of human rights violations. It also appointed country rapporteurs—individual experts assigned to conduct on-site investigations in countries suspected of systematic gross violations. The institutionalized human rights violations in Chile and Argentina were central to these important steps taken to strengthen monitoring. The creation of the position of United Nations High Commissioner for Human Rights in 1993 gave the UN's human rights commitment a higher profile.[15]

Paralleling the development of international organizations' monitoring agencies was the rise of NGOs with international purviews. Some, such as the International Commission of Jurists, founded in 1952 and based in Geneva, and the Lawyers Committee for Human Rights, founded in 1978 and headquartered in New York, are specialized in membership and function. The most visible human rights NGO was, and still is, Amnesty International, founded in London in 1961. Operating with a large membership base, Amnesty International works to secure the liberty of individual prisoners of conscience, monitors human rights conditions around the world, and issues annual reports and special reports as needed. Amnesty International won the Nobel Peace Prize in 1977. Human Rights Watch, founded in 1978, investigates and publicizes human rights violations and brings pressure against offending governments. In 1981, it established the first of its regional divisions, Americas Watch, in response to the spread of repression and state terrorism from South to Central America.[16]

Amnesty International and Human Rights Watch have been constantly engaged in Latin America since their founding. Unfettered by the constraints and slow pace inherent in intergovernmental agencies, they have been scrupulous and aggressive in their monitoring work. Because their reports are public and widely circulated, Amnesty International and Human

Rights Watch have been able to pressure the intergovernmental agencies to respond to flagrant cases of human rights violations.

The establishment of monitoring agencies was a significant step forward in developing the international human rights framework. With the monitoring in place, world opinion could be informed of violations; governments could respond as they desired, or not respond at all; and domestic human rights organizations could gain information, support, and legitimacy from the work of the international agencies. Yet, in the 1970s, when state terrorism appeared in Latin America, the international human rights regime was incomplete and virtually untested.

New Challenges to Human Rights

Even as the monitoring system took shape and decolonization neared completion in Asia, Africa, and the Caribbean, a number of events severely challenged the progress that the UN, the OAS, and the NGOs had made. The brutality of the South African system of apartheid penetrated the international consciousness with the 1960 Sharpeville massacre. The Vietnam War acquainted a worldwide TV audience with atrocities against noncombatants. Civil and international wars in Africa involving Angola, Sudan, Congo, Nigeria, Ethiopia, Eritrea, and other countries were conducted with little regard to the established rules of war. Repressive regimes that routinely violated human rights came to power in Africa, Asia, Latin America, and Greece. The genocide of up to half a million Indonesians in 1965–1966 and nearly two million Cambodians, perpetrated by the Khmer Rouge between 1975 and 1979, shocked the world. In the 1990s, atrocities in Kosovo and East Timor and the genocides in the ex-Yugoslavia and Rwanda were further reminders of the growing gap between principle and practice in the human rights sphere. These developments called into question the value of the numerous human rights declarations and treaties adopted since World War II.[17]

Latin America was one of the areas most deeply affected by repression during the second phase of the human rights revolution. From the early 1960s into the early 1980s, despite widespread ratification of UN and OAS human rights instruments, democratically elected governments were replaced by military dictatorships, or, in some cases, the elected governments themselves embraced repression of their citizenry. By the mid-1970s, repression in several countries had risen to the level of state terrorism.

State terrorism is one of two forms of terrorism, the other being terrorism against the state. In the early twenty-first century, it is the latter that pervades the public consciousness. It is the attacks on civilians and state agents by terrorist groups such as the Irish Republican Army (IRA), the Basque Euskadi ta Askatasuna (ETA, Basque Homeland and Freedom), Hamas, and more recently Al Qaeda that make the news and rivet attention on terrorism. After the experience of terrorism at home in the 1995 Oklahoma City bombing and the 2001 attacks on the World Trade Center and the Pentagon, Americans' perception of terrorism as the work of antistate groups has been strengthened.

The two forms of terrorism share essential characteristics. At the risk of appearing arbitrary, let us borrow, from among the thousands of definitions of terrorism devised by academics, journalists, and policy makers, one of the broader, more inclusive ones.[18] In the words of Frederick H. Gareau, "Terrorism consists of deliberate acts of a physical and/or psychological nature perpetrated on select groups of victims. Its intent is to mold the thinking and behavior not only of these targeted groups, but more importantly, of larger sectors of society that identify [with] or share the view and aspirations of the targeted groups or who might easily be led to do so. The intent of the terrorists is to intimidate or coerce both groups by causing them intense fear, anxiety, apprehension, panic, dread, and/or horror."[19] Terrorism against the state is designed to force the government to modify its policies, to overthrow the government, or even to destroy the state. The intent of terrorism by the state is to eliminate some or all of the people who are considered actual or potential enemies of the regime, and to marginalize those not eliminated through the fear that terrorism instills.

The results of terrorism by the IRA, ETA, Hamas, Timothy McVeigh, and Al Qaeda are terrible and lamentable; yet none has been entirely successful in forcing the desired changes in government policy, and none has come even close to destroying a state. By contrast, state terrorism has taken huge tolls in human life and has succeeded in its purpose of eliminating or marginalizing the regime's enemies. The greatest mass killings of civilians in the twentieth century were conducted by state terrorist regimes: Stalin's forced starvation and purges and Hitler's Holocaust killed millions of people and intimidated potential enemies into silence and passivity. The government that marshals the will and resources to defeat terrorism or minimize its impact has a strong possibility of success; it is much more difficult to oppose terrorism by the state, particularly without outside aid.

A look at human rights under the two varieties of terrorism can be instructive. Countries living under threat of antistate terrorism may restrict human rights, especially civil liberties such as freedom of speech and press and habeas corpus, as a tactic for fighting terrorism. Their governments may modify or suspend constitutional protections that appear to give the terrorists an advantage.

This lesson has been learned in the United States where, since September 11, 2001, civil libertarians and ordinary citizens alike have been concerned that, under the terms of the Patriot Act, protections traditionally afforded by the Bill of Rights have been eroded in the name of fighting terrorism. They fear that ordering or condoning interrogation techniques that involve torture, although directed at the "enemy," may erode the country's moral values and weaken standards of conduct for the state's treatment of its own citizens.[20]

While terrorism against the state may negatively affect human rights, state terrorism extinguishes them. When the state employs terrorism as a means of ruling, it recognizes no constraints on its power to deal with individuals and groups it considers the enemy or potential enemy and with other persons who may accidentally run afoul of the authorities. A terrorist state may tolerate some elements of constitutional rule, so long as these do not interfere with its arbitrary use of power. Those people not considered enemies of or dangers to the regime may be well served by the criminal justice system and need not worry about their welfare and security. But should they cross the line or mistakenly be identified as a dissident or a potential subversive, nothing stands between the individual and the state.[21]

In Latin America, state terrorism in the 1970s and 1980s produced an unprecedented crisis of human rights. It systematically violated the human rights of millions of people. It took hundreds of thousands of lives and left millions of people grieving, often without the solace of having a body to bury and mourn. It left hundreds of thousands permanently scarred—emotionally and physically—by torture. It forced huge numbers of people to flee their countries for safety and spend years in exile. State terrorism made millions of people live with fear so acute that it paralyzed them. And it left legacies that still deeply divide the societies in which it was practiced.[22]

Among the legacies of state terrorism are the human rights movements that came into existence to fight repression. Today, whether large and dynamic or small and weak, these movements still search for truth about the period of severe repression and seek justice for the victims of human rights violations and for the families of those victims who perished. They foster preservation of the memory of state terrorism in many ways, in the mold of Holocaust commemoration and education. They lobby for measures of all kinds that may help to prevent a recurrence of the 1970s–1980s crisis, from human rights education to weeding out known repressors from military ranks and public office. In some countries, reckoning with the legacies of state terrorism is still central to national politics.[23]

Latin America's experience of state terrorism has seeped into the universal consciousness. Chile's secret police, the DINA (Dirección de Inteligencia

Nacional, the National Directorate of Intelligence); the emblematic Argentine human rights group, the Madres de Plaza de Mayo (Mothers of Plaza de Mayo); the Guatemalan Mayan Nobel Peace Laureate, Rigoberta Menchú; the assassination of Salvadoran archbishop Oscar Romero; and General Augusto Pinochet's arrest in London are remembered around the world. Latin America bequeathed the truth commission and the forensic anthropological team to the growing number of countries that have reckoned with past human rights violations. And revulsion at the practices of Latin American state terrorism contributed to the refinement of international human rights law, including conventions against torture and the disappearance of persons. In these and other ways, the Latin American experience was important to the development of the third, contemporary stage of international human rights.

The Contemporary International Human Rights Regime

The resurgence of war, repression reaching the level of state terrorism, ethnic cleansing, and genocide heightened the world's consciousness of human rights thanks in large part to the work of existing human rights monitoring organizations in publicizing the violations. In response, human rights organizations proliferated, and a number of additional international covenants were drawn up and ratified. In some countries, new legislation granted the courts jurisdiction over human rights crimes committed outside the countries' borders.[24] Intergovernmental agencies and NGOs pushed vigorously to influence domestic courts to accept new international jurisprudence and implement the provisions of the international human rights treaties that their governments had ratified; in some cases, governments have responded by explicitly incorporating the treaties into law or by even giving them constitutional standing.[25] These developments underpinned the third stage of the post–World War II revolution in human rights, a phase that one author calls "an era of institutionalization of international justice."[26]

Following Nuremberg precedents, the UN created special tribunals for prosecuting those accused of genocide in the former Yugoslavia and Rwanda. After improvising in those cases, the UN opened the International Criminal Court (ICC) at The Hague, Netherlands, in 2003. The new court is charged with rendering judgment on the types of offenses prosecuted at the Nuremberg and Tokyo Tribunals following World War II: war crimes, genocide, and crimes against humanity, a category that includes systematic acts such as murder, torture, and enforced disappearance against civilian populations. The ICC's authority is not retroactive. The body assumes jurisdiction if the country where the offenses occurred does not take responsibility; if the country is not a party to the Rome Statute of the ICC, the UN Security Council's recommendation must precede the court's involvement. The ICC works on the basis of the two key principles of the new international human rights jurisprudence: crimes against humanity cannot be amnestied, and the perpetrators of such crimes are subject to universal jurisdiction.[27]

The new international human rights regime is not lacking in critics. The United States under the George W. Bush administration has led the resistance to acceptance of the recent changes. It has argued that the execution of legitimate foreign policy could lead to indictments on charges of war crimes or crimes against humanity, such as those widely alleged to have been committed by former secretary of state Henry Kissinger through his roles in Vietnam and Latin America.[28] Bush rescinded the U.S. commitment to participate in the ICC made by his predecessor, President Bill Clinton, citing the potential peril to U.S. foreign policy initiatives involving armed force. The Bush administration vigorously pursued bilateral treaties with a number of countries to ensure that U.S. nationals are not delivered to the ICC. In 2002, it successfully pressured the UN Security Council to exempt U.S. peacekeepers from ICC jurisdiction for a year, with the option of annual renewal of the exemption. Under pressure from the Bush administration, Belgium in 2003 narrowed the scope of its law on universal jurisdiction. Clearly, Bush's unilateralism was intended to undermine the greatest step yet taken toward making international human rights treaties enforceable.[29]

These setbacks notwithstanding, the international constellation of treaties, institutions, jurisprudence, and practice constructed over the course of half a century, along with the domestic human rights movements around the world, has begun to undermine the impunity of human rights violators. The amnesties that state terrorist regimes gave themselves upon returning governance to civilians have, in some countries, become ineffective in protecting repressors against prosecution. The 1998 arrest in London of former Chilean dictator General Augusto C. Pinochet on human rights charges gave the world an instant education on this shift in international norms. The 2003 extradition of former Argentine naval officer Ricardo Miguel Cavallo from Mexico to Spain on charges of crimes in Argentina—the first case in which a person was sent from one country to trial in a second for human rights crimes committed in a third—further underscored the recent changes in international jurisprudence.[30] In 2005, the ICC began investigating human rights violations in the Darfur region of Sudan, a possible prelude to prosecution; later that year it issued its first indictments, against the rebel Lord's Resistance Army in Uganda.[31] If U.S. or other opposition to an effective international human rights regime does not slow this momentum, a new world order with effective deterrents to crimes against humanity and genocide may have a chance to develop. In such an ideal world, human rights nightmares such as those endured in Latin America in the 1970s and 1980s would be a thing of the past.

Notes

1. Richard J. Goldstone, "Advancing the Cause of Human Rights: The Need for Justice and Accountability," in *Realizing Human Rights: Moving from Inspiration to Impact*, ed. Samantha Power and Graham Allison (New York: St. Martin's Press, 2000), 196.

2. Inter-American Commission on Human Rights, *Report on the Situation of Human Rights in Argentina* (Washington, DC: Organization of American States, 1980), 27.

3. For a list of UN declarations, conventions, and treaties regarding human rights, see the website of the UN High Commissioner for Human Rights: www.unhchr.ch.

4. The late Sergio Vieira de Mello, UN High Commissioner for Human Rights, used this terminology in his "Message of the High Commissioner on Human Rights Day, December 10, 2002," mimeo. See Paul Gordon Lauren, *The Evolution of International Human Rights: Visions Seen*, 2nd ed. (Philadelphia: University of Pennsylvania Press, 2003); Jack Donnelly, *Universal Human Rights in Theory and Practice*, 2nd ed. (Ithaca, NY: Cornell University Press, 2003); and Geoffrey Robertson, *Crimes against Humanity: The Struggle for Global Justice* (New York: New Press, 2000).

5. See G. S. Graber, *Caravans to Oblivion: The Armenian Genocide, 1915* (New York: Wiley, 1996); Thomas P. Anderson, *Matanza: El Salvador's Communist Revolt of 1932* (Lincoln: University of Nebraska Press, 1971); J. Arch Getty and Oleg V. Naumov, *The Road to Terror: Stalin and the Self-Destruction of the Bolsheviks, 1932–1939*, trans. Benjamin Sher (New Haven, CT: Yale University Press, 1999); Chris Ward, *Stalin's Russia*, 2nd ed. (New York: Oxford University Press, 1999).

6. Carlos Santiago Nino, *Radical Evil on Trial* (New Haven, CT: Yale University Press, 1996), 8. See also Robert K. Woetzel, *The Nuremberg Trials in International Law* (New York: Praeger, 1962).

7. Scott Davidson, *The Inter-American Human Rights System* (Aldershot, Hants, England: Dartmouth Publishing Co., 1997); David J. Harris and Stephen Livingstone, eds., *The Inter-American System of Human Rights* (New York: Oxford University Press, 1998). The American Declaration of the Rights and Duties of Man is found at www.cidh.oas.org/Basicos/basic2.htm (accessed August 24, 2005).

8. Lauren, *The Evolution of International Human Rights*, 135–270; Robertson, *Crimes against Humanity*, 1–114. The Universal Declaration of Human Rights is reprinted in many places, including Lauren, *The Evolution of International Human Rights*, 299–303; and www.un.org/Overview/rights.html (accessed September 13, 2005).

9. Natalie Hevener Kaufman, *Human Rights Treaties and the Senate: A History of Opposition* (Chapel Hill: University of North Carolina Press, 1990). While several

presidents have signed treaties, the Senate, concerned about sovereignty and the Cold War, had ratified only three human rights treaties as of 1990. It finally ratified the UN Convention on Civil and Political Rights in 1992.

10. The Cuban Revolution of 1959 temporarily introduced the Cold War into the OAS. Cuba was expelled from the organization in 1962.

11. Davidson, *The Inter-American Human Rights System*; Harris and Livingstone, *The Inter-American System of Human Rights*. Each of the OAS human rights agencies has its own website.

12. Jack Donnelly, *International Human Rights*, 2nd ed. (Boulder, CO: Westview Press, 1998), 10.

13. Donnelly, *International Human Rights*, 53.

14. Howard Tolley Jr., *The U.N. Commission on Human Rights* (Boulder, CO: Westview Press, 1987); Kirsten A. Young, *The Law and Process of the U.N. Human Rights Commission* (Ardsley, NY: Transnational Publishers, 2002).

15. Tolley, *The U.N Commission*; Young, *The Law and Process*.

16. Claude E. Welch Jr., *NGOs and Human Rights: Promise and Performance* (Philadelphia: University of Pennsylvania Press, 2001); Jonathan Power, *Like Water on Stone: The Story of Amnesty International* (Boston: Northeastern University Press, 2001); Aryeh Neier, *Taking Liberties: Four Decades in the Struggle for Rights* (New York: Public Affairs, 2003), 149–286.

17. Geoff Simons, *Indonesia, the Long Oppression* (New York: St. Martin's, 2000), 170–85; Ben Kiernan, *The Pol Pot Regime: Race, Power, and Genocide in Cambodia under the Khmer Rouge, 1975–79* (New Haven, CT: Yale University Press, 2002); Gérard Prunier, *The Rwanda Crisis: History of a Genocide* (New York: Columbia University Press, 1995); Michael Anthony Sells, *The Bridge Betrayed: Religion and Genocide in Bosnia* (Berkeley: University of California Press, 1996). See also Eric D. Weitz, *A Century of Genocide: Utopias of Race and Nation* (Princeton, NJ: Princeton University Press, 2003); Kurt Jonassohn with Karin Solveig Björnson, *Genocide and Gross Human Rights Violations in Comparative Perspective* (New Brunswick, NJ: Transaction Publishers, 1998); Robert Gellately and Ben Kiernan, eds., *The Specter of Genocide: Mass Murder in Historical Perspective* (Cambridge: Cambridge University Press, 2003).

18. A November 18, 2006, Google search turned up approximately 1,110,000 entries for definitions of terrorism.

19. Frederick H. Gareau, *State Terrorism and the United States: From Counterinsurgency War to the War on Terrorism* (London: Zed Books, 2004), 14.

20. Among hundreds of studies of the Patriot Act are Stuart A. Baker, ed., *Patriot Debates* (Chicago: American Bar Association, 2005); and Amitai Etzioni, *How Patriotic Is the Patriot Act? Freedom versus Security in the Age of Terrorism* (New York: Routledge, 2004).

21. General studies of state terrorism include P. Timothy Bushnell et al., eds., *State Organized Terror: The Case of Violent Internal Repression* (Boulder, CO: Westview Press, 1991); Jeffrey A. Sluka, ed., *Death Squad: The Anthropology of State Terror* (Philadelphia: University of Pennsylvania Press, 2000); and Brenda K. Uekert,

Rivers of Blood: A Comparative Study of Government Massacres (Westport, CT: Praeger, 1995).

22. Studies of state terrorism in Latin America include Juan E. Corradi et al., eds., *Fear at the Edge: State Terror and Resistance in Latin America* (Berkeley: University of California Press, 1992); Cecilia Menjívar and Néstor Rodríguez, *When States Kill: Latin America, the U.S., and Technologies of Terror* (Austin: University of Texas Press, 2005); and Kees Koonings and Dirk Kruijt, *Societies of Fear: The Legacy of Civil War, Violence and Terror in Latin America* (London: Zed Books, 1999).

23. Edward L. Cleary, *The Struggle for Human Rights in Latin America* (Westport, CT: Praeger, 1997); Marjorie Agosín, *Surviving beyond Fear: Women, Children and Human Rights in Latin America* (Fredonia, NY: White Pine Press, 1993).

24. Tolley, *The U.N. Commission*, 55–186. As an example of changes in national jurisprudence, Spain, which would become a major factor in Latin American human rights, enacted legislation in 1985 granting Spanish courts universal jurisdiction in certain categories of crime, including genocide and those whose prosecution is mandatory under international treaties: Richard Wilson, "Prosecuting Pinochet: International Crimes in Spanish Domestic Law," *Human Rights Quarterly* 21, no. 4 (1999): 927–79. Belgium also incorporated universal jurisdiction into its domestic law.

25. See chapters 5 and 6 for the incorporation of international treaties in Argentina and Chile.

26. Naomi Roht-Arriaza, "The Role of International Actors in National Accountability Processes," in *The Politics of Memory: Transitional Justice in Democratizing Societies*, ed. Alexandra Barahona de Brito, Carmen González-Eníquez, and Paloma Aguilar, 40–64 (Oxford: Oxford University Press, 2001).

27. Howard Ball, *Prosecuting War Crimes and Genocide: The Twentieth-Century Experience* (Lawrence, KS: University of Kansas Press, 1999); William Driscoll et al., *The International Criminal Court: Global Politics and the Quest for Justice* (New York: International Debate Education Association, 2004); and Marlies Glasius, *The International Criminal Court: A Global Civil Society Achievement* (New York: Routledge, 2005). See also the entire issue of *The International Review of the Red Cross*, no. 845 (March 2002), titled "Impunity—The International Criminal Court."

28. See Christopher Hitchens, *The Trial of Henry Kissinger* (London: Verso, 2001).

29. Julie A. Mertus, *Bait and Switch: Human Rights and U.S. Foreign Policy* (New York: Routledge, 2004), 51–72 (esp. 51–62); Naomi Roht-Arriaza, *The Pinochet Effect: Transnational Justice in the Age of Human Rights* (Philadelphia: University of Pennsylvania Press, 2005), 190–91.

30. Roht-Arriaza, *The Pinochet Effect*, 140–49; *Los Angeles Times*, January 11, 2004.

31. www.icc-cpi.int/press/pressreleases/107.html (accessed August 8, 2006); *New York Times*, October 7, 2005.

CHAPTER TWO

~

The Latin American
Human Rights Crisis

In some countries of Latin America [the Doctrine of National Security] justifies itself as the defender of the Christian civilization of the West. It elaborates a repressive system, which is in line with its concept of "permanent war."

—Third Conference of Latin American Bishops,
"The Puebla Document," 1979[1]

There are many people in the country and abroad who, erroneously interpreting the sense of counter-revolutionary warfare, have believed that this action is directed against the people or against important sectors of the population. . . . Nothing is further from the truth.

—Argentine military leadership, 1962[2]

As demonstrated by the incidences of state terrorism and genocide that have occurred over the past four decades, statements of principle such as the Universal Declaration of Human Rights are little more than empty rhetoric or meaningless pieces of paper unless reinforced by the proper political framework. Even in normal times, in countries where respect for human rights is most deeply ingrained, access to the full exercise of civil and political rights is rationed: the powerful, wealthy, and influential can command respect for the rights promised in their countries' constitutions, while the poor, the minorities, and the uneducated struggle, and often fail, to obtain the same protections. In times of economic, social, or political crisis or perceived danger to the national polity, the human rights guaranteed in national constitutions and international covenants are easily suppressed. Authoritarian governments routinely trample these rights.

Much of Latin America in the 1970s and 1980s experienced a profound crisis of human rights. This resulted fundamentally from the prevailing political climate, both domestic and international. In countries accounting for over half of Latin America's population, regimes that institutionalized grave human rights violations came to power; in some cases, the repression rose to the level of state terrorism. During this period, all but two South American countries fell under military governance, while in several Central American countries, weak elected governments served at the pleasure of dominant military establishments. Authoritarian rule and the armed forces' commitment to eradicating the political left in their countries, which they perceived as a severe threat to the status quo and the privileges of the elites, led in some cases to the formal suspension of constitutional guarantees, and in others to extraofficial but equally effective suppression of civil and political rights. Political parties, interest groups, and civic institutions opposed to military policies were too weak to offer effective resistance. Moreover, at the onset of the period of repressive rule, there were almost no human rights organizations, and certainly nothing that could be termed a human rights movement, to resist repression and aid its victims.

The alignment of international political forces during the Cold War was likewise detrimental to human rights. The top priority of U.S. Latin American policy from 1959 to 1990 was to dampen the influence of the Cuban Revolution and the appeal of revolution in the hemisphere. Except during the presidency of Jimmy Carter (1977–1981), the United States offered virtually unconditional support to the regimes that suppressed human rights as they persecuted leftist parties and groups. During this period, moreover, there was no international influence capable of countering U.S. hegemony over Latin America.[3] The existence of the Inter-American, UN, and nongovernmental framework of standards and monitoring provided a means for disseminating information to the world and bringing pressures to bear for improvements in human rights policies, but the international jurisprudence and institutions for enforcement of human rights law had not yet developed; thus the perpetrators of human rights abuses had little concern about being held accountable for their crimes, and victims had little recourse to outside aid.

Impact of the Cuban Revolution

The catalyst of Latin America's human rights crisis was the Cuban Revolution. The impact of the Cuban Revolution on Latin America posed an unprecedented challenge to the status quo, to the stability of governments, and to the privileges of the elites. The potential spread of Cuban-style revolution beyond the island represented the gravest threat the United States had experienced to its continued economic and geopolitical dominance of the Western Hemisphere. In sum, the Cuban Revolution resounded like an earthquake on the Latin American scene.[4]

In the words of journalist Herbert Matthews, a close observer of Latin America, "January 1, 1959, when Fidel Castro triumphed, began a new era in Latin America."[5] For the next thirty years, the Cuban Revolution would be the driving force in Latin American politics, first inspiring revolutionary movements and then engendering a strong reaction against both revolution and reform. Particularly in its first five years, Fidel Castro's revolution brought Latin America's social, economic, and political problems into sharp focus. It inspired broad segments of the population—particularly workers, peasants, and youth—to believe that a similar revolution was possible in their countries. Social unrest, the radicalization of politics, mass mobilizations, and insurrections destabilized governments and kept the region in a high state of agitation.[6]

There were several reasons for the Cuban Revolution's enormous impact on Latin America. First, Castro's road to power offered an explicit methodology for successful insurrection: guerrilla warfare. Although greatly oversimplifying the history of the movement that put Castro into power, the generally accepted explanation of his success credited a guerrilla band in the Sierra Maestra mountains, originally numbering no more than twenty men, with defeating the dictatorship of Fulgencio Batista (1952–1958) and its U.S.-trained and equipped forty-thousand-man army after only twenty-five months in the field. This story of the heroic guerrilla, replete with sacrifice, self-abnegation, and steely determination, became central to the lore of the revolution and an irresistible siren song in Latin America. Ernesto (Che) Guevara, the Argentine medical doctor who fought alongside Castro, published a book, *Guerrilla Warfare*, in 1960. Essentially a how-to manual on the guerrilla method of fighting, Che's book became an instant best seller in Latin America. Although *Guerrilla Warfare* argued that the rural guerrilla method could work only against dictatorships such as Batista's, Che quickly modified his position by asserting that Cuban-style insurrection would be effective anywhere in Latin America if there were willing revolutionaries to carry it out. The story of the Sierra Maestra odyssey, Che's writings, and Castro's repeated exhortations to take up arms, sometimes backed by aid to insurgent movements, constituted a powerful call to revolutionary insurrection. When Castro said, "The duty of every revolutionary is to make the revolution," many Latin Americans listened, and more than a few responded.[7]

Cuba's was Latin America's most thorough social revolution, far surpassing the Mexican Revolution of 1910 in the degree of change it wrought. Moving at impressive speed, Castro essentially extinguished capitalism in Cuba within three years, replacing it with a socialist economy that, despite many shortcomings, delivered work for all, provided free education and health care, subsidized food and housing, and gave a sense of dignity to the common Cuban. His agrarian reform, which expropriated the dominant, largely foreign-owned estates and created an agrarian economy of state farms and individual smallholdings, was a beacon for Latin America's land-starved *campesinos*. As a result of these accomplishments, many among Latin America's poor majority—*campesinos*, workers, and the marginalized masses lacking any semblance of a decent life—came to believe that utopia could be seized by following the Cuban example.[8]

Another major attraction of Castro's revolution was its success in breaking free of U.S. domination. For the first time since the United States had established its hegemony over Latin America in the period between the Spanish American War (1898) and the Great Depression, a country, in this case a small and very proximate country, was successfully able to defy the dictates of Washington and Wall Street by expropriating all U.S. property on the island and forging an alliance with the Cold War nemesis of the United States, the Soviet Union. Given the general Latin American view of the United States as an imperialist power, this was indeed a notable feat in the David-and-Goliath mold. When Castro's forces defeated the U.S.-sponsored Bay of Pigs invasion in April 1961, Castro's popularity with many Latin Americans soared to new heights; he acquired the stature of a second Bolívar—a new liberator of Latin America.[9]

Finally, the style of the revolution complemented its concrete accomplishments, deepening its impact on Latin America. Castro himself was a very charismatic leader whose martial appearance and moving speeches captivated audiences at home and abroad. His flair for publicity, his appetite for taking on the greatest challenges, and his impatience for change kept him and his revolution constantly in the news. The timing of the revolution was also important. It occurred in a period when the great majority of Latin American countries and people lived under democratic rule, a circumstance that allowed the relatively free flow of information and the opportunity to advocate revolutionary positions openly. Further, the recent advent of the cheap transistor radio circumvented the need for electricity and transcended the barrier of illiteracy, allowing news of Cuba to penetrate the most remote corners of the hemisphere.[10]

The revolution that freed the island from U.S. domination and established a new society based on an egalitarian model continued, and soon deepened, the suppression of civil and political liberties initiated under the Batista dictatorship that it replaced. As Castro moved further into the Soviet orbit through the 1960s, Cuba's government increasingly adopted the trappings and the substance of its patron. Castro integrated his 26th of July Movement with Cuba's communist party, the Partido Socialista Popular, in 1961. Four years later, he established the Cuban Communist Party as the only authorized political party and continued to suppress civil and political liberties in the name of defending the revolution against its internal and external enemies.

Castro eventually formalized his regime in 1976 with the adoption of a new constitution. In its treatment of human rights, the constitution accurately reflected the realities of the new socialist state. The basic economic, social, and cultural rights enumerated in the Universal Declaration were fully guaranteed without equivocation, and they were quite effectively implemented until the economic crisis of the 1990s: All Cubans have the right to a job (article 44.1), fair pay (article 44.2), free health care (article 49), free education (article 50), and protection in old age (article 47). On the other hand, the constitution lists the essential civil and political rights found in the Universal Declaration, but in each case with caveats that effectively deny their exercise. Free speech and press are recognized "in keeping with the objectives of socialist society" (article 52). Freedom of association is limited to the officially sanctioned mass organizations (article 53). Religious freedom is recognized, but "it is illegal for a faith or religious belief to oppose the Revolution" (article 54). No right recognized in the constitution may be exercised "against the existence and objectives of the socialist state nor against the decision of the Cuban people to construct socialism and communism" (Article 61).[11] The widely noted and criticized April 2003 crackdown on dissident human rights activists indicates that the status of civil and political rights in Cuba remains essentially unchanged after more than forty-five years of Castro's rule.[12]

The Antirevolutionary Reaction

Long before the 1976 constitution, the regime's move toward communism, with the concomitant extinction of civil and political rights, disappointed many Latin Americans who applauded the changes in Cuban society and the island's liberation from U.S. domination. Indeed, within two or three years of Castro's accession to power, much of the Latin American democratic left—those who believed social reform and national liberation to be compatible with political democracy—became ambivalent or hostile toward the Castro regime. The human rights issue was important in steering important reformist parties such as Peru's Alianza Popular Revolucionaria Americana (American Popular Revolutionary Alliance, APRA); Venezuela's Acción Democrática (Democratic Action, AD); and Chile's Partido Demócrata Cristiano (Christian Democratic Party, PDC) into opposition against Castro and against the groups within their own countries that advocated Cuban-style revolution.[13]

The democratic left groups were but one element in a broad array of forces opposed to the Cuban Revolution and its influence. The wave of revolution that shook the hemispheric status quo to its foundations spawned a potent wave of reaction. Latin America's wealthy and privileged saw their Cuban counterparts lose their property and status and opt for exile over life under socialism. The religious witnessed the revolution's persecution of the Catholic Church. The Latin American militaries observed the dissolution of the Cuban military and its replacement with Castro's own revolutionary armed forces.

Thus the same Cuban Revolution that mobilized broad segments of the Latin American population for change engendered in other sectors an equally strong determination to fight against revolution—some to prevent the eclipse of the civil and political rights suppressed in Cuba, and others to preserve their privileges and way of life. Whether by conviction or by convenience, opponents of revolution united behind slogans praising democracy and individual rights—to highlight the negative side of the Cuban Revolution. In their zeal to prevent revolution, and in some cases with premeditation, they opened the way for regimes of state terrorism that instituted policies toward civil and political liberties that were as oppressive as Castro's, or more so. And unlike Castro's, these regimes did not trade civil and political rights for economic, social, and cultural rights; they extinguished them all.

The Latin American antirevolutionary reaction relied on the support of the U.S. government, which spared no resource or effort to thwart the spread of revolution beyond Cuba, in alliance with Latin America's elites and armed forces. The Latin American militaries had traditionally played dual roles in national life. Their primary role, according to constitutions and laws, was defense against external threats. Military curricula, training, and equipment were oriented to protecting the country's borders against invasion. In Latin America, however, there was relatively little history of warfare between neighbors. In the twentieth century, only the 1932–1935 Chaco War that pitted Bolivia versus Paraguay can be counted as a full-scale war.[14]

The other role of the armed forces involved national political life. At times, ambitious and self-serving officers seized power in pursuit of their own ends; more commonly, officers took power to guide their countries through times of crisis. For example, the armed forces seized power in many Latin American countries between 1930 and 1932, when the Great Depression caused severe economic dislocations, social tensions, and political instability that existing governments were unable to handle. The military's tutelary role in national political life had deep roots. In some countries, the military considered itself to be the founder of the nation through wars of liberation from Spanish colonial rule, and hence the very essence of the country's identity. Even in those countries that gained independence without war, including Central America and Brazil, the militaries viewed themselves as the guardians of national values and as the ultimate arbiters of the national good. "Most of Latin America, even those nations governed by popularly elected presidents with democratic values, expects the armed forces, 'in crises,' to exercise their 'historical mission' to 'save the patria.'"[15] Most countries' constitutions and laws, moreover, placed these responsibilities in the military's hands.

In the crisis created by the Cuban Revolution, the militaries' role was not to defend borders against Cuban troops. The problem was Cuban-inspired forces within their national borders. While the armed forces were prepared to save the patria again, as they had done previously, the degree of mobilization and radicalization, and in many countries the threat or reality of guerrilla warfare, presented unprecedented challenges. Determined to prevent the spread of revolution, the United States responded with a program to prepare Latin America's militaries for the era of wars of national liberation in the Cold War context. Preparation for defense against the internal enemy had two components: military training in counterinsurgency warfare and the teaching of national security doctrine.

National security doctrine was not unknown in Latin America prior to the 1960s. French theorists had written extensively on the new approaches adopted in their country's nonconventional colonial wars in Vietnam and Algeria. Homegrown concepts of national security had been formulated in professional military schools and war colleges in several Latin American countries. But the ascendancy of national security doctrine within Latin America's armed forces was, above all, the result of U.S. resolve to prevent communist revolution in the hemisphere.[16]

Even before Fidel Castro's accession to power, the United States had begun adjusting its military doctrines to the new times. At the onset of the

Cold War, U.S. defense doctrine had focused on the external threat from the Soviet Union. The 1947 Rio Pact had been adopted to implement the concept of collective hemispheric security against potential external aggression by the USSR. But by the early 1950s, a new kind of threat to the regional status quo had emerged. In Guatemala, the reformist Jacobo Arbenz government (1950–1954) violated the two pillars of U.S. foreign policy: it expropriated large tracts of land owned by a U.S. corporation, United Fruit Company, without offering compensation satisfactory to the company; and it showed a softness toward communism by allowing Communist Party members to hold positions of influence in government and by purchasing arms from Communist Czechoslovakia.

To justify the overthrow of Arbenz, the Eisenhower administration pressured the Latin American countries to endorse a Cold War corollary of the Monroe Doctrine, a foreign policy extension of McCarthyism. The 1954 Declaration of Caracas substituted "international communism" for the European monarchies that President Monroe in 1823 had declared incompatible with the institutions of the Western Hemisphere and warned to stay away. The Caracas document stated that "the domination or control of the political institutions of any American state by the international communist movement . . . would constitute a threat to the sovereignty and political independence of the American states, endangering the peace of America."[17] By equating internal subversion with international communist penetration, the Declaration of Caracas shifted the military's focus from external defense to internal security.

The United States viewed the Cuban Revolution's threat to Latin America through the prism of the Caracas Declaration. It was not an invasion by Cuban forces but the rise of militantly pro-Castro "subversives" that constituted the threat to U.S. interests and the Latin American establishment. The U.S. objective, in the words of President John F. Kennedy's Secretary of Defense, Robert McNamara, was "to guard against external covert intrusion and internal subversion designed to create dissidence and insurrection."[18] This required modernization of the traditional guardianship role.

The transformation of the enemy from external to internal meshed easily with the Latin American military tradition of intervening at times of crisis to protect the homeland. In a region notable for its lack of foreign wars, and hence of conventional combat experience, the Latin American militaries enthusiastically embraced the new assignment that promised hands-on experience in a different but equally patriotic kind of warfare. As an Argentine colonel put it, the new doctrine was "a hope for the Argentine army. It was destined to fill the void produced by the almost complete disappearance of possibilities of war between our country and some of its neighbors."[19] From the 1960s through the 1980s, safeguarding the national interest became synonymous with stamping out leftist subversives intent on replicating the Cuban Revolution.

The United States provided the Latin American militaries with extensive training in the means of combating the internal threat. By 1975, over seventy thousand soldiers had been trained at over one hundred service schools in the United States, in the Panama Canal Zone, and in their own countries. The United States, just learning about counterinsurgency in Vietnam, trained Latin Americans to fight guerrilla outbreaks using the guerrillas' own tactics, but aided by sophisticated weaponry and supporting equipment. Special elite units, based on the U.S. Army's Green Beret model, were formed in many countries; their efficacy was demonstrated in the defeat of Che Guevara's guerrillas in Bolivia in 1967—and their brutality in the massacres in El Salvador and Guatemala in the 1980s. In a parallel approach to internal security, the U.S. Agency for International Development provided training for police in riot control, intelligence, and interrogation techniques, which critics called torture.[20]

The thousands of Latin American officers who received counterinsurgency and police training also took courses in national security doctrine. These classes taught about the communist threat and the methods of subversion that Marxists employed. The early success of the instruction in national security doctrine was reflected in a 1962 Argentine army report: "The armies of the free countries of America have taken part in studies of this nature in the Inter-American Course on Counter-Revolutionary Warfare. . . . These joint studies . . . bring out clearly that the principal enemy of our civilization and way of life is to be found in the very heart of our national communities."[21] Another measure of success was the reputation of the U.S. Army's Southern Command's School of the Americas in the Panama Canal Zone, which trained over twenty thousand officers in the 1960s; so many of its graduates applied their lessons after returning home that it became known as the "school of assassins."[22]

In some of the countries that would fall under military domination in the aftermath of the Cuban Revolution, particularly in South America, the military's analysis of the threat to national security involved both political and economic issues. On the political front, the threat was leftist subversion. National security required the control or elimination of subversives. In some cases, the military would push for civic reeducation of the populace to root out all ideas of Marxism, class conflict, and even the concepts of liberal democracy that permitted Marxism to compete freely with other ideologies in the political system. On the economic side, a thorough reorientation of the economy would be needed to promote rapid economic development so as to eliminate the poverty upon which revolutionaries preyed. Unlike earlier crises that had prompted military intervention, the profound crisis provoked by the Cuban Revolution would not be susceptible to a quick fix. The patriotic mission of the armed forces would be accomplished only when the country had been thoroughly immunized against revolution.[23]

While the economic program was normally left in the hands of civilian technocrats, and reeducation was the domain of intellectuals and bureaucrats, the immediate mission of the officer corps was to fight the new enemy of the patria: Marxist subversion. Marxist operatives not only engaged in guerrilla warfare; they were found throughout society, in political parties, universities, secondary schools, labor unions, the mass media, the social activist wing of the Catholic Church, the professions, and even in the home. As depicted during the McCarthy era in the United States, Marxists were not only disloyal to their country; they were duplicitous, clever, amoral, and capable of subverting organizations and using them for their devious purposes. The Argentine military report cited above confirmed this view: "The enemy is tremendously dangerous. We are not attacked from outside . . . but subtly undermined through all channels of the social organization. It poisons the minds, it weakens the spirit, it fabricates Pharisees and false prophets, and distorts everything in an imperceptible process of time."[24] Similarly, Chilean dictator Augusto Pinochet called Marxism "permanent aggression at the service of Soviet imperialism [which] gives rise to an unconventional war in which territorial invasion is replaced by attempts to take over states from within." To parry this threat, he concluded, "it is necessary to place power in the armed forces, since only they have the organization and means to counter it."[25]

In several countries, the armed forces felt it necessary to modify, suspend, or even destroy the institutions of democracy that made it possible for revolutionary ideas to circulate and for subversive groups to operate. Imposing states of siege or emergency, they suspended habeas corpus, censored the media, purged judiciaries and legislatures, and banned political parties and unions. Where the perceived threat was grave, the military would go further. It would go to war against subversion using its ultimate weapon: state terrorism.

In its 1991 report, the Chilean truth commission, established after the restoration of civilian government to investigate human rights violations during the Pinochet dictatorship, cogently spelled out the connections between national security doctrine, counterinsurgency, and the extreme repression that the military applied in that country. The explanation is equally applicable to Argentina and other Latin American countries. Counterinsurgency forces must fight guerrillas and subversives with their own unorthodox methods in order to keep the country from succumbing to forces directed from Cuba and the Soviet Union. Counterinsurgency training thus teaches secrecy, special methods of combat, and sophisticated interrogation techniques (torture). These and related exercises "gradually accustomed the students [of counterinsurgency] to the fact that ethical limits were receding and diminishing, sometimes to the vanishing point." Conventional warfare was subject to the "rules of war"; war on subversives knew no rules at all. Because of the life-or-death importance of defending the homeland's Western Christian civilization against communist subversion, national security became "a supreme value . . . regarded as being above ethics. . . . In extreme cases (designated as such by the authorities) the rights of individuals could be violated by reason of an alleged general interest."[26] This reasoning legitimized repression without restraint. Moreover, it did not require a majority of ranking officers to force this logic on the entire military institution; a determined minority could sometimes impose its extremist agenda, its task facilitated by the fact that the more moderate majority had undergone the same training and indoctrination.

On August 3, 1976, Undersecretary of State for Latin American Affairs Harry W. Shlaudeman delivered a secret report to Secretary of State Henry Kissinger entitled "The 'Third World War' and South America." The report sheds further light on the driving forces behind state terrorism: "The military regimes of the southern cone of South America see themselves as embattled: on one side by international Marxism and its terrorist exponents, and on the other by the hostility of the uncomprehending industrial democracies misled by Marxist propaganda." They are cooperating to "eradicate 'subversion,' a word which increasingly translates into non-violent dissent from the left and center-left. . . . This siege mentality shading into paranoia is perhaps the natural result of the convulsions of recent years in which the societies of Chile, Uruguay and Argentina have been badly shaken by assault from the extreme left. But the military leaders, despite near decimation of the Marxist left in Chile and Uruguay, along with the accelerating progress toward that goal in Argentina, insist that the threat remains and the war must go on. Some talk of the 'Third World War,' with the countries of the southern cone as the last bastion of Christian civilization."[27]

The Terrorist States

The rise of revolutionary movements throughout Latin America in the wake of the Cuban Revolution had a destabilizing effect on the region's predominantly elected, civilian governments. The growth of demands for reform, the creation or expansion of revolutionary groups, the rise in demonstrations and strikes, the *campesino* occupations of hacienda lands, and in several countries the appearance of guerrilla bands compromised governments' ability to maintain order and preserve citizens' security. Weakened by the growth of mobilization and by increasing challenges to the status quo, several Latin American governments fell to military coups between 1959 and 1963.[28]

The March 1964 coup in Brazil was an important milestone along the way to Latin America's human rights crisis. Beset in the early 1960s by worker unrest and a massive peasant mobilization, both supported by populist President João Goulart, Brazil became increasingly unstable. The military's coup aimed not only to remove Goulart but to curb the left's influence in the political system. During the following five years, the military ruled within the framework of civilian institutions, reserving the presidency for military officers and curtailing the left parties and unions, but maintaining a congress and state governments with restricted powers. However, in response to the outbreak of urban guerrilla war in 1969, the military shut down the remaining civilian institutions and began a period of rule through severe repression. In addition to attacking the guerrillas, the government adopted the strategy—later refined in Chile and Argentina—of targeting their actual and potential supporters in order to isolate the guerrillas. Arbitrary detention, torture, and assassination became standard instruments of government policy in the fight against subversion; in addition to its own police and military units, the government sanctioned or condoned private death squads.

Because the guerrillas were easily defeated, the Brazilian military government did not employ its repressive powers to the full extent possible; in contrast to their Chilean and Argentine counterparts, the Brazilian officers attempted to weaken and marginalize the left, not eradicate it. By 1974, the military began to rein in its repressive apparatus. Yet the Brazilian armed forces had created the first Latin American national security state and had institutionalized state terrorism.[29]

State terrorism in Uruguay began only six months after the military and police had delivered the coup de grace to the Tupamaros, the original Latin American urban guerrilla movement. Responding to a deteriorating economy and an increasingly unresponsive political system, the Tupamaros formed in the early 1960s and began operations against the government in 1968. At the height of their power, between 1969 and 1972, they had hundreds of fighters, an extensive support network, and a "people's prison" for high-profile detainees. The Tupamaro threat was so serious that the government in April 1972 declared an "internal state of war"; within months, the military had broken the organization and had captured its leaders.[30]

After the defeat of the gravest insurrectionary challenge since Castro's victory in Cuba, the Uruguayan officers, following the prescriptions of national security doctrine, turned to rooting out the subversives who might share the Tupamaros' goals. They began with a "soft" coup in February 1973, and four months later, acting through a civilian figurehead president, they dissolved Congress, replaced it with an advisory council of state, and brought the public administration under military control. Thereafter, the military followed the Brazilian pattern by progressively stripping the hybrid civilian-military government of all substantive citizen participation and creating an apparatus of state terrorism to use against the left. As in Brazil, state terrorism exacted a heavy toll in imprisonment, exile, and torture. Yet in terms of deaths and disappearances, the records of the Brazilian and Uruguayan military dictatorships were mild in comparison with those of the Chilean and Argentine regimes.[31]

Chile became the third Latin American country to institutionalize state terrorism. Unlike their counterparts in Brazil and Uruguay, the Chilean military did not temporize. They were not interested in preserving even a facade of civilian governance, and upon overthrowing the elected government of Salvador Allende on September 11, 1973, they quickly abolished or appropriated virtually every institution that had the potential to oppose them. Unlike their Brazilian counterparts, they did not embrace state terrorism as a last recourse; they launched a wave of terrorism on the day of the coup. In contrast to the Brazilians and Uruguayans, the Chileans were very public about their objectives and their methods; there was nothing subtle about rounding up thousands of prisoners, the extensive use of torture, executions following sham courts-martial, and shootings in cold blood. After the initial wave of open terrorism, the Chilean armed forces constructed a sophisticated apparatus for the secret application of state terrorism that lasted until the dictatorship's end.[32]

The impact of the Chilean coup reached far beyond the country's borders. Through their aid in the overthrow of Allende and their support of the Pinochet dictatorship, President Richard Nixon and his national security adviser, Henry Kissinger, sent a clear signal to all of Latin America that anti-revolutionary regimes employing repression, even state terrorism, could count on the support of the United States. The U.S. government, in effect, gave a green light to Latin America's right wing and its armed forces to eradicate the left and use repression to erase the advances that workers—and in some countries, *campesinos*—had made through decades of struggle. This "September 11 effect" was soon felt around the hemisphere.[33]

Thirty months after the Chilean coup, the Argentine military struck. Facing a guerrilla war that they were handily winning, the armed forces overthrew President Isabel Perón and immediately escalated a "dirty war" that was already under way against the left, both guerrillas and noncombatants. The Argentines learned from the Chilean experience; desiring to avoid the near-universal condemnation that had greeted the bloodbath across the Andes, they devised a manner of eliminating the left without overflowing the prisons, holding mock trials, or leaving bodies to be collected and identified. They perfected the forced disappearance of persons—a method of killing that left no trace of the victims.[34] After the Argentine coup, over two-thirds of the population of South America lived under repressive dictatorships as the tide of reaction swept over the region.

Institutionalized terrorism arrived in Peru early in the 1980s when the ruthless insurgency of the Sendero Luminoso, a rural-based guerrilla organization inspired by Mao Zedong and by indigenist sentiments, used terrorism against Andean villagers in its effort to seize power. During a decade of counterinsurgency, the Peruvian government responded with terrorism, effectively trapping civilians between two repressive forces. A Peruvian truth commission reported in 2003 that some seventy thousand people were killed in the struggle, half by the insurgents and a third by the government forces.[35]

In the late 1970s and the 1980s, the human rights crisis reached Central America. After an eighteen-year struggle, in the only successful guerrilla war since Castro's, the Frente Sandinista de Liberación Nacional (Sandinista National Liberation Front, FSLN) toppled the venerable Somoza family dictatorship in 1979. The Sandinista victory and subsequent implementation of its revolutionary program galvanized the left in neighboring countries and in response triggered the use of state terrorism in defense of elite privileges and national security.[36]

While Honduras experienced heightened repression in the aftermath of the Sandinista victory and collaborated in the U.S.-sponsored Contra War against the Nicaraguan government, El Salvador and Guatemala were the most severely affected by state terrorism. In El Salvador, a coalition government of the country's economic elite and the military, which ruled through electoral fraud and repression, had been challenged by a small guerrilla movement in the 1970s. Energized by the Sandinista victory and support from Cuba, the fragmented insurgency united in 1980 as the Frente Farabundo Martí de Liberación Nacional (Farabundo Martí National Liberation Front, FMLN) after government operatives assassinated Archbishop Oscar Arnulfo Romero, a vocal critic of government-sponsored death squads and human rights violations. With the 1981 inauguration of the Reagan administration, the U.S. government, labeling the FMLN as communist subversives directed by a Moscow-Havana-Managua axis, deepened its involvement in the conflict. U.S.-financed and trained counterinsurgency battalions and paramilitary death squads turned their weapons against civilians as well as guerrillas, repressing prodemocracy organizations, driving peasants off the countryside, and massacring entire villages. By the mid-1980s, the civil war had reached equilibrium, with the government holding the main cities and keeping the highways open by day and the FMLN operating freely by night.[37]

A conjuncture of events in 1989 and 1991 brought the war to a close as both sides lost international support. A government death squad's highly publicized 1989 brutal murder of six Jesuit priests, their housekeeper, and her daughter swayed U.S. public opinion against continuing support of the government, while the Sandinistas' electoral loss in 1990, combined with the 1991 collapse of the Soviet Union and the resulting economic crisis in Cuba, undercut moral and financial support for the FMLN. Brokered by the UN, a January 1992 peace accord ended the armed conflict after at least seventy-five thousand people, mostly civilians, had been killed. The war also created hundreds of thousands of refugees and launched the migration stream that made Salvadorans the fastest-growing Latino group in the United States in the late twentieth century.[38]

In neighboring Guatemala, the escalation of repression in the late 1970s and 1980s had its roots in a long-smoldering guerrilla conflict. After the U.S.-sponsored invasion that overthrew the progressive Arbenz government in 1954 and the rollback of reforms enacted in the previous decade, many Guatemalan leftists, including workers and peasants, were receptive to Fidel Castro's call to revolution. From 1960 to 1970, guerrillas operated with minimal success, and the government used troops and paramilitary death squads against them and all potential collaborators, including peasants, left and moderate politicians, students, and union leaders. In the wake of the Sandinista victory, guerrilla activity grew, and the government responded with unprecedented state terrorism.[39]

Heading civilian governments, two generals, Romeo Lucas García (1978–1982) and José Efraín Ríos Montt (1982–1983) unleashed a policy of village massacres and scorched earth that drove Maya peasants out of entire regions, into Mexican refugee camps, and in many cases on to the United States. While all elements of the left were targeted, the brutality directed toward the Maya and the number of victims from their ranks validated the application of the term "genocide" to the repression of this period. The one-sided conflict dragged on until 1996, when the UN finally succeeded in arranging a peace accord. Over two hundred thousand people, primarily Mayan peasants, had been killed, and hundreds of thousands were displaced.[40]

The toll of Latin America's human rights crisis was massive. The guerrillas were responsible for numerous and heinous human rights violations; but governments, using their overwhelmingly superior power, and aided by the United States, were responsible for the great majority of the crimes. Over four hundred thousand people were killed, many of them disappeared, in the name of national security—the great majority of them innocent civilians caught up in the conflagration. The number of persons arbitrarily imprisoned, tortured, and exiled, while impossible to ascertain, clearly reached several million. The dreams shattered, careers truncated, families sundered, and lives ruined by state terrorism cannot possibly be quantified.

Owing to the worldwide publicity it received and the reaction against it, the Latin American human rights crisis contributed to the strengthening of the international human rights regime. It was an important stimulus to the exponential growth of human rights activism, both national and international, that began in the mid-1970s. Repression in Latin America, as well as elsewhere in the world, led to the founding of additional human rights organizations, both intergovernmental and NGOs, and to the adoption of new treaties and conventions. Latin America, in sum, played a major role in the development of tougher human rights standards and the tools necessary to enforce those standards.[41]

The Legacies of State Terrorism

By 1990, Latin America's human rights crisis was winding down. The military dictatorships that had institutionalized state terrorism in South America were replaced by civilian governments: Argentina's in 1983, Uruguay's in 1984, Brazil's in 1985, and Chile's in 1990. Ecuador had returned to elected government in 1979, Bolivia in 1982, and in Paraguay, the Stroessner dictatorship ended after thirty-five years in 1989. In Peru, the Sendero Luminoso was essentially defeated by 1992, and repression eased. With the end of war in El Salvador in 1992 and Guatemala in 1996, the era of state terrorism was largely over. In the new millennium, the human rights situation in Cuba remains essentially the same as it has been for nearly half a century. In Haiti, an established tradition of human rights violations has continued. Colombia, in the throes of an intensified guerrilla war and drug-driven violence, is the only country whose human rights situation has worsened since 1990.[42]

The transition from rule by repression—whether under military or civilian regimes—to governments democratically elected and committed to the rule of law was profoundly challenging. Most importantly, the weakness of democratic culture in most of Latin America was an obstacle to the construction or reestablishment of civic institutions and stable civilian governments. In addition, the creation of democratic rule was negatively impacted by the global economic contraction of the 1980s and was further threatened by the neoliberal policies imposed by the International Monetary Fund and the World Bank that fostered growing economic disparities and further impoverished the poor. A quarter of all Latin Americans in 1993 lived on a dollar per day or less, a number that had increased by 20 percent since 1987. In those countries moving from regimes of state terrorism to democracy, the challenges were compounded by the legacies of grave human rights violations.[43]

Upon relinquishing political power, the armed forces left behind profoundly divided societies. Deep fissures separated the armed forces and the groups that had supported their rule from the individuals and groups who had suffered the wrath of state terrorism and who were backed by human rights movements that had been formed during the period of repression. The central issue dividing societies was justice versus impunity. Would the amnesty laws left in place by exiting military regimes hold up? Would the victims, their families, and the human rights movements settle for an accounting of what had occurred in their countries? For admissions of culpability or requests for forgiveness? For the remains of the disappeared? Or would they demand investigations and trials for the alleged perpetrators of human rights violations? Would the armed forces submit to investigations and prosecution after, in their view, saving their countries from Marxism? Would the new civilian governments, fearing military reprisals, choose to sacrifice justice and close a terrible chapter in their national histories in the interest of shoring up their fragile democracies?[44]

In practice, in societies undergoing the transition from repressive to democratic governments, justice is neither absolute nor unidimensional. There are both judicial and nonjudicial responses to human rights crimes and various ways of promoting reconciliation. In this complex process, called transitional justice, governments are rarely capable of, and often are not interested in, bringing repressors to trial. Even where there is the will, there are complicating factors such as whether to prosecute the actual killers and torturers or only those whose orders they obeyed, and whether to adopt a statute of limitations on trials so as to avoid prolonging the tensions and divisiveness they create.

There are several nonjudicial approaches that can help to heal societies following severe repression. These include establishing investigative bodies, normally called truth commissions, to ascertain the facts about the repression and identify the victims; in addition to aiding individuals and societies in the healing process, truth commissions provide the basis of memory and truth that human rights advocates use to contest the official histories implanted and left behind by the repressor regimes. Other nonjudicial approaches include offering material reparations to victims and their families; reforming institutions that violated human rights or were complicit in the violations, such as military and police forces and courts; and building a new culture of respect for human rights.[45]

Just as the period of massive, institutionalized human rights violations was shaped by the constellation of domestic and international political forces, so was the period of transition during which the legacies of state terror were addressed. The most important single factor shaping the human rights climate was the establishment or reestablishment of democratic political systems. The period from 1990 to the present is unprecedented in Latin American history: With the exceptions of Cuba and Haiti, democratic governments, defined as those chosen by "free, open, and fair elections," held uninterrupted sway throughout the region.[46] The new culture of democracy is in large measure a reaction against the excesses of the period of state terror. The hemispheric commitment to democracy was formalized in the 2001 Inter-American Democratic Charter, which requires all OAS members to maintain democratic, constitutional governments. While fragile, the new democracies have survived several tests: when presidents have resigned or been driven from office, as occurred seven times in Ecuador between 1997 and 2005, four times in Argentina, three times in Bolivia, and once in Peru and Paraguay, the armed forces respected the constitutional order of succession and refrained from seizing power.[47]

Human rights observance is imperfect in any democratic country, but with the freedoms and the balance of powers implicit in democratic governance, civil and political rights have a much better chance of being recognized and practiced than in authoritarian systems. Moreover, democracy allows the human rights organizations formed during the period of repression to function freely. While they seek justice for past violations, they also vigorously push for strict observance of human rights in the present.

The international political situation is likewise very different from the 1970s and 1980s. With the collapse of the Soviet Union in 1991, the threat of the spread of Cuban-style revolution evaporated—and with it the rationale for a U.S. policy of supporting state terrorist regimes. Since then, except for dealing with perceived threats or problems such as the war in Colombia, the Chávez government in Venezuela, and the perennial aggravation of Fidel Castro, the United States has paid little attention to its southern neighbors beyond pushing its neoliberal economic agenda. As a signatory to the Inter-American Democratic Charter, the U.S. government is formally committed to supporting democracy in Latin America.[48]

Another major difference from the earlier period that affects the observance of human rights is the nature of the international human rights regime. When Latin America entered its human rights crisis, international institutions were still in the stage of standard setting, monitoring agencies were relatively new and untested, and domestic institutions were essentially nonexistent. But in response to the repression and state terrorism, numerous human rights organizations were established, and powerful human rights movements developed in some Latin American countries. International human rights NGOs multiplied. In addition, during its rapid evolution in the 1990s, human rights jurisprudence essentially ruled out amnesties in any form for human rights crimes, and international enforcement mechanisms were established. International jurisprudence has helped domestic human rights organizations establish higher standards and compel compliance with human rights law in Latin American countries. The 1998 arrest of General Pinochet in London, despite the eventual refusal of Great Britain to allow his extradition to Spain, graphically showed the world that a new era in human rights had arrived.[49]

While the political conjuncture of the postrepression period clearly tilted in favor of improved human rights practices, it did not guarantee redress for the massive human rights violations of the recent past. Indeed, victims and their families were often victimized again after the repressive regimes ended. The winners in the war on subversion reminded the losers of their feats and merits through holidays, ceremonies, speeches, and publications. When victims were commemorated, former repressors often countered by glorifying their own past deeds in saving the patria. Encounters with former torturers and the murderers of family members, who enjoyed their freedom and flouted their impunity, were acid reminders of state terrorism. Reports of truth commissions and unscripted events such as repressors' public confessions or Pinochet's arrest triggered memory and reopened wounds suffered years earlier. There was also the limited scope of investigations, reparations, and justice. Most civilian governments, if they did anything, limited their efforts to the most egregious crimes: murder and disappearance. This approach, dictated by the need to limit provocations to the military, implicitly suggested that indiscriminate detention, torture, rape, and forced exile were unimportant.

The greatest obstacle to justice was the continuing power of the militaries. Although out of office, the militaries continued to exercise their traditional tutelage over national politics, either directly as in Chile, or indirectly through pressures and sometimes threats, even rebellions. Antidemocratic military culture appeared to have hardened during the militaries' antisubversive campaigns. Many officers felt that their mission of national purification was unfinished and resented suggestions that they had committed excesses in the holy crusade to save the patria from Marxism.[50] For these officers and their civilian allies, the victims, whether evil or merely misguided, were responsible for their fate. Thus the militaries and their allies raised obstacles to investigations and prosecutions and harassed human rights groups; in Guatemala, unknown assailants—presumably linked to the military—went so far as to murder Bishop Juan Gerardi, head of the Catholic Church's Recovery of Historical Memory project. This happened in April 1998, two days after the church released the report of its truth commission's findings.[51]

Public indifference was another impediment to the quest for justice in the transitional period. Despite the large numbers of victims of human rights violations, a majority of the citizens of the countries that experienced state terrorism had not lost family members or close friends; most had not undergone arbitrary arrest and torture. Many of the same persons who had hidden behind a feigned ignorance of the human rights violations occurring around them during the period of repression continued to be disengaged, perhaps shamed by the reminders of their earlier denial of reality. Others, particularly the rural and small-town poor, were neutralized by the lingering memories of state terrorism and the enduring fear it instills; even if they lost family and friends, they often grieved in silence rather than making dangerous waves. These large segments of the countries' populations were marginal to the human rights movements' quest for justice. With the passage of time and the onset of "issue fatigue," they could even turn against the human rights movements, whose demands, shrill voices, and street demonstrations were unwelcome reminders of times best forgotten and impediments to the easy solution of closing the book on a difficult period and getting on with individual lives and national priorities.[52]

The complexities of pluralistic politics also contributed to the difficulty of achieving justice. In addition to the indifference of large segments of the population, advocates of justice had to deal with the substantial numbers of citizens who had supported the repression out of the conviction that the perceived threats to their way of life posed by Cuban-inspired leftists fully justified a war on subversion. Even the political parties sympathetic to victims and intent on achieving justice had multiple agendas, justice being one among many, whereas victims and their families tended to be single-issue political actors. Lacking the common enemy that had united them during the period of repression, the human rights movements themselves sometimes split over goals and strategy, thereby losing their cohesiveness and diluting their voices. They also lost much of their international financial support following the end of institutionalized repression. Those governments that were most committed to seeking justice for human rights violations were forced to compromise in the political arena; they also had to compromise with the militaries, which implicitly or explicitly threatened to disrupt the delicate process of democratic consolidation if subjected to investigation or prosecution.

The difficulty of achieving justice within democracy was poignantly illustrated by developments in Uruguay following the end of its period of repression in 1984. In the only case of its kind, the Uruguayan electorate passed direct judgment on the question of justice versus impunity. After the national congress, threatened by the military and its supporters, enacted a 1986 law forbidding prosecutions for human rights crimes, citizens gathered sufficient signatures to subject the law to a referendum. After much delay, in the April 1989 poll, they lost: military pressures, support for the past repression, public indifference, pluralistic politics, and the continuing state of fear instilled by state terrorism prevailed over the sentiment for justice by 53 to 41 percent.[53]

The contest between justice and impunity continues today in all countries that experienced state terrorism during Latin America's human rights crisis. This is particularly true in Chile and Argentina, where Latin America's most powerful human rights movements actively push investigations and trials of alleged repressors. Supported by the rapidly evolving international jurisprudence of human rights, even in Uruguay the issue supposedly settled by popular vote has been resurrected. "True reconciliation," in the words of Nelson Mandela, "does not consist in merely forgetting the past."[54] Despite efforts to impose collective amnesia, the past is very much alive today; and thanks to the persistence of human rights movements and victims of past dictatorships and their families, and to the human rights revolution launched by the Nuremberg trials, it is likely to be remembered for a very long time.

Notes

1. John Eagleson and Philip Scharper, eds., *Puebla and Beyond: Documentation and Commentary*, trans. John Drury (Maryknoll, NY: Orbis Books, 1979), 200.

2. "Report to Foreign Military Attachés by Argentine Armed Forces Leaders after Frondizi Overthrow," confidential U.S. Foreign Service Dispatch, April 16, 1962, quoted in Martin Edwin Andersen, *Dossier Secreto: Argentina's Desaparecidos and the Myth of the "Dirty War"* (Boulder, CO: Westview Press, 1993), 44.

3. John D. Martz, ed., *United States Policy in Latin America: A Quarter Century of Crisis and Challenge, 1961–1986* (Lincoln: University of Nebraska Press, 1988); Peter H. Smith, *Talons of the Eagle: Dynamics of U.S.-Latin American Relations*, 2nd. ed. (New York: Oxford University Press, 2000), 117–218.

4. Timothy P. Wickham-Crowley, *Guerrillas and Revolution in Latin America: A Comparative Study of Insurgents and Regimes since 1956* (Princeton, NJ: Princeton

University Press, 1992); Thomas C. Wright, *Latin America in the Era of the Cuban Revolution*, rev. ed. (Westport, CT: Praeger, 2001); Boris Goldenberg, *The Cuban Revolution and Latin America* (New York: Praeger, 1966).

5. Herbert Matthews, *The Cuban Story* (New York: George Braziller, 1961), 273–74.

6. Donald C. Hodges, *The Latin American Revolution: Politics and Strategy from Apro-Marxism to Guevarism* (New York: William Morrow, 1974).

7. Che Guevara, *Guerrilla Warfare*, 3rd ed., rev. and updated by Brian Loveman and Thomas M. Davies Jr. (Wilmington, DE: Scholarly Resources, 1997); Rolando Bonachea and Marta San Martín, *The Cuban Insurrection, 1952–1958* (New Brunswick, NJ: Transaction Books, 1974); Rolando Bonachea and Nelson P. Valdés, eds., *Revolutionary Struggle 1947–1958: Volume I of the Selected Works of Fidel Castro* (Cambridge, MA: MIT Press, 1972); Che Guevara, *Reminiscences of the Cuban Revolutionary War*, trans. Victoria Ortiz (New York: Grove Press, 1968); Jorge G. Castañeda, *Compañero: The Life and Death of Che Guevara*, trans. Marina Castañeda (New York: Knopf, 1997); Jon Lee Anderson, *Che Guevara: A Revolutionary Life* (New York: Grove Press, 1997).

8. Rolando E. Bonachea and Nelson P. Valdés, eds., *Cuba in Revolution* (Garden City, NY: Anchor Books, 1972); Edward Boorstein, *The Economic Transformation of Cuba* (New York: Monthly Review Press, 1968); Jorge I. Domínguez, *Cuba: Order and Revolution* (Cambridge, MA: Harvard University Press, 1978).

9. Philip W. Bonsal, *Cuba, Castro, and the United States* (Pittsburgh: University of Pittsburgh Press, 1972); Jorge I. Domínguez, *To Make the World Safe for Revolution: Cuba's Foreign Policy* (Cambridge, MA: Harvard University Press, 1989); Richard E. Welch Jr., *Response to Revolution: The United States and the Cuban Revolution, 1959–1961* (Chapel Hill: University of North Carolina Press, 1985); Peter Wyden, *Bay of Pigs* (New York: Simon & Schuster, 1979).

10. Martin Kenner and James Petras, eds., *Fidel Castro Speaks* (New York: Grove Press, 1969); and Tad Szulc, *Fidel: A Critical Portrait* (New York: William Morrow, 1986).

11. The original 1976 constitution is found at www.georgetown.edu/pdba/Constitutions/Cuba/cuba1976.html (accessed June 6, 2005).

12. Amnesty International, *Cuba, "Essential Measures": Human Rights Crackdown in the Name of Security* (London: Amnesty International, 2003).

13. Harry Kantor, *The Ideology and Politics of the Peruvian Aprista Movement* (New York: Octagon Books, 1966); John D. Martz, *Acción Democrática: Evolution of a Modern Political Party in Venezuela* (Princeton, NJ: Princeton University Press, 1966); Michael Fleet, *The Rise and Fall of Chilean Christian Democracy* (Princeton, NJ: Princeton University Press, 1985).

14. Brian Loveman and Thomas M. Davies Jr., *The Politics of Antipolitics: The Military in Latin America*, rev. and updated ed. (Wilmington, DE: Scholarly Resources, 1997); Frederick M. Nunn, *The Time of the Generals: Latin American Professional Militarism in World Perspective* (Lincoln: University of Nebraska Press, 1992); Bruce W.

Farcau, *The Chaco War: Bolivia and Paraguay, 1932–1935* (Westport, CT: Praeger, 1996).

15. Brian Loveman, "Human Rights, Antipolitics, and Protecting the *Patria*: An (Almost) Military Perspective," in *The Politics of Antipolitics*, ed. Loveman and Davies, 402.

16. Roger Trinquier, *Guerre, subversion, révolution* (Paris: R. Laffont, 1968); Genaro Arriagada Herrera, *El pensamiento político de los militares: estudios sobre Chile, Argentina, Brasil y Uruguay* (Santiago: Centro de Investigaciones Socioeconómicos de la Compañía de Jesús en Chile, 1981), 169–207; Instituto de Estudios Políticos para América Latina y Africa, *La ideología de la seguridad nacional en América Latina* (Madrid: Instituto de Estudios Políticos para América Latina y Africa, 1977); Manuel Antonio Garretón, *The Chilean Political Process*, trans. Sharon Kellum with Gilbert W. Merkx (Boston: Unwin Hyman, 1989), 68–84; David Pion-Berlin, "National Security Doctrine, Military Threat Perception and the 'Dirty War,'" *Comparative Political Studies* 21 (October 1988): 382–407.

17. Quoted in Graham H. Stewart and James L. Tigner, *Latin America and the United States*, 6th ed. (Englewood Cliffs, NJ: Prentice-Hall, 1975), 804–5; John Child, *Unequal Alliance: The Inter-American Military System, 1938–1978* (Boulder, CO: Westview Press, 1980); Richard M. Immerman, *The CIA in Guatemala: The Foreign Policy of Intervention* (Austin: University of Texas Press, 1982); Stephan Schlesinger and Stephen Kinzer, *Bitter Fruit: The Untold Story of the American Coup in Guatemala* (Garden City, NJ: Doubleday & Co., 1982).

18. Quoted in Guevara, *Guerrilla Warfare*, 26; Cole Blasier, *The Hovering Giant: U.S. Responses to Revolutionary Change in Latin America, 1910–1985*, rev. ed. (Pittsburgh: University of Pittsburgh Press, 1985).

19. Mario Horacio Orsolini, *La crisis del ejército* (Buenos Aires: Ediciones Arayú, 1964), 45. Writing also about Argentina, Eduardo Tiscornia noted that, in the absence of wartime combat between the Paraguayan War (1865–1870) and the Falklands/Malvinas conflict (1982), "it became necessary to create artificial conditions to preserve the martial spirit and construct the internal corporative pride that real wartime actions provide." Eduardo Tiscornia, *El destino circular de la Argentina, 1810–1984* (Buenos Aires: Librería Sarmiento, 1983), 142.

20. Lesley Gill, *The School of the Americas: Military Training and Political Violence in the Americas* (Durham, NC: Duke University Press, 2004); Child, *Unequal Alliance*; Michael T. Klare, *War without End: American Planning for the Next Vietnams* (New York: Vintage Books, 1972); Loveman and Davies, eds., *The Politics of Antipolitics*, 130–31.

21. "Report to Foreign Military Attachés by Argentine Armed Forces Leaders after Frondizi Overthrow," confidential U.S. Foreign Service Dispatch, April 16, 1962, quoted in Andersen, *Dossier Secreto*, 44.

22. Jack Nelson-Pallmeyer, *School of Assassins: Guns, Greed, and Globalization* (Maryknoll, NY: Orbis Books, 2001); Michael T. Klare and Cynthia Arnson, *Supplying Repression: U.S. Support for Authoritarian Regimes Abroad* (Washington, DC: Institute for Policy Studies, 1981).

23. David Collier, ed., *The New Authoritarianism in Latin America* (Princeton, NJ: Princeton University Press, 1979); Abraham F. Lowenthal and J. Samuel Fitch, eds., *Armies and Politics in Latin America*, rev. ed. (New York: Holmes & Meier, 1986); Joseph Ramos, *Neoconservative Economics in the Southern Cone of Latin America, 1973–1983* (Baltimore, MD: Johns Hopkins University Press, 1986); Karen Remmer, *Military Rule in Latin America* (Boston: Unwin Hyman, 1989); Alain Rouquié, *The Military and the State in Latin America*, trans. Paul Sigmund (Berkeley: University of California Press, 1987).

24. Quoted in Andersen, *Dossier Secreto*, 44.

25. From a 1976 speech, quoted in Genaro Arraigada Herrera, *Por la razón o la fuerza: Chile bajo Pinochet* (Santiago: Editorial Sudamericana, 1998), 63.

26. Chile, *Report of the National Commission on Truth and Reconciliation*, trans. Phillip E. Berryman (Notre Dame, IN: University of Notre Dame, 1993), 1:61. A scholar of the Argentine dirty war wrote: "Cold War crusaderism allied to extralegal tactics taught that morality could be suspended in the 'higher cause' of defending the nation, the West, or Christianity." Paul H. Lewis, *Guerrillas and Generals: The Dirty War in Argentina* (Westport, CT: Praeger, 2002), 143.

27. Peter Kornbluh, *The Pinochet File: A Declassified Dossier on Atrocity and Accountability* (New York: New Press, 2003), 187.

28. Goldenberg, *The Cuban Revolution*; Irving Louis Horowitz, Josué de Castro, and John Gerassi, eds., *Latin American Radicalism* (New York: Vintage Books, 1969); Henry A. Landsberger, ed., *Latin American Peasant Movements* (Ithaca, NY: Cornell University Press, 1969).

29. Wilfred A. Bacchus, *Mission in Mufti: Brazil's Military Regimes, 1964–1985* (Westport, CT: Greenwood Press, 1990); Peter McDonough, *Power and Ideology in Brazil* (Princeton, NJ: Princeton University Press, 1981); Maria Helena Moreira Alves, *State and Opposition in Military Brazil* (Austin: University of Texas Press, 1985); Thomas E. Skidmore, *The Politics of Military Rule in Brazil* (New York: Oxford University Press, 1988).

30. María Esther Gilio, *The Tupamaro Guerrillas*, trans. Anne Edmondson (New York: Ballantine Books, 1973); James Kohl and John Litt, eds., *Urban Guerrilla Warfare in Latin America* (Cambridge, MA: MIT Press, 1974); Arturo C. Porzecanski, *Uruguay's Tupamaros: The Urban Guerrilla* (New York: Praeger, 1973).

31. Servicio Paz y Justicia, Uruguay, *Uruguay Nunca Más: Human Rights Violations, 1972–1985*, trans. Elizabeth Hampsten (Philadelphia: Temple University Press, 1992); Saúl Sosnowski and Louise B. Popkin, eds., *Repression, Exile, and Democracy: Uruguayan Culture*, trans. Louise B. Popkin (Durham, NC; Duke University Press, 1993).

32. See chapter 3.

33. See chapter 3, 49, 56, 74–79, 82–83, on the U.S. role in Chile.

34. See chapter 4.

35. Cynthia McClintock, *Revolutionary Movements in Latin America: El Salvador's FMLN and Peru's Shining Path* (Washington, DC: United States Institute of Peace

Press, 1998); David Scott Palmer, ed., *The Shining Path of Peru* (New York: St. Martin's Press, 1992); Steve J. Stern, ed., *Shining and Other Paths: War and Society in Peru, 1980–1995* (Durham, NC: Duke University Press, 1998). The truth commission's report is available on the Internet at www.cverdad.org.pe/ingles/ifinal/conclusiones.php (accessed October 16, 2005).

36. John A. Booth, *The End and the Beginning: The Nicaraguan Revolution*, 2nd ed. (Boulder, CO: Westview Press, 1985); Thomas W. Walker, ed., *Nicaragua: The First Five Years* (New York: Praeger, 1985); Henri Weber, *Nicaragua: The Sandinista Revolution*, trans. Patrick Camiller (London: Verso Editions, 1981).

37. Americas Watch, *El Salvador's Decade of Terror: Human Rights since the Assassination of Archbishop Romero* (New Haven, CT: Yale University Press, 1991); Tommie Sue Montgomery, *Revolution in El Salvador: Origins and Evolution*, 2nd ed. (Boulder, CO: Westview Press, 1989); McClintock, *Revolutionary Movements*.

38. Tommie Sue Montgomery, *Revolution in El Salvador: From Civil Strife to Civil Peace*, 2nd ed. (Boulder, CO: Westview Press, 1995).

39. J. L. Fried et al., eds., *Guatemala in Rebellion: Unfinished Revolution* (New York: Grove Press, 1982); Eduardo Galeano, *Guatemala: Occupied Country*, trans. Cedric Belfrage (New York: Monthly Review Press, 1969).

40. Ricardo Falla, *Massacres in the Jungle: Ixcán, Guatemala, 1975–1982*, trans. Julia Howland (Boulder, CO: Westview Press, 1994); Daniel Wilkinson, *Silence on the Mountain: Stories of Terror, Betrayal, and Forgetting in Guatemala* (Boston: Houghton Mifflin, 2002); Susanne Jonas, *Of Centaurs and Doves: Guatemala's Peace Process* (Boulder, CO: Westview Press, 2000); Rachel Sieder, ed., *Guatemala after the Peace Accords* (London: Institute of Latin American Studies, 1998).

41. See chapters 3 and 4.

42. Wright, *Latin America in the Era*, 194–202; Amnesty International, *Cuba, "Essential Measures."* For up-to-date coverage of Colombia, see *Colombia Journal Online* at www.colombiajournal.org. Annual reports on human rights in Cuba and Haiti, as well as all other Latin American countries, are published by Human Rights Watch (http://hrw.org) and Amnesty International (www.amnesty.org).

43. The literature on transitions is voluminous. See Guillermo O'Donnell and Philippe Schmitter, *Transitions from Authoritarian Rule: Tentative Conclusions about Uncertain Democracies* (Baltimore, MD: Johns Hopkins University Press, 1986); Guillermo O'Donnell, Philippe Schmitter, and Laurence Whitehead, eds., *Transitions from Authoritarian Rule: Latin America* (Berkeley: University of California Press, 1988); James M. Malloy and Mitchell A. Seligson, eds., *Authoritarians and Democrats: Regime Transition in Latin America* (Pittsburgh: University of Pittsburgh Press, 1987). On Latin America's impoverishment, see Albert Berry, ed., *Poverty, Economic Reform, and Income Distribution in Latin America* (Boulder, CO: Lynne Rienner, 1998); Douglas A. Chalmers et al., eds., *The New Politics of Inequality in Latin America: Rethinking Participation and Representation* (New York: Oxford University Press, 1997); Michel Chossudovsky, *The Globalisation of Poverty: Impacts of IMF and World Bank Reforms* (London: Zed Books, 1997). Wright, *Latin America in the Era*, 203.

44. Luis Roniger and Mario Sznajder, *The Legacy of Human-Rights Violations in the Southern Cone: Argentina, Chile, and Uruguay* (Oxford: Oxford University Press, 1999), 109–35. Chilean writer Ariel Dorfman aptly sums up the challenges in the afterword to his play *Death and the Maiden* (New York: Penguin, 1992), 73–74.

45. Ruti Teitel, *Transitional Justice* (New York: Oxford University Press, 1999); A. James McAdams, ed., *Transitional Justice and the Rule of Law in New Democracies* (Notre Dame, IN: University of Notre Dame Press, 1997); Alexandra Barahona de Brito, Carmen González-Enríquez, and Paloma Aguilar, eds., *The Politics of Memory: Transitional Justice in Democratizing Societies* (Oxford: Oxford University Press, 2001); Mark R. Amstutz, *The Healing of Nations: The Promise and Limits of Political Forgiveness* (Lanham, MD: Rowman & Littlefield, 2005); Alexandra Barahona de Brito, *Human Rights and Democratization in Latin America: Uruguay and Chile* (Oxford: Oxford University Press, 1997), 1–32; Manuel Antonio Garretón, "Human Rights in Democratization Processes," in *Constructing Democracy: Human Rights, Citizenship, and Society in Latin America*, ed. Elizabeth Jelin and Eric Hershberg (Boulder, CO: Westview Press, 1996), 39–58. *NACLA Report on the Americas* 32, no. 2 (September–October 1998), titled "Unearthing Memory: The Present Struggle over the Past," is devoted to memory and truth contestation.

46. The definition of democratic elections is from Samuel P. Huntington, *The Third Wave: Democratization in the Late Twentieth Century* (Norman: University of Oklahoma Press, 1991), 9. Note that Mexico's 1988 presidential election (for the 1988–1994 term) was fraudulent, but reforms made the process more transparent thereafter.

47. Roderick Ai Camp, ed., *Democracy in Latin America: Patterns and Cycles* (Wilmington, DE: Scholarly Resources, 1996); Jorge I. Domínguez, ed., *Constructing Democratic Governance: Latin America and the Caribbean in the 1990s* (Baltimore, MD: Johns Hopkins University Press, 1996); John Peeler, *Building Democracy in Latin America* (Boulder, CO: Lynne Rienner, 1998); Christopher Sabatini, "Plowing the Sea? International Defense of Democracy in the Age of Illiberal Democracy," in *Democracy and Human Rights in Latin America*, ed. Richard S. Hillman, John A. Peeler, and Elsa Cardozo da Silva (Westport, CT: Praeger, 2002), 77–101. See the Inter-American Democratic Charter at www.oas.org/charter/docs/resolution1_en_p4.htm (accessed October 4, 2005).

48. Jonathan Hartlyn, Lars Schoultz, and Augusto Varas, eds., *The United States and Latin America in the 1990s: Beyond the Cold War* (Chapel Hill: University of North Carolina Press, 1992); Smith, *Talons of the Eagle*, 219–352; *NACLA Report on the Americas* 34, no. 3 (November–December 2000), an issue titled "Minding the Backyard: Washington's Latin America Policy after the Cold War," offers a critical assessment of U.S. policy.

49. See chapter 6, 202–7.

50. See chapter 5, 151–57, and chapter 6, 181–85, 194–96, 198.

51. *NACLA Report on the Americas* 32, no. 2 (September–October 1998): 33–34.

52. See chapters 5 and 6 for analyses of the political impediments to justice discussed in this and the following paragraph.

53. Robert K. Goldman and Cynthia G. Brown, *Challenging Impunity: The Ley de Caducidad and the Referendum Campaign in Uruguay* (New York: Americas Watch, 1989); Lawrence Weschler, *A Miracle, a Universe: Settling Accounts with Torturers* (New York: Pantheon Books, 1990), 173–236; Servicio Paz y Justicia, Uruguay, *Uruguay Nunca Más*, xxi–xxiv.

54. www.ethics.org.au/things_to_read/email_newsletter_04_04.shtm (accessed August 30, 2006).

PART TWO

THE DIRTY WARS

~

CHAPTER THREE

Chile under State Terrorism

The annihilation of Marxism could not be achieved in a democratic climate; the annihilation of Marxism and of everyone who considered
themselves pro-Marxist, neutral, lukewarm, undefined, was carried out
with brutal methods of repression that had no limits.

—General Horacio Toro, Chilean Army[1]

In the minds of the world at large, we are closely associated with this
junta, ergo with fascists and torturers.

—Richard J. Bloomfield, U.S. Embassy staff, Santiago[2]

Prior to 1973, Chile was one of Latin America's most stable and democratic
countries. In contrast to most countries of the region, Chile developed a
strong tradition of civilian rule following its independence from Spain in
1818. Beginning in the 1920s, the elite-dominated political system had
opened, with a brief period of political turbulence, to accommodate new parties and interest associations representing Chile's middle and working classes.
By the late 1930s, the Chilean electorate had coalesced into three roughly
equal right, centrist, and left blocs, the latter represented by the Socialist
Party and Latin America's most powerful Communist Party. The middle-class
Radical Party held the balance of power between 1938 and the late 1950s.
The last military intervention before 1973 occurred in 1932, when elements
of the military held or shared power for four months after the civilian gov-
ernment collapsed under the weight of the Great Depression.[3]

When revolutionary insurgency gripped much of Latin America in the 1960s, the Cuban Revolution's impact on Chile reflected the country's unique political history. As it did throughout Latin America, Castro's revolution inspired the radicalization of politics, increased demands for change, and triggered mobilization for land reform. But with the exception of the antisystem Movimiento de Izquierda Revolucionaria (Movement of the Revolutionary Left, MIR), founded in 1965 by students at the University of Concepción, the radicalization of Chilean politics occurred primarily within the existing institutional framework. As a result of the leftward shift of electoral politics between the 1961 and 1965 congressional elections, the right's share of the vote fell from 30.4 percent to 12.5 percent. The center benefited most from the right's decline, particularly the new and dynamic Christian Democratic Party, which rapidly won over the Radicals' constituency as well as votes from both left and right. Meanwhile, both the center and the left had incorporated ideas from the Cuban Revolution, and in the 1964 presidential election, voters were offered a choice between two versions of revolution: the Marxist program of Socialist Salvador Allende, and the "revolution in liberty" of Christian Democrat Eduardo Frei. The right bloc supported Frei, the lesser of the evils in their view, in order to prevent Allende's election. Frei won with 56.1 percent to Allende's 38.9 percent.[4]

Frei's administration (1964–1970) was progressive, even radical compared to previous Chilean governments. It legalized the unionization of agricultural workers; launched an ambitious land reform; invested in education, housing, and health; and took over a half interest in the U.S. copper companies that dominated Chile's export economy. Frei's reform program, however, was a political failure: it was far too radical for conservatives, most of whom had voted for Frei and thus felt betrayed, and too slow and timid for the left. In 1970, the refurbished right presented its own candidate against the Christian Democrats and the left candidate, Salvador Allende, who headed the Unidad Popular (Popular Unity, UP) coalition of Socialists, Communists, and four smaller non-Marxist parties. A longtime leader in the Socialist Party, Allende ran on a platform of accelerating change and moving Chile quickly to socialism. He won with 36.3 percent of the vote versus 34.9 for the right candidate and 27.8 for the Christian Democrat.[5]

Salvador Allende, a medical doctor and veteran politician, was the world's first, and only, freely elected socialist who was committed to eliminating large-scale capitalism in his country. He had first been elected to Congress in 1937; between 1966 and 1970, he served as president of the Senate. He had been a presidential candidate in 1952, 1958, and 1964. A decade after the Cuban Revolution had shown the possibility of radical change, Allende's election stunningly brought home to Chile the reality of revolution: revolution by the ballot box, the "Chilean road to socialism," or as Allende called it, the "revolution of red wine and empanadas" (traditional meat and onion pies), evoking the ingredients of Chilean popular celebrations. Despite Allende's pledge to work within the boundaries of Chile's 1925 constitution, his commitment to socialism threatened the elites' economic privileges, their land, and their very way of life. To many of Chile's *campesinos* and workers, the election of their "*compañero presidente*" was the prelude to a previously unimaginable utopia of abundance and equality. The contestation of these opposing and irreconcilable views of the future exacerbated the polarization begun in the 1960s and rapidly eroded the Chilean traditions of compromise and civility, endangering the shared value of democracy as the guiding principle of politics and ultimately straining the political system to the breaking point.[6]

U.S. governments throughout the 1960s had watched the radicalization of Chilean politics with growing concern. From the early 1960s through the 1970 presidential election, U.S. administrations spent millions of dollars to strengthen the opposition to the Chilean left. Having failed to prevent Allende's election, Nixon and his national security adviser, Henry Kissinger, set out to prevent the president-elect from being inaugurated. The CIA pursued dual strategies to accomplish this. Track I involved creating a climate for a military coup—a highly improbable occurrence in a country whose armed forces respected civilian governance and the 1925 constitution. Track II focused on the constitutional requirement that Congress formally elect the president in the absence of a majority in the popular vote—a very common occurrence given Chile's multiparty system. Although Congress had always elected the candidate who obtained the greatest number of votes, the CIA attempted to bribe Christian Democratic legislators to vote for the runner-up, who would resign immediately, making way for Frei to be reelected. Neither approach worked, and Allende was inaugurated on November 4. Two days later, the National Security Council met in Washington to discuss how to "bring him down."[7]

Although hampered by the UP's minority status in both chambers of Congress, Allende quickly threw down the gauntlet to Chilean and foreign capitalists by vigorously pursuing his campaign promise to expropriate large-scale business, industry, landholdings, and copper mining. Initially stunned and disoriented by Allende's victory, the Chilean right regrouped and within a year had forged an alliance with the centrist Christian Democrats, whose largely middle-class constituency balked at the uncertainties and discomforts of rapid change. The right-center alliance used its congressional majority and control of the judiciary to block the president's legislative agenda wherever possible, while Allende, unwilling to back down, used his executive powers and obscure laws from the Depression era to forge ahead. By Allende's second year, confrontation replaced dialogue. By his third year, the stakes were higher: the survival of the constitutional regime.[8]

The widening chasm between pro- and anti-Allende Chileans was based on more than ideological and programmatic disagreements. The MIR along with radicalized elements of Allende's coalition, particularly members of his own Socialist Party, proselytized and agitated ceaselessly, hoping to push the revolution beyond Allende's legal prescriptions and establish a revolutionary society beyond bourgeois law, while rightists responded with armed groups and sabotage. Hypermobilization in both the countryside and the large cities brought peasants and workers face to face with landowners and bosses in ways that were inconceivable to either side just a few years earlier. Occupations of haciendas and factories by their workers spawned a virulent reaction on the part of owners and managers, culminating in two "bosses' strikes" organized by the country's business interest associations, or gremios, and subsidized by the CIA: the first, in October 1972, shut down the country's economy while sparking even more occupations, and the second, in August 1973, was not lifted until Allende's overthrow.

During Allende's third year in office, "polarization became the dominant feature of political language and interaction, and the more violent sectors in that polarization . . . came to the fore."[9] The extreme left talked stridently about arming their followers and replacing the armed forces with popular militias; on the right, Patria y Libertad (Fatherland and Liberty) destroyed infrastructure, assassinated leftists, and painted "Djakarta," an allusion to the slaughter of Indonesian Communists following Sukarno's 1965 overthrow, on walls and buildings. As the lines hardened, families, friends, and organizations split. Constant agitation, shortages, violence, name-calling, and press sensationalism became a way of life. To Allende supporters, the economic elites and political right were anachronisms—supercilious "momios," or mummies, whose day had passed. To Allende opponents, the left was made up of extremists, criminals, and subversives intent on establishing a Soviet-style dictatorship. The lexicon of the time included "it's us or them," "you can't make an omelet without breaking a few eggs," and "the cancer has to be rooted out." This language of vilification employed by both sides, in the words of the truth commission that probed human rights violations under the Pinochet dictatorship, "paved the way for fear which engenders hatred and hence brutality and death."[10] Chile, in short, had become a "nation of enemies."[11]

The Coup and Its Aftermath

When it came on September 11, 1973, the coup surprised few people, even in a country where the military's adherence to law and constitution had long been taken for granted. Allende's revolution had spun out of control; Chile was virtually bankrupt, beset by shortages and runaway inflation, and increasingly ungovernable. Both sides had openly discussed a military uprising; in late August, the opposition majority in Congress had passed a resolution that in effect called for the military to remove Allende. Many UP loyalists fully expected a coup; some naively thought they were prepared for it. Weary of daily confrontation and permanent crisis, many ordinary Chileans welcomed military intervention, with the expectation that the armed forces would follow a conventional Latin American script: seize control, detain and deport top government officials, hold power for a year or two, and then call elections to restore civilian rule. Much of the officer corps anticipated the same. Many Christian Democrats, members of Chile's largest party, fully expected Eduardo Frei, whom the constitution had barred from seeking a second consecutive term in 1970, to be elected president again.[12]

The armed forces along with the Carabineros, Chile's national police, rose on the morning of September 11. Following the navy's seizure of the principal port of Valparaíso, rebel forces quickly occupied strategic points throughout the country. After President Allende rejected an ultimatum to surrender, Hawker-Hunter jets strafed the Moneda, Chile's historic presidential palace, leaving it in flames. Allende took his life inside the burning building. In Santiago's industrial belt and shantytowns, where large-scale resistance was expected, the few armed clashes that occurred ended within forty-eight hours. The military sealed Chile's borders for eleven days, turning the country into a huge prison camp for thousands of Allende supporters, and imposed an around-the-clock curfew. Radio broadcasts announced lists of persons required to turn themselves in to the new authorities. Many people complied with these orders in order to clear their names; some were never seen again.[13]

After the first day, with Allende dead and the expected resistance having failed to materialize, the military had won virtually complete control of Chile. Yet for several weeks a brutal crackdown filled makeshift jails, hospitals, and morgues. Allende supporters, whose political beliefs and organizations had been perfectly legal until the morning of September 11, were ex post facto criminals in the eyes of Chile's new masters. Stunned by the display of military might and the severity of the repression, thousands of leftists went underground, sought asylum in embassies, or attempted to flee the country after the borders reopened. Many people were shot on the spot for defying the curfew; others, the authorities claimed, were killed resisting arrest or attempting to escape after detention—explanations for murder that the dictatorship would use for years to come. Bodies were left on streets and roads and dumped into rivers, including the Mapocho, which runs through the heart of Santiago; others were buried in secret graves, beginning the soon-to-be routine practice of "disappearing" the regime's enemies.[14]

The highest-profile Allende supporters, including cabinet ministers and party leaders, were arrested and flown to an improvised prison on Dawson Island in the icy Straits of Magellan. Another fifty thousand persons throughout the country were rounded up and held in soccer stadiums, military bases, government buildings, and navy ships. The National Stadium, where some seven thousand prisoners were held, and the navy ship *Esmeralda*, anchored at Valparaíso, became enduring symbols of the postcoup repression. Many prisoners were tortured and hundreds executed in these and other locales throughout the country during the first weeks of the new regime.

Almost two thousand people were tried by hastily assembled military war tribunals, which lacked the minimum guarantees for a fair trial. Some three hundred were executed immediately; others were sentenced to prison camps. In addition to military repression, right-wing vigilantes in rural areas exacted revenge on *campesinos* who had challenged the traditional social order by joining unions, agitating for land, and occupying haciendas. These and other class and personal scores were settled in the atmosphere of bloodshed and revenge that dominated after September 11.[15]

In one of its first statements, the junta declared that it would hold power "only as long as circumstances require[d]" for it to restore Chile's "broken institutionality."[16] Despite this discourse of democratic restoration, it was clear from the outset that the military was not following the standard coup script. Attacking and burning the Moneda palace, the most visible and venerated symbol of Chilean democracy, revealed the military leadership's determination to reject any limits on the use of force to destroy their enemies—an ominous prelude to the establishment of the terrorist state. On the evening of September 11, the commanders of the army, navy, air force, and Carabineros swore themselves in as a governing junta and decreed a state of siege befitting a "state or time of war," which suspended civil liberties and greatly expanded the jurisdiction of the military courts. The declaration of war, the use of force far out of proportion to what was needed to dislodge the Allende government, and the prolonged application of massive repression reinforced the message of the bombing of the Moneda.[17]

As the junta coalesced, it gave additional signals that its agenda extended well beyond the overthrow of Allende and that its rule would be lengthy. In addition to granting itself absolute authority to govern without restrictions, the junta began dismantling all institutions that might stand in the way of its consolidation of power. It replaced UP provincial governors with military officers, removed all mayors and city councilors, banned left parties and suspended the others, and closed Congress. The junta instituted strict censorship, dissolved the national labor federation, appointed military rectors for the universities, and restricted the activities of professional organizations. Within weeks, almost no institutions remained as counterweights to absolute military rule. In November the junta declared the country's election registries null; they were later burned. Meanwhile, just days after the coup, the junta had appointed a committee to study reforming the 1925 constitution.[18]

At the junta's first public appearance, on the night of September 11, air force commander in chief General Gustavo Leigh had declared that it was the military's duty to extirpate the "Marxist cancer."[19] While the other three junta members spoke that night in more conciliatory tones, their words and actions soon revealed their commitment to Leigh's proposition. General Augusto C. Pinochet, army commander in chief and leader of the junta, initially assured Chileans that there would be "neither victors nor vanquished," that the military's mission was to "salvage the country"; but in an October speech, he claimed in messianic tones that the coup had been God's work, and he committed himself to the "heroic struggle" to carry out a "moral cleansing" in order to "extirpate the root of evil from Chile."[20]

In order to justify its massive crackdown on Allende supporters and the emerging crusade against Marxism, the junta announced on September 17 that it had discovered Plan Z, and later it printed the *White Book of the Change of Government in Chile* to make its case.[21] Widely distributed at home and abroad, the *White Book* used assorted documents, photographs of arms caches, and bold claims in an attempt to convince the world that in the sinister Plan Z, the Allende government, aided by Cuban operatives, had planned to assassinate top military officers and opposition political figures. The *White Book* stated, "The Unidad Popular and Salvador Allende, not satisfied with trampling upon the majoritarian will of the country, with violating the substance and the form of the constitution and of the laws, with disregarding the condemnation and the warnings of the other Powers of the State, with ruining the country economically and financially, and with having sown and spread hate, violence and death throughout the nation, was prepared and ready to carry out this self-coup designed to conquer an absolute power based on force and crime, and installing the 'people's dictatorship.'"[22] In addition to justifying the overthrow of Allende, by demonizing the left as assassins, servants of Moscow, and enemies of the country, the *White Book* clearly laid the groundwork for a holy crusade against the left.

On September 11, the military had declared itself at war, but by all indications it had won the war in a matter of hours. The decisive actions of September eliminated any possibility of effective resistance and restored a state of order that Chile had not experienced in months, even years. Plan Z had been concocted to justify the violent repression of the left, but despite a search for the arsenals and training camps alleged in the junta's booklet, little evidence was found to substantiate the claims of grave threats to the fatherland. However, as the junta's commitment to eradicating the left deepened, it required the fiction of war to justify the extreme measures it would need to employ. Thus, to validate its existence, rally public support, and unify the military around its mission, the junta invented a war that it would fight for sixteen and a half years.

In order to convince the country of the gravity of the Marxist threat, intensify the wartime atmosphere, and spread anti-Marxist fervor to the provinces, where the takeover had encountered virtually no resistance, the junta staged an event that became known as the "Caravan of Death" in late September and October. General Sergio Arellano Stark was dispatched on a helicopter tour of eight cities and towns where he was to convene war tribunals to quickly try and sentence detainees and increase the sentences of those already convicted but not executed. While on this mission, Arellano's party also summarily shot seventy-five people and buried them in secret graves.[23]

The Caravan of Death made regional commanders and other ranking officers take a position: either they stood with the hard line emanating from the junta, they retired, or they faced severe consequences. Lieutenant Colonel Olagier Benavente, stationed at Talca when Arellano visited his base, recalled, "That fear that General Arellano aroused in Talca spread quickly throughout Chile. I understood that you had to be tougher if you wanted to survive."[24] The exercise was a success: in addition to sowing terror among civilians, it enabled the junta to weed out the small number of pro-Allende officers, the larger number who favored a quick return to civilian government, and weak-willed officers who balked at the measures taken. It ensured the ascendancy of the mission to eradicate the left.[25]

By the end of 1973, sixteen weeks after the coup, the military, abetted by a small number of civilians including members of Patria y Libertad, had exacted a heavy toll on the human rights of Chileans. Tens of thousands had been arrested without warrants, thousands had been tortured, and hundreds were tried and sentenced in war tribunals. Nearly two thousand people had been killed outright or had disappeared following detention.[26] The exodus of leftists, which would become a true diaspora, was well under way. The junta had unleashed state terrorism on the Chilean people on September 11 in order to establish control rapidly and completely. During the ensuing sixteen weeks, terrorism was an instrument of policy, but it was driven also by hatred, vengeance, pent-up rage, an air of triumphalism, and perhaps by the taste of absolute power over the enemy—an enemy described by Pinochet on the morning of the coup as "those filthy people (*mugrientos*) who want to ruin the country."[27]

Almost immediately, both domestic and international institutions raised concerns as the need for defense of human rights became apparent. The severity of the repression, the hardening of the military's mission, and the junta's dismantling of virtually all institutions of civil society made it impossible for individuals to act on their own or to form groups to offer aid on the scale required. As a result, the Chilean human rights movement developed under the auspices of the only institutions capable of carving out space for human rights work: the churches. While the dominant Roman Catholic Church was the most visible defender of human rights, denominations representing small numbers of Chileans—the Methodist and other Protestant churches, the Greek Orthodox Church, and the Jewish community—also played a central role, aided by financial support from the World Council of Churches and other international sources.[28]

The churches responded within weeks, first by setting up a Comité Nacional de Ayuda a los Refugiados (National Committee for Aid to Refugees, CONAR)—also known as Committee 1—to help find refuge for the thousands of leftists being hunted down, including many foreigners. They worked with the Intergovernmental Committee for European Migration, the UN high commissioner for refugees, and the International Red Cross to first get the persecuted into embassies and then to arrange safe conduct and passage to countries willing to accept them as refugees. By the end of October, some four thousand safe conducts had been issued, and another five thousand were pending. On October 6, the churches founded Committee 2—the Comité de Cooperación para la Paz en Chile (Committee for Cooperation for Peace in Chile, COPACHI)—to provide legal, material, and spiritual assistance to the persecuted and the growing numbers of unemployed. These two church-based organizations functioned for nineteen and twenty-seven months, respectively, during the period of the most violent repression, despite being labeled Marxist and being constantly harassed by the regime.[29]

Complementing the struggle of the incipient domestic human rights movement were the efforts of human rights advocates around the world. From the day of the coup, human rights in Chile were the subject of global concern. News and images of soldiers herding unarmed civilians at rifle point, stadiums packed with prisoners, bodies washed up on the banks of the Mapocho, and a grim General Pinochet looking sinister in dark glasses filled newspapers and television screens. Within days of the coup, Amnesty International and the International Commission of Jurists requested UN intervention to save lives. The International Red Cross sent an inspection team less than two weeks after the coup. Other human rights NGOs sought permission to visit but were initially denied. Several embassies, including the Mexican, Venezuelan, Argentine, Swedish, Italian, and French, opened their doors to provide temporary sanctuary for the hunted. The dictatorship expelled Swedish ambassador Harald Edelstam in December for his exceptionally active role in offering asylum.[30]

Before the end of 1973, the executive secretary of the Inter-American Commission on Human Rights, a delegation from Amnesty International, and several other groups of lawyers and human rights advocates visited Chile. While the Nixon administration embraced the new regime and renewed aid and loans it had cut to undermine Allende, the U.S. Congress discussed human rights in Chile within a week of the coup and held full-scale hearings in December. Other visits, investigations, and hearings were announced. To counter the negative foreign reaction, the junta established the Dirección de Información Exterior (Foreign Information Directorate) to purchase favorable coverage in media around the world through U.S. public relations firms.[31]

Background to the Terrorist State

Historically, no South American country had a less politicized military than Chile. Yet the transformation of a military institution removed from partisan and ideological politics into a political machine with an ideological mission and the will to use any means to accomplish it did not happen overnight. There had been currents of political activism in the armed forces at least since the 1920s: individual officers collaborated with right-wing organizations, and military lodges such as Línea Recta (Straight Line) and Por un Mañana Auspicio (For an Auspicious Tomorrow, PUMA) of the 1950s brought together officers who supported antidemocratic rightist agendas. While there were moderate and leftist officers in the ranks, overall the military had a "continual and longstanding tradition of anticommunism dating practically back to the Russian Revolution."[32]

From the onset of the Cold War, and particularly in the wake of the Cuban Revolution, the Chilean military, along with their counterparts throughout the Americas, had been bombarded with national security doctrine and its centerpiece, anti-Marxism. From outside the barracks, however, it was difficult to gauge the degree to which the anti-Marxist lesson had been absorbed because, unlike the militaries of most other countries, the Chilean officer corps accepted a constitutionally sanctioned division of labor: the politicians talked while they trained to defend the country. Moreover, in a country where Marxist parties had enjoyed legality since the 1920s, had held cabinet posts since 1938, and represented a third of the electorate, military pronouncements about the dangers of Marxism were out of bounds. But the evidence from after September 11 suggests that long before Allende's election, anti-Marxist indoctrination had penetrated deeply. When tested by the Allende administration, the military's anti-Marxism proved stronger than its time-honored tradition of constitutionalism.[33]

Among some officers, the experience of the UP years translated intellectual opposition to Marxism into a visceral hatred. In addition to many of Allende's policies, the polarization, hypermobilization, and growing chaos that characterized Allende's last year and a half could not have pleased an institution that valued order and hierarchy. The greatly exaggerated but loudly trumpeted existence of armed leftist groups during Allende's administration naturally concerned the institutions that officially monopolized armed force. The ultraleft's talk of abolishing the armed forces and replacing them with people's militias, as happened in Cuba, and its alleged attempts to provoke rebellion in the military ranks, seemed to challenge the very survival of the armed forces. Some officers worried about a civil war and its potentially divisive impact on the military.

Breaking with Chilean tradition, Allende in desperation had brought officers into his cabinet during two periods of political crisis in order to provide an image of probity and stability. Resentment at being used to prop up a government that appeared to tolerate antimilitary words and actions further stoked the anti-Marxist fires. Had General Carlos Prats, a committed constitutionalist and friend of Allende, not been army commander during most of Allende's presidency, the coup might well have come earlier. Ultimately, the UP years put the military's anti-Marxism and its tradition of nonintervention on a collision course. That collision occurred on September 11, 1973.[34]

Developments in the coup's aftermath also help explain the institutionalization of state terrorism. Those military men who had been convinced of the imminence of a Marxist takeover—the thesis of Plan Z—fully expected important groups inside and outside the country to embrace their cause and express gratitude for the salvation of Chile. But rather than thanking the military, most of the Western democracies, the Chilean Catholic Church, and the Christian Democrats—most of whom initially endorsed the coup—condemned the brutality of the repression. This lack of comprehension and support frustrated the military leaders and left them resentful; rather than modifying their attitudes and behavior, the hard-liners dug in to shoulder the task of fighting World War III. This reaction reinforced their mistrust of all "politics" and led them to shun even the mainstream conservative political establishment that might have been able to exercise a moderating influence over their actions.[35]

Fundamental also to the development of state terrorism was a small but aggressive group of advocates of countersubversive warfare, mostly majors and colonels who, in the fluid situation following the coup, were able to impose their vision of a holy crusade. The "DINA group" of virulently anti-Marxist officers, so named for the secret police agency they would create and run, was operating cohesively even before the coup. Led by Colonel Manuel Contreras, the group moved quickly and ruthlessly after September 11 to promote its cause and extend its power. It soon achieved disproportionate influence with the military command, particularly with Pinochet, who had assumed command of the army only three weeks before the coup. As a last-minute convert to the plot to overthrow Allende, he seized upon the extremist agenda and the influence of the DINA group to firm up his position and unify the military around himself. Those who questioned the ascendancy of the DINA group were outmaneuvered, forcibly retired, and in some cases even killed.[36]

Though executed by the military and police, the coup of September 11, 1973, and the state terrorism that ensued did not take place in a political vacuum. A majority of Chileans may have welcomed the coup. After the Christian Democrats withdrew their support in reaction to the degree of repression and to the military's emerging plans for systemic change, Pinochet still retained the backing of large numbers of rightist civilians who either endorsed state terrorism or acquiesced in it, although normally denying its existence. Some went beyond supporting the regime. Many collaborated as cabinet ministers, administrators, policy consultants, and bureaucrats; as owners of mass media, editors, and writers; or as judges. Some worked directly in the terror apparatus. Others, including influential individuals who lent their names and prestige to the regime, collaborated in less direct ways.

In common with other Latin American countries, Chile had had extreme right groups and movements throughout the twentieth century, but they did not prosper because elite interests were effectively represented and protected by two political parties—the Conservatives and Liberals—and by interest associations such as the Sociedad Nacional de Agricultura (National Society of Agriculture, SNA) and similar organizations for other economic sectors. Even after losing their supremacy in the 1920s, these rightist parties, relying on their large landowner base to control the rural vote, were able to deflect threats to their interests. But with the mobilization and radicalization catalyzed by the Cuban Revolution—and an unrelated reform that introduced the secret ballot in 1958—the right's control of the crucial rural vote evaporated. Realizing this, the right had supported Christian Democrat Eduardo Frei in the 1964 presidential election to prevent a likely victory by Salvador Allende in a three-way race. Elections the following year decimated the right's power in Congress, leaving the two parties with 7 of 45 seats in the Senate and only 9 of 147 in the Chamber of Deputies. The worst nightmare of the right then followed: an aggressive program of agrarian reform that not only took landowners' property but further undermined their political power, leading the traditional elites to feel "on the verge of extinction."[37]

After regrouping in 1966 under a new name, the Partido Nacional (National Party), the right approached the 1970 presidential election with a degree of optimism. But when Allende won and launched his program to establish socialism, a large part of the right withdrew its allegiance to democratic politics—an allegiance that had been fraying since the mid-1960s as the right's political power plummeted—and embraced the heretofore minor currents of the antidemocratic right. Even while contesting Allende in Congress, in the media, and in the streets, some rightists opted for a military solution to their crisis. In the words of a scholar of the extreme right, "in moments of crisis the boundaries between moderate and extreme right fade."[38] The trajectory of politics from the early 1960s through the Allende administration was such a crisis for the traditionally moderate Chilean right. Thus, in addition to supporting the coup, much of the right would endorse any methods the dictatorship might use to persecute the left and restore the elites' tattered status and power—even state terrorism.

Following the coup, a small but influential coterie of extreme right-wing civilians, known as *gremialistas* for their role in marshaling Chile's business and professional associations, or *gremios*, in the right's struggle against Allende, came to the fore. They made themselves readily available to the military government in order to guide it toward their ideal: a Chile run by the upper class, free of social conflict, and bound by a Catholic nationalist or integralist ideology. Led by Catholic University law professor Jaime Guzmán, this group found a receptive audience among the officers. The *gremialist* view of politics, already shared by some within the military, was that the Chilean political system, from values to constitution to elections, was fatally flawed because it had allowed Marxism to flourish for decades and had opened the door to Allende's election. Under these influences, the military's mission broadened beyond eradicating the left; it included rolling back the clock to the early twentieth century, to a time before Chile's social struggles had begun in earnest and when oligarchic rule was uncontested.[39]

Having seized and consolidated power, the commanders realized that they possessed a historic opportunity to recast the country in fundamental ways. Within a few months, Pinochet's and the junta's vision, largely shaped by the *gremialistas*, had begun to jell. The government's March 1974 "Declaration of Principles," written primarily by Guzmán, proclaimed, "Chile is not neutral toward Marxism, and the present government does not fear or hesitate to declare itself anti-Marxist." The armed forces would hold power indefinitely "because the task of reconstructing the country morally, institutionally, and materially requires profound and prolonged action." To accomplish this, "it is absolutely necessary to change the mentality of Chileans" by extirpating Marxism and its doctrine of class struggle and replacing it with the values of conservative Catholicism, class harmony, and Chilean nationalism.[40] The institutional rebuilding would require the elimination of virtually all existing political institutions, save the courts, and the eventual construction of a "protected democracy" that would prevent the resurgence of leftist influence.

After some initial debate, the regime decided that the economic rebuilding would follow the neoliberal model advocated by the so-called Chicago Boys, a cadre of Catholic University economists trained by Milton Friedman at the University of Chicago. This version of unfettered capitalism, suitable to the emerging global economy, required not only undoing all of Allende's economic measures, but stripping away the many accretions of state economic control and ownership that had accumulated since the Great Depression—a monumental task. The free market model involved shrinking government budgets, cutting social programs, eliminating the high tariffs that protected Chilean industry, and selling off state-owned enterprises.[41]

The government's plan to construct what would be essentially a new country was extremely ambitious. With the exception of Fidel Castro's Cuban Revolution, no twentieth-century Latin American regime had ever set forth such a far-reaching agenda. Taking his cues from the Soviet Union, which had struggled in the 1930s to create the "New Soviet Man"—people with attitudes and values of socialist solidarity rather than capitalist individualism—Castro tried to create a "New Cuban Man" in the early 1960s through Marxist education, censorship of alternate views, and suppression of dissent.[42] Obviously, such a complete transformation, whether in the Soviet Union or Cuba, could not be accomplished within a framework of democracy and civil liberties; it had to be forced.

Pinochet's task would be similar to Castro's. Ridding Chile of politics, inculcating new values, building new institutions, and coping with the consequences of a new economic dogma could not be accomplished by persuasion. Like Castro's overwhelming challenge, the recasting of Chile would need to be forced. Although the "cancer of Marxism" had infected only part of Chilean society, albeit a major one, Pinochet's use of force would be far more systematic and brutal than Castro's: Pinochet would rely upon state terrorism to effect a final solution to the problems of Marxism and subversion.[43]

State Terrorism Institutionalized

By early 1974, observers noted a change in the repression. Large-scale arrests became rarer, bodies turned up less frequently, and fewer soldiers patrolled the streets. The truth commission established after the dictatorship's end noted the difference: "Many disappearances took place in the latter months of 1973, but for the most part these were efforts to evade responsibility for murder by hiding the bodies. By contrast, the instances of disappearance after arrest in the 1974–1977 period reflect a pattern of prior planning and centralized coordination."[44] The regime was shifting from the ad hoc but lethal terrorism it unleashed on September 11 to institutionalized terrorism. To increase its efficiency and parry the world reaction to the brutality of the postcoup period, the regime developed a new approach to eradicating the left that was designed to cover up the practices of state terrorism and offer plausible deniability to charges of gross human rights violations: the disappearance.

Although disappearance became the preferred method of eradicating subversives, some people were still killed outright, either by design or as the result of bad information, botched abductions, or resistance to arrest. When dealing with corpses, the secret police invariably explained the deaths as resulting from prisoners' attempting to escape (the *ley fuga*), armed attacks on the police, or shootouts among rival bands of subversives. The formal terror apparatus that was functioning before the beginning of 1974 reaped its greatest harvest in the following three and a half years, but it remained intact and continued to function to the regime's final days.

State terrorism was directed at a wide range of people, almost all of them associated with the left. Indeed, no one defined by the regime as a leftist, even if unaffiliated with the UP government or the Marxist parties, could consider him- or herself exempt from persecution. Many were targeted for the ex post facto crimes of having embraced Marxist ideology or having belonged to Marxist organizations, both perfectly legal prior to September 11,

1973. Some victims of state terrorism had violated laws under the Allende government, such as occupying factories and farms or possessing weapons prohibited by arms control laws. Others were targeted because they belonged to broad categories of people automatically suspected of disaffection from the regime—students, teachers, intellectuals, journalists, members of several professions, workers, union members and leaders, and slum dwellers. Some people were accidental or random victims of repression.[45]

Chile's poor were constantly in the repressors' sights, initially because they were assumed to be Allende supporters, and later because, as the primary victims of the new economic model, they had to be tightly controlled to prevent protests that might embarrass or even threaten the regime. The consequences of the Chicago Boys' radical policies for Chile's workers were massive unemployment, contracting real wages, and, with their unions emasculated and government social programs cut, little hope for remedying their dire situation. Thus, at the time of the coup and again during the regime's economic "shock" measures of 1974–1976 and the economic crisis of 1982–1985, slums were especially targeted for close control. Troops and police conducted *allanamientos*, or sweeps, of the areas by surrounding them to prevent escape, searching house by house for weapons and subversive materials, and detaining men, some of whom were sent to prison camps where they became hostages to the correct comportment of their families and neighbors.[46]

Campesinos lost out through the reversal of one of Latin America's most ambitious agrarian reform programs. The military immediately halted land distribution and returned much expropriated property to its former owners. It slashed government technical and financial aid to the new family-farm sector created under Frei and Allende, making it unable to compete in the new free market. With landowner control restored and *campesino* leaders persecuted, the rural poor were thoroughly intimidated and constituted no threat to the praetorian peace.[47]

As a rule, Christian Democrats were marginalized but left alone so long as they respected the ban on political activity. Dissidents were harassed, sometimes exiled, but rarely killed or disappeared. Rightists had no reason to worry; indeed, the peace and, for some, the prosperity they enjoyed after 1973 were the fruits of state terrorism.[48]

The dictatorship utilized all the elements at its command to impose terror. Each military branch and the Carabineros had their own intelligence service that was used both to gather information on "subversives" and to carry out much of the day-to-day repression. New formations, such as a shadowy Comando Conjunto (Joint Command) death squad run by the air force in 1975–1976, appeared and disappeared during the dictatorship. Even after the creation of the Dirección Nacional de Inteligencia (National Directorate of Intelligence, DINA), the junta's new secret police, the apparatus of state terrorism continued to experience rivalries and overlapping tasks and jurisdictions.[49]

The DINA was the core of the state terror apparatus. By November 1973, as the junta's mission and long-term ambitions were taking shape, Colonel Manuel Contreras, leader of the hard antileft faction, was beginning to operate a new "super" intelligence agency, institutionally independent of existing ones, under the junta's direct authority. Decree law 521 formally established the DINA a few months later. Its published articles seemed innocuous enough; they charged the agency with "gathering all information . . . needed for policy formulation and planning and for the adoption of those measures required for the protection of national security and the development of the country." In three secret, unpublished articles, the law established DINA's primacy among intelligence services and authorized the new secret police agency to conduct raids and make arrests without restraints.[50]

Creation of the DINA put the most extreme of the military's anti-Marxists in charge of the emblematic instrument of state terrorism. As director of the DINA, Contreras recruited like-minded individuals from within the military and police for this elite secret police dedicated to the "total extermination of Marxism"; he also hired civilians, including some from the paramilitary Patria y Libertad.[51] Eventually reaching some four thousand agents, the DINA also had thousands of informants and collaborators. Although it officially reported to the junta, the DINA quickly became Pinochet's personal instrument. Several ranking officers clashed with Contreras over the DINA's methods and power; one general, in a letter to Pinochet, referred to it as "a true Gestapo."[52] Doubters and opponents of the DINA expressed themselves at considerable peril, for this "state within a military state" was central to the enhancement of Pinochet's personal power over the junta and the country, which allowed him in June 1974 to elevate his status from head of the junta to "supreme head of the nation," and in December to president of the republic.[53]

The DINA was a multifaceted secret organization that used its "practically unlimited power" to "conceal its actions and assure its impunity."[54] Its repressive apparatus consisted of two intelligence brigades—the Metropolitan Brigade for Santiago and another for the rest of the country—that reported through Contreras to Pinochet. The Metropolitan Brigade assumed greater importance because leftists, since it was almost impossible for them to avoid detection and detention in the smaller cities and towns, usually sought refuge in the sprawling capital with its three million people and the possibility of clandestine existence. The Metropolitan Brigade was divided into the Caupolicán and Purén units, each of which was further divided into operations groups, among them the Halcón, Aguila, and Vampiro (Hawk, Eagle, and Vampire) groups, which conducted the repressive operations using their own offices, vehicles, and weaponry. They operated without constraints, taking advantage of the state of siege and the curfew, which, though gradually shortened, remained in force for several years, giving the DINA the upper hand against the enemy trapped for several hours each night in safe houses that became increasingly unsafe.[55]

The DINA's efforts focused on the regime's most dangerous enemies: the MIR and the Socialist and Communist parties. The Socialists and Communists had lost much of their upper ranks to prison, execution, or exile in the months following the coup, but both parties succeeded in establishing underground units. These clandestine groups lacked offensive capability and posed no threat to military control, but they served the exiled leadership by smuggling out intelligence and keeping alive the hope of mounting resistance. The MIR leadership initially rejected the option of exile and went underground, determined to resist. The regime considered the MIR especially dangerous because of its radicalism, its claims to have armed fighters, and its successful proselytizing among *campesinos* and slum dwellers. Ultimately, all three underground organizations and their real or potential collaborators were targeted because, despite their weakness, they stood in the way of the complete extermination of the left inside Chile.[56]

In pursuing the left underground, the DINA refined the methods of repression that had characterized the first few months after the coup and had led to international investigations and condemnations of the junta's human rights policies. It immediately established a number of secret detention and torture centers around the country. Among those in and around the capital were Cuatro Alamos, an exclusive DINA facility inside the Tres Alamos prison camp set up to hold political prisoners; Londres 38, the former downtown offices of the Socialist Party's Santiago section; and a house at José Domingo Cañas 1367. After it opened in mid-1974, Villa Grimaldi was the DINA's most important secret detention center until its closing in 1977.[57]

A three-acre site with a luxurious main house and numerous outbuildings, Villa Grimaldi was confiscated by the military after the coup from a wealthy friend and supporter of President Allende. It was located in the Andean foothills near Santiago. The DINA used Villa Grimaldi, which it called Terranova Barracks, as headquarters of the Metropolitan Brigade, and built cells and torture rooms in various buildings on the property. Approximately five thousand enemies of the regime passed through Villa Grimaldi; of those, at least 240 were tortured to death, murdered, or disappeared.[58]

The DINA's modus operandi began with a detention, usually but not always under cover of the curfew. Detainees were not taken to regular jails where they would have become part of the public record; thus, when family members inquired about missing loved ones, the authorities had no arrest record and hence no knowledge of the victim's whereabouts. Instead, detainees were driven, handcuffed and hooded or stuffed into the trunks of cars, to Villa Grimaldi or another DINA detention center, where records were secret. This procedure gave a modicum of credibility to government denials of responsibility, such as that issued by Interior Minister Sergio Fernández in 1978: "It is likely that the great majority of the presumed disappeared have gone underground or have been killed in confrontations, and the false documents they used prevented their identification."[59]

Following abduction, prisoners were interrogated under torture in specially equipped chambers to extract intelligence that could be used for more arrests and to break their will to resist the military state. A Chilean human rights organization catalogued seventeen categories of torture used by the DINA specialists. Among the more standard were the electric cattle prod applied to sensitive areas such as the genitals, anus, nipples, and eyes; "the grill," the application of electricity to an individual strapped to a metal bed frame; the "submarine," submerging the head in toilet water until the victim nearly drowns, and then repeating it; the "dry submarine," near suffocation using a plastic bag; the "telephone," the application of extremely loud noise to the ear; "the parrot's perch," hanging prisoners by the wrists and ankles, which were bound together; prolonged beatings; repeated rape; drugs; and infinite varieties of psychological torture, the worst of which was being forced to watch or hear the torture of a loved one. In the words of a woman forced to hear the screams of her brother under torture, that experience was "the most profound terror that a human being can feel."[60] Of course, the more sadistic torturers invented specialties all their own. Medical doctors often supervised these sessions to monitor victims' condition so as to maximize torture without causing death, at least until the torturers decided to conclude their work with murder.[61]

Gladys Díaz reputedly spent a longer time in Villa Grimaldi than anyone else who survived to describe the experience. A radio journalist and MIRista, Díaz experienced three months of torture at Villa Grimaldi after being arrested with her husband in 1975. They were forced to watch each other being tortured the first few days, until he was removed from Villa Grimaldi and disappeared. She was then confined in a former water tower in a space so small that she could not lie down. In the torture chamber, she was subjected to electricity, drugs, the submarine, and the telephone, and was beaten by a karate expert who broke her hip. The days when she was not physically tortured were filled with psychological torture: the playing of tapes of children's voices to make her believe the DINA had her son, and the hours of anticipating the next torture session. She was also made to witness two murders: one a beating by chains, the other a shooting.

Discussing her survival, Gladys remembered, "The ways that one finds to defend oneself are unlimited. I sometimes dreamed about beautiful things. . . . I remember having awakened to the sound of a little bird that was outside, and how I was able to keep the sound of the bird's singing in my ears for days." On torture, she reflected, "The worst part of torture is not the physical pain that you suffer—I think that the worst part of torture is to have to realize in such a brutal way that human beings are capable of doing something so aberrant to another person as torturing them." Although always blindfolded, Gladys learned her torturers' identities; she saw them all after the end of the dictatorship.[62]

Among them was Osvaldo "guatón" (big belly) Romo. A street thug and police informant, he was recruited by the DINA for his useful sadism. Interviewed by journalist Nancy Guzmán, the completely unrepentant Romo proudly proclaimed, "I destroyed whole families." When electricity was applied, he reported, the person strapped to the grill "jumps, yells, twists, sometimes pisses and shits on themselves, really. But nothing happens to them, they don't die. They think they are dying but no, what happens is their heart jumps out their ears, but sometimes it even does them good." Asked about rape of torture victims, he responded, "That's a tale that Marxists invent. Who was going to rape those disgusting, dirty, urine-covered women with blood running down their legs and covered with filth?" Despite his intimate knowledge of torture, Romo said, "I have not violated anyone's human rights." Justifying everything, Romo maintained, "There was a war here. . . . I was a combatant."[63] While publicly denying that government agents tortured, Pinochet reportedly told two religious leaders privately, "You have to torture them, because without it, they don't sing. Torture is necessary to extirpate communism."[64]

After gaining all the information they could—sometimes none—and often severely and permanently damaging prisoners' bodies and minds, DINA operatives decided the victims' fate. Some were released with severe warnings against discussing their ordeals; they were usually dropped at some remote locale at night to be found the next morning by passersby. Others were transferred to official prisons, where they were documented, could receive visitors, and enjoyed much-improved treatment. Others were murdered and their bodies disappeared so as to leave no record of the death or burial. The bodies were disposed of in various ways: they were buried in secret individual or mass graves; they were interred in cemeteries as unknown persons (N/N); they were thrown into rivers; or they were dropped from aircraft into the ocean or onto inaccessible Andean peaks.[65]

The DINA and torturers like Romo added layers to a culture of fear that had gripped Chile since the Allende years.[66] During the UP government, people on the right feared radicals, violence, and losing their property, and some feared living under a Marxist dictatorship. On September 11, fear shifted to the other side and intensified exponentially as draconian economic measures made the poor fear for their livelihood and the extreme repression made leftists fear for their lives and those of their loved ones. Most intimidating was the knowledge that there was no shield from state terrorism; anticipating the fate that awaited one after falling into the DINA's hands paralyzed and isolated people. Said a former Socialist organizer, "You would confide only in people you were absolutely sure of, and even then there was always a seed of doubt."[67] In the words of one who lived it, "Our fear makes us live half-lives, repressed and suffocated."[68] Even grieving over killed or disappeared loved ones was done "in complete solitude and in fear, which made the situation more terrible."[69] Reflecting nearly thirty years after the coup, a woman whose son was disappeared said, "Fear, fright, horror endure in the consciousness. Terror cannot be removed from the collective memory."[70]

Fear did not end at Chile's borders, for the DINA recognized no territorial limits to its mission. In November 1975, Contreras hosted his counterparts from Argentina, Uruguay, Bolivia, and Paraguay at the "First Inter-American Conference on National Intelligence," at which all agreed to collaborate across borders in the hunt for Marxists. In honor of the Chilean initiative, they named their plan "Operation Condor" after the Chilean national bird. Thus was formally launched "the most sinister state-sponsored terrorist network in the Western Hemisphere, if not the world," a South American anti-Marxist axis which Brazil would join the following year and Ecuador and Peru in 1978.[71] Yet an informal Operation Condor had already been working for over a year; it had harassed and killed Chilean and Uruguayan exiles in Argentina, including former army commander and Allende loyalist General Carlos Prats and his wife, blown up outside their Buenos Aires apartment in September 1974.[72]

Operation Condor involved cross-border coordination, intelligence gathering, and repression of leftists in member countries and beyond, including Europe and the United States. Agents from targets' home countries worked side by side with agents of fellow Condor countries to track, torture, and kill exiled "subversives." Among Condor's prominent victims were Christian Democratic leader Bernardo Leighton and his wife, both severely wounded in Rome; former UP cabinet member Orlando Letelier, killed with his assistant in Washington, D.C.; and MIR leader Edgardo Enríquez, abducted in Argentina in a joint operation, sent to Villa Grimaldi, tortured, and disappeared. U.S. intelligence and the State Department knew about Operation Condor and collaborated in various ways.[73]

Exile

Forced exile—a violation of two articles of the Universal Declaration of Human Rights—was a hallmark of the Pinochet regime.[74] Exile was a central stratagem for securing absolute control and eradicating the left within Chile. The regime expelled several thousand and offered exile as an alternative to long prison terms. More commonly, although exile was forced, individuals had some control over its timing. Some were among the thousands of public- and private-sector employees who were purged and blacklisted to prevent their finding other employment in Chile. Others lost their jobs as the economy contracted. Many chose exile after harassment, detention, or torture. Others sensed the approaching repression, as did a nonpartisan leftist radio and television journalist in 1974: "We met at Lucho's apartment and began to talk about which of our friends were still free, which . . . were already prisoners, and which . . . were dead. Then we began to realize that the circle was closing in on us. . . . I said, 'Well, I'll go to Peru for six months and come back.'" From Peru she moved to Canada, unable to return to Chile for eleven years.[75]

Some two hundred thousand Chileans, nearly two percent of the national population, went into exile for political reasons in at least 110, and possibly as many as 140, countries on all continents. Chileans went to such geographically and culturally distant places as Kenya, Bangladesh, and even the Cape Verde Islands and Greenland.[76] A major reason for the exiles' global dispersal was the rise of repressive governments in neighboring South American countries and the actions of Operation Condor. Most of the thousands of Chileans who fled across the Andes to Argentina, the nearest original haven, moved on as the danger level rose following the death of Argentine president Juan Perón in 1974. In Latin America, only Venezuela, Mexico, and Cuba took in large numbers of exiles. The Soviet bloc countries welcomed many refugees, and the Western European countries, along with Canada and Australia, offered sanctuary to the greatest number. The United States accepted relatively few.

Life in exile was difficult, regardless of one's destination. Exiles carried heavy psychological baggage: the bitterness of defeat; feelings of guilt for leaving behind jailed, dead, or disappeared comrades; and memories of torture. They arrived with dreams shattered, families torn apart, careers destroyed. These and other traumas had to be borne without the comfort and solidarity provided by the typical Chilean extended family. As a result, exiles suffered high rates of depression, divorce, alcoholism, and suicide. Almost all exiles, even those who stayed abroad for the entire sixteen and a half years of the dictatorship, experienced the syndrome of "living with the suitcases packed"—a situation of suspended reality, of living neither in Chile nor in their host country.

What kept many of the exiles going was the political struggle. Having lost the battle at home, they sought to undermine Pinochet from the "external front." Upon arriving at their exile destinations, militants of the Socialist and Communist parties, the MIR, and the major national labor union, under the umbrella of the UP in exile, reconstituted their organizations. At the local level, the parties disseminated information, organized demonstrations, and sold empanadas to raise money and consciousness. To mobilize support among the citizenry of the host countries, the exiles worked with parties and student, labor, church, and human rights groups; founded solidarity committees; and launched campaigns to free selected political prisoners and ban trade with Chile. The exiles' intense and uncompromising political activity carried a risk: owing to the long reach of Operation Condor, "an entire generation of political exiles [was] forced to look over their shoulder wherever they were in the world."[77] Exiles' efforts were crucial to keeping the regime's dark side in the world's consciousness and in countering the influence of powerful multinational business interests that supported the dictatorship for reopening Chile to their capital.

The Pinochet regime constantly vilified the exiles. Since most left through normal channels, on scheduled flights with papers in order, the regime portrayed exile as voluntary. It attempted to discredit exiles by concocting the image of a "golden exile"—a comfortable existence that contrasted harshly with the economic hardship that ordinary Chileans faced at home in the early part of the dictatorship. They were denounced as subversives and foreign agents: "Every exiled Marxist is an agent of international subversion." They were traitorous turncoats responsible for the campaign of calumny—not against the regime, but against Chile: "The jet set of exile dedicate themselves full-time to anti-Chilean activism."[78] Exiles could not return without the written permission of the interior ministry; many carried passports stamped with the letter L, signifying that they were on the list of those prohibited from returning. This policy remained in force until 1984.

The Judiciary and Mass Media

The suppression of human rights under the military boot was greatly facilitated by the collaboration of two important national institutions: the judiciary and the mass media. Despite closing down all other potentially independent governmental institutions upon seizing power, the military left the court system intact, affirming early on that "the powers of the judicial branch [remain] fully in force."[79] Yet two factors in effect gave the DINA and their collaborators free rein. First, under the state of siege, the military justice system enjoyed sweeping authority that infringed on the judiciary's normal jurisdiction. Second, the civilian courts turned a blind eye to the suppression of human rights.

From the Supreme Court down, the justices consistently refused to intervene to stop the terror. When presented with habeas corpus petitions related to disappearances, which they were obligated to act upon within twenty-four hours, judges simply accepted the word of security forces that the individual was not under detention. When the authorities admitted to having the individual under arrest, judges accepted the official version of events, approving the arrest. Of the nearly nine thousand habeas corpus petitions filed by the Catholic Church, only twenty-three were accepted, most of them after 1984.[80] When presented with overwhelming evidence of crimes, such as the case of fifteen *campesinos'* bodies found in an abandoned mine at Lonquén, judges declared themselves incompetent under the state of siege, referring the case to military justice, with predictable results. In the words of the report of the Chilean National Commission on Truth and Reconciliation, "The judicial branch as a whole proved ineffective in both protecting human rights and punishing their violation."[81]

Why did the Chilean judges, heirs to a well-respected legal tradition with a solid reputation for integrity and a history of independence from political pressures, abet the regime in its suppression of human rights? There are several answers. The Supreme Court had engaged in bitter battles with Allende over property rights and governmental powers; as a result, the justices welcomed the coup and cooperated with the new regime. Also, the judicial system was hierarchical and authoritarian; the Supreme Court controlled the career prospects of lower court judges, leading most to fall silently into line. Legal training in Chile emphasized literal interpretation of the law, and having embraced the military junta as the government, judges acquiesced in the decree laws that the military government issued. Any lingering issues of the legitimacy of governance by decree were canceled by the adoption of Pinochet's new constitution in 1980. Finally, in the words of a repentant former prosecutor for the dictatorship, "The country was full of hatred. We all became part of it."[82]

The mass media likewise supported, by commission or omission, the exercise of state terrorism. All pro-UP newspapers, magazines, and radio and television stations were shut down at the time of the coup. The government also controlled several newspaper, television, and radio outlets directly. Most of the remaining media, including the powerful Agustín Edwards empire which published Chile's largest and most influential newspaper, *El Mercurio*, were enthusiastic in their support of the regime and served as its apologists. After a period of prior censorship, the surviving media were allowed to publish freely so long as they exercised self-censorship to filter out criticism of the dictatorship's core policies and key personalities. Those that crossed the line of the acceptable, primarily Christian Democratic–affiliated media, were suspended periodically from publishing or broadcasting or were shut down for good. Further control was exercised by the requirement of government authorization for new media to begin operations. Although policy was slightly liberalized in 1984, the bulk of the media decisively supported the dictatorship and abetted the suppression of human rights to the regime's end.[83]

Government and progovernment media published as fact the disinformation that constantly flowed from government sources—even stories as bizarre and transparent as the 1975 Operation Colombo, the dictatorship's most elaborate story about leftists killing fellow leftists in internecine feuds to cover disappearances carried out by the DINA. Operation Colombo was intended to blunt international condemnations of human rights policy by attempting to substantiate the government's repeated assertions that most of the missing had gone into exile. Since the disappeared could not be located among the living exiles, the DINA produced cadavers that it claimed were those of individuals whose families had reported them as missing. In collaboration with Argentine security forces, it placed several mutilated bodies on Argentine streets with fake Chilean documents; pinned to their clothes were notes indicating that the MIR had done the killing. The DINA created a fictitious magazine in Argentina and appropriated an obscure newsletter in Brazil to publish lists totaling 119 Chilean "extremists," all reported as missing by their families, who had reportedly been killed in internecine fighting with fellow Marxists.[84]

The media docilely or enthusiastically printed the story without questioning the sources. One newspaper ran the headline "MIRistas exterminated like rats." *El Mercurio* smugly editorialized, "The politicians and foreign newsmen who asked themselves so many times about the fate of these members of the MIR and blamed the Chilean government for the disappearances of many of them, now have the explanation that they refused to accept. Victims of their own methods, exterminated by their own comrades, every one of them demonstrates with tragic eloquence that violent people end up falling victims to the blind and implacable terror that they provoke."[85]

The Human Rights Movement: Domestic and International

The original church-based, ad hoc human rights organizations that had formed within weeks of the coup gave rise to the two organizations that formed the backbone of the human rights movement. The ecumenical Fundación de Ayuda Social de las Iglesias Cristianas (Social Aid Foundation of the Christian Churches, FASIC) was founded in April 1975 and continues its work today. The Vicaría de la Solidaridad (Vicariate of Solidarity), a ministry of the Archbishopric of Santiago, was created on January 1, 1976. It was dissolved after the return of civilian government, but the foundation that it created prior to disbanding supports ongoing human rights work. Alongside these organizations and those founded later, numerous individual priests and progressive religious orders also ministered to the people of the shantytowns and poor rural areas, doing everything possible to protect them against the dual onslaught of repression and hunger, often at grave risk to their own personal safety.[86]

The Vicaría de la Solidaridad assumed the most visible role of moral opposition to the regime and defender of human rights. The Chilean Catholic Church's commitment to the defense of human rights, which was supported by a majority of Chile's twenty-eight bishops, reflected the liberalization of the hierarchy—a long process driven by domestic concerns beginning in the 1930s and by the reorientation of the universal church after 1958 under popes John XXIII and Paul VI. The 1966 Conference of Latin American Bishops in Medellín, Colombia, had been the decisive event in the rise of a more active and compassionate church committed to social change to benefit the poor. The spread of liberation theology in Latin America dated from the Medellín conference. While the hierarchy had not embraced liberation theology in its more radical formulations, the Chilean bishops, not without considerable dissent, had adopted progressive views on social issues by the late 1960s.[87]

Despite the government's hostility to its work and its very existence, the Vicaría was able to survive and conduct important work for two reasons: legally, it was not an autonomous agency but an integral unit of the archdiocese of Santiago; and its founder and patron, Cardinal Archbishop Raúl Silva Henríquez, was an astute and compassionate churchman who considered the defense of human rights a logical extension of his longtime work in defense of Chile's poor and downtrodden. By virtue of the church's power and prestige, the Vicaría was able to carve out space for its work. During the dictatorship's first decade, when political opposition inside the country was essentially nonexistent, the Vicaría acted as "the voice of the voiceless."[88] Cardinal Silva Henríquez skillfully set the course of the Vicaría's mission. Without directly challenging military rule, the Vicaría pragmatically sought to ameliorate the regime's worst human rights abuses. It placed a high value on each political prisoner freed, each torture session avoided, and each life saved. It also collaborated in relief efforts for impoverished slum dwellers and unemployed workers. The Vicaría offered a wide range of material, moral, psychological, and legal services to victims and their families and offered education and training in the meaning and promotion of human rights. It gathered voluminous evidence of human rights abuses, and, despite the courts' consistent refusal to cooperate, its lawyers filed thousands of habeas corpus and other legal briefs. Its bimonthly *Solidaridad* bulletin detailing its legal actions provided documentation for international human rights efforts. The Vicaría created a large archive that would prove invaluable to investigations following the return of civilian government.

FASIC, less known in Chile and abroad, complemented the work of the Vicaría. FASIC maintained a lower profile because it was more vulnerable than the Vicaría to regime pressures: it did not enjoy the protection of the Catholic Church, and it was denied legal status throughout the dictatorship. It functioned as a branch of the Methodist Church and received funding from the World Council of Churches and other international sources. In addition to general human rights advocacy and aid to the poor, FASIC developed several specialized programs. Among these were family reunification, which helped families of exiles regroup abroad; services for children of the repressed; and counseling for torture victims and families of the killed and disappeared. Beginning in 1983, it played a central role in the effort to end the ban on exiles' return.[89]

From the beginning, the religious-based organizations fostered the creation of new, specialized human rights organizations, sheltered them insofar as possible from the regime's harassment, and provided material and moral support. Some organizations focused on human rights education; others were organizations of family members of victims of specific types of human rights violations. The first established was the Agrupación de Familiares de Detenidos Desaparecidos (Group of Families of the Detained Disappeared, AFDD), founded in 1974. Among the many others were the Agrupación de Familiares de Presos Políticos (Group of Families of Political Prisoners, AFPP, 1976); the Agrupación de Familiares de Ejecutados Políticos (Group of Families of

Those Executed for Political Reasons, AFEP, 1978); the Comité Pro Retorno de Exiliados (Committee for the Return of Exiles, CPRE, 1978); Protección a la Infancia Dañada por los Estados de Emergencia (Protection of Children Damaged by the States of Emergency, PIDEE, 1979); the Comité de Defensa de los Derechos del Pueblo (Committee for the Defense of the People's Rights, CODEPU, 1980); and the Comisión Nacional Contra la Tortura (National Commission against Torture, 1983). The Comisión Chilena de Derechos Humanos (Chilean Human Rights Commission), a general advocacy group with a large and diverse membership, was established in 1978. By the end of the military regime, there were fifteen freestanding general and specialized human rights organizations functioning in Chile, and over thirty subsidiary groups.[90]

The dictatorship did all it could to limit the impact of the domestic human rights movement. Through censorship and intimidation, it limited media coverage of human rights issues and organizations. It denounced human rights activists as antipatriotic tools of the international Marxist conspiracy against Chile. A regime spokesman in 1976, for example, vilified those who "sling mud at the fatherland, and join in the foreign conspiracy."[91] The ban on public demonstrations was strictly enforced; when groups challenged this policy, they were forcefully dispersed and often arrested. The dictatorship harassed the human rights organizations by breaking into their offices and destroying their files and by threatening, beating, exiling, and in a few cases murdering their activists. Despite these measures, the human rights movement survived and grew. Its actions likely helped to prevent the toll of state terror from being greater than it was, and over time the movement contributed to eroding the omnipotence and legitimacy of military power.[92]

The international response to Chilean state terrorism was so potent that it resulted in transcendent changes in international human rights advocacy. The reaction was based in part on the nature of the overthrown government: Allende was popular, his experimental road to socialism was widely admired, and he had taken Chile into the Non-Aligned Movement, a large group of developing countries that joined to develop a voice outside the Cold War Soviet-U.S. polarity. The brutality of the coup in a democratic country with a long tradition of civilian governance, along with the death of Allende, which most believed was murder, galvanized people, organizations, and governments around the world.

Revelations about the Nixon administration's involvement in trying to prevent Allende's election and subsequently trying to undermine his government launched the human rights movement in the United States: membership in the U.S. section of Amnesty International grew from three thousand to fifty thousand between 1974 and 1976. The Washington Office on Latin America, an influential new voice for defending human rights in Latin America, was founded in 1974, and a coalition of groups established the Human Rights Working Group in January 1976. In addition, the U.S. Congress took unprecedented steps to punish a country for human rights violations and to change American foreign policy to include human rights norms.[93]

The Chilean coup and its aftermath also brought about major changes in the UN's approach to human rights. Reflecting governments' unwillingness to grant the international body power to interfere with their treatment of their own citizens, before 1973, the UN's human rights agencies had employed arcane, confidential procedures that produced little or no publicity about governments that violated human rights, and they took no corrective action. The UN had consistently and publicly condemned only two governments, South Africa and Israel, of gross human rights violations—for apartheid and for treatment of Palestinians in the occupied territories. Despite the existence of governments that routinely violated their citizens' human rights, such as the repressive colonels' dictatorship in Greece (1967–1974) and the state terrorist regime of Idi Amin in Uganda (1971–1979), the UN had not taken a strong stand against governments that violated rights for political reasons.

This changed with Chile, when the UN for the first time recognized arbitrary mass detention, torture, and murder as gross human rights violations and sidestepped its rules to make Chile a very public issue. In 1974, the UN Human Rights Commission invited Hortensia Bussi, the widow of Salvador Allende, to address it and established an Ad Hoc Working Group on Chile. The same year, the UN General Assembly issued the first of its annual condemnations of the dictatorship. In 1975, it issued the UN's first declaration against torture in response to the Chilean situation. The UN Human Rights Commission demanded permission to visit Chile but was stalled until 1978. When it finally occurred, the visit was the first ever on-site investigation by the commission. In 1978, the commission went so far as to establish a special trust fund for Chilean victims of torture. Following the 1978 visit, the UN replaced its working group with a special rapporteur, a position it renewed until 1990, and in another precedent-setting move, it appointed a rapporteur specifically to investigate disappearances in Chile. The UN helped keep Chile in the international spotlight for the duration of the military regime.[94]

After the initial barrage of criticism and condemnation, the military government was reluctant to open Chile to inspection by international human rights organizations. After initially denying their requests for on-site visits, the government allowed the Inter-American Commission on Human Rights and the International Commission of Jurists to send delegations in 1974; these visits added to the volume of reports that had resulted from visits by Amnesty International and other NGOs in the weeks and months following the coup. Although the Inter-American Commission on Human Rights was not allowed additional on-site investigations, it produced critical reports in 1976 and 1977 based on information received and interviews with exiles.[95]

Determined to accomplish its mission of eradicating the left at any cost, the dictatorship normally ignored or responded dismissively to international pressures, attributing them to an anti-Chilean campaign by exiled traitors in league with international communism. At every opportunity, it claimed the moral high ground. In November 1974, for example, when it offered exile to political prisoners in order to reduce the prison population, a regime spokesman attributed the move to "humanitarian sentiments."[96] It routinely denied the existence of serious human rights problems, attributing any irreg- ularities to the state of war against Marxism. The regime sometimes reacted defiantly to specific reports of human rights violations; an ad in the *Wash- ington Post*, for example, alleged that the second negative report by the In- ternational Commission of Jurists in 1974 "demonstrates [the organization's] relationship with the Soviet Union and its allies in pursuance of identical objectives."[97] When the government granted permission for human rights in- vestigations within Chile, usually after considerable stalling, it limited ac- cess, intimidated potential witnesses, moved prisoners, and closed known de- tention sites to minimize damage.

For domestic consumption, the regime portrayed international human rights advocacy as illicit intervention in Chile's internal affairs and as attacks on national sovereignty. In January 1978, following the UN General Assem- bly's fourth annual condemnation, Pinochet held a plebiscite on the follow- ing proposition: "In the face of international aggression unleashed against our country, I support President Pinochet in his defense of the dignity of Chile and I reaffirm the legitimacy of the government of the Republic to lead with sovereignty the process of the country's institutionalization." The yes box was a Chilean flag; the no was a black flag. In a vote without debate, op- position, or an electoral registry (it had been burned), the yes won with 75 percent support.[98]

Pinochet's defiance of international pressures rested on solid foundations. He counted on the efficacy of the DINA to keep the ongoing repression se- cret so that charges of human rights violations could not be conclusively proven. He also counted on the lucrative opportunities for trade and invest- ment that the Chicago Boys' model offered to developed capitalist countries to blunt their criticism of his human rights policies and avoid the inconvenience of diplomatic isolation. Despite a steady stream of negative reports and resolutions by both intergovernmental agencies and NGOs, most Western governments maintained correct diplomatic relations and supplied needed capital directly or through multinational agencies. The unflagging economic and diplomatic support of Nixon and his successor, Gerald Ford, who retained Henry Kissinger as secretary of state, helped buffer the regime against its critics, even as the Ford administration gently pressured Pinochet to clean up his government's image if not its substance.

The dictatorship also counted on the shifting political climate in Latin America, and hence in the OAS, to weather the international condemnation. From the early 1970s to the mid-1980s, the number of repressive governments grew dramatically. As a result of the decline of democracies and the rise of dictatorships, the Chilean approach to human rights became closer to the norm than the exception in Latin America. Thus, in contrast to the UN General Assembly, the OAS General Assembly failed to take action on the reports of its human rights commission on conditions in Chile.[99]

An early indication of the shift in the hemispheric political climate, and a diplomatic triumph for Pinochet, was the OAS's decision to hold a meeting of its general assembly in Santiago in June 1976. This would allow the regime to demonstrate that Chile was, as the propaganda machine repeatedly proclaimed, "an island of peace." While this involved obvious risks, the military's control over the country was so complete that the gamble seemed worthwhile. To prepare for the conference, the regime cracked down on potential sources of trouble just as it intensified the hunt for the last surviving underground opposition, the Communists. Human rights concerns were not absent at the meeting: a few brave dissident Chilean lawyers addressed a damning letter to the delegates, and Henry Kissinger himself, more concerned with appearance than reality, both publicly and privately asked Pinochet to make changes. The government allowed some public debate in an attempt to show that freedom existed; then, after the conference ended, it exiled two of the dissident lawyers, Christian Democrats Jaime Castillo Velasco and Eugenio Velasco Letelier. The assembly considered the second report of the Inter-American Commission on Human Rights on the situation in Chile, and the government responded by rebutting the critical report point by point. Overall, hosting the OAS less than three years after the coup demonstrated that the regime was capable of surmounting international attacks on its human rights performance with minimal damage.[100]

The remainder of 1976, however, did not go so smoothly for the regime. In September, the DINA overreached itself by conducting an assassination in the heart of Washington, D.C.'s Embassy Row, a few blocks from the White

House. Orlando Letelier, Allende's first ambassador to Washington, who also served as his minister of foreign affairs and later of defense, had been held a year at Dawson Island with other top UP leaders and expelled from Chile upon his release. He returned to Washington, where he became the most prominent figure lobbying against the Pinochet regime. The dictatorship decided to silence him and put the DINA in charge of the assassination. Led by U.S. citizen and DINA operative Michael Townley, the team attached a bomb to Letelier's automobile and detonated it by remote control, killing Letelier and his American assistant, Ronni Moffitt. Despite the Chilean government's energetic denials of complicity and its claims that leftists had done it to sour relations between Santiago and Washington, the DINA's hand was soon revealed. U.S. demands for the extradition of all those involved in the assassination, including DINA head Contreras, would muddle Chilean-U.S. relations for years to come.[101]

Six weeks later, Jimmy Carter was elected president. Strongly committed to human rights, Carter was able to build upon the work that Congress had done beginning with the postcoup hearings in late 1973. Led by Democrat representatives Don Fraser and Michael Harrington and senators Ted Kennedy and Tom Harkin, Congress had first targeted the normal flow of military aid to Chile. By June 1976, it enacted legislation to establish an office for human rights in the State Department, which was required to produce annual reports on human rights in all countries that received U.S. aid; negative reports could have financial consequences.

Whereas the Ford administration had tried to evade congressional restrictions, Carter's election brought Congress and the White House into alignment. Declaring in his inaugural address that "our commitment to human rights must be absolute," Carter made the observance of human rights a central tenet of U.S. foreign policy. He appointed Patricia Derian, an aggressive human rights advocate, to the upgraded position of assistant secretary of state for human rights and humanitarian affairs. Under Carter, relations with Pinochet cooled, aid dropped, and the U.S. voted against Chile in the UN and in some international lending agencies. U.S. attempts to sabotage Allende, previous administrations' tolerance of human rights violations under Pinochet, and the personal convictions of a new president and key members of Congress altered U.S. foreign policy in ways that directly affected Chile as well as other Latin American countries.[102]

The Letelier assassination and Carter's election triggered changes in the Pinochet regime. Two weeks after the U.S. election, Pinochet released 302 political prisoners. Meeting with Admiral Patricio Carvajal at the OAS in May 1977, Secretary of State Cyrus Vance urged additional concrete actions such as ending the state of siege, dissolving the DINA, and moving toward reestablishing civilian government.[103] The last suggested change received lip service, but the first two occurred within a year, abetted by internal pressures from regime members and supporters who favored the improvement of Chile's international image.

On August 13, 1977, Pinochet dissolved the DINA. The Letelier assassination and Carter's human rights policies had turned Contreras and the DINA, heretofore Pinochet's greatest assets, into liabilities. But despite U.S. pressure, it is unlikely that Pinochet would have acted if the DINA had not essentially accomplished its mission. The decimation of the Communist Party's underground in December 1976, following the earlier destruction of the MIR and Socialist clandestine units, had eliminated the last potential resistance inside Chile. This allowed the regime to announce in June 1977 that it held no more prisoners detained under the state of siege—conveniently ignoring those held in secret. Although he could have, Pinochet did not declare victory over the Marxists, for that would have undermined the rationale for his continuation in power.[104]

Seizing the opportunity to refurbish the regime's image while placating Carter, Pinochet replaced the DINA with the less sinister-sounding Centro Nacional de Informaciones (National Information Center, CNI), which the general announced would have a purely informational character. In reality, the CNI was a virtual replica of the DINA, with a new name and a new boss, but essentially the same personnel, duties, and techniques of terrorism. Pinochet also ended the state of siege on March 10, 1978, four and a half years after its inception on the day of the coup, replacing it with a "state of exception," which jurists found to be little different. Although the DINA and the state of siege were gone, the apparatus of state terrorism remained intact and continued functioning to the end of the regime.[105]

A final gesture symbolically closed an era in the military's governance: the amnesty decree of April 19, 1978. Decree law 2191 amnestied the authors of crimes committed from September 11, 1973, through March 10, 1978—the duration of the state of siege—along with their accomplices and accessories. It applied to crimes by agents of the state and, for the appearance of fairness, crimes committed against the state. To avoid further eroding relations with the United States, the Letelier assassination was not amnestied.[106]

Pinochet's amnesty established impunity for four and a half years of state terrorism and grave human rights violations. The sixteen weeks following the coup had cost 1,823 lives according to the official investigation, as well as uncounted other violations. From early January 1974, when the DINA began functioning, through the end of the state of siege—the symbolic truce in an invented war—nearly eight hundred more people were killed, many of them disappeared.[107] Thousands more were harassed, blacklisted, jailed, tortured, and forced into exile.

Following the cosmetic changes, the amnesty, and the reduction in the level of repression, Pinochet's advisers convinced the general to allow the long-stalled visit of the UN Human Rights Commission. Arriving in July 1978, the delegation met with government officials, church leaders, and families of the disappeared. It visited Villa Grimaldi, which had been converted to an officers' club. The commission's detailed report confirmed earlier reports and allegations and, though highly critical, noted some improvement in human rights conditions.[108]

While the UN Human Rights Commission's visit was a historic first, it was but one of many that occurred in response to Chilean state terrorism. The UN, the OAS, and the international human rights NGOs had established an unprecedented level of cooperation over Chile. Together with the domestic human rights movement and the exiles, the international organizations for the first time shone a spotlight on a politically motivated regime of state terrorism. In the words of one author, "Rarely, if ever before, in world history had so many international actors reacted so strongly to human rights abuses."[109] The continuous negative publicity that the dictatorship received, together with the practice of interorganization cooperation, provided an important impetus toward strengthening the global human rights framework that would bear additional fruit in the late 1970s and the 1980s as state terrorism spread first to Argentina and then to Central America. Yet while the international and domestic pressures may have ameliorated the repression within Chile—an unmeasurable proposition—they could not stop it.

Apogee and Denouement of the Regime: April 1978–March 1990

The period from the amnesty through most of 1981 constituted the dictatorship's halcyon years. Under the Chicago Boys' tutelage, the economy began to boom, growing by 7.5 percent annually, and fortunes were made; this was the "Chilean miracle." The economic miracle won Chile international accolades for pioneering the model, which, according to free market economists, all of Latin America should follow. Chilean entrepreneurs labeled themselves the "jaguars"—the smaller but equally dynamic counterparts of the Asian "tigers" of those years. The miracle's trickle down eased the plight of workers, although, without unions and a supportive state, they did not regain their former levels of employment and income.[110]

With the left defeated and the economy booming, repression eased. A minor threat to the regime emerged after 1978 when the MIR sought to reestablish a presence inside Chile. "Operation Return" involved clandestine entry, recruitment, and organization, an attempt to establish a guerrilla training camp in the southern Andean foothills, and bombings and bank robberies in Santiago that briefly shook the reigning tranquility in 1980 and 1981. The regime responded with heightened repression, but rather than conduct a broad crackdown, it pursued the MIR selectively. Thus, from 1978 through 1980, the toll in murdered and disappeared fell to the lowest level of the entire dictatorship.[111]

After years of preparation, Pinochet submitted a new constitution to the nation in 1980. Following a government propaganda campaign—opponents of the constitution were allowed a single public forum, without television coverage—the new charter was approved in a plebiscite on September 11, 1980, the seventh anniversary of the coup, by an announced 67 percent of the voters. When implemented in March 1981, Pinochet's "Constitution of Liberty" locked in military rule and his own immense powers for eight more years. It also provided for a plebiscite within eight years that could extend his rule for an additional eight-year term. The constitution established the institutional basis of a "protected democracy" designed to prevent the resurrection of the left, preserve the free market economic model, and assure impunity for Pinochet and the military for their human rights crimes after the eventual return of civilian government.[112]

In late 1981, a severe economic crisis precipitously ended the economic miracle and brought forth the first open opposition to military rule since the coup. Beginning in 1983, the illegal center and left parties mobilized in periodic "national days of protest," attempted general strikes, formed a broad alliance, and called for a national dialogue to discuss terms of a return to democracy ahead of Pinochet's timetable. In addition to the economic crisis, the end of military rule in Peru, Bolivia, Argentina, Uruguay, and Brazil between 1980 and 1985 further stoked the opposition to Pinochet's continuance in power.[113]

Concurrently with the rise of civic opposition, Communist Party operatives returned clandestinely to Chile to establish a second armed opposition group, the Frente Patriótico Manuel Rodríguez (Manuel Rodríguez Patriotic Front, FPMR). By 1984, the FPMR was launching terrorist attacks on military and police targets, bombing power transmission towers and the Santiago metro, and organizing extensively in the slums to form a large cadre of youthful fighters bent on toppling the regime by armed insurrection.[114]

In response to the two-pronged civic and armed assault on his rule, Pinochet on November 6, 1984, ratcheted up the state of exception to a new state of siege and increased the repression to a level unseen since 1976. Contested in the streets for the first time, the regime could no longer keep the repression out of sight. It routinely used unnecessary levels of force and brutality in breaking up the days of protest and other peaceful but illegal demonstrations. It resurrected the neighborhood sweeps of the early post-coup period, surrounding the shantytowns, searching them house by house, and arresting thousands. Among the most notable and highly publicized human rights violations of this period was the March 1985 abduction and murder of three Communists whose throats were slashed (the *degollados*) and their bodies dumped along a road near Santiago by the Carabineros intelligence service. In June 1986, two children, apprehended by a military patrol carrying a bucket of liquid paraffin to ignite wood during a demonstration, were doused with the liquid and set on fire; one died, the other was horribly disfigured, and their photographs appeared around the world. Atrocities that might have seemed routine in the dictatorship's early years had returned, but times had changed: Chileans had grown accustomed to lighter repression, and the democratization of Chile's neighbors made the dictatorship seem anachronistic. Repression from the beginning of the protests in 1981 to the regime's end in March 1990 took a heavy toll: 467 killed or disappeared, unknown numbers arrested and tortured, and more people exiled.[115]

The domestic human rights movement responded to the recrudescence of repression with renewed commitment and energy. The Vicaría continued its legal representation and other activities, and the newer organizations created under its protection sought to ease the crackdown and free the huge numbers of people arrested in demonstrations and sweeps. The human rights organizations suffered the regime's wrath in the form of harassment, beatings, and expulsions.[116]

International pressures also mounted in response to the renewed human rights violations after 1981. The UN, the OAS, and the NGOs reported and denounced the government's tactics in countering the protests. The United States, under the presidency of Ronald Reagan since January 1981, had reverted to a foreign policy of realpolitik; Carter's concern for human rights was subordinated to U.S. economic and strategic interests. By 1985, however, the State Department began to view the Chilean situation as dangerous. Continued uncritical U.S. support of the regime might strain relations with the new democracies that had replaced dictatorships in most neighboring countries, including South America's largest powers, Brazil and Argentina. Moreover, the deepening U.S. involvement in Central America brought into focus a relevant lesson from Nicaragua: prolonged civic protest and armed conflict in Chile, the resurgence of the once-defeated left, and

Pinochet's intransigence were reminiscent of the formula that had led in 1979 to the Sandinistas' ouster of the Somoza dynasty. Thus the Reagan administration began employing economic pressures and even denunciations of the human rights situation to force Pinochet to ease the repression and, above all, to adhere to the constitution's 1988 deadline for a plebiscite on the extension of his rule.[117]

The protests ended abruptly after September 7, 1986, when the FPMR attempted to assassinate Pinochet. The dictator survived a spectacular shootout that killed five military escorts and injured another ten. The reaction was ferocious: another state of siege, numerous arrests, neighborhood sweeps, expulsions, heightened censorship, and vigilante-style executions of opposition figures. Recognizing that Pinochet could neither be overthrown by arms nor forced to speed up the transition to civilian rule, and hoping to avoid the further heightening of repression in the assassination attempt's aftermath, the center and left parties dropped the strategy of protest in favor of gearing up for the plebiscite. Moreover, they wished to avoid giving Pinochet any pretext for canceling the plebiscite. They had been forced to play by the dictator's rules and, in so doing, to concede tacitly the legitimacy of his institutions.[118]

At the height of the protests in 1983 and 1984, Pinochet had reluctantly granted his opponents a few concessions. The most important of these were a slight but significant opening for opposition media; permission for the student and professional organizations to elect their leadership, and thus to recover a degree of independence; and a relaxation of the ban on exiles' return. These concessions proved costly to the regime, as new politically oriented magazines appeared, the opposition won most elections in the professional and student associations, and repatriated exiles brought their convictions and energy with them to the "internal front." The 1983–1984 opening, paid for in blood, was important to the opposition's success in the plebiscite.[119]

Pinochet's rules for the plebiscite made it difficult for the opposition to mount a campaign against him. However, as the lone military dictator left from the wave that had engulfed South America in the 1960s and 1970s, he came under intense pressure from friendly sources—the U.S. government, much of the Chilean right, and even some within his own military—to hold an election that, unlike his previous plebiscites, would meet minimal standards of fairness and would thus be seen as legitimate. Energized by returned exiles and the long-frustrated desire for change, the center and left parties formed the broad "Concertación por el No" (Coalition for the No) that registered voters, held massive demonstrations, and produced convincing ads for the limited television time allotted. The no won the October 5, 1988, plebiscite with 53.3 percent of the vote; Pinochet's enraged attempt to throw out the results was thwarted by his fellow commanders. In a peculiarly Chilean twist, the dictatorship, so foreign to national tradition, was ended by a quintessentially Chilean exercise: a massive, peaceful vote in a democratic election.[120]

The dictatorship was not finished yet, however. As specified in constitution and law, seventeen months would transpire before an elected president took office. Pinochet was pressured by both the opposition and his supporters to negotiate some amendments to his constitution in order to soften slightly its unworkably authoritarian provisions. But the general remained firmly in control during the transition. While allowing a few concessions, he also changed the rules for the incoming elected government in ways that strengthened the shield of impunity for the human rights crimes that he and the military had committed during sixteen and a half years. The political system he bequeathed to the nation, a faithful incarnation of his concept of protected democracy, would successfully thwart the quest for justice for years to come.

Notes

1. General Horacio Toro, quoted in Sergio Marras, *Palabra de soldado: entrevistas de Sergio Marras* (Santiago: Ornitorrinco, 1989), 137.

2. Richard J. Bloomfield, memorandum to Assistant Secretary of State for Latin America William D. Rogers, July 11, 1975, in Peter Kornbluh, ed., *The Pinochet File: A Declassified Dossier on Atrocity and Accountability* (New York: New Press, 2003), 258–59.

3. The best general history of Chile in English is Brian Loveman, *Chile: The Legacy of Hispanic Capitalism*, 3rd ed. (New York: Oxford University Press, 2001). For the nineteenth and twentieth centuries, see Simon Collier and William F. Sater, *A History of Chile, 1808–2002*, 2nd ed. (Cambridge: Cambridge University Press, 2004); and Leslie Bethell, ed., *Chile since Independence* (Cambridge: Cambridge University Press, 1993).

4. The Radical Party candidate received 5 percent. Collier and Sater, *A History of Chile*, 309, has election results from 1958 through 1973.

5. Michael Fleet, *The Rise and Fall of Chilean Christian Democracy* (Princeton, NJ: Princeton University Press, 1985); Arturo Olavarría Bravo, *Chile bajo la Democracia Cristiana*, 6 vols. (Santiago: Editorial Nascimento, 1966–1971); Cristián Gazmuri et al., *Eduardo Frei Montalva y su época*, 2 vols. (Santiago: Aguilar, 2000). Note that since the Chilean electoral system did not require a runoff in the event that no candidate received a majority, and since there was normally a minimum of three candidates, often more, Allende's relatively small percentage of the vote was not unprecedented.

6. There is a large body of literature on the UP years. Among the more useful books in English are Sergio Bitar, *Chile, Experiment in Democracy*, trans. Sam Sherman (Philadelphia: Institute for the Study of Human Issues, 1986); Stefan de Wylder, *Allende's Chile: The Political Economy of the Rise and Fall of the Unidad Popular* (Cambridge: Cambridge University Press, 1976); Paul E. Sigmund, *The Overthrow of Allende and the Politics of Chile, 1964–1976* (Pittsburgh: University of Pittsburgh Press, 1977); Arturo Valenzuela, *The Breakdown of Democratic Regimes: Chile* (Baltimore: Johns Hopkins University Press, 1978). For broader studies that cover both the Allende administration and the Pinochet dictatorship, see Lois Hecht Oppenheim, *Politics in Chile: Democracy, Authoritarianism, and the Search for Development*, 2nd ed. (Boulder, CO: Westview Press, 1999); and Manuel A. Garretón Merino, *The Chilean Political Process*, trans. Sharon Kellum with Gilbert W. Merkx (Boston: Unwin Hyman, 1989).

7. Kornbluh, *The Pinochet File*, 119 (quoting Secretary of Defense Melvin Laird). This book reproduces dozens of recently declassified documents on U.S. relations with Allende and Pinochet. Jonathan Haslam, *The Nixon Administration and the Death of Allende's Chile: A Case of Assisted Suicide* (London: Verso, 2005); Paul E. Sigmund, *The United States and Democracy in Chile* (Baltimore, MD: Johns Hopkins University Press, 1993), 11–84. Pamela Constable and Arturo Valenzuela, *A Nation of Enemies: Chile under Pinochet* (New York: W. W. Norton, 1991), 9, refers to Chile's "culture of austere, enlightened civility."

8. Bitar, *Experiment in Democracy*; de Wylder, *Allende's Chile*.

9. Chile, *Report of the Chilean National Commission on Truth and Reconciliation*, trans. Phillip E. Berryman (Notre Dame, IN: University of Notre Dame Press, 1993), 1:48.

10. *Report of the Chilean National Commission*, 1:53.

11. From the title of Constable and Valenzuela, *Nation of Enemies*.

12. Fleet, *Rise and Fall*, 176–81. María Elena Carrera, a senator and member of the Socialist Party's central committee, admitted later that, although her party was certain that the coup was coming, "all of our preparations were more plans than realities." Thomas C. Wright and Rody Oñate, *Flight from Chile: Voices of Exile* (Albuquerque: University of New Mexico Press, 1998), 14. This chapter draws from several studies of the dictatorship and its human rights violations, including Rodrigo Atria et al., *Chile, la memoria prohibida: las violaciones a los derechos humanos, 1973–1983*, 3 vols. (Santiago: Pehuén Editores, 1989); Ascanio Cavallo Castro, Manuel Salazar Salvo, and Oscar Sepúlveda Pacheco, *Chile, 1973–1988: la historia oculta del régimen militar* (Santiago: Editorial Antártica, 1989); Genaro Arriagada, *Por la razón o la fuerza: Chile bajo Pinochet* (Santiago: Editorial Sudamericana, 1998); Constable and Valenzuela, *Nation of Enemies*; Mary Helen Spooner, *Soldiers in a Narrow Land: The Pinochet Regime in Chile*, updated ed. (Berkeley: University of California Press, 1999); J. Samuel Valenzuela and Arturo Valenzuela, *Military Rule in Chile: Dictatorship and Oppositions* (Baltimore, MD: Johns Hopkins University Press, 1986); and Garretón, *The Chilean Political Process*, 117–212.

13. This description of the coup and its aftermath draws on numerous sources, including Atria et al., *Memoria prohibida* 1: 77–212; Ernesto Ekaizer, *Yo, Augusto* (Buenos Aires: Aguilar, 2003), 31–177; Constable and Valenzuela, *Nation of Enemies*, 15–39; Patricia Verdugo, *Interferencia secreta: 11 de septiembre de 1973*, with CD (Santiago: Editorial Sudamericana, 1998). General Augusto Pinochet, who would become junta leader, refers to the skirmishes in the capital as "the battle of Santiago," in Pinochet, *Camino recorrido: biografía de un soldado* (Santiago: Instituto Geográfico Militar de Chile, 1990), 1:293–300.

14. This and the following paragraphs rely on *Report of the Chilean National Commission*, 1:129–468; Atria et al., *Memoria prohibida*, 1:77–404; Amnesty International, *Informe sobre presos políticos retenidos en campos secretos de detención en Chile, marzo de 1977* (Barcelona: La Faya-Ciencia, 1977); Amnesty International, *Chile, Torture and the Naval Training Ship the "Esmeralda"* (London: International Secretariat, 2003); Manuel Ahumada Lillo, *Cerro Chena testimonio* (Santiago: Ediciones Tierra Mía, 2003).

15. *Report of the Chilean National Commission*, 1:99–116; Atria et al., *Memoria prohibida*, 1:213–77; Arriagada, *Por la razón*, 24. One of the most notorious cases of rural repression, which dated from October 1973, came to light in 1978 when fifteen bodies were discovered in a mine at Lonquén. Cavallo, Salazar, and Sepúlveda, *Historia oculta*, 255–64. Isabel Allende's novel, *Of Love and Shadows*, trans. Margaret Sayers Peden (New York: Dial Press, 2005), is based on that discovery.

16. Bando no. 5, in Arriagada, *Por la razón*, 22.

17. Collier and Sater, *A History of Chile*, 358, called the attack on the Moneda "the most dramatic and tragic moment in the modern history of Chile." *Report of the Chilean National Commission*, 1:79. See Brian Loveman, *The Constitution of Tyranny: Regimes of Exception in Spanish America* (Pittsburgh: University of Pittsburgh Press, 1993), for an overview of the use of states of exception throughout the region.

18. *Report of the Chilean National Commission*, 1:74–80. Arriagada, *Por la razón*, 19–40.

19. Augusto Pinochet U., *El día decisivo*, 5th ed. (Santiago: Editorial Andrés Bello, 1984), 260.

20. Ekaizer, *Yo, Augusto*, 142–43; Constable and Valenzuela, *Nation of Enemies*, 19, 39.

21. Sigmund, *The United States and Democracy*, 86–87, discusses the differing views of the CIA's involvement in Plan Z.

22. The *White Book of the Change of Government in Chile: 11th of September* (Santiago: Empresa Editora Nacional Gabriela Mistral, n.d.), 29 (the language is that of the book's English edition). Circulation of the *White Book* was so massive that even a very junior assistant professor, the author of this book, received a complimentary copy in the mail. David Kohut, Olga Vilella, and Beatrice Julian, *Historical Dictionary of the "Dirty Wars"* (Lanham, MD: Scarecrow Press, 2003) is a useful reference work on the state terrorist regimes of Chile, Argentina, and Uruguay.

23. Patricia Verdugo, *Chile, Pinochet, and the Caravan of Death*, trans. Marcelo Montecino (Coral Gables, FL: North-South Center Press, 2001).

24. Verdugo, *Caravan of Death*, 24.

25. *Report of the Chilean National Commission*, 1:57–59; Atria et al., *Memoria prohibida*, 1:283–90, 413–14; Constable and Valenzuela, *Nation of Enemies*, 54–57.

26. Corporación Nacional de Reparación y Reconciliación, *Informe sobre calificación de víctimas de violaciones de derechos humanos y de la violencia política* (Santiago: Corporación Nacional de Reparación y Reconciliación, 1996), 579. The exact number of deaths and disappearances established for 1973 was 1,823.

27. Verdugo, *Interferencia secreta*, 121–22; *Report of the Chilean National Commission*, 1:129–146; Patricia Politzer, *Fear in Chile: Lives under Pinochet*, trans. Diane Wachtell (New York: Pantheon, 1989), 3–19, 69–92, 140–88, 214–45.

28. This and the following paragraph are based on Patricio Orellana and Elizabeth Q. Hutchison, *El movimiento de derechos humanos en Chile, 1973–1990* (Santiago: Centro de Estudios Políticos Latinoamericanos Simón Bolívar [CEPLA], 1991), esp. 11–23, 91–94, 162–66; Brian H. Smith, *The Church and Politics in Chile* (Princeton, NJ: Princeton University Press, 1982), 287–94; Pamela Lowden, *Moral Opposition to Authoritarian Rule in Chile, 1973–1990* (London: Macmillan Press, 1996), 27–51.

29. Cavallo, Salazar, and Sepúlveda, *Historia oculta*, 40. Pinochet said of Cardinal Archbishop Raúl Silva Henríquez, "He appeared to have more Marxist or socialist ideas than any leftist political leader." Pinochet, *Camino recorrido*, 2:24.

30. Wright and Oñate, *Flight from Chile*, 39–54; Mark Ensalaco, *Chile under Pinochet: Recovering the Truth* (Philadelphia: University of Pennsylvania Press, 2000), 31–36.

31. Sigmund, *The United States and Democracy*, 85–107; Heraldo Muñoz, *Las relaciones exteriores del gobierno militar chileno* (Santiago: Ornitorrinco, 1986), 23–25; Lars Schoultz, *Human Rights and United States Policy toward Latin America* (Princeton, NJ: Princeton University Press, 1981), 52–58; Cavallo, Salazar, and Sepúlveda, *Historia oculta*, 78–79.

32. *Report of the Chilean National Commission*, 1:55; Frederick M. Nunn, *The Military in Chilean History: Essays on Civil-Military Relations, 1810–1973* (Albuquerque: University of New Mexico Press, 1976), esp. 242–308; Genaro Arriagada Herrera, *El pensamiento político de los militares (estudios sobre Chile, Argentina, Brasil y Uruguay)* (Santiago: Editorial Aconcagua, 1986), 84–107; Gregory Weeks, *The Military and Politics in Postauthoritarian Chile* (Tuscaloosa: University of Alabama Press, 2003), 31–42.

33. Nunn, *The Military in Chilean History*, 242–308; Arriagada, *El pensamiento político*, 84–107. Note that the Communist Party had been outlawed between 1948 and 1958, at the onset of the Cold War.

34. Nunn, *The Military in Chilean History*, 253–308.

35. This interpretation draws from Arriagada, *Por la razón*, 35–36.

36. *Report of the Chilean National Commission*, 1:57–65; Cavallo, Salazar, and Sepúlveda, *Historia oculta*, 66–70, cites the deaths of Generals Augusto Lutz and Oscar Bonilla as likely results of their opposition to the growing influence of the DINA. Air force general Alberto Bachelet, father of Chile's president Michelle Bachelet, died following torture in the air force hospital in Santiago.

37. Alexandra Barahona de Brito, *Human Rights and Democratization in Latin America: Uruguay and Chile* (Oxford: Oxford University Press, 1997), 41; Sandra McGee Deutsch, *Las Derechas: The Extreme Right in Argentina, Brazil, and Chile, 1890–1939* (Stanford, CA: Stanford University Press, 1999), 11–25, 59–77, 143–92; Thomas C. Wright, *Landowners and Reform in Chile: The Sociedad Nacional de Agricultura, 1919–1940* (Urbana: University of Illinois Press, 1982), 171–97. The candidate whom the right had originally committed to support, Julio Durán of the Radical Party, stayed in the race but drew only 5 percent of the vote.

38. Deutsch, *Las Derechas*, 338.

39. Paul S. Reinsch, "Parliamentary Government in Chile," *American Political Science Review* 3 (1909): 508, described the Chilean elites in the early twentieth century as "an aristocracy of birth and wealth [which] has unquestioned control of social and political life. This society constitutes at the present time the only aristocracy in the world which still has full and acknowledged control of the economic, social, and political forces of the state in which they live." Those Chilean rightists who in the 1970s desired to return to these ideal conditions had, according to one scholar, "an unarticulated vision of a kind of regressive utopia." Barahona de Brito, *Human Rights and Democratization*, 56; Garretón, *Chilean Political Process*, 75–81; Armand Mattelart, *La burguesía en la escuela de Lenín: el gremialismo y la línea de masas de la burguesía chilena* (Lima: Centro de Documentación MIEC-JECI, 1974).

40. Quoted in Thomas G. Sanders, "Military Government in Chile," in *The Politics of Antipolitics: The Military in Latin America*, ed. Brian Loveman and Thomas M. Davies Jr., 1st ed. (Lincoln: University of Nebraska Press, 1978), 274.

41. Juan Gabriel Valdés, *Pinochet's Economists: The Chicago School in Chile* (Cambridge: Cambridge University Press, 1995).

42. See Richard R. Fagen, *The Transformation of Political Culture in Cuba* (Stanford, CA: Stanford University Press, 1969).

43. If one calculates the Marxists' strength on the basis of support for the UP, it would be around 40 percent of Chile's population (based on the 1970 presidential and 1973 congressional elections). Membership in the Marxist parties, of course, was much smaller.

44. *Report of the Chilean National Commission*, 2:469. Human rights advocate José Zalaquett testified before the U.S. Congress in 1976 that "after February 1974, the methods changed suddenly. The intelligence services no longer announced deaths and detained persons began to disappear." Atria et al., *Memoria prohibida*, 1:389.

45. There is an abundance of testimonial literature that reveals the diversity among victims. Examples include Hernán Valdés, *Diary of a Chilean Concentration Camp*, trans. Jo Labanyi (London: Gollancz, 1975); Aníbal Quijada, *Cerco de púas* (Santiago: Fuego y Tierra, 1990); Otilia Vargas V., *La dictadura me arrebató cinco hijos* (Santiago: Editorial Mosquito Comunicaciones, 1991); Comité de Defensa de los Derechos del Pueblo (CODEPU), *Todas íbamos a ser reinas: estudio sobre nueve mujeres embarazadas que fueron detenidas y desaparecidas en Chile* (Santiago: Quimo Impre-

sores, 1990); and Rosario Rojas de Estudillo et al., *Memorias contra el olvido* (Santiago: Amerinda Ediciones, 1987).

46. Peter Winn, ed., *Victims of the Chilean Miracle: Workers and Neoliberalism in the Pinochet Era, 1973–2002* (Durham, NC: Duke University Press, 2004); Joseph Collins and John Lear, *Chile's Free Market Miracle: A Second Look* (Oakland, CA: Institute for Food and Development Policy, 1994); Marjorie Agosín, *Tapestries of Hope, Threads of Love: The Arpillera Movement in Chile, 1974–1994* (Albuquerque: University of New Mexico Press, 1996) documents a shantytown form of protest in which women wove their reactions to repression in burlap.

47. Lovell S. Jarvis, *Chilean Agriculture under Military Rule: From Reform to Reaction, 1973–1980* (Berkeley: Institute of International Studies, University of California, 1985); Patricio Silva, *Estado, neoliberalismo y política agraria en Chile, 1973–1981* (Amsterdam: CEDLA, 1987); Crístobal Kay and Patricio Silva, eds., *Development and Social Change in the Chilean Countryside: From the Pre-Land Reform Period to the Democratic Transition* (Amsterdam: Centre for Latin American Research and Documentation, 1992).

48. Only twelve Christian Democrats were identified among the total of 3,197 persons certified as killed or disappeared by government investigative bodies following the dictatorship's end. See Corporación Nacional de Reparación y Reconciliación, *Informe*, 591; Fleet, *Rise and Fall*, 182–207.

49. *Report of the Chilean National Commission*, 2:478–83; Atria et al., *Memoria prohibida*, 2:271–347.

50. The testimonies of two leftists who became DINA agents are among the best firsthand accounts of the agency's workings: Marcia Alejandra Merino Vega, *Mi verdad: "más allá del horror, yo acuso . . ."* (Santiago: Printed at A.T.G., S.A., 1993); and Luz Arce, *The Inferno: A Story of Terror and Survival in Chile*, trans. Stacey Alba Skar (Madison: University of Wisconsin Press, 2004). Also, *Report of the Chilean National Commission*, 2:471–505; Cavallo, Salazar, and Sepúlveda, *Historia oculta*, 51–60, 113–22, 133–42; Constable and Valenzuela, *Nation of Enemies*, 90–114; Ekaizer, *Yo, Augusto*, 215–37; Manuel Salazar Salvo, *Contreras: historia de un intocable* (Santiago: Grijalbo, 1995).

51. Constable and Valenzuela, *Nation of Enemies*, 91.

52. Cavallo, Salazar, and Sepúlveda, *Historia oculta*, 50. Referring to the twentieth century's other paradigmatic secret police organization, a U.S. defense attaché in Santiago wrote in January 1974, before the DINA's existence had been made public, that the DINA "is becoming a KGB-type organization." Kornbluh, ed., *The Pinochet File*, 163.

53. The term "state within a military state" was used by Covey Oliver, a member of an International Commission of Jurists delegation that visited Chile in 1974, in testimony before the U.S. House of Representatives' Committee on Foreign Affairs. It is cited in Ensalaco, *Chile under Pinochet*, 110. Pinochet's consolidation of power over the junta and the army is chronicled in Genaro Arriagada Herrera, *Pinochet: The Politics of Power*, trans. Nancy Morris (Boston: Unwin Hyman, 1988); and Arturo

Valenzuela, "The Military in Power: The Consolidation of One-Man Rule," in *The Struggle for Democracy in Chile*, ed. Paul W. Drake and Iván Jaksić, rev. ed. (Lincoln: University of Nebraska Press, 1995), 21–72. See also Constable and Valenzuela, *Nation of Enemies*, 64–89.

54. *Report of the Chilean National Commission*, 2:472.

55. *Report of the Chilean National Commission*, 2:471–505; Nicolás Sánchez Albornoz, *The Population of Latin America: A History* (Berkeley: University of California Press, 1974), 247.

56. The MIR's resistance is chronicled in Carmen Rojas, *Recuerdos de una MIRista* (Montevideo: Ediciones del Taller, 1988). See also Pinochet, *Camino recorrido*, 2:287–349; Wright and Oñate, *Flight from Chile*, 70–90; Cavallo, Salazar, and Sepúlveda, *Historia oculta*, 51–60.

57. *Report of the Chilean National Commission*, 2:483–92.

58. An insider's view of Villa Grimaldi is found in Merino Vega, *Mi verdad*, 65–104. See also *Report of the Chilean National Commission*, 2:485–87; and Wright and Oñate, *Flight from Chile*, 79–84. See the Derechos Chile website, www.derechoschile.com (accessed June 3, 2003) and the pamphlet by Pedro Alejandro Matta, "A Walk through a 20th-Century Torture Center: Villa Grimaldi, Santiago de Chile; A Visitor's Guide" (2000).

59. Eugenio Hojman, *1973–1989 Memorial de la dictadura: cronología de 16 años de pesadilla* (Santiago: Editorial Emisión, 1990), 105.

60. Chile, *Informe de la Comisión Nacional sobre Prisión Política y Tortura*, 281. This report may be seen at www.latinamericanstudies.org/chile/informe.htm (accessed November 18, 2005).

61. The seventeen categories of torture were compiled by the National Commission against Torture and are cited in Ensalaco, *Chile under Pinochet*, 91. See also Katia Reszczynski, Paz Rojas, and Patricia Barceló, *Tortura y resistencia en Chile: estudio médico-político* (Santiago: Editorial Emisión, 1991); Eric Stover, *The Open Secret: Torture and the Medical Profession in Chile* (Washington, DC: American Association for the Advancement of Science, 1987); Carlos Basso, *El último secreto de Colonia Dignidad* (Santiago: Editorial Mare Nostrum, 2002); Deyanira Corvalán interview, Santiago, November 15, 2002.

62. Gladys Díaz interview, in Wright and Oñate, *Flight from Chile*, 79–84.

63. Nancy Guzmán, *Romo: confesiones de un torturador* (Santiago: Editorial Planeta, 2000), 153, 159, 161, 172. Also, Nancy Guzmán interview, Santiago, November 15, 2002.

64. Helmut Frenz, "Porqué este era el único camino," in Atria et al., *Memoria prohibida*, 1:xxvii.

65. *Report of the Chilean National Commission*, 2:501–3; Guzmán, *Romo*, 163–65. See also chapter 6, 207–9, for more on the disposal of bodies. On the disappeared in general, see Vicaría de la Solidaridad, *Informe sobre 384 casos de personas desaparecidas, Julio '76*, 5 vols. (Santiago: Arzobispado de Santiago, Vicaría de la Solidaridad, 1976); León Gómez Araneda, *Tras la huella de los desaparecidos* (Santiago: Ediciones Caleuche, 1990).

66. For an excellent study of fear under state terrorism, see Juan E. Corradi, Patricia Weiss Fagen, and Manuel Antonio Garretón, eds., *Fear at the Edge: State Terror and Resistance in Latin America* (Berkeley: University of California Press, 1992), esp. 1–89; Constable and Valenzuela, *Nation of Enemies*, 140–65.

67. Constable and Valenzuela, *Nation of Enemies*, 148.

68. Politzer, *Fear in Chile*, xiii.

69. Guzmán, *Romo*, 106, quoting Patricia García.

70. Juana Shanahan interview, Santiago, November 20, 2002; *Report of the Chilean National Commission*, 2:788–89.

71. Kornbluh, *The Pinochet File*, 328.

2. John Dinges, *The Condor Years: How Pinochet and His Allies Brought Terrorism to Three Continents* (New York: New Press, 2004); J. Patrice McSherry, *Predatory States: Operation Condor and Covert War in Latin America* (Lanham, MD: Rowman & Littlefield, 2005); Edwin Harrington and Mónica González, *Bomba en una calle de Palermo* (Santiago: Editorial Emisión, 1987); Alejandro Carrió, *Los crímenes del Cóndor: el caso Prats y la trama de conspiraciones entre los servicios de inteligencia del Cono Sur* (Buenos Aires: Sudamericana, 2005).

73. Dinges, *The Condor Years*, 130–33, 142–43, 175–98.

74. The discussion of exile is based primarily on Wright and Oñate, *Flight from Chile*. Article 9 says, "No one shall be subjected to arbitrary arrest, detention, or exile." Article 13.2 says, "Everyone has the right to leave any country, including his own, and to return to his country." The regime also used internal exile, or *relegación*, as a form of punishment.

75. Ana Laura Cataldo interview in Wright and Oñate, *Flight from Chile*, 62.

76. Clodomiro Almeyda, *Reencuentro con mi vida* (Santiago: Ornitorrinco, 1987), 274.

77. Dinges, *The Condor Years*, 229.

78. *Qué Pasa*, April 2–8, 1981, 7; *La Nación*, November 26, 1982.

79. *Report of the Chilean National Commission*, 1:117–26 (quotation 117); Alejandra Matus, *El libro negro de la justicia chilena* (Santiago: Editorial Planeta, 1999).

80. Lowden, *Moral Opposition*, 151. The numbers of habeas corpus writs filed and accepted vary from source to source, but Lowden's figures are within the common range. See, for example, Cynthia G. Brown, *Human Rights and the "Politics of Agreements": Chile during President Aylwin's First Year* (New York: Americas Watch, 1991), 36–37.

81. *Report of the Chilean National Commission*, 1:119.

82. Constable and Valenzuela, *Nation of Enemies*, 116.

83. Constable and Valenzuela, *Nation of Enemies*, 152–59; Cavallo, Salazar, and Sepúlveda, *Historia oculta*, 167–76.

84. Atria et al., *Memoria prohibida*, 2:101–39.

85. *El Mercurio*, July 25, 1975, quoted in Kornbluh, *The Pinochet File*; http://friends oflatinamerica.typepad.com/hocofola/2005/08/demanding_the_m.html (accessed November 8, 2005).

86. Chile lost 380 clerics in the first two years after the coup, 314 of whom were foreigners. Many were expelled or pressured to leave the country. Some were tortured, and a few were murdered. Smith, *The Church and Politics*, 329–33.

87. Smith, *The Church and Politics*, 67–161; Lowden, *Moral Opposition*, 13–25.

88. Atria et al., *Memoria prohibida*, 2:473. See Lowden, *Moral Opposition*, 53–149; Cynthia G. Brown, *The Vicaría de la Solidaridad in Chile* (New York: Americas Watch, 1987); Jaime Esponda F., "Objetivos y criterios estratégicos aplicados por la Vicaría de la Solidaridad del Arzobispado de Santiago en su tarea de defensa de los derechos humanos," in *Represión política y defensa de los derechos humanos*, ed. Hugo Frühling E. (Santiago: Centro de Estudios Sociales-CESOC, 1986), 107–31; Oscar Pinochet de la Barra, *El Cardenal Silva Henríquez: luchador por la justicia* (Santiago: Editorial Salesiana, 1987).

89. Mario Garcés D. and Nancy Nicholls L., *Para una historia de los derechos humanos en Chile: historia institucional de la Fundación de Ayuda Social de las Iglesias Cristianas FASIC, 1975–1991* (Santiago: LOM Ediciones, 2005); Orellana and Hutchison, *Derechos humanos*, 143–94; Elizabeth Lira K., "Psicología y derechos humanos en una situación represiva: la experiencia de la FASIC," in *Represión política*, ed. Frühling, 269–91.

90. Orellana and Hutchison, *Derechos humanos*, 5–68, 204–25; Hernán Vidal, *Dar la vida por la vida: la Agrupación Chilena de Familiares de Detenidos Desaparecidos* (Minneapolis: Institute for the Study of Ideologies and Literature, 1982); Silvia Fernández Ramil and Jorge Osorio Vargas, "Notas sobre algunas experiencias de educación para los derechos humanos en Chile," in *Represión política*, ed. Frühling, 185–209; Patricia M. Chuchryk, "Subversive Mothers: The Opposition to Military Rule in Chile," in *Surviving Beyond Fear: Women, Children and Human Rights in Latin America*, ed. Marjorie Agosín (Fredonia, NY: White Pine Press, 1993), 86–97. Most of the organizations published—and some continue to do so—periodic reports on their activities.

91. Ensalaco, *Chile under Pinochet*, 120.

92. Orellana and Hutchison, *Derechos humanos*, 51–52.

93. Long-time human rights advocate and leader Aryeh Neier wrote, "Pinochet's coup, and the role played by Richard Nixon, Henry Kissinger, and the CIA in bringing it about, were crucial in the emergence of the human rights movement in the United States." Neier, *Taking Liberties: Four Decades in the Struggle for Rights* (New York: Public Affairs, 2003). See also Margaret E. Keck and Kathryn Sikkink, *Activists beyond Borders: Advocacy Networks in International Politics* (Ithaca, NY: Cornell University Press, 1998), 89–90; and Darren G. Hawkins, *International Human Rights and Authoritarian Rule in Chile* (Lincoln: University of Nebraska Press, 2002), 57, 81.

94. Howard Tolley Jr., *The U.N. Commission on Human Rights* (Boulder, CO: Westview Press, 1987), 63–66, 70–82, 86, 104, 111–33; Ensalaco, *Chile under Pinochet*, 98–124, 163–67; Muñoz, *Relaciones exteriores*, 191–97, 309–15; Hawkins, *International Human Rights*, 61–62; Iain Guest, *Behind the Disappearances: Argentina's Dirty War against Human Rights and the United Nations* (Philadelphia: University of

Pennsylvania Press, 1990), 95–98. Guest writes, "The Chilean coup had a dramatic impact on the U.N." (97).

95. Inter-American Commission on Human Rights, *Report on the Status of Human Rights in Chile: Findings of "On the Spot" Observations in the Republic of Chile July 22–August 2, 1974* (Washington, DC: OAS, 1974); Inter-American Commission on Human Rights, *Second Report on the Situation of Human Rights in Chile* (Washington, DC: OAS, 1976); Inter-American Commission on Human Rights, *Third Report on the Situation of Human Rights in Chile* (Washington, DC: OAS, 1977); Arriagada, *Por la razón*, 22–23.

96. *Las Ultimas Noticias*, November 12, 1974, quoted in Orellana and Hutchison, *Derechos humanos*, 168.

97. Quoted in Schoultz, *Human Rights and United States Policy*, 53–54.

98. Cavallo, Salazar, and Sepúlveda, *Historia oculta*, 178–88.

99. Muñoz, *Relaciones exteriores*, 197–200; Schoultz, *Human Rights and United States Policy*, 132–34.

100. Atria et al., *Memoria prohibida*, 2:245–70; Cavallo, Salazar, and Sepúlveda, *Historia oculta*, 146–51; Ensalaco, *Recovering the Truth*, 117–24. Kornbluh, *The Pinochet File*, 234–37, makes it clear that Kissinger was interested in image, not substance, in human rights matters.

101. John Dinges and Saul Landau, *Assassination on Embassy Row* (New York: McGraw-Hill, 1980); Taylor Branch and Eugene M. Proper, *Labyrinth* (New York: Viking Press, 1982); Alejandra Matus Acuña and Francisco Javier Artaza, *Crimen con castigo* (Santiago: La Nación Ediciones B, 1996).

102. Schoultz, *Human Rights and United States Policy*, 109–34.

103. Atria et al., *Memoria prohibida*, 2:413–17; Sigmund, *the United States and Democracy*, 110–11.

104. Atria et al., *Memoria prohibida*, 3:9–47; Arriagada, *Por la razón*, 87–90.

105. Atria et al., *Memoria prohibida*, 3:9–47; Hojman, *Memorial de la dictadura*, 91; Sigmund, *The United States and Democracy*, 110–18.

106. *Diario Oficial*, April 19, 1978. Brian Loveman and Elizabeth Lira, *Las ardientes cenizas del olvido: vía chilena de reconciliación política 1932–1994* (Santiago: LOM Ediciones, 2000), 451–65.

107. Corporación Nacional de Reparación y Reconciliación, *Informe*, 577.

108. Guest, *Behind the Disappearances*, 167–68.

109. Hawkins, *International Human Rights*, 3. Hawkins also writes, "While international human rights norms were developed on paper from the 1940s to the 1960s, the Chilean coup triggered one of the first and most extensive efforts to translate those norms into practice" (55).

110. Winn, *Victims of the Chilean Miracle*; Arriagada, *Por la razón*, 75–87, 289.

111. Corporación Nacional de Reparación y Reconciliación, *Informe*, 577; Cavallo, Salazar, and Sepúlveda, *Historia oculta*, 290–98, 343–52.

112. José Luis Cea Egaña, *Tratado de la Constitución de 1980: características generales, garantías constitucionales* (Santiago: Editorial Jurídica de Chile, 1988); Cavallo,

Salazar, and Sepúlveda, *Historia oculta*, 309–32. For more detail on the constitution and institutions, see chapter 6, 181–85.

113. Drake and Jaksić, eds., *The Struggle for Democracy*, 1–304; Cavallo, Salazar, and Sepúlveda, *Historia oculta*, 376–98; Gonzalo de la Maza and Mario Garcés, *La explosión de las mayorías: protesta nacional, 1983–1984* (Santiago: Editorial ECO, 1985).

114. Hernán Vidal, *Frente Patriótico Manuel Rodríguez: el tabú del conflicto armado en Chile* (Santiago: Editorial Mosquito, 1995). The Communist Party adopted the insurrectionary line in 1980.

115. Corporación Nacional de Reparación y Reconciliación, *Informe*, 577; Patricia Verdugo, *Quemados vivos* (Santiago: Aconcagua, 1986); Cathy Lisa Schneider, *Shantytown Protest in Pinochet's Chile* (Philadelphia: Temple University Press, 1995), 153–90.

116. Orellana and Hutchison, *Derechos humanos*, 51–52; Lowden, *Moral Opposition*, 93–116.

117. Sigmund, *The United States and Democracy*, 132–78; Muñoz, *Relaciones exteriores*, 133–34.

118. Arriagada, *Pinochet*, 67–78. Constable and Valenzuela, *Nation of Enemies*, 271–95; Cavallo, Salazar, and Sepúlveda, *Historia oculta*, 499–508.

119. Arriagada, *Pinochet*, 64–66; Wright and Oñate, *Flight from Chile*, 171–97.

120. Arriagada, *Por la razón*, 217–64; Cavallo, Salazar, and Sepúlveda, *Historia oculta*, 565–88; Constable and Valenzuela, *Nation of Enemies*, 296–320.

~

CHAPTER FOUR

The Dirty War in Argentina

While Videla governs, I kill.

—General Luciano Menéndez, commander, Third Army Corps[1]

The Armed Forces responded to the crimes of the terrorists with a terrorism infinitely worse than the terrorism they fought, because from the 24th of March, 1976, they used the power and impunity of the absolute State, abducting, torturing and murdering thousands of human beings.

—*Nunca más: Informe de la Comisión Nacional sobre la Desaparición de Personas*[2]

Between 1860 and 1930, Argentina went from a backwater struggling with the legacies of Spanish colonialism to the wealthiest country in Latin America, one with aspirations to challenge the United States for leadership of the Western Hemisphere. New technology, foreign capital, and five million European immigrants allowed Argentina to integrate into the new world economy and become its greatest beef exporter and a major supplier of grains. The rise of the export economy underpinned the development of a stable, constitutional, elite-controlled political system, to which the middle classes gained access following electoral reform in 1912. In the contest among capital cities to become the Paris of Latin America, Buenos Aires clearly claimed the trophy.[3]

The year 1930 was a watershed in Argentine history. The Great Depression ended both the meteoric rise of the Argentine economy and the country's sixty-eight years of uninterrupted civilian rule. The long-term economic decline that began in 1930 featured periodic crises that contributed to undermining governmental stability and continuity. Between 1930 and 1976, Argentina experienced nine successful military coups and twenty-one different presidential administrations; only two elected governments completed their constitutional terms, none after 1952. The 1930 turning point began what is often called the Argentine "riddle": how and why a prosperous, dynamic country lost its way and never recovered.[4]

Juan D. Perón, an army colonel, was elected president in 1946 and was re-elected in 1951. An admirer of Mussolini and an Axis sympathizer in World War II, Perón built his regime on the sometimes grudging support of his fellow officers and, with the astute collaboration of his wife Evita, the enthusiastic support of Argentina's workers. By promoting unionization and aligning the state with workers in labor disputes, Perón managed to redistribute income sharply in labor's direction, solidifying his base but alienating the economic and social elites. The regime nationalized foreign-owned railroads and utilities and promoted industrialization, creating a large state economic sector. After Evita's death in 1952, the Perón regime lost much of its magic. Declining prices for Argentina's exports reduced its ability to deliver economic and social benefits to its base, and a conflict with the Catholic Church and growing opposition within the armed forces led to Perón's overthrow in 1955.[5]

Perón's legacies profoundly influenced Argentina for decades and still reverberate today. Although an elected president, his authoritarianism and selective repression of opponents helped to ingrain both traits in the country's political culture. His prolabor policies left in place Latin America's strongest labor movement, a militantly Peronist force. His populism and antielite rhetoric fostered intransigent anti-Peronism among the socioeconomic elites, much of the middle class, and most of the officer corps. Thus Perón's ultimate legacy: a country so deeply and bitterly divided that it was essentially ungovernable except by force.[6]

Between 1955 and Perón's return to the presidency in 1973, Argentina alternated between civilian and military governments that averaged less than twenty-two months in duration. The concomitant lack of continuity in economic policy exacerbated the post-1930 decline, while antilabor policies eroded workers' living standards. This made the memory as well as the myth of the Peronist halcyon days all the more appealing and consequently hardened the Peronist resistance. Meanwhile, the influence of the Cuban Revolution was manifested in the growth of radical groups and the appearance, beginning in 1959, of three rural guerrilla movements based on Che Guevara's formula, all of which were quickly suppressed. The aging Perón remained active, directing his masses of followers from exile in Madrid and preparing for an eventual return to power. The military itself was divided between moderates who favored civilian government, without the Peronists, and hard-liners who had little tolerance for civilians of any stripe. The two factions alternated in power and occasionally took up weapons to settle their conflicts.[7]

In 1966, General Juan Carlos Onganía overthrew an elected government and established a repressive regime based on the national security state concept, similar in broad outlines to the military government established in Brazil two years earlier. Upon seizing power, he pledged to combat "ideological infiltration, subversion and chaos."[8] Unlike his post-Perón predecessors, Onganía moved decisively to consolidate control by banning political parties and activity, repressing the labor movement, purging the universities, and silencing the independent press. His economic policies, a radical brand of neoliberalism, also foreshadowed the model that the military would try to impose in the 1970s.[9]

The "Cordobazo," a massive but short-lived uprising of workers and students, occurred in May 1969 in the industrial city of Córdoba in reaction to Onganía and his policies. The Cordobazo catalyzed a rapid radicalization of large sectors of Argentine society. Already under the influence of the Cuban Revolution, labor unions and university students moved rapidly to the left, and secondary students became increasingly radicalized and mobilized. Although constituting a small minority of Argentina's clergy, the Movimiento de Sacerdotes para el Tercer Mundo (Movement of Priests for the Third World), inspired by liberation theology, exerted an influence disproportionate to its numbers.[10]

The most dramatic outcome of the Cordobazo was the rise of a powerful urban guerrilla movement. Inspired by the example of the Tupamaro urban guerrillas in neighboring Uruguay, six guerrilla groups began operating in Argentine cities in 1970. After attrition and consolidation, two major guerrilla organizations emerged: the Trotskyist/Guevarist Ejército Revolucionario del Pueblo (People's Revolutionary Army, ERP), led by Mario Roberto Santucho, and the larger pro-Perón Montoneros, headed by Mario Firmenich. In order to cultivate public support, the guerrillas carried out Robin Hood–style actions such as dispensing stolen food in slums and forcing foreign companies to rehire dismissed workers. They raised funds through bank robberies and kidnappings for ransom; attacked police, military posts, and locales associated with the elites; and assassinated important figures, including the strongly anti-Peronist General Pedro Eugenio Aramburu, who had headed the second post-Perón government.[11]

In response to this unprecedented challenge, which led to General Roberto Levingston's overthrow of Onganía in June 1970, the military and police fought back with both legal and extralegal methods. Upon his assumption of power in February 1971, Levingston's successor, General Alejandro Lanusse, initiated a state of siege that allowed the military to supplement the police in fighting terrorism and subversion and to set up a special court to expedite trials of guerrillas. The new court proved effective, convicting some six hundred accused terrorists in two years. Simultaneously, the regime used torture, executions, and disappearance to counter the surging leftist mobilization.[12]

The urban guerrillas added a new element to the complexity of Argentine politics. While the ERP wanted nothing to do with Perón, the Montoneros were fighting to force the military to permit Perón's return. Illustrating the aging leader's amazingly broad appeal as well as his capacity for manipulation, Perón encouraged the guerrillas, whom he called his "special formations," by promising to create a socialist Argentina upon his return. This cynical ploy triggered the rapid expansion and radicalization of the Peronist Youth movement that supported the Montoneros but did not use arms. Added to a new economic crisis and heightened labor militancy, the successes of the urban guerrillas and the growth of the Peronist Youth made it clear that Argentina finally had become ungovernable without Perón. Bowing to escalating pressures, Lanusse called for elections in 1973 in which Peronists were permitted to participate, although a residency requirement prohibited Perón from running. After a brief Peronist caretaker government, which amnestied all of the hundreds of jailed guerrillas and other leftists and abolished the antiterrorist court, Perón returned in June 1973. He was elected president in September with 62 percent of the vote and inaugurated in October.[13]

Perón's return ended eighteen years of myth accretion and his ability to be everything to everyone among his partisans. It also ended the Peronist left's illusions. Formerly united by their goal of Perón's return, the factions within the heterogeneous movement split following his election as they competed for influence in the new government. Forced to choose between his union core and the left fringe, Perón reneged on his promises to the Montoneros and the Peronist Youth and sided firmly with the mainstream labor organizations. The ERP's continued terrorist actions targeting police, military personnel, and union and rightist political leaders provided a pretext for a crackdown on the left in general, including the Montoneros, who had suspended their armed struggle upon Perón's return.

Repression of the left was directed by Perón confidant and social services minister José López Rega, a sinister character known as "the sorcerer" for his trafficking in the occult. He created the Alianza Anticomunista Argentina (Argentine Anticommunist Alliance, AAA), an extraofficial death squad made up largely of military and police. During Perón's eight-and-a-half-month presidency, the AAA and the military intelligence units were used sparingly, at least in comparison with their later levels of activity. Nonetheless, the ingredients were in place for the emergence of the full-scale dirty war.[14]

Beginnings of the Dirty War

The dirty war began in earnest following Perón's death in July 1974, during the twenty-one-month administration of his vice president and widow, Isabel Perón. Weak willed, politically inexperienced, and facing mounting economic and political crises, she allowed herself to be controlled by López Rega, who ran the AAA from his ministry. In response to the Montoneros' resumption of armed insurrection in September 1974, the AAA heightened its activity, and the government enacted increasingly tough antiterror laws and a state of siege that empowered the military and silenced the press. By late 1974, dozens of "subversives" were being murdered monthly, among them intellectuals, journalists, union leaders, and students identified with the left. Exiles who had fled repression in Chile and Uruguay following the coups in their countries became favorite targets. Leftist terror and rightist counterterror grew exponentially in late 1974, to become much worse in 1975.[15]

The army became formally involved in the war against the left in February 1975 when Isabel Perón authorized it to launch "Operation Independence" against a rural guerrilla campaign that the ERP had begun the previous year in the poor sugar-growing province of Tucumán. Tucumán became the proving ground for the military's nationwide dirty war that would follow its coup in March 1976. Military reports from the remote province deliberately inflated the numbers of ERP fighters and casualties on both sides in order to create a false sense of grave national danger; a news blackout assured an absence of competing accounts. Rather than attempting to wipe out the small number of rebels in the countryside, army units in civilian dress stalked and abducted people identified as leftists in the towns. In an ominous prelude to the dirty war, the army set up its first secret detention center where it tortured and killed not only guerrillas but also members of groups it labeled subversive.[16]

Explaining this approach, General Acdel Vilas, commander of the Tucumán operation, described the rationale for dirty war: "The offensive against subversion presupposes in the first place freedom of action in all areas . . . a series of special procedures, an instantaneous response, a persecution to the death." A Tucumán provincial commission that later investigated the army's operations concluded, "The repressive system put together had a basic objective: the mass diffusion of terror in order to paralyze any attempt at opposition."[17] The military prolonged its war in Tucumán into 1976, six months after the ERP guerrilla force deployed there had been essentially defeated, setting another precedent for the conduct of the dirty war at the national level. With the army's exercise in Tucumán, in the words of a historian, "the genocide was under way."[18]

While the army experimented in Tucumán, the AAA and the guerrillas intensified their terrorist campaigns, pushing the monthly political murder toll beyond one hundred several times in 1975. On October 3, Isabel Perón was hospitalized for a reported gall bladder ailment. Three days later, Peronist Italo Luder, who as president of the Senate became acting president of Argentina, issued decree 2772, which ordered the armed forces "to carry out the military and security operations that may be necessary to annihilate the activities of subversive elements in all the country's territory."[19] This unpublished presidential decree officially gave the military carte blanche to wage war however they saw fit, not only against the guerrillas but against whomever they deemed subversive.

As the violence escalated and the economic crisis deepened, society became increasingly polarized, and support for the president virtually evaporated. Thus, when it came, as in Chile, the coup surprised no one. Accustomed to military intervention, and clearly living in a time of crisis, a majority of Argentines welcomed the coup of March 24, 1976, believing that a military government was necessary to restore order and reverse the economic decline. The *Buenos Aires Herald* expressed a common view: "The entire nation responded with relief. . . . This was not just another coup, but a rescue operation. These are not men hungry for power, but men with a duty."[20] But as in Chile, many of those who welcomed the *golpe* (coup) would see their satisfaction turn to nightmare.

When it seized power, the new junta, comprising the army, navy, and air force commanders, proclaimed an ambitious program, El Proceso de Reorganización Nacional (The Process of National Reorganization). Shortly after the coup, the junta leader and new president of Argentina, General Jorge Rafael Videla, announced, "The events which took place on March 24, 1976, represent more than the mere overthrow of a government. On the contrary, they signify the final closing of a historical cycle and the opening of a new one."[21] In order to meet a challenge of this magnitude, the officers moved quickly to dismantle all institutions capable of opposing them and to assume direct control of the Argentine state at all levels. They suspended the constitution and political parties; extended the state of siege; closed Congress, provincial legislatures, and city councils; banned union activity; purged the courts, universities, and secondary schools; and severely limited press freedom. Officers replaced civilians as ministers, provincial governors, mayors, administrators of state enterprises, and union officials—even as director of Buenos Aires' famous opera house, the Teatro Colón. The junta divided the country into security zones and subzones under the control of high-ranking officers. Although personal and interbranch rivalry and competition negatively affected governmental efficiency, the Argentine military regime remained a joint venture of the three branches in close cooperation with Argentina's multiple police forces, never becoming a personal dictatorship such as Pinochet's.[22]

Despite its appropriation of sweeping powers, the new government initially appeared fairly moderate. Unlike Chile following the coup, in Argentina there was no curfew and no black ink on newspaper pages revealing a censor's heavy hand; there were few soldiers on the streets, and the bodies that turned up were identified as dead guerrillas. The general sense was that the military had swept away an unpopular, incompetent, and ineffectual government in order to save the country from violence and decay. The appearance and tone of Videla and his colleagues were reassuring, not threatening. Nonetheless, Argentines might have detected something sinister in Videla's speech announcing that "it is precisely to ensure the just protection of the natural rights of man that we assume the full exercise of authority: not to infringe upon liberty but to reaffirm it; not to twist justice but to impose it."[23] Their concern might have heightened if they had recalled part of a speech he had given just five months earlier at a conference of Latin American and U.S. military officers in Montevideo: "As many persons as necessary will have to die to achieve the country's [Argentina's] security."[24] They might have worried even more if they noticed the many medical references liberally sprinkled through the discourse of military leaders: "diagnosis," "cancer," "social pathology," "surgery," "extirpation of diseased tissues."[25]

In contrast to their Chilean counterparts, who initially had differing objectives until the DINA group and Pinochet set the junta's agenda, the Argentine officers took power with a clear purpose. Even as Videla spoke, unprecedented repression, ordered and coordinated from inside the governing junta, was being unleashed. Although no one outside the high military circles realized it until later, the seizure of power was the initial step toward implementing a method of repression concocted by the military command beginning in September 1975, when Isabel Perón had appointed Videla as army commander. The military's plan drew heavily on national security doctrine as espoused by French, U.S., and Argentine strategists. Under the guise of a war on the guerrillas, a program with broad support among a populace tired of violence, the military launched its dirty war on subversion. As they would remind the judges at their trial nine years later, Italo Luder's decree 2772 had ordered them to eradicate subversion, a term that the secret order did not define.[26]

By the time of the coup, the battle against the guerrillas was actually winding down. The number of guerrillas in the field, according to an authoritative source, is "a matter of guesswork."[27] Estimates vary from forty thousand armed fighters to between two thousand and three thousand. Despite these irreconcilable differences, the trajectory of the guerrilla struggle is clear. The larger Montoneros had suffered heavy losses and had revealed their weakness as a fighting force in a failed October 1975 attack on Infantry Regiment 29 in Formosa Province. After its defeat in Tucumán, the ERP lost more fighters in a December 1975 attack on an army garrison in Monte Chingolo in Buenos Aires Province, leaving it with few combatants. Assessing these developments, army commander Videla wrote in January 1976, nearly two months before the coup, that the "terrorist organizations" were "absolutely impotent," that they had "little fighting capability" and were unable to "reach a military level," although they were still capable of terrorist acts such as kidnappings, bombings, and assassinations.[28]

Following the coup, the military continued to decimate the guerrillas. ERP leader Santucho was ambushed and killed in July 1976, and most of the group's survivors fled the country by the following year. The Montoneros hung on longer, carrying out sporadic terrorist actions, but they reportedly lost the bulk of their remaining fighting force by mid-1978. Montonero leader Firmenich fled in 1977, and the remaining cadre followed in 1979. It is clear that at no time after the coup were the guerrillas a threat to capture territory or overthrow the government.[29]

Casualties among government forces confirm the guerrillas' early demise: 29 military and police reportedly died fighting the guerrillas in 1973, 54 in 1974, 137 in 1975, and the number peaked at 156 in 1976. Fatalities then plummeted to 43 in 1977, 6 in 1978, and none thereafter.[30] Despite this reality, the military would publicly claim throughout their nearly eight years in power, and thereafter, that the grave threat posed by the guerrillas justified all their repressive actions, and that any noncombatant casualties were collateral damage, the result of errors or isolated excesses.

Why, under the guise of fighting guerrillas, did the military leadership intensify the dirty war to the point of abducting, torturing, disappearing, and murdering thousands of noncombatants? What motivated them to institutionalize state terrorism and turn its fury on their unarmed compatriots? This is the conundrum of the dirty war. With all political power in its hands, the military after March 1976 had alternatives to the path it chose. There was the precedent of Lanusse's success in prosecuting captured guerrillas and their collaborators between 1971 and 1973. Moreover, upon seizing power, the military not only purged the judiciary to eliminate opponents of its hard line; it also reinstated the death penalty, subjected noncombatants suspected of subversion to military courts, and provided a legal basis for indefinite detention without trial. Since the military expected to hold power indefinitely, the guerrillas and subversives who would be sentenced to prison could not expect to be pardoned as they had been in 1973. Yet the military did not trust the legal solution; in the words of a naval officer, if subversives were turned over to the courts rather than being exterminated, "we'd be allowing a twenty year old terrorist to stay alive and maybe receive amnesty in ten to fifteen years. . . . He'd be only thirty or thirty-five, the age of a good military or political leader, with the added appeal of having been a martyr in his youth."[31]

The junta clearly possessed powerful tools to complement its purely military advantage over the left; together, the military and judicial approaches should have allowed the regime to finish off the remaining guerrillas, along with their collaborators, in a relatively short time. Yet putting an end to Argentina's cycle of antistate violence was just the first step on the officers' agenda. Envisioning an exorcism, a final solution to the problem of subversion, they made the conscious decision to conduct war on their fellow citizens—guerrillas, collaborators, suspected subversives, and others.

The Context of State Terrorism

Underlying the dirty war, as well as the other Latin American wars against human rights, were the threat of revolution and its antidotes: national security doctrine and counterinsurgency warfare. National security doctrine had begun to influence the Argentine armed forces even before the United States pushed it throughout the hemisphere in response to the Cuban Revolution. As a result of many officers' strong aversion to the Peronists, whom they considered an internal enemy, Argentine officers were quite receptive to ideological indoctrination in national security. From the early 1950s, Argentine officers had imbibed French concepts of counterinsurgency developed during colonial wars in Vietnam and Algeria. Argentina also had homegrown theoreticians of national security doctrine, among them Professor Jordán Bruno Genta, who preached the necessity of fighting the internal enemy and published on counterrevolutionary warfare in the 1960s. Throughout the 1960s, the military branches and police units greatly expanded their intelligence capabilities, preparing for their enhanced role in defending Argentina against domestic enemies, for "the timely intervention of a surgeon to eradicate the evil before the body becomes too weak and is totally diseased."[32]

While Argentina in the 1960s was turbulent, from 1970 on it was a textbook case for the establishment of a national security state and the application of counterinsurgency warfare. A government-commissioned 1971 poll found that half the population of Argentina's three largest cities supported the guerrillas. In addition to a guerrilla war, the powerful, radicalized Peronist Youth movement; the leftward shift within the labor movement; the unprecedented mobilization of university and secondary students; and the impact of the Third World priest movement had undermined three military governments and had defeated eighteen years of military policy with the successful push for Perón's return. The Montoneros' declarations that after their victory their fighters would replace the defeated regular army and the Peronist Youth's claims to be forming "popular militias" strengthened the resolve of many officers to crush the left.[33]

To military men trained in national security, Argentina by 1976 appeared to require a large dose of very strong medicine. While the waning guerrilla movement was still something of a challenge, the root cause of the Argentine problem, in their eyes, was much larger: ideas that inspired the guerrillas and their supporters and threatened the capitalist system. The means to fight this enemy were not to be found in Argentina's laws and its courts—not even the draconian laws and purged courts of the Proceso. The solution was state terrorism.[34]

The military was far from alone in embracing extreme measures against the left. Like Chile, Argentina had a history of extreme right currents within its political system. However, reactionary elements in Argentina—often grouped under the label "nationalists"—were both stronger and more extreme than their Chilean counterparts. The far right emerged in the late nineteenth century as a backlash against the massive wave of immigration that transformed Argentina between the 1870s and World War I; Chile, by contrast, received a much smaller influx of immigrants. Among the immigrants to Argentina were large numbers of Eastern European Jews, who created Latin America's largest Jewish community and gave rise to a strong strain of anti-Semitism in the extreme right. The resettlement of hundreds of German Nazi fugitives in Argentina following World War II bolstered nationalism and anti-Semitism and strengthened the extreme right. Jews and the left became convenient scapegoats for Argentina's problems, which mounted after 1930 and reached crisis proportions in the 1970s.[35]

The Argentine elites lost control of national politics much earlier than did their Chilean counterparts. After the rise to power of a middle-class

party, the Unión Cívica Radical, in 1916 and the growth of left-wing ideologies and groups, some of the elites and their allies embraced antidemocratic solutions to defending their interests, including varieties of integralism
and fascism. The far right extended its influence within the military, the
church, the media, the professions, and in politics, and every government
from 1930 on came under some degree of nationalist influence. The powerful extreme right embedded in Argentina's mainstream institutions was supportive of the military's hard line on the left, and, given the degree of crisis
in the 1970s, the distinction between moderate and extreme right became
blurred. Thus the Proceso had large numbers of civilian collaborators and
even more supporters.[36]

There is no doubt that many within the armed forces, as well as the supporting cast of civilians, saw the 1976 institutionalization of military power
as an opportunity to implement a final solution to the threat of a Marxist
seizure of power that had hung over Argentina and Latin America since the
Cuban Revolution.[37] Argentines had seen their neighbors struggle with the
same threat—Che Guevara in Bolivia, the Tupamaros in Uruguay, and Allende in Chile—and had watched General Pinochet recast his country's political and economic systems in a bid to rid Chile of the Marxist threat once
and for all. Despite the fact than no guerrilla movement, rural or urban, had
duplicated Castro's feat in the seventeen years since the Cuban insurrection,
developments in Argentina from the Cordobazo to 1976 made a Marxist victory appear possible. Clearly, to officers schooled in national security doctrine, absolute military control provided the best means of eliminating the
threat.

Former political prisoner Jacobo Timerman reduced the military mind-set
to its basics: "World War III had begun; the enemy was left-wing terrorism;
and Argentina was the initial battleground chosen by the enemy." The apoc-
alyptic language that laced the discourse of ranking officers—the medical references and the oft-repeated belief that Argentina was on the front lines of
a world war between Western Christian civilization and communism—reflected their will to mount a campaign of eradication, unfettered by limitations on the use of force or barbarity, while the armed forces held the reins.
This was the driving force behind the dirty war.[38]

More mundane considerations also elucidate the reasons for the dirty war.
Unlike their Chilean counterparts, Argentine military men since 1930 had
demonstrated a thirst for political power—for the good of the nation, in their
opinion, and clearly for their own good. Although internally divided over
material interests and strategy, the armed forces had come to constitute what
one scholar has called a "military party."[39] Despite the ambitions of some of

its leaders, however, the military had been unable to consolidate its political power and form stable, lasting governments. If they sought to hold power over the long run, getting rid of their most implacable enemies, the guerrillas and other subversives, would be the first order of business, followed by the taming of the powerful Peronist unions.

The Argentine military and police were notoriously corrupt institutions—another marked contrast to their Chilean counterparts. For years, some of their leaders and units had operated extensive extortion, kidnapping, and drug rackets. Direct governance without any outside oversight allowed the established corrupt practices to flourish and become more profitable. Indeed, in the militarized state, officers were placed in charge of the numerous enterprises in the large state sector, giving them unprecedented opportunities for graft and other forms of enrichment. Military and ranking police officers were also offered lucrative seats on boards of directors in the private sector. Lower down in the hierarchy, soldiers who abducted people to disappear them routinely looted their victims' homes, making off with what was called "war booty," which was shared with their superiors. In addition, victims were made to sign over titles to their homes, automobiles, and other assets. Some individuals, in fact, were abducted for financial rather than political motives.[40]

There was also the revenge motive: for every military or police victim of guerrilla terrorism, from the humble patrolman to General Aramburu, who was murdered by the Montoneros, there would be a score to settle.

Once initiated, the dirty war took on a life of its own. The enemies of the fatherland were numerous, an infinitely expandable pool; the task was therefore potentially interminable. Power, from power over the country to power over the life or death of an individual, was a potent narcotic, as reflected in a colonel's self-description: "I am the lord of life and death."[41] As their human rights crimes accumulated and the number of their victims grew, military men had to consider the possibility, however remote, of investigations and prosecution under a future civilian government. Moreover, the financial bonanza they enjoyed from exercising political power could not continue under civilian rule. Thus there were multiple motives for prolonging state terrorism under the guise of a war on the guerrillas.

Having decided on a broad, one-sided "war" against noncombatants, the military had to determine who the subversives were and how to attack them. Subversives were defined in various dehumanizing ways. For Videla, they were those "we do not consider Argentine" and who hold "ideas contrary to our western, Christian civilization." For the police chief of Rosario, a reputed sadistic torturer, subversives were outside "the family of man." And for general and later junta leader Reynaldo Bignone, they were not only "anti-fatherland" but were also "agents of the anti-Christ."[42] Precise definitions were unnecessary, of course, because the officers were both judge and jury. In practice, any degree of real or imputed dissidence from the military's mission and values made one a potential target. Given the radicalization of Argentine society in the 1960s and 1970s, the number of potential victims was immense. So when grieving parents protested that their missing child was not a guerrilla, a collaborator of the guerrillas, or even a political activist, that he or she had done nothing illegal or wrong, they were missing the real point of state terrorism.

In its war on subversion, the dictatorship organized a system of repression that recognized no legal or moral boundaries or constraints on the military's power. As Lieutenant Colonel Hugo Pascarelli asserted, "The fight in which we are engaged does not recognize moral limits; it is conducted beyond good or evil."[43] General Ibérico Saint Jean, governor of Buenos Aires Province after the coup, once articulated his strategic understanding of the dirty war: "First we will kill all the subversives, then we will kill their collaborators, then . . . their sympathizers, then . . . those who remain indifferent; and, finally, we will kill the timid." General Ramón Camps, chief of police of Buenos Aires Province, likewise envisioned concentric rings of victims, properly understood if "subversives" is substituted for "guerrillas": "First, we will kill the guerrillas. Then, we will kill the guerrillas' families. Then we will kill the friends of their families, and the friends of their friends, so that there will be no one left to remember who the guerrillas were." General Luciano Menéndez, commander of the Third Army Corps based in Córdoba, put his approach in quantitative terms: "We are going to have to kill 50,000 people: 25,000 subversives, 20,000 sympathizers, and we will make 5,000 mistakes."[44] These Dantesque rings of hell may have overstated the actual reach of state terrorism in Argentina, but they offer a chilling insight into the minds and ambitions of three of the dirty war's most powerful and feared repressors.

Long before the coup, the beefed-up military and police intelligence services had compiled lists of leftist suspects, readying them to become targets. Family members were often taken, as Camps proposed, with the result that some parents lost two, three, or more children and a grandchild or two. Other victims were identified from address books, photographs, or school albums taken from victims, named under torture, or spotted on the streets by collaborators. Many people were targeted because they belonged to categories of persons that were suspect, to which were attributed tendencies toward radicalism, liberalism, or merely a lack of sympathy with the military's mission of cleansing Argentina. These included union members and leaders, students, teachers and professors, journalists, actors, artists, and other professionals, particularly psychiatrists and defense lawyers. Interbranch rivalry, personal ambitions, incompetence, greed, and the opportunity to settle personal scores under cover of the antisubversive crusade yielded still more victims, including some not even suspected of subversion. Some were victimized randomly, while others were collateral damage of murders or disappearances.[45]

The Disappeared

When they seized power in March 1976, the Argentine military commanders were keenly aware of the international outcry against human rights violations in Chile. They had observed the almost overnight strengthening of the world's human rights lobby, the unprecedented steps that the UN had taken to condemn the Pinochet regime, and the response of the U.S. Congress and the new, burgeoning U.S. human rights movement. Yet rather than being deterred from their mission of eradicating the left, the Argentines selected a method that they believed would allow them to go undetected and thus avoid the international pressures directed at the Chilean military government.[46]

The military regime detained, tortured, and exiled many thousands of people. It murdered over 3,800 individuals whose bodies were recovered for burial. But the Argentine dirty war became synonymous with disappearances; the Argentine military regime made the term "disappear" a sinister transitive verb. The Inter-American Commission on Human Rights called disappearance "a true form of torture for the victim's family and friends, because of the uncertainty they experience as to the fate of the victim and because they feel powerless to provide legal, moral, and material assistance." *Nunca más*, the report of the Comisión Nacional sobre la Desaparición de Personas (National Commission on the Disappearance of Persons, CONADEP), which was established after the end of military rule, likened the effect of disappearances on loved ones to "permanently leaning over the abyss of a horror without limits." The mother of a disappeared person explained the impact of this method of state terror: "Disappearance is inexplicable. You are left with a void that is never filled."[47]

The disappearance served the regime's purposes because, since there were neither publicly accessible arrest records nor corpses, the government enjoyed plausible deniability. Disappearance served to intensify and prolong the general state of terror by which the military ruled. It was a means of discouraging public outcries and the formation of a cohesive opposition; as long as one's family member was missing rather than certified as dead, as long as even a ray of hope continued for the loved one's safety, family and friends were neutralized, afraid that speaking out or aggravating the authorities would result in his or her death. Further, the regime's frequently repeated explanations of the whereabouts of the disappeared—that they had gone underground, were in voluntary exile, or had been killed in internecine fighting among terrorist bands—could not be disproved and thus provided a means of denial in which many Argentines took refuge. For these reasons, as well as an extreme perversity on the part of some who would deny families the solace of mourning and burying a body, the Argentine military dictatorship perfected the disappearance.[48]

Nunca más, publications of human rights groups, testimonies of survivors of detention centers and a few repressors, and the trials of the former rulers allow us to establish the anatomy of a disappearance, from start to finish. All branches of the military and police were involved in disappearances, but hands-on practitioners were relatively few. In the military's arrangement for territorial administration, Argentina was divided into security zones that coincided with the jurisdiction of the four army corps, with smaller zones for the navy and air force. These jurisdictions were further divided into some forty subzones and hundreds of areas. Under general orders from the top, zone, subzone, and area commanders set up *grupos de tareas*, task groups of military and police personnel that operated semiautonomously in conducting disappearances. Officers not connected to task forces were sometimes assigned to participate in them or were given duties as executioners in order to spread responsibility and establish a "blood pact" of silence.[49]

The task group, which carried out abductions that initiated disappearances, consisted normally of between half a dozen and a dozen men, usually dressed in civilian clothes and using unmarked cars, particularly Ford Falcons. The majority (62 percent) of abductions that were witnessed by a survivor and verified by CONADEP were conducted at night; a majority (also 62 percent) of abductions occurred in the victim's domicile, while others took place on public thoroughfares (24.6 percent), in workplaces (7 percent), or in places of study (6 percent).[50]

In the case of abductions at home, the task groups informed local police of impending actions so that they would stay clear; this was known as the "green light." The kidnappers would enter the victim's home, rough him or her up, and beat or threaten family members or others found on the premises. If the intended victim was not present, the abductors normally waited, holding other residents or unwitting visitors captive until the victim arrived. They routinely sacked the home for war booty. To enhance and extend the sense of terror that abductions caused, the task groups sometimes flouted their impunity, calling attention to their actions throughout the neighborhood by making loud noises, firing weapons, or blocking traffic while executing the abduction. A report on a 1976 case indicated that the perpetrators went "into the street with their prisoners, in the middle of the morning, in the sight of neighbors and passersby, pointing hand guns and rifles and waiting unhurriedly and with complete impunity."[51]

Abducted persons were not taken to regular police facilities to be booked, where their detention would become a matter of public record, but to secret detention centers whose existence could be and was consistently denied.[52] The regime set up approximately 380 of these facilities throughout the country, many located in secured areas within military bases and police stations. Others were in such diverse settings as hospitals, government offices, automobile repair shops, schools, farms, and even the basement of the upscale Galerías Pacífico on Buenos Aires' downtown Florida shopping street. Thus many people were held and tortured within feet or even inches of normal life. As one prisoner recalled, "I could hear people walking by, cars and buses passing, life going on as usual, with us disappeared in a concentration camp. We were in the world but not part of it, alive in the realm of death."[53]

The five largest secret detention centers were the Escuela de Mecánica de la Armada (Navy Mechanics School, ESMA) and the Club Atlético, a federal police facility, both in very visible Buenos Aires locations; the Campo de Mayo army base and Vesubio, a former summer residence, both in the province of Buenos Aires; and La Perla, a military base in Córdoba Province. Among them, these five facilities are estimated to have received some 14,500 prisoners. Regardless of size, all the detention centers housed torture facilities, prisoners' quarters, military or police personnel, and, commonly, living quarters for the torturers themselves. The secret detention centers were conceived "more than for the sheer physical suppression of the victims, for submitting them to a meticulous and planned despoilment of the attributes of any human. Because entering them meant in every case CEASING TO EXIST [sic]."[54]

Such was the case of ESMA, known as the Argentine Auschwitz, the most vivid symbol of state terrorism, located on Buenos Aires' busy Avenida Libertador San Martín. Occupying a prime site, the school was a well-kept, tranquil-appearing symbol of navy pride where junta member Admiral Emilio Massera ran one of the most feared task groups, GT 3/32. While ESMA's normal functions as an engineering school continued, the officers' living quarters were remodeled to accommodate a torture center, hospital, and photography laboratory in the basement, and cubicles on the third floor and the loft where prisoners were kept following torture. The second floor held a large storeroom for war booty. GT 3/32 headquarters was on the ground floor, and officers lived on the second floor and part of the third. Both ambitious and ruthless, Massera urged his men in GT 3/32 to take on the enemy "with the maximum violence," and he reportedly engaged directly in the torture along with a list of sadists including lieutenants Antonio Pernía, Alfredo Astiz, and Juan Carlos Rolón. ESMA became notorious also for its "death flights" in which prisoners were thrown from aircraft into the Atlantic Ocean. Over five thousand abducted persons passed through ESMA; most perished.[55]

Upon arriving at a detention center, prisoners were assigned numbers, like Jews in Nazi extermination camps, and were taken immediately to the torture chambers, which in some centers were called *quirófanos*, or operating theaters, as found in hospitals. One survivor described the *quirófano* in the following terms: "This was a very sinister place, the walls were so covered with blood and stains that you could barely make out that it had once been painted yellow. The smell of burned flesh, blood, sweat, and excrement . . . made the air heavy, suffocating."[56] Prisoners faced a wide range of physical and psychological torture, as in the Chilean DINA's centers. As reported by prisoners detained in five different centers, there was a standard regimen of torture that varied according to the victim's value to the repressors, the quality of information extracted, and his or her ability to resist; it usually lasted between one and ten days. The most commonly used instrument was the electric cattle prod, or *picana*, an earlier Argentine invention that served as effectively for torture as for herding. Prisoners were strapped to a metal table and tortured with the *picana* for hours on the most sensitive body parts, occasionally being wetted down for greater effect. These torture sessions were called "a chat with Susan" in some detention centers. Medical doctors supervised the torture, calling off the sessions when victims approached death, then reviving them with serums and vitamins to face more torture.[57]

Alternating with the *picana* were the submarine, hanging by the feet, rape, burning with cigarettes, mock executions, beatings with clubs or chains, and deafening noises. Sadists invented torture instruments of their own, including a thick broom handle with 220 volt wires attached called the "Carolina" and a rectal torture device called the *rectóscopo*.[58]

Psychological torture took various forms. Some repressors allowed prisoners to speak with or write to their families and even visit them; this prolonged the family's and the victim's agony by kindling hopes of survival that were almost never realized. Psychological torture also included reassurance to the prisoners that they would eventually be sent to rehabilitation camps or legal prisons—a rare occurrence. And the uncertainty of one's fate and the inability to influence it were a psychological torture that all prisoners had to endure.

Perhaps the cruelest psychological torture was making one witness, visually, aurally, or both, the physical torture of a spouse, child, or parent.[59]

After the period of intense torture, prisoners were moved to a holding area called the *capucha*, or hood, for the hoods prisoners wore. There, in the words of a survivor, "Hell awaited them . . . , permanent terror, isolation and impotence in the face of constant humiliation."[60] Typically, they were handcuffed and shackled in spaces so tiny they were called *tubos*, or tubes. They continued to receive physical abuse in the form of beatings, continuous bright light, and loud music; some were returned to the operating theater for more torture. Hygienic and dietary conditions were miserable: all lost weight and many got sick, but if they were deemed worthy of keeping alive, doctors attended them. The isolation, terror, subhuman conditions, and the knowledge that there was little chance of leaving alive drove some prisoners insane.[61]

Pregnant women received different treatment if they and their fetuses survived the initial torture. As their delivery time approached, they were taken from the *tubos* to an infirmary, where they received improved nutrition, and ultimately to a facility that had birthing service, such as ESMA. After giving birth, they were separated from their child and were sometimes killed straight away or were returned to the *tubos* to await the common fate. The infants born in captivity, along with small children captured with their parents, were given, along with false documentation, to childless military couples or others favored by the regime to raise as their own. To the military mind, being raised in a Christian and patriotic family would be a blessing for children otherwise headed for perfidy under the influence of their subversive parents.[62]

Jews suffered disproportionately, in part because of their overrepresentation in some of the "subversive" or suspect categories and professions, and in part owing to virulent anti-Semitism within the military and police and within the extreme right in general. The common notion that Argentina was fighting to protect its Western Christian heritage in itself demonized Jews and legitimized anti-Semitic actions. With the largest Jewish community in Latin America, Argentina had seen several waves of anti-Semitism since the era of mass immigration in the late nineteenth century, some involving serious violence. Moreover, the military contained professed admirers of Hitler for whom the dirty war provided the opportunity to indulge their proclivities.[63]

Jews accounted for less than 2 percent of Argentina's population but 10 percent of the disappeared. According to much evidence, they suffered even greater abuse and humiliation than non-Jews. Jews were very commonly subjected to treatment such as being called "dirty Jews" and "the Antichrist"; being lectured on the evils of Jews and told repeatedly that "the only good Jew is a dead Jew"; being forced to kneel before portraits of Hitler, to listen to recordings of his speeches, and to shout "Heil Hitler"; and having swastikas painted on their bodies. In addition, they often suffered harsher physical treatment because of their Jewishness.

The fate of prisoners held in secret detention centers was exclusively in the hands of the repressors. There was no access to attorneys or courts and no possibility of appeal. In the overall scheme of the dirty war, the authority over life and death was decentralized, residing in the hands of zone and sub-zone commanders or their subordinates unless a prisoner's case received notice at the top of the hierarchy. Thus, the colonel's boast that he was the angel of life and death was far from hyperbole. There were three options for the living disappeared: liberation, transfer to the legal prison system, or death. Prisoners were graded on official documents in three categories based on their degree of dangerousness: "potentially dangerous," "dangerous," and "extremely dangerous." Some of those rated "potentially dangerous" were freed or sent to the regular prison system; those in the other two categories were normally slated for death.[64]

As a prisoner explained, "One learned rapidly: One is only in the detention center for a period of time that is hard to predict: Then, the 'transfer.'"[65] The transfer was the repressors' term for execution. Prisoners were told that most of them would be transferred either to legal prisons, which would be a major step toward freedom, or to rehabilitation camps. This fiction provided but a thin hope of survival, another uncertainty that eroded their condition as humans, because they knew that for most, transfer meant execution. Prisoners did not know when transfers would occur, nor who among them would be transferred. A full facility was dangerous—a prelude to transfer. A heightened presence of intelligence officials who graded the prisoners signaled a transfer within a week or so and exacerbated the level of anxiety. Who would be selected? How would they be killed?[66]

The arrival of special units from outside the center launched the transfer, which culminated in murder and disposal of the bodies in ways designed to continue the regime's plausible deniability and impede future investigations. Many were shot by firing squads or at close range with pistols. Some were shot standing before prepared trenches, as on Loma del Torito outside the La Perla army base in Córdoba; others were later buried in mass graves on bases or in clandestine common graves in cemeteries throughout the country, where their remains, often with hands cut off, would commingle over time, making identification difficult. Corpses were also buried in cemeteries in individual paupers' graves, under the symbol N/N (no name). Some bodies were dynamited, others incinerated. In urban areas, tires were sometimes burned along with the bodies to disguise the smell of burning flesh. In coastal areas, these methods of killing and disposal were supplemented by the practice of dropping prisoners into the ocean from aircraft. This was the preferred procedure for those held at ESMA. Some had their bellies slit before being ejected to minimize the danger that they might float; they were referred to as "fish food." After bodies washed up on both the Argentine and Uruguayan shores, pilots flew further out into the Atlantic before making the drops. Some transferred prisoners served government propaganda purposes: their corpses were exhibited as dangerous guerrillas shot in "confrontations" or while "trying to escape" so as to corroborate the military's claim that it was continuing to fight a major guerrilla war—the justification for the regime's existence.[67]

Who were the disappeared? CONADEP established the disappearance of 8,960 people; further government investigations have added some four thousand to the list of the documented disappeared. Human rights organizations estimate that thirty thousand were disappeared under the military regime. The exact number of disappeared persons will never be known, but CONADEP's figures provide a profile of the 8,960 originally documented cases that gives a general picture of the demography of disappearance. Seventy percent of the disappeared were men, 30 percent women; 10 percent of the women, or about 270, were pregnant. Three-fourths were between twenty-one and thirty-five years of age; youth between sixteen and twenty accounted for 10.6 percent, while children under sixteen (1.65 percent) and persons over fifty-five (2.58 percent) were not exempt from disappearances. By occupation, 30.2 percent of the disappeared were workers, 21 percent students, 17.9 percent white collar employees, 10.7 percent professionals, 5.7 percent teachers, 3.8 percent housewives, 2.5 percent police and military, 1.6 percent journalists, and 0.3 percent religious professionals. At least a dozen disabled persons, some completely paralyzed, were disappeared. Urban areas, particularly greater Buenos Aires, were most heavily affected, but people disappeared in every corner of the country. La Plata, a university center and the capital of Buenos Aires Province, lost the greatest proportion of its youth of any part of the country.[68]

CONADEP also established the chronology of the disappearances among the 8,960 victims it identified. The first year to surpass one hundred was 1975, when some 350 persons disappeared. The coup year of 1976 was the peak, with nearly 4,200 disappearances, followed by 1977 with over 3,200. In 1978, just over one thousand disappeared. The last year to top one hundred was 1979, with 225, but disappearances occurred in small numbers through the regime's end.[69] As in Chile, the greatest number of atrocities occurred in the period immediately after the coup. Unlike Chile, where some of the human rights violations were attributable to high emotional states of hatred and a lust for revenge, disappearances in Argentina from the beginning were calculated, planned, and executed on government orders. State terrorism was institutionalized from the moment of the coup.

A State of Fear

Although disappearances peaked in 1976–1977, the intense sense of terror they produced remained. The military had deliberately created a climate of extreme fear in order to secure and extend its control. As a naval officer said, "If we exterminate them all [the subversives], there'll be fear for several generations."[70] Fear explains people's passivity in the face of violence, as in the abduction of Susana Barros from Buenos Aires bus 128 in broad daylight. Rather than protesting or resisting, passengers and the driver averted their gaze as the young woman was hauled away to ESMA; passively, they continued to their destinations. Commenting on the behavior of her friends, a rural woman complimented the military's effectiveness in instilling fear: "The military taught them well: Fear us, fear each other, fear yourselves."[71] Said a woman who lost a child, "Fear is a jail without bars."[72]

State terrorism was so effective in Argentina because initially no institutions opposed it, and society at large feared, denied, and even justified it, leaving the affected individuals and families helpless and isolated. Particularly in the first couple of years, most parents and spouses did not understand that the government itself was conducting the disappearances. The methods of abduction; the absence of records and bodies; and government explanations about subversives going underground, going into exile, or being killed by other terrorists made it impossible for them to see their situation in clear focus. Thus they filed reports with the authorities and made the rounds of police stations, hospitals, military bases, ministries, and morgues searching for their lost ones. The standard government response to their inquiries was that the missing were "persons who are not recorded as detained."[73]

Beyond that fruitless exercise, they were paralyzed and neutralized by the sheer terror of knowing that they were completely at the mercy of forces they did not understand, but which held absolute power over their loved one, the rest of their family, their friends, and themselves. And the repressors did everything to enhance the pervasive sense of their omnipotence and impunity, and hence fear. They singled out very prominent persons, including former congressmen, a diplomat, and a newspaper publisher, for murder or disappearance in order to promote the "general understanding that nothing and no one could alter the course of predetermined events."[74]

Many Argentines sought refuge in denial: "We knew but we didn't know"—a sentiment expressed by ordinary Germans about the removal of

Jews in their midst en route to extermination—epitomized the response of many who were not directly affected by the disappearances.[75] In the absence of proof, reports of disappearances could be discounted as rumor or attributed to the excesses of a few rogue bands of military or police that the government would surely bring under control. Alternatively, one could believe the regime's disinformation. When convinced that someone had really disappeared, people commonly responded, "por algo será" (there must be a reason). Parents of disappeared children were extremely frustrated by their inability to convince even their closest friends that the government had abducted their son or daughter.[76] In the words of a mother who lost a child, "We tried to explain this ineffable reality, which our compatriots were unable to understand unless they had been touched by it either directly or indirectly."[77] Friendships became strained or broken; parents who spoke out about their children's fate were often ostracized and labeled *resentidos*, or resentful ones. This reaction drove parents deeper into retreat and despair until, as one explained, "the outside world became opaque."[78]

Accomplices in the Dirty War

Afflicted families had nowhere to turn for succor. On the day of the coup, the military rulers purged the Supreme Court, the state prosecutor's office, and the provincial high courts and required both continuing and new judges to swear loyalty to the Proceso. A large part of the judiciary either supported the dirty war or looked the other way; the state of siege severely limited the powers of those judges inclined to protect individuals' rights. The large-scale imprisonment, exile, murder, and disappearance of lawyers who took human rights cases soon made it almost impossible for families to secure legal assistance. As a result of these conditions, only one writ of habeas corpus filed during the Proceso was successful. The common knowledge that there was no recourse in the courts only exacerbated the generalized sense of terror.[79]

The mass media were also complicit in the dirty war. Official communiqué number 19 made it a serious crime to publish anything designed to "perturb, jeopardize, or diminish the prestige of the military or security and police forces." Journalists who showed independent tendencies were harassed, jailed, and murdered; over 150 were disappeared. Most of the media willingly or enthusiastically supported the Proceso; they regularly published disinformation provided in government-disseminated packets and churned out stories of fake prison escapes and guerrilla terrorist attacks along with exaggerated figures on military and police casualties in order to reinforce the fiction of a continuing war against the guerrillas. In a 1977 event that became an international incident, the press published without comment the official story that two French nuns were abducted by the Montoneros, when in reality they were being held at ESMA in preparation for their murder. The media also reported as fact the regime's most absurd misrepresentations of the human rights situation.[80]

Another institution that might have provided defense for the victims of human rights violations, at least for its own members, was the labor movement, one of the most powerful institutions in Argentina since Perón's first government. Whereas previous military governments had been forced to bargain with the Peronist trade unions, the leaders of the Proceso were determined to neuter them, for three main reasons. With their power to command the streets and paralyze the economy, the unions were potential obstacles to the military's aspirations for total power. The de-Peronization of Argentina had to begin with the unions, which constituted the core of the Peronist Party. In addition, the junta's neoliberal economic agenda required the reduction of labor costs, and hence the suppression of union bargaining power, in order to control inflation, make Argentine production more competitive in international markets, and attract large-scale foreign investment.[81]

The unions thus suffered immediate and ferocious repression. The regime banned strikes, shut down the major national labor federation, took control of hundreds of locals, and detained thousands of shop stewards and ordinary workers, murdering many. Troops occupied some factories and utilities, empowering owners to cut wages, suspend work and safety rules, and generally restore nineteenth-century working conditions. Combined with the neoliberal policies being implemented by Economy Minister José Martínez de Hoz, this direct assault on unions reduced workers' real income by over one-third within ten months of the coup, further reducing unions' ability to resist. Nearly a third of the persons disappeared were workers, many of them union activists.[82]

Unlike their trans-Andean counterparts, the Argentine military did not face a church hierarchy committed to protecting human rights. Indeed, with only a few dissenting voices, the Argentine Council of Bishops was a collaborator in the dirty war. Bishop Victorio Bonamín spoke for many of his colleagues in calling the dirty war "a struggle to defend morality, human dignity, and ultimately a struggle to defend God."[83] In the words of a leading critic, "The bishops knew the truth and they hid it in order to aid the military government. Faced with a choice between God and Caesar, they chose Caesar."[84] A human rights activist said of Argentina's bishops, "One hand was enough to count those who supported us."[85]

The church's support of the dirty war was based on its conservative tradition and its anti-Marxist and anti-Peronist views. The intellectual training of many Argentine priests was rooted in the most conservative strain of Catholicism, similar to that which underpinned Franco's dictatorship and informed lay organizations such as Opus Dei. In addition, the Catholic Church enjoyed a privileged position as Argentina's official religion and received a substantial state subsidy for salaries and the vast system of Catholic education.[86]

The role of military vicars was central to the collaboration. These chaplains, whose lives and careers were normally spent within the military institution, identified closely with their martial comrades. In 1976, the president of the Conference of Bishops, Archbishop Adolfo Tortolo, was also head of the military vicariate. Mirroring the broader society, the church had become polarized by the early 1970s between progressives and the traditionalists who considered the Third World priest movement a challenge to the bishops' authority and to the status quo. Thus, when the military declared war on subversion, the religious hierarchy not only failed to take a vigorous stand for human rights; it stood by while the military targeted progressive church people, killing over forty, from two bishops to lay persons, disappearing at least 120, and jailing and expelling hundreds more.[87]

The complicity of the church went beyond its failure to nurture and shield a human rights movement. A number of priests, particularly military vicars, played active roles in the repression. A few were accused of actually engaging in torture. Vicar Christian von Wernich consoled a soldier following the murder of three detainees by telling him that "what [he] had done was necessary, that it was a patriotic act, and that God knew that it was for the good of the country."[88] Priests regularly blessed the crews of the aircraft used to drop people into the ocean and assured them they had administered "a Christian death."[89] A ranking general said of Bishop José Miguel Medina, "His advice clearly pointed the military sword in the right direction."[90] The archbishop of Buenos Aires, Cardinal Juan Carlos Aramburu, was a supreme apologist for the dirty war. Upon the discovery of mass graves in 1982, he declared, "In Argentina there are no mass graves; each body has its own casket. Everything was registered in the proper books. The common graves are of persons whom the authorities were unable to identify after they died. Disappeared? Things should not be mixed up. Do you know that there are some 'disappeared' persons who today are living quite contentedly in Europe?"[91]

Rise of a Human Rights Movement

The initial response of the international human rights community to the Argentine junta was muted in comparison to its reaction to the Pinochet regime, for several reasons: the Chilean coup had violently shattered Latin

America's strongest democratic tradition; Allende's experiment in democratic socialism had been widely admired in the socialist bloc, the developing world, and Western Europe; the massive roundups and summary executions in Chile made sensational news and caused revulsion around the globe; and the large number of Chilean exiles worked incessantly to rally world opinion against Pinochet. Argentina, by contrast, was accustomed to military rule; the coup had overthrown an incompetent, corrupt, and unpopular regime; and the Argentine military's tactic of disappearance, combined with the presence of a serious though waning guerrilla war, made reality difficult to decipher and disclaimers plausible. Moreover, the USSR and Argentina had a profitable trade relationship, and because Argentina's Communist Party was minuscule, the Soviet Union had little stake in Argentine politics. As a result, the USSR did not marshal its allies, and, in contrast to the reaction against Chile, an anti-Argentine bloc did not develop in the UN.[92]

Despite the less hostile reaction, the international human rights NGOs took note of the Argentine situation, increased their monitoring, and released damning reports. Several governments protested the disappearance of their citizens, totaling nearly six hundred, some of whom held dual citizenship with Argentina. Meanwhile, the burgeoning exile population spread the news about human rights violations. In 1978, the UN General Assembly weighed in with an expression of concern about disappearances, although neither Argentina nor Chile was named.[93]

At the onset of the military dictatorship, Argentina had three human rights organizations. The Liga Argentina por los Derechos del Hombre (Argentine League for the Rights of Man) had been founded in 1937 primarily to defend Communists from government persecution. As political violence rose in the run-up to the 1976 coup, two additional organizations were established. The Servicio Paz y Justicia (Peace and Justice Service, SERPAJ) was created in 1974 as a branch of an ecumenical, religious-based international group dedicated particularly to social justice for the poor and marginalized. The Asamblea Permanente por los Derechos Humanos (Permanent Assembly for Human Rights, APDH), established in December 1975, specialized in legal action and documentation of human rights violations. In the face of the relentless repression after March 24, 1976, however, there was almost nothing these organizations could do to curtail human rights violations.[94]

In response to the massive harvest of state terrorism, several new domestic human rights organizations appeared in Argentina within a year and a half of the *golpe*. The Movimiento Ecuménico por los Derechos Humanos (Ecumenical Movement for Human Rights) was founded in 1976 by dissident Catholic clerics who rejected the hierarchy's passivity in the face of repression. In the same year, family members of victims began founding organizations to publicize their cause and pressure the authorities for redress. The first of these was the Familiares de Detenidos y Desaparecidos por Razones Políticas (Families of the Detained and Disappeared for Political Reasons), founded in September 1976.[95]

Thirteen months after the coup, on April 30, 1977, fourteen mothers of disappeared persons met in the Plaza de Mayo in front of the presidential palace, the Casa Rosada, with the intention of petitioning junta leader Videla for information about their children. From this humble beginning developed the emblematic Argentine human rights organization, the Madres de Plaza de Mayo (Mothers of the Plaza de Mayo). These extraordinarily brave and determined women, who had met each other in their grim and desperate routine of searching for their children, surmounted their fears and launched a movement that gradually grew into the hundreds and became one of the world's best-known human rights organizations. They soon settled on a routine of symbolic protest that continues today: at 3:30 on Thursday afternoons they marched around the obelisk in the Plaza de Mayo wearing shawls made to look like baby diapers, to symbolize their children and their condition as mothers, carrying placards with photographs and names of their children and the question, "¿dónde están?" (where are they?) One Madre explained the photographs: "Because people didn't believe, it was necessary to use photos to show that our children existed."[96]

The testimony of a woman's first Thursday afternoon march captures both the Madres' agony and their solidarity. "Like all new arrivals, they asked me who my 'disappeared person' was and for how long he had been gone. My answer was broken by sobs: 'a daughter and my son-in-law . . . four months ago.' [Then] I heard their replies: 'Three of my children a year ago'; 'Me, a daughter, an invalid, eight months ago'; 'My parents and my sister . . . she was pregnant.'"[97]

The regime tried to marginalize the Madres by branding them the "locas (crazy ones) de Plaza de Mayo," a label constantly repeated in the media. They were depicted as part of the "anti-Argentine campaign" that underlay any questioning of the human rights situation. The regime used direct repression, breaking up their marches, beating and arresting them, and disappearing several members, including three of the founders, and more of their children. Though often discouraged and fearful, the Madres fought back. As their numbers grew, they were able to carve out some space for their actions. They established chapters in over a dozen cities, support groups abroad, and connections with foreign media; they sometimes traveled abroad to make their case, meeting with political leaders and support groups. They met briefly with Pope John Paul II during his 1980 visit to Brazil. They eventually acquired an office and became a prominent part of the Buenos Aires scene. In 1980, they received the People's Peace Prize, an alternative recognition for nominees for the Nobel Peace Prize.[98]

Another key human rights organization, the Abuelas de Plaza de Mayo (Grandmothers of the Plaza de Mayo) was founded in October 1977 by women whose born or unborn grandchildren had been disappeared along with their daughters or daughters-in-law, and sometimes their sons or sons-in-law as well. Recognizing the probability that their daughters were dead, the grandmothers focused on the brighter possibility of being reunited with their potentially surviving grandchildren. The Abuelas became one of the most active and widely recognized organizations in the expanding universe of Argentine human rights organizations.[99]

Although constantly repressed, the human rights movement continued to expand with the addition in 1979 of the Centro de Estudios Legales y Sociales (Center for Legal and Social Studies, CELS), an organization dedicated to legal action and documentation. CELS was founded by lawyer Emilio Mignone, whose daughter had been disappeared. Having worked at the OAS in Washington in the 1960s, Mignone was able to call on his international connections to increase cooperation between domestic and international human rights groups. CELS provided legal aid to families of the disappeared, including thousands of writs of habeas corpus, and collected a vast archive of documentation, which, along with information supplied by APDH, formed the basis of investigations and trials after the return of civilian government.[100]

Despite the growth of domestic and international pressures, the military regime remained unfazed. Two years into the Proceso, a large segment of the population supported or at least tolerated the government and its mission. The guerrillas' defeat had restored tranquility, except among the "subversives" that the regime continued to exterminate. The military's economic policies had produced a short-lived period of "sweet money" for the middle classes and well-to-do. The Madison Avenue public relations giant Burson-Marsteller, hired by the junta six months after the coup, had done a good job of planting positive information about Argentina in the world media to offset the growing suspicions about the human rights situation. The Argentine foreign ministry used assiduous and sometimes dirty diplomatic maneuvering to keep the UN Human Rights Commission at bay, in marked contrast to the Pinochet regime's failure in this area. Like the Chilean dictatorship, the junta skillfully parried criticism from abroad by assuming the mantle of defender of Argentine sovereignty. These factors, combined with the methodology of the disappearance, the fiction of the ongoing guerrilla struggle, and the collaboration of church, judiciary, and media, continued to shield Argentina from the full force of the energized international human rights lobby.[101]

The quadrennial international soccer championship, the World Cup, was held in Argentina in May and June 1978, when the regime was at the peak of its power and prestige. Hosting the World Cup was a big gamble for the regime because, as the Mexican government discovered in hosting the 1968 Olympics, the legions of foreign journalists sent to cover the sporting event were likely to look beyond the athletic arenas for stories and footage.[102] The Madres and other groups extended themselves to take advantage of this opportunity to disseminate news of the disappearances to the world.

Nonetheless, as hosting the OAS had done for Pinochet, the regime's gamble paid off. The government turned out large crowds to protest against the Madres and affirm the regime's claims about human rights. The regime adroitly harnessed Argentina's "soccer nationalism" and translated it into support for the dictatorship. Prior to the matches, military leaders had identified their personas, and hence the regime, with Argentine success: Videla was photographed kicking a ball with Diego Maradona, the Argentine successor to Pelé as the world's soccer superstar, and Massera claimed victory for the Argentine team in advance. When the Argentine team won the championship, its victory validated the regime and its policies.[103]

Many foreign journalists—predominantly sports writers, not political analysts—persuaded by the reigning calm, regime propaganda, and the smooth running of the World Cup, concluded that human rights concerns were unfounded. The president of the Fedération Internationale de Football Association (FIFA), the governing association of world soccer, opined, "The World Cup was more than soccer. It served to change Argentina's image abroad and showed that things published in the foreign press are a fantasy."[104] In the Southern Hemisphere in late fall of 1978, sport trumped human rights: Argentina won the world's most prestigious trophy, the rulers took credit, and the concerns of the "*locas*" were swept aside. A Madre lamented, "The people were happy, enjoying the football; and I was in tears, thinking what indifferent people we Argentines are. Young people are being taken away and they are celebrating as if it were a party."[105]

The cause of human rights in Argentina, and in the world, found a powerful ally in U.S. President Jimmy Carter. Inaugurated ten months after the coup, Carter made Argentina a priority test of his human rights–based foreign policy. His assistant secretary of state for human rights and humanitarian affairs, Patricia Derian, made several visits to Argentina, where she met with dissidents and human rights activists and questioned the military rulers directly in efforts to penetrate the official veil of secrecy. U.S. embassy personnel in Buenos Aires received families of the disappeared and recorded their stories. On a November 1977 visit to Argentina, Secretary of State Cyrus Vance handed Videla a list of 7,500 names of persons alleged to have disappeared. The U.S. Congress in 1978 prohibited military sales, aid, and loans to Argentina. The Carter administration consistently voted against Argentine requests for loans from international financial institutions.[106]

After three years in which the military regime snuffed out human rights with near-absolute impunity, the mutually reinforcing work of the domestic human rights movement, international human rights organizations, governments whose citizens were killed and disappeared, and the Carter administration began to bear fruit. In 1978, the Argentine government's desire for U.S.-made equipment for a major dam project clashed with Carter's refusal to approve the necessary financing owing to the regime's human rights record. In a compromise crafted by the U.S. administration, Argentina got the equipment in exchange for approving a visit by the Inter-American Commission on Human Rights. In preparation for the visit, the first by an official international human rights agency to Argentina, the junta closed some secret detention centers, destroyed documents, moved prisoners, and threatened human rights organizations. Nonetheless, during two weeks in September 1979, the commission's delegation met with government officials, including the junta members, church leaders, human rights organizations, political parties, lawyers' associations, unions, business and professional organizations, judges, and representatives of the media. It also visited several legal prisons. Before arriving, the commission had secured permission to announce in the press that it would receive denunciations of individual cases of human rights violations; 4,153 people availed themselves of this opportunity in four cities, filing 5,580 complaints.[107]

Anticipating a damaging assessment, the military government rushed to publish its own version of truth in *Evolution of Terrorist Delinquency in Argentina*, which it presented to the commission as justification for its actions. This report documented numerous left terrorist attacks and argued that terrorists introduced the "ideology of death" that had come to dominate "education, culture, the workers, the economy and justice" prior to the Proceso. Cleansing the country of subversion, therefore, had become absolutely necessary.[108] But the regime's report rang hollow to the commission and to most Argentines.

Released in April 1980, the commission's 266-page report listed names and described in detail individual cases of torture, murder, and disappearance. Without giving its own estimate of the number of disappearances, the report concluded that of the various lists that had been produced, one containing 5,818 names collected by human rights organizations was the most accurate. The commission's reputation for impartiality and thoroughness and its conservative methodology for establishing facts made its findings authoritative. And, for the first time, it described the human rights violations as what they were: deliberate policy set by the junta, not just actions against the guerrillas, excesses, or mistakes. Banned in Argentina, the report was smuggled in and widely circulated, providing a growing number of Argentines with the confirmation of their worst fears: the government had intentionally killed their children, spouses, and friends.[109]

The impact of the Inter-American Commission on Human Rights report illustrates the newly acquired ability of the international human rights lobby, energized by the Chilean coup, to affect a state terrorist regime. Two other developments outside Argentina also contributed to the weakening of the military government. After successfully resisting for four years, the junta suffered a blow when the UN Human Rights Commission established a Working Group on Enforced or Involuntary Disappearances in February 1980. This was clearly a response to conditions in Argentina as well as Chile. And later in the year, Adolfo Pérez Esquivel, founder of the human rights organization SERPAJ, received the Nobel Peace Prize. Together with the Inter-American Commission on Human Rights report, these developments placed Argentina under a spotlight. The international condemnation that the junta had dodged for so long began to take a toll. The Proceso's raison d'être, liberating the country from terrorism, had been unmasked as a fiction. Against this backdrop, human rights groups pressed their case more vigorously, the level of repression fell, disappearances virtually ceased, and fear began to recede. These developments opened the way for the rise of an overt opposition movement for the first time since the military seized power.[110]

While international human rights advocacy clearly impacted the Argentine dictatorship, so did the experience of state terrorism in Argentina influence the development of international human rights. This influence built upon the dramatic impact of the Chilean coup and the lesser but important role of the Brazilian and Uruguayan state terrorist governments in pushing international human rights advocacy forward. Several of the innovations in international advocacy occurred in the United States, to the point that by 1977, in the opinion of one observer, the interest groups pressing for improvements in the Latin American human rights situation had become "one of the largest, most active, and most visible foreign policy lobbying forces in Washington."[111] That assessment did not factor in the influence of a dynamic new organization, Human Rights Watch, founded in 1978—the same year in which the journal *Human Rights Quarterly* was established, reflecting the growing centrality of the theme to activists, policy makers, journalists, and academics. In 1981, after state terrorism had spread to El Salvador and Guatemala, Human Rights Watch established its first regional affiliate, Americas Watch. And there is no mistaking the stamp of Chile and Argentina in a series of international declarations and conventions on torture and disappearance whose gestation dates from the 1970s: the 1984 UN Convention against Torture and Other Cruel, Inhuman, or Degrading Treatment or Punishment; the 1985 Inter-American Convention to Prevent and Punish Torture; the 1992 UN Declaration on the Protection of All Persons from Enforced Disappearance; and the 1994 Inter-American Convention on Forced Disappearances of Persons.[112]

The Collapse of Military Rule, 1980–1983

By the terms of the Proceso, General Videla's presidential term was five years. In March 1981, General Roberto Viola replaced him. With Ronald Reagan in the White House, Argentina no longer faced U.S. pressure on the human rights front. But Viola's accession to the presidency coincided with the onset of a severe economic crisis caused by global conditions and, in large part, by the military's corruption and mismanagement. The crisis involved mushrooming international debt, growing trade deficits, capital flight, hyperinflation, a severe contraction of real wages, and the near collapse of the banking system. The gross domestic product fell precipitously. In response to the Inter-American Commission on Human Rights report and the economic crisis, events that would have been unthinkable during the previous five years unfolded rapidly. The business elites' associations openly criticized the government, the banned national labor federation called a general strike, and the political parties jointly issued a call for a return to civilian government. Protest marches drew thousands, and while many were repressed, the degree of force employed was moderated. Faced with these developments, which sparked intense personal and interbranch contention within the military, the government lost stability and coherence. When Viola began a dialogue with the nascent opposition, discussing a possible transition to civilian government, the hard-liners quickly replaced him with one of their own, General Leopoldo Galtieri, in December 1981.[113]

Desperate to rally support for the faltering regime, Galtieri decided to invade the Falkland (Malvinas) Islands, some nine hundred miles southeast of Buenos Aires. Claimed by Argentina but occupied by Britain since 1833, the islands had long been a bone of contention between the two countries and a proven generator of nationalistic fervor. The invasion, launched on April 2, 1982, was a disaster for Argentina and the third junta. The Argentine military sent poorly trained and equipped conscripts to the theater while most of the ranking officers remained at their desks. The fundamental miscalculation was that Britain would not contest the remote islands occupied by some 1,800 people and 600,000 sheep. However, living up to her "iron lady" sobriquet, Prime Minister Margaret Thatcher immediately dispatched troops, ships, and planes to the South Atlantic. The tide quickly turned in Britain's favor, and after having some 10,000 men captured and around 650 killed, Argentina's remaining troops on the islands surrendered on June 14.[114]

Galtieri's gambit utterly failed as the patriotic fervor that initially rallied support for the regime gave way to massive demonstrations blaming the military for a national disaster. Galtieri was replaced in July 1982 by retired General Reynaldo Bignone, whose charge was to execute an exit strategy. This fourth and final junta called for elections and prepared to return the military to the barracks.

Before exiting, the armed forces took precautions to protect themselves against both truth and justice. They bulldozed or dismantled the remaining secret detention centers and destroyed records and other evidence of their crimes. On April 28, 1983, the junta issued a "Final Document" that was read on television while images of leftist terrorist actions played in the background. The Final Document repeated the assertions on which the dirty war had been based: that there had been a real war, legally authorized by acting president Italo Luder against fifteen thousand combatants "technically trained and ideologically fanaticized to kill." The military had sacrificed itself to save the nation. Talk of disappeared persons was "a lie used for political ends, since there are no secret places of detention in the country." As for the persons alleged to be missing, the Final Document claimed that some were in exile and others were living secretly in Argentina. Those killed in confrontations with the military carried false documents, and since their identities could not be established, they were buried as N/N. The different terrorist groups killed each other and buried or destroyed the bodies.

The Final Document went on to declare that all actions of the armed forces in the war were "acts of service." Only the judgment of history, not the courts, could determine responsibilities for any accidents committed during the war. Equating military self-interest with the national will, the Final Document stated, "It is the desire of the entire nation to put an end to a painful period of our history." Thousands of people demonstrated against the Final Document, and the human rights movement rejected the military's feeble attempt to justify state terrorism.[115]

As the election approached, the human rights organizations and Raúl Alfonsín, the presidential nominee of the Unión Cívica Radical (Radical Civic Union, UCR)—the moderate party that was the Peronists' principal rival—demanded that the courts, rather than history, judge the human rights violations committed under military rule. Worried about this prospect, the government issued an amnesty for crimes committed during the Proceso; attempting to appear evenhanded, decree law 22, 924/83, applied the amnesty to guerrillas as well as to the military and police. Learning of the military's decision to amnesty itself, antiregime and human rights groups carried out a massive twenty-four-hour "march of resistance" at the Plaza de Mayo. The decree was issued two days later, on September 22.[116]

Raúl Alfonsín was elected president on October 30, 1983, with 52 percent of the vote versus 40 percent for Peronist stalwart Italo Luder. During the campaign, Luder, the man who had issued the October 1975 decree giving the military carte blanche to annihilate subversion, had vacillated on the validity of the military's self-amnesty. Alfonsín was inaugurated on December 10. The Argentine military left office in complete disgrace after losing its bid for the Malvinas and amid unfolding discoveries of mass graves of its victims around the country. In contrast to Chile's transition, controlled all the way by Pinochet, in Argentina the military left via the back door, assuming that the amnesty and the memory of terror would assure its impunity. Despite the circumstances of its departure, however, the military still had the weapons and the ability to use them.[117]

Notes

1. General Luciano Menéndez, quoted in William C. Smith, *Authoritarianism and the Crisis of the Argentine Political Economy* (Stanford, CA: Stanford University Press, 1989), 232.

2. Comisión Nacional sobre la Desaparición de Personas (CONADEP), *Nunca más: Informe de la Comisión Nacional sobre la Desaparición de Personas*, 5th ed. (Buenos Aires: Editorial Universitaria de Buenos Aires, 1999), 7.

3. General histories of Argentina in English include David Rock, *Argentina 1516–1987: From Spanish Colony to Alfonsín* (Berkeley: University of California Press, 1987); Daniel K. Lewis, *The History of Argentina* (Westport, CT: Greenwood Press, 2001); and Jonathan C. Brown, *A Brief History of Argentina* (New York: Facts on File, 2003). On the twentieth century, see Luis Alberto Romero, *A History of Argentina in the Twentieth Century*, trans. James P. Brennan (University Park: Pennsylvania State University Press, 2002).

4. On Argentina between 1930 and 1976, see Romero, *A History of Argentina*, 59–214; Gino Germani, *Política y sociedad en una época de transición: de la sociedad*

tradicional a la sociedad de masas (Buenos Aires: Paidós, 1971); and Alain Rouquié, *Poder militar y sociedad política en la Argentina*, trans. Arturo Iglesias Echegaray, 2 vols. (Buenos Aires: Emecé Editores, 1981–82), 1:181–337, 2:9–421. Scott Mainwaring, "Authoritarianism and Democracy in Argentina," *Journal of Interamerican Studies and World Affairs* 26, no. 3 (August 1984): 415–31 (quote 415), describes Argentine political culture as "golpista." Argentina was among the top countries of the world in terms of per capita income in 1928; in 1991, it ranked near the hundredth: Emilio F. Mignone, *Derechos humanos y sociedad: el caso argentino* (Buenos Aires: Centro de Estudios Legales y Sociales [CELS], 1991), 26.

5. On Perón and his rise to power and first government, see Robert J. Alexander, *Juan Domingo Perón* (Boulder, CO: Westview Press, 1979); Daniel James, *Resistance and Integration: Peronism and the Argentine Working Class, 1946–1976* (Cambridge: Cambridge University Press, 1988); Félix Luna, *Perón y su tiempo* (Buenos Aires: Sudamericana, 1986); Nicholas Fraser and Marysa Navarro, *Evita*, rev. ed. (New York: W. W. Norton, 1996). Perón quadrupled the number of unionized workers between 1946 and 1951, to over 2.3 million. James, *Resistance and Integration*, 9.

6. On the Peronist legacies, see Félix Luna, *Argentina de Perón a Lanusse, 1943–1973* (Barcelona: Planeta, 1972); James, *Resistance and Integration*.

7. Marcelo Cavarozzi, *Autoritarismo y democracia* (Buenos Aires: Ariel, 1997); Rouquié, *Poder militar*, 2: 112–251; Romero, *A History of Argentina*, 131–72; Rock, *Argentina*, 320–66; Juan Corradi, *The Fitful Republic* (Boulder, CO: Westview Press, 1985).

8. Martin Edwin Andersen, *Dossier Secreto: Argentina's Desaparecidos and the Myth of the "Dirty War"* (Boulder, CO: Westview Press, 1993), 52.

9. Guillermo O'Donnell, *Bureaucratic Authoritarianism: Argentina, 1966–1973, in Comparative Perspective*, trans. James McGuire and Rae Flory (Berkeley: University of California Press, 1988); Gregorio Selser, *El onganiato*, 2 vols. (Buenos Aires: C. Samonta, 1972–1973).

10. Claudia Hilb and Daniel Lutzky, eds., *La nueva izquierda argentina: 1960–1980* (Buenos Aires: Centro Editor de América Latina, 1984); James Brennan, *El Cordobazo* (Buenos Aires: Sudamericana, 1996); Gustavo Pontoriero, *Sacerdotes para el Tercer Mundo: "El fermento en la masa" (1967–1976)* (Buenos Aires: Centro Editor de América Latina, 1991); Paul H. Lewis, *Guerrillas and Generals: The Dirty War in Argentina* (Westport, CT: Praeger, 2002), 19–81.

11. On the guerrillas, see James Kohl and John Litt, eds., *Urban Guerrilla Warfare in Latin America* (Cambridge, MA: MIT Press, 1974); Richard Gillespie, *Soldiers of Perón* (Oxford: Oxford University Press, 1982); María José Moyano, *Argentina's Lost Patrol: Armed Struggle, 1969–1979* (New Haven, CT: Yale University Press, 1995); María Seoane, *Todo o nada* (Buenos Aires: Planeta, 1991); Lewis, *Guerrillas and Generals*, 1–197.

12. Alfredo Pucciarelli, ed., *La primacía de la política: Lanusse, Perón, y la nueva izquierda en tiempos del GAN* (Buenos Aires: Editorial Universitaria de Buenos Aires, 1999); Lewis, *Guerrillas and Generals*, 71–73.

13. Liliana De Riz, *Retorno y derrumbe: el último gobierno peronista* (Mexico City: Folios Ediciones, 1981); Andersen, *Dossier Secreto*, 68–96; Gillespie, *Soldiers*, 89–122.

14. Ignacio González Janzen, *La Triple-A* (Buenos Aires: Editorial Contrapunto, 1986).

15. Andersen, *Dossier Secreto*, 103–23; González Janzen, *La Triple-A*.

16. Andersen, *Dossier Secreto*, 124–41; Lewis, *Guerrillas and Generals*, 105–13.

17. Donald C. Hodges, *Argentina's "Dirty War": An Intellectual Biography* (Austin: University of Texas Press, 1991), 125; Andersen, *Dossier Secreto*, 135.

18. Romero, *A History of Argentina*, 213.

19. *Argentina: juicios a los militares. Documentos secretos, decretos-leyes, jurisprudencia. Cuadernos de la Asociación Americana de Juristas*, no. 4 (1988), 15.

20. *Buenos Aires Herald*, March 25, 1976, quoted in Patricia Marchak, *God's Assassins: State Terrorism in Argentina in the 1970s* (Montreal: McGill-Queen's University Press, 1999), 212; Andersen, *Dossier Secreto*, 142–72; Lewis, *Guerrillas and Generals*, 115–29.

21. Brian Loveman and Thomas M. Davies, eds., *The Politics of Antipolitics: The Military in Latin America*, rev. ed. (Wilmington, DE: Scholarly Resources, 1997), 160.

22. Peter Waldmann and Ernesto Garzón Valdéz, *El poder militar en la Argentina, 1976–1981* (Buenos Aires: Editorial Galerna, 1983); Enrique Vásquez, *La última: origen, apogeo y caída de la dictadura militar* (Buenos Aires: Editorial Universitaria de Buenos Aires, 1985).

23. Loveman and Davies, *The Politics of Antipolitics*, 162.

24. *Clarín*, October 24, 1975, in Mignone, *Derechos humanos y sociedad*, 65–66.

25. Juan Corradi, "Military Government and State Terrorism in Argentina," in *Politics of Antipolitics*, ed. Loveman and Davies, 230–31. For incisive analysis of the discourse of state terrorism in Argentina, see Marguerite Feitlowitz, *A Lexicon of Terror: Argentina and the Legacies of Torture* (New York: Oxford University Press, 1998).

26. CONADEP, *Nunca más*, 56.

27. Lewis, *Guerrillas and Generals*, 46.

28. Videla's statement appeared in *Clarín*, January 31, 1976. By late 1977, the government was putting out its view that the Montoneros were almost defeated: *La Opinión*, December 7, 1977; *La Nación*, December 21, 1977. The dictatorship maximized the numbers while human rights groups tend to minimize their estimates. The highest estimate I have seen is forty thousand armed fighters, a figure offered by the U.S. public relations firm Burson-Marsteller, employed by the junta, in a propaganda piece in the U.S. media. The low figure, two to three thousand, was offered by human rights groups. Another point of disagreement is between total membership in guerrilla organizations, which included support personnel, and actual trained fighters.

29. See Gillespie, *Soldiers*; Moyano, *Lost Patrol*; Seoane, *Todo o nada*; and Lewis, *Guerrillas and Generals*, 46–48.

30. Figures on military and police deaths are published by the military officers' organization, the Círculo Militar, in *In Memoriam* (Buenos Aires: Círculo Militar, 1998–1999), 2:369–81. The dictatorship acknowledged that leftist terrorist attacks

peaked in 1975 and that only one occurred after 1976: República Argentina, Poder Ejecutivo Nacional, *Evolution of Terrorist Delinquency in Argentina* (Buenos Aires: Poder Ejecutivo Nacional, 1980), 168–72.

31. Quoted in Jacobo Timerman, *Prisoner without a Name, Cell without a Number*, trans. Tony Talbot (New York: Vintage Books, 1988), 49.

32. Quoted in Andersen, *Dossier Secreto*, 44; Hodges, *Argentina's "Dirty War,"* 125–71; David Pion-Berlin, *The Ideology of State Terror: Economic Doctrine and Political Repression in Argentina and Peru* (Boulder, CO: Lynne Rienner, 1989), 98–104; Jordán Bruno Genta, *Guerra contrarevolucionaria: doctrina política* (Buenos Aires: Nuevo Orden, 1965).

33. Hodges, *Argentina's "Dirty War,"* 87–123; Hilb and Lutzky, *La nueva izquierda*; Pontoriero, *Sacerdotes para el Tercer Mundo*; Lewis, *Guerrillas and Generals*, 83–87. The poll is cited in Andersen, *Dossier Secreto*, 73.

34. A naval officer, asked about using the death penalty against guerrillas, said simply, "It is very slow." Ilda Micucci interview, Buenos Aires, December 9, 2002.

35. While Argentina received far fewer immigrants than the United States during the great wave of 1880 to 1914, immigration transformed the country more thoroughly than it did the United States because Argentina's pre-1880 population was much smaller. See Carl E. Solberg, *Immigration and Nationalism, Argentina and Chile, 1890–1914* (Austin: University of Texas Press, 1970); Sandra McGee Deutsch and Ronald H. Dalkart, eds., *The Argentine Right: Its History and Intellectual Origins, 1910 to the Present* (Wilmington, DE: Scholarly Resources, 1993); David Rock, *Authoritarian Argentina: The Nationalist Movement, Its History, and Its Impact* (Berkeley: University of California Press, 1993); Sandra McGee Deutsch, *Las Derechas: The Extreme Right in Argentina, Brazil, and Chile, 1890–1939* (Stanford, CA: Stanford University Press, 1999), 26–37, 78–106, 193–247.

36. Deutsch and Dalkart, eds., *The Argentine Right*; Rock, *Authoritarian Argentina*; Deutsch, *Las Derechas*, 26–37, 78–106, 193–247; Eduardo Luis Duhalde, *El estado terrorista argentino: quince años después, una mirada crítica* (Buenos Aires: Editorial Universitaria de Buenos Aires, 1998), 88–120.

37. The Argentine military's anti-Marxist ambitions clearly extended beyond Argentina's boundaries. In addition to participating in Operation Condor, the junta was a sponsor of the Contra war against the Sandinista government in Nicaragua prior to the Reagan administration's involvement. See Ariel C. Armomy, *Argentina, the United States, and the Anti-Communist Crusade in Central America, 1977–1984* (Athens: Ohio University Center for International Studies, 1997).

38. Timerman, *Prisoner without a Name*, 101; Hodges, *Argentina's "Dirty War,"* 124–71, offers an incisive discussion of the military's conception of World War III and the defense of Western civilization against communism.

39. The term was used by Jorge A. Sábato, cited in Mignone, *Derechos humanos y sociedad*, 38.

40. CONADEP, *Nunca más*, 282–92; Alvaro Abós, *Delitos ejemplares: historias de la corrupción argentina, 1810–1997* (Buenos Aires: Grupo Editorial Norma, 1999),

231–61; Diego Masera Cerutti interview, Mexico City, September 12, 2003; Andersen, *Dossier Secreto*, 55–56.

41. Mignone, *Derechos humanos y sociedad*, 68. One of imprisoned Jacobo Timerman's interrogators told him, "Only God gives and takes life. But God is busy elsewhere, and we're the ones who must undertake this task in Argentina." Timerman, *Prisoner without a Name*, 31.

42. *Clarín*, December 18, 1977, in Mignone, *Derechos humanos y sociedad*, 66; Feitlowitz, *A Lexicon of Terror*, 24. See María Seoane and Vicente Muleiro, *El dictador: la historia secreta y pública de Jorge Rafael Videla* (Buenos Aires: Sudamericana, 2000).

43. Eduardo Luis Duhalde, *El estado terrorista argentino* (Barcelona: Editorial Argos Vergara, 1983), 79.

44. The quotations, in order, are found in Feitlowitz, *A Lexicon of Terror*, 32; Judith Laikin Elkin, "Recoleta: Civilization and Barbarism in Argentina," *Michigan Quarterly Review* 27 (1988): 235; and Lewis, *Guerrillas and Generals*, 147. A naval officer confirmed this approach to Jacobo Timerman, saying that it would be necessary to "exterminate" all the subversives: "All . . . about twenty thousand people. And their relatives, too—they must be eradicated—and also those who remember their names." Timerman, *Prisoner without a Name*, 50. See also Marchak, *God's Assassins*.

45. Duhalde, *El estado terrorista argentino*, offers an excellent analysis of the methodology of state terrorism in Argentina. See also CONADEP, *Nunca más*, 293–390; and Andersen, *Dossier Secreto*, 175–204.

46. "Even before the military coup of March 1976, international human rights pressures had influenced the Argentine military's decision to cause political opponents to 'disappear,' rather than imprisoning them or executing them publicly." Margaret E. Keck and Kathryn Sikkink, *Activists beyond Borders: Advocacy Networks in International Politics* (Ithaca, NY: Cornell University Press, 1998), 103–4. The intent to avoid Pinochet's fate was explicit. One officer reportedly said, "We are not going to use the firing squad like Franco (Spain's dictator, 1939–75) and Pinochet, because then everyone up to the Pope will ask us not to do it." Mignone, *Derechos humanos y sociedad*, 60.

47. The quotations, in order, are from Inter-American Commission on Human Rights, *Report on the Situation of Human Rights in Argentina* (Washington, DC: Inter-American Commission on Human Rights, 1980), 53; CONADEP, *Nunca más*, 246; and Mercedes Colas de Meroño interview, Buenos Aires, December 5, 2002. The estimate of the number of bodies recovered is from Inés Izaguirre, "Secuestros y desaparición: las tácticas de la guerra de clases del capital financiero," in *La desaparición forzada como crimen de lesa humanidad: el "nunca más" y la comunidad internacional*, by Coloquio de Buenos Aires (Buenos Aires: Coloquio de Buenos Aires, 1989), 111.

48. It is also suggested that disappearances were inspired by Hitler's order to disappear potential resisters in the occupied territories into the "night and fog." The strong Nazi sympathy within the Argentine military makes this credible. See Hodges, *Argentina's "Dirty War,"* 187–91; and Frank Graziano, *Divine Violence: Spectacle, Psychosexuality, and Radical Christianity in the Argentine "Dirty War"* (Boulder, CO: Westview Press, 1992).

49. Centro de Estudios Legales y Sociales (CELS), *Terrorismo de estado: 692 responsables* (Buenos Aires: CELS, 1986), 263–339; Comisión Argentina de Derechos Humanos, *Ex-ayudante del General Harguindeguy acusa: testimonio del inspector de la Policía Federal Argentina (R. O.) Rodolfo Peregrino Fernández* (Buenos Aires: Comisión Argentina de Derechos Humanos, 1983) (pamphlet), 41, says the method of sealing the blood pact started with General Luciano Menéndez, commander of the Third Army Corps headquartered in Córdoba Province, who made "each and every one" of his ranking officers execute prisoners. Pion-Berlin, *Ideology of State Terror*, 102–4. Miguel Bonasso, *Recuerdo de la muerte* (Mexico City: Ediciones Era, 1984) is a fictional but realistic portrayal of a disappearance.

50. CONADEP, *Nunca más*, 16–26; Sergio Verbitsky, *Rodolfo Walsh y la prensa clandestina, 1976–1978* (Buenos Aires: Ediciones de la Urraca, 1985), 56.

51. Inter-American Commission on Human Rights, *Report on the Situation of Human Rights in Argentina*, 98. The taking of war booty was blatant. In one reported case, an army truck with uniformed soldiers arrived at an abduction site half an hour after the event to haul off the loot. Inter-American Commission on Human Rights, *Report on the Situation of Human Rights in Argentina*, 58.

52. General Videla, for example, said in December 1977, "I flatly deny that concentration camps exist in Argentina." CONADEP, *Nunca más*, 55.

53. Feitlowitz, *A Lexicon of Terror*, 166; Amnesty International, "Testimonio sobre campos secretos de detención en Argentina," n.d., mimeo in Centro de Estudios Legales y Sociales (CELS), Centro de Documentación, 21. CONADEP, *Nunca más*, 54–223, has detailed descriptions of dozens of secret detention camps. CONADEP reported in 1984 that its investigations had uncovered approximately 340 secret detention centers. Twenty years later, the number had risen to approximately 380: Raúl Alfonsín, *Memoria política: transición a la democracia y derechos humanos* (Buenos Aires: Fondo de Cultura Económica, 2004), 39. See also Norberto Pedro Urso, *Mansión Seré: un vuelo hacia el horror* (Buenos Aires: Ediciones de la Memoria, 2002); and Carlos Gabetta, *Todos somos subversivos* (Buenos Aires: Bruguera, 1983).

54. CONADEP, *Nunca más*, 55.

55. Centro de Estudios Sociales y Legales (CELS), *Testimonio sobre el centro clandestino de detención de la Escuela de Mecánica de la Armada Argentina (ESMA)* (Buenos Aires: CELS, 1984) is the testimony of an ESMA survivor who spent four and a half years there; as part of the inmate staff, he had much opportunity to observe, and he identifies naval personnel who worked in ESMA as well as dozens who disappeared there. See also Ana María Martí et al., *ESMA "trasladados": testimonio de tres liberadas, octubre de 1979* (Buenos Aires: Abuelas de Plaza de Mayo, Familiares de Desaparecidos y Detenidos por Razones Políticas, and Madres de Plaza de Mayo, Línea Fundadora, 1995); Claudio Eduardo Martyniuk, *ESMA: fenomenología de la desaparición* (Buenos Aires: Prometeo Libros, 2004); CONADEP, *Nunca más*, 126–44 (quotation from Massera, 128); Asociación Madres de Plaza de Mayo, *Massera: el genocida* (Buenos Aires: Editorial La Página, 1999).

56. Quoted in Feitlowitz, *A Lexicon of Terror*, 57–58.

57. Amnesty International, "Testimonio sobre campos secretos," 20–21. See also Centro de Estudios Legales y Sociales (CELS), *Patti: manual del buen torturador* (Buenos Aires: CELS, 1999); CONADEP, *Nunca más*, 26–54; Timerman, *Prisoner without a Name*, 6–7. Note that torture was not new to the dirty war; it had been practiced selectively since at least 1930, but never institutionalized as in the secret detention centers: Ricardo Rodríguez Molas, *Historia de la tortura y el orden represivo en la Argentina*, 2 vols. (Buenos Aires: Editorial Universitaria de Buenos Aires, 1984–1985). Feitlowitz, *A Lexicon of Terror*, 53–60, has a glossary of the dirty war terminology.

58. CELS, *Testimonio sobre ESMA*, 21; Feitlowitz, *A Lexicon of Terror*, 58; Iain Guest, *Behind the Disappearances: Argentina's Dirty War against Human Rights and the United Nations* (Philadelphia: University of Pennsylvania Press, 1990), 40–41.

59. CONADEP, *Nunca más*, 26–54; Amnesty International, "Testimonio sobre campos secretos," 20–25; Andersen, *Dossier Secreto*, 205–13.

60. Amnesty International, "Testimonio sobre campos secretos," 21: Martyniuk, *ESMA*; CONADEP, *Nunca más*, 59–69.

61. CELS, *Testimonio sobre ESMA*; CONADEP, *Nunca más*, 59–69.

62. Abuelas de Plaza de Mayo, *Niños desaparecidos en Argentina desde 1976* (Buenos Aires: Madres de Plaza de Mayo, 1990); Julio Nosiglia, *Botín de guerra* (Buenos Aires: Abuelas de Plaza de Mayo, 1985); CONADEP, *Nunca más*, 299–313; Amnesty International, "Testimonio sobre campos secretos," 34–35. The acclaimed 1985 film *La historia oficial* [The Official Story], directed by Luis Puenzo, deals with the consequences of baby kidnapping.

63. This and the following paragraph are based on Timerman, *Prisoner without a Name*, which offers keen insights into the dilemmas of Argentine Jews during the dirty war. See also Marisa Braylan, *Report on the Situation of the Jewish Detainees-Disappeared during the Genocide Perpetrated in Argentina* (Buenos Aires: Social Research Center of DAIA-Argentinean Jewish Community Centers Association, 2000); CONADEP, *Nunca más*, 69–75; Feitlowitz, *A Lexicon of Terror*, 89–109.

64. Amnesty International, "Testimonio sobre campos secretos," 25–32. One prisoner who was eventually freed wrote, "I never discovered why the military spared my life." Alicia Partnoy, *The Little School: Tales of Disappearance and Survival in Argentina*, trans. Alicia Partnoy with Lois Athey and Sandra Braunstein (Pittsburgh: Cleis Press, 1986), 15.

65. Amnesty International, "Testimonio sobre campos secretos," 25.

66. Amnesty International, "Testimonio sobre campos secretos," 25–32; CONADEP, *Nunca más*, 68–69.

67. CONADEP, *Nunca más*, 223–47; Horacio Verbitsky, *The Flight: Confessions of an Argentine Dirty Warrior*, trans. Esther Allen (New York: New Press, 1996) deals with death flights from ESMA. It was more of a challenge to kill victims held in legal prisons with a paper trail. The terms "shot trying to escape" and "killed in confrontations" were often used to explain the killings of these nondisappeared "subversives."

68. CONADEP, *Nunca más*, 293–390; Feitlowitz, *A Lexicon of Terror*, 178–79.

69. CONADEP, *Nunca más*, 298.

70. Timerman, *Prisoner without a Name*, 50.

71. Feitlowitz, *A Lexicon of Terror*, 136, 149–50.

72. Mercedes Colas de Meroño interview, Buenos Aires, December 5, 2002. See Juan E. Corradi, Patricia Weiss Fagen, and Manuel Antonio Garretón, eds., *Fear at the Edge: State Terror and Resistance in Latin America* (Berkeley: University of California Press, 1992), esp. 1–89.

73. Inter-American Commission on Human Rights, *Report on the Situation of Human Rights in Argentina*, 71.

74. CONADEP, *Nunca más*, 248; Andersen, *Dossier Secreto*, 214–19.

75. Feitlowitz, *A Lexicon of Terror*, 107.

76. Ilda Micucci interview, Buenos Aires, December 9, 2002; CONADEP, *Nunca más*, 9–10.

77. Amnesty International, *"Disappearances," a Workbook* (New York: Amnesty International, 1982), 117.

78. Andersen, *Dossier Secreto*, 218; Marta Vásquez interview, Buenos Aires, December 10, 2002; Inter-American Commission on Human Rights, *Report on the Situation of Human Rights in Argentina*, 117–18.

79. Enrique Groisman, *La Corte Suprema de Justicia durante la dictadura (1976–1983)* (Buenos Aires: CISEA, 1989); Eduardo S. Barcesat, "Defensa legal de los derechos a la vida y la libertad personal en el régimen militar argentino," in *Represión política y defensa de los derechos humanos*, ed. Hugo Frühling E. (Santiago: Centro de Estudios Sociales [CESOC], 1985), 141–62; CONADEP, *Nunca más*, 250, 391–441. Lawyers' professional associations estimated that 23 of their members were murdered and 109 disappeared, while many more were imprisoned and exiled.

80. Andrew Graham-Yool, *The Press in Argentina, 1973–1978* (London: Writers and Scholars Educational Trust, 1979); CONADEP, *Nunca más*, 296, 367–74; *La Nación*, December 18, 1977. *La Opinión*, the newspaper founded and run by Jacobo Timerman, and the English-language *Buenos Aires Herald* dissented from the official line insofar as possible; Timerman paid with imprisonment and banishment.

81. Alvaro Abós, *Las organizaciones sindicales y el poder militar (1976–1983)* (Buenos Aires: Centro Editor de América Latina, 1984).

82. Abós, *Las organizaciones sindicales*; CONADEP, *Nunca más*, 296, 375–90; Andersen, *Dossier Secreto*, 175–83.

83. Emilio Mignone, *Witness to the Truth: The Complicity of Church and Dictatorship in Argentina, 1976–1983*, trans. Phillip Berryman (Maryknoll, NY: Orbis Books, 1988), 6; CONADEP, *Nunca más*, 259–63.

84. Mignone, *Witness to the Truth*, 71.

85. Marta Vásquez interview, Buenos Aires, December 10, 2002.

86. Mignone, *Witness to the Truth*, 71–96; Deutsch, *Las Derechas*, 102–5, 240–44; Patrick Rice interview, Buenos Aires, December 9, 2002.

87. Andersen, *Dossier Secreto*, 54–55, 184–93; CONADEP, *Nunca más*, 347–60; Mignone, *Witness to the Truth*, 128–50.

88. CONADEP, *Nunca más*, 260; Mignone, *Witness to the Truth*, 110–18.

89. Verbitsky, *The Flight*, 30.

90. Mignone, *Witness to the Truth*, 8.

91. Mignone, *Witness to the Truth*, 36. Cardinal Aramburu earlier had denied the human rights group Madres de Plaza de Mayo the use of the cathedral for a meeting place. Marguerite Guzmán Bouvard, *Revolutionizing Motherhood: The Mothers of the Plaza de Mayo* (Wilmington, DE: Scholarly Resources, 1994), 72.

92. Alison Brysk, *The Politics of Human Rights in Argentina: Protest, Change, and Democratization* (Stanford, CA: Stanford University Press, 1994), 51–56; Aldo César Vacs, *Discreet Partners: Argentina and the USSR since 1917* (Pittsburgh: University of Pittsburgh Press, 1984), 24–126.

93. Brysk, *Politics of Human Rights*, 51–58; Guest, *Behind the Disappearances*, 64; Amnesty International, *Report on the Mission to Argentina, November 6–15, 1976* (London: Amnesty Publications, 1977); Amnesty International, *The "Disappeared" of Argentina: List of Cases Reported to Amnesty International, March 1976–February 1979* (London: Amnesty International, 1979); Carlos Slepoy interview, Madrid, November 13, 2001.

94. Raúl Veiga, *Las organizaciones de derechos humanos* (Buenos Aires: Centro Editor de América Latina, 1985); Brysk, *Politics of Human Rights*, 45–51; Graciela Fernández Meijide, "Historia de las organizaciones de derechos humanos en la Argentina y su rol en la democracia," in *Represión política*, ed. Frühling, 59–77; María Sondereguer, "El trabajo de las organizaciones de derechos humanos con sectores populares: areas de actividad y perspectivas hacia el futuro," in *Represión política*, ed. Frühling, 79–95.

95. Veiga, *Las organizaciones*; Brysk, *Politics of Human Rights*, 49–51.

96. Ilda Micucci interview, Buenos Aires, December 9, 2002. See Bouvard, *Revolutionizing Motherhood*; Jo Fisher, *Mothers of the Disappeared* (Boston: South End Press, 1989); John Simpson and Jana Bennett, *The Disappeared and the Mothers of the Plaza* (New York: St. Martin's Press, 1985); Matilde Mellibovsky, *Circle of Love over Death: Testimonies of the Mothers of the Plaza de Mayo*, trans. Maria Proser and Matthew Proser (Willimantic, CT: Curbstone Press, 1997); Marjorie Agosín, *Circles of Madness: Mothers of the Plaza de Mayo=Círculos de locura: Madres de la Plaza de Mayo* (Fredonia, NY: White Pine Press, 1992) is a book of poems and photographs.

97. Inter-American Commission on Human Rights, *Report on the Situation of Human Rights in Argentina*, 117.

98. Bouvard, *Revolutionizing Motherhood*; Fisher, *Mothers of the Disappeared*; Mellibovsky, *Circle of Love*.

99. Rita Arditti, *Searching for Life: The Grandmothers of the Plaza de Mayo and the Disappeared Children of Argentina* (Berkeley: University of California Press, 1999).

100. CELS, "Brochure," n.d., has a brief history of the organization; Inter-American Commission on Human Rights, *Report on the Situation of Human Rights in Argentina*, 257–62; Brysk, *Politics of Human Rights*, 52–53.

101. Guest, *Behind the Disappearances*, 89–332; Vacs, *Discreet Partners*, 74–82; Feitlowitz, *A Lexicon of Terror*, 41–46; Joseph S. Tulchin, *Argentina and the United States: A Conflicted Relationship* (Boston: Twayne, 1990), 146–49. Tulchin wrote that, "by 1979, the refutation and rejection of the international 'campaign' against Argentina had become an obsessive issue in foreign policy," in "The Impact of U.S. Human Rights Policy: Argentina," in *Latin America, the United States, and the Inter-American System*, ed. John D. Martz and Lars Schoultz (Boulder, CO: Westview Press, 1980), 228.

102. The opening of the Mexican Olympiad was preceded by what is called the "Tlatelolco massacre," a savage repression of protesting students that killed several hundred. Scenes of the massacre were broadcast around the world. See Elaine Carey, *Plaza of Sacrifices: Gender, Power, and Terror in 1968 Mexico* (Albuquerque: University of New Mexico Press, 2005).

103. Pablo Alabarces, *Fútbol y patria: el fútbol y las narrativas de la nación en la Argentina* (Buenos Aires: Prometeo, 2002), 119–36; Feitlowitz, *A Lexicon of Terror*, 35–37; Duhalde, *Estado terrorista argentino: quince años después*, 115–17.

104. *Página 12*, December 30, 1990.

105. Elisa de Landín, quoted in Fisher, *Mothers of the Disappeared*, 73.

106. Guest, *Behind the Disappearances*, 151–243; Andersen, *Dossier Secreto*, 250–69; Cynthia Brown, ed., *With Friends Like These: The Americas Watch Report on Human Rights and U.S. Policy in Latin America* (New York: Pantheon, 1985), 99–100. Guest writes, "Argentina came to symbolize Carter's confrontational approach to human rights" (xiv). Many Argentines expressed their gratitude to Carter, including Emilio Mignone, *Derechos humanos y sociedad*, 58.

107. Inter-American Commission on Human Rights, *Report on the Situation of Human Rights in Argentina*; Guest, *Behind the Disappearances*, 164–79; CELS, *Testimonio sobre ESMA*, 4–5.

108. República Argentina, Poder Ejecutivo Nacional, *Evolution of Terrorist Delinquency in Argentina* (Buenos Aires: Poder Ejecutivo Nacional, 1980), 3.

109. Inter-American Commission on Human Rights, *Report on the Situation of Human Rights in Argentina*; Guest, *Behind the Disappearances*, 176–79.

110. The commission reported that it had received no new denunciations of disappearances between its September 1979 visit and the April 1980 publication of its report. Inter-American Commission on Human Rights, *Report on the Situation of Human Rights in Argentina*, 264. Guest, *Behind the Disappearances*, 190–201; Lewis, *Guerrillas and Generals*, 179–90. Tulchin, *Argentina and the United States*, 148, refutes the idea of Carter's and Derian's influence by arguing that the military stopped disappearances because there were few if any "subversives" left.

111. Schoultz, *Human Rights and U.S. Foreign Policy*, 75.

112. See the UN and OAS websites for human rights treaties.

113. Smith, *Authoritarianism and the Crisis of the Argentine Political Economy*, 239–61; Lewis, *Guerrillas and Generals*, 179–90.

114. Rubén Moro, *The History of the South Atlantic Conflict: The War of the Malvinas* (New York: Praeger, 1989); Horacio Verbitsky, *Malvinas: la última batalla de la Tercera Guerra Mundial*, rev. ed. (Buenos Aires: Editorial Sudamericana, 2002); Martin Middlebrook, *The Fight for the Malvinas: The Argentine Forces in the Falklands War* (New York: Viking, 1989).

115. Reprinted in *La Prensa*, April 29, 1983.

116. Romero, *A History of Argentina*, 247–54.

117. Laura Tedesco, *Democracy in Argentina: Hope and Disillusion* (London: Frank Cass, 1999), 51–58; Alfonsín, *Memoria política*, 37.

PART THREE

JUSTICE VERSUS IMPUNITY

CHAPTER FIVE

Argentina: The Sinuous Path of Transitional Justice

The disappearance of people was useful. Besides, it wasn't people who disappeared, but subversives.

—General Ramón Camps, commander,
Buenos Aires Provincial Police[1]

Disappearances, then, are a "continuing offense" and not only or strictly in legal terms. For as long as the uncertainty remains, they are an open wound in the fabric of society that is not healed by amnesty laws or clemency decrees and much less by lofty calls to "reconciliation" lamely uttered from time to time by political and religious leaders. Without public acknowledgment, reconciliation is an empty gesture, or worse, another name for impunity.

—Juan Méndez, general counsel, Human Rights Watch[2]

From 1964, when Brazil inaugurated a new form of repressive antileftist dictatorship designed to counter the revolutionary impulse unleashed by the Cuban Revolution, to 1996, when a peace accord ended state terrorism in Guatemala, Latin America experienced a prolonged and profound crisis of human rights. Beginning in 1978 with the end of General Hugo Banzer's seven-year Bolivian dictatorship, much of Latin America entered a transition from rule by repression—whether under military or civilian regimes—to governments democratically elected and constrained, however imperfectly, by law.[3] The transitions brought about the restoration of human rights, but

they also ushered in difficult periods of dealing with the human rights violations of the past and developing the means of protecting those rights in the
future so as to prevent a recurrence of the recent crisis. The postterror years
in Argentina and Chile fully illustrate the challenges and complexities of
transitional justice.

The Ascendancy of Truth and Justice, 1983–1985

Argentina began its transition with the presidential and congressional elections of October 30, 1983. As the first Latin American country to emerge
from a period of extreme state terrorism, Argentina faced the questions and
dilemmas of transition without a blueprint. In the words of President Raúl
Alfonsín, "We were aware that it was an unprecedented historical situation."[4] Moreover, the weakness of Argentina's democratic tradition and culture, evidenced by the predominance of dictatorial regimes from 1930
through 1983, constituted a monumental obstacle to the development of stable civilian government. However, the incoming government had an enormous advantage over most of the other Latin American countries involved
in similar transitions: Having abandoned the halls of government in disgrace,
the military would have to defend itself against the quest for truth and justice from a weakened position.[5]

During his presidential campaign, Alfonsín promised to restore human
rights in Argentina, calling for "a democracy with real power to defend the
rights of all." Within days of his December 10 inauguration, he launched
initiatives to investigate human rights violations under the dictatorship, to
achieve justice for victims and the families of those who did not survive,
and to protect human rights in the future by breaking what he called Argentina's "historic cycle of impunity."[6] He met with the human rights organizations; submitted a bill to rescind the military's amnesty decree, which
the new Congress passed as its first law; began freeing political prisoners;
and drafted legislation to increase the penalty for torture and to heavily pe-
nalize both military men and civilians for plotting the forceful overthrow
of a government. He also pushed for quick approval of international human
rights instruments that Argentina had not previously ratified, including the
UN's covenants on civil and political rights and on economic, social, and
cultural rights and the American Convention on Human Rights. The most
sensational of Alfonsín's initiatives were the establishment of a truth commission and his decision to prosecute the members of the first three juntas—six generals and three admirals—for crimes committed during their
tenure in office.[7]

While these measures were bold and even dangerous, Alfonsín's approach to transitional justice was designed to balance the quest for truth and justice with the military's sensitivity to what it perceived as persecution. Although thoroughly discredited, the military retained the ability to disrupt the delicate process of constructing democracy by overtly challenging governmental and judicial authority, by rebelling, and by threatening or even executing another coup. Initially the climate favored the demands of the human rights groups, but from the beginning, Alfonsín's policies were carefully calculated to avoid unnecessary provocations that could put the country's fledgling democracy in peril.[8]

Alfonsín and the human rights movement agreed that discovering truth was a necessary precondition to justice and reconciliation. To establish the facts about the primary method of state terrorism in Argentina and the toll it had taken, Alfonsín named a Comisión Nacional sobre la Desaparición de Personas (National Commission on the Disappearance of Persons, CONADEP). Despite his generally cautious approach to transitional justice, he did not compromise on the composition of CONADEP: its ten members were selected because of their "firm attitude toward the defense of human rights."[9] The human rights organizations had argued that Congress was the appropriate investigative body, as its powers of subpoena would be necessary to command testimony and retrieve relevant documents. In a compromise, Alfonsín invited each chamber of Congress to appoint three members to the commission, but the Senate, where his Radical Party was in the minority, refused to cooperate.

Alfonsín's approach to the truth commission reflected his commitment to balance. He created CONADEP without subpoena powers—the stated reason why Nobel Peace Laureate Adolfo Pérez Esquivel declined an appointment to the commission; instead, he ordered the military to cooperate with the investigations. He gave CONADEP just 180 days to finish its work. And while disappearance was clearly the most egregious of the human rights violations employed by the military, CONADEP was not charged with investigating the other widespread grave human rights violations committed between 1976 and 1983, including prolonged arbitrary detention, rape, torture, baby stealing, and extrajudicial execution not preceded by disappearance.[10]

CONADEP elected the distinguished writer Ernesto Sábato as its president, hired staff, and began its task before the end of 1983. Owing to the limitations on the commission's purview and powers, the Madres de Plaza de Mayo refused to collaborate with it. The remaining human rights organizations lent their support by supplying experts, witnesses, and documents; the files of the Centro de Estudios Legales y Sociales (Center for Legal and Social Studies, CELS) and the Asamblea Permanente de Derechos Humanos

(Permanent Assembly of Human Rights, APDH) were particularly useful to the search for truth. The human rights organizations also quickly flooded the courts with cases implicating hundreds of military and police in criminal activity.[11]

In addition to working in Buenos Aires, CONADEP opened offices and took testimony in cities throughout the country and urged exiles to testify in Argentine consulates in the countries where they resided. It interviewed some 1,500 survivors of the secret detention centers, inspected a number of locations where the centers had functioned, and visited mass burial sites. These activities elicited death threats against CONADEP's personnel and several bombings of its provincial offices. In July 1984, CONADEP presented a two-hour television program featuring interviews with detention camp survivors and relatives of disappeared persons that was broadcast over Alfonsín's reservations. The program resulted in the bombing of a government television station and menacing saber rattling by troops on bases near the capital, testing Alfonsín's balancing act and foreshadowing the military's future reactions to human rights investigations and trials.[12]

CONADEP worked quickly but thoroughly. Employing a rigorous methodology, it required incontrovertible proof of a person's disappearance at the hands of government agents for the individual to be included in its tally. After receiving a three-month extension of its mandate, the commission delivered its report to the president on September 20, 1984. In November, it published a summary of its findings under the dramatic title *Nunca más* (Never Again). The book began with an unmistakable allusion to the Holocaust: "Many of the episodes described here will be difficult to believe. That is because the men and women of our country have only known such horrors through chronicles from other latitudes." It also quoted President Alfonsín's indictment of national security doctrine: "Thousands of persons were illegally deprived of their liberty, tortured and killed as a result of the application of those methods of fighting inspired by the totalitarian Doctrine of National Security."[13] *Nunca más* became an instant best seller and was reprinted several times.

Nunca más described in detail the methods of abduction, the secret detention centers where victims were held, and the means of execution and disposal of bodies. CONADEP substantiated the existence of 340 secret detention centers and named 8,960 disappeared persons, a figure that exceeded the numbers documented by the human rights organizations. *Nunca más* reported that, in addition to the guerrillas disappeared by the military, "there are thousands of victims who were never linked with such activity but yet were subjected to horrific punishments because of their opposition to the military dictatorship, their participation in union or student struggles, for being recognized intellectuals who questioned state terrorism, or simply for being family members, friends, or for being included in the address book of someone considered subversive"—a description of victims that confirmed the rings-of-hell approach prescribed by generals Camps and Saint Jean.[14] CONADEP also cited the obstacles it had faced: the brevity of its investigations; the remoteness of some areas where repression had occurred; the reluctance of some victims' relatives, particularly those of lower socioeconomic status, to testify; and the military's failure to cooperate. It concluded that the number of disappeared was substantially greater than the 8,960 it had documented. Although the testimony it received reportedly contained the names of some 1,300 to 1,500 individuals directly involved in the disappearances, CONADEP did not make their names public, citing the limits of its charge and the jurisdiction of the courts to prosecute the repressors. The commission submitted the list of repressors to the president and sent over one thousand cases to the courts.[15]

Beyond describing disappearances and enumerating victims, *Nunca más* was a mechanism for contesting the military's official history of its nearly eight years in power. For those who rejected the military version of the truth but did not comprehend the big picture, *Nunca más* provided an alternate understanding. Through attention to detail and rigor in documentation, it provided concrete information that countered the military's secrecy and denial and its insistence that any deaths were the result of "excesses" in a just war on subversion. For the victims and their families, testifying before CONADEP and having the names and, in some cases, the stories of their loved ones' ordeals published in *Nunca más* was a first step in a long and difficult process of healing—a process still far from complete in many individuals today.[16]

Owing to its success in discovering and documenting the facts about disappearances and to the resulting moral authority that it acquired, CONADEP became a model for truth commissions around the world. The Argentine experience established the truth commission as an essential part of transitional justice in countries going from repressive regimes to democracies, wherever this occurred; the phrase "*nunca más*" would resonate in many languages as the rallying cry for societies struggling to heal rifts caused by grave human rights violations. In the thirty years following the establishment of CONADEP, over thirty countries instituted truth commissions. In Latin America alone, Uruguay, Chile, Ecuador, El Salvador, Guatemala, Honduras, Haiti, Panama, Peru, and Paraguay followed the Argentine approach. Argentina supplied personnel to advise and participate in some of these commissions. Beyond Latin

America, truth commissions were created to facilitate transitions in countries as disparate as Nigeria, East Timor, and Germany. The best known of these is the Truth and Reconciliation Commission established in South Africa following the end of the apartheid regime.[17]

Another element in the establishment of truth involved identifying the thousands of disappeared persons whose remains, in varying condition, were discovered beginning in 1982 in hundreds of mass graves and in cemetery plots with markers bearing the designation N/N (no name). Recovery of some remains, including those thrown into the ocean from the death flights, was impossible; many of the disappeared remained unaccounted for, as those who knew their disposal sites remained silent. The gruesome task of identifying the dead got a boost from eminent U.S. forensic scientist Dr. Clyde Snow, who arrived in June 1984 to conduct exhumations and instruct his Argentine counterparts in the most advanced methodology for identifying remains. Exhumations did more than identify the dead; in some cases, the scientists were able to determine that women had given birth before being killed. If an infant's remains were not found with those of the mother, the Abuelas de Plaza de Mayo added another child to their list of kidnapped babies. Each such discovery gave an aging woman the hope that she might have a living grandchild.[18]

While most families welcomed the opportunity to identify and bury their loved ones, the Madres de Plaza de Mayo as a group opposed exhumations. Some Madres preferred to hold on to the hope of finding their children alive, and the group's stance was to link the identification of remains to punishment of the killers. Thus they withheld permission to exhume remains that might be those of their children until they could be assured of proper investigations, trials, and sentences for the murderers. Given Alfonsín's intention to limit trials in order not to push the military into a violent reaction, the Madres assumed that the actual murderers of their children would remain free. On at least one occasion, the Madres physically blocked exhumations. Their intransigence distanced the Madres not only from the government but from other human rights groups and contributed to a split in their ranks in 1986.

Adding misery to the macabre process of recovering remains, unknown persons mailed a box of bones in November 1984 to a couple with a note indicating that the contents belonged to their disappeared daughter who had been executed for "treason" and collaboration with the Montonero guerrillas. A forensic scientist later found that the bones were those of a male.[19]

Dr. Snow helped form the Equipo Argentino de Antropología Forense (Argentine Forensic Anthropology Team), which conducted many of the exhumations in the 1980s and 1990s. Just as Argentina exported the truth commission, so it did the forensic team to countries around the world that had undergone large-scale murder and genocide. By 2004, the team had worked on recovering and identifying remains and on training local forensic scientists in thirty-one countries on five continents—a grim testimonial to the barbarity of the late twentieth century.[20]

Having ordered the trial of the juntas, the Alfonsín administration made it clear that it did not plan to try the military as an institution for human rights crimes. In addition to the nine leaders of the three juntas, the government preferred to limit trials to ranking officers in positions of command. Prosecuting the thousands of military and police personnel involved in the repression, Alfonsín later reflected, "would have placed the whole process of transition at serious risk."[21] He also believed that, in the interest of prudence, the entire judicial process should be as brief as possible. Pursuing his goal of balance, the president also ordered seven surviving Montonero and ERP leaders to stand trial. Some human rights groups condemned this approach as a nefarious "theory of the two devils" that blamed the guerrillas and the military equally for the horrific toll of state terrorism, thus implicitly trivializing the military's record of human rights violations.[22]

A crucial question in the pursuit of justice was which courts had the authority to try the junta members and their subordinates who were likely to be indicted. Traditionally, the military judged its own in all matters—a continuation of the colonial *fuero militar*—but neither the president nor the public had faith in that approach. To rectify this, Alfonsín introduced legislation reforming the Code of Military Justice to establish an automatic appeal of military courts' verdicts in civilian courts. By the law passed in February 1984, the military court, the Consejo Supremo, was given 180 days to complete each trial after receiving the documented criminal complaint. If it failed to meet this requirement or engaged in "negligence or unjustifiable delay," the case would automatically move to a federal appellate court. By retaining the Consejo Supremo's jurisdiction in the first instance, Alfonsín offered the military an opportunity to clean its own house, avoid public trials, and begin refurbishing its image.[23]

In order to minimize the military backlash against prosecution, Alfonsín sought to block the human rights movement's attempt to bring all known hands-on repressors of any rank to justice. He hoped to contain the number of trials by applying his concept of "due obedience" based on three degrees of responsibility: those who planned and oversaw the repression, those who committed "excesses" in carrying out the general orders, and those who simply obeyed their superiors' direct orders. Military men lacking decision-making authority would benefit from a presumption that they had perceived the orders they followed as legitimate. Thus, as part of his proposed reform of the Code of Military Justice, he asked Congress to exempt from prosecution everyone outside the highest levels of responsibility. In the Senate, however, an opposition lawmaker who had lost two children to disappearance added a crucial amendment. As enacted, law 23.049 failed to exempt from prosecution personnel implicated in "atrocious and aberrant acts"—which it defined as torture, rape, murder, and child stealing. The amendment thwarted Alfonsín's intentions of limiting trials, leaving hundreds of military personnel subject to prosecution.[24]

The Consejo Supremo pursued the trial of the three juntas in desultory fashion, failing to meet the 180-day deadline for completion. Then, in late September 1984, it announced that it could not judge the junta members because the orders they had issued in the "war against subversion" were "unobjectionable." Issued just days after CONADEP had submitted its report with its compelling evidence of massive, institutionalized human rights violations, this defiant military claim of impunity caused a major uproar in public opinion; it also revealed the dismal failure of Alfonsín's policy of allowing the military to deal with its crimes and reclaim its institutional legitimacy. In fact, after almost three years and over two thousand cases, the Consejo Supremo convicted no one and acquitted numbers of notorious repressors. Among these was Navy Lieutenant Alfredo Astiz, known as the "Blond Angel of Death," one of whose most nefarious deeds was infiltrating the Madres de Plaza de Mayo by posing as the brother of a *desaparecido* and then detaining twelve of the Madres and two French nuns working with them, all of whom were subsequently disappeared.[25]

In response to the military's intransigence, the Buenos Aires federal appellate court took over the case of the junta members. The trial began in April 1985. Journalists, academics, and human rights activists from around the world joined the Argentine audience in attending or watching on television what was billed "the trial of the century."[26] The generals and admirals were charged with over seven hundred separate cases of illegal detention, torture, and murder. The court heard seventy-eight days of testimony from over eight hundred witnesses for the defense and the prosecution.[27]

The defense produced prominent civilians and ranking military officers who testified to the high degree of threat posed by the guerrillas at the time of the coup and argued that Interim President Italo Luder's October 6, 1975, executive decree authorizing the armed forces to conduct the "operations that may be necessary" to annihilate subversives provided the legal basis for their actions. According to the defense, the military deserved gratitude for defeating the Marxists and making Argentina's new democracy possible. Defense attorneys portrayed any human rights violations as collateral damage of a real war on subversion, an unconventional, decentralized war lacking coordinated direction from the top, and consistently impugned prosecution witnesses' testimony by tying them to the guerrillas. Admiral Massera on the witness stand painted the proceedings as absurd: "I didn't come here to defend myself. No one has to defend himself for having won a just war, and the war against terrorism was a just war."[28]

The prosecution selected witnesses to the crimes, family members of the disappeared, and survivors of the secret detention camps to provide details of some of the most grisly and inhuman of the military's crimes. Among the detention center survivors who testified was Iris Etelvina Pereyra de Avellaneda, a thirty-seven-year-old woman abducted with her fourteen-year-old son in suburban Buenos Aires. She was forced to listen to her son's torture, which ended in a "terrifying silence." In one of the centers where she was subsequently held, she was forced to cry "viva Hitler" in order to use the bathroom. Only when she was released after twenty-seven months did she learn that her son's body, hands and feet tied and neck broken, had been found floating off the coast of Uruguay a month after the abduction. Another was Haydée García de Candeloro, a psychologist, who was abducted with her husband and five other labor lawyers in Mar del Plata in what was known as the "Night of the Neckties." She testified that treatment in the detention centers aimed to "undermine the prisoner, destroy his identity systematically." She heard her husband's death cry from an adjoining room. Pablo Díaz testified about one of the most notorious of Argentina's disappearances, the "Night of the Pencils," in which seven high school students in La Plata were abducted after protesting the elimination of reduced student fares on the city's buses. Díaz was the only survivor.[29]

Prosecutors argued that the evidence proved a criminal plan at the junta level and that the alleged state of war was a fabrication. Further, if a real war had existed, the Argentine military would be guilty of violating internationally recognized rules of war. Summing up, chief prosecutor Julio César Strassera argued, "Either there was no war, as I believe, and we have before us common criminals; or there was—and we have before us war criminals." He concluded the prosecution's case with the phrase "*nunca más.*"[30]

On December 9, 1985, the panel of judges ruled unanimously that the methods of repression used during the dictatorship—abduction, disappearance, torture in secret detention centers, and murder—had been selected in a conscious decision of Argentina's military leadership and carried out under its orders. They found that, having established the methodology of repression, the commanders gave their subordinates discretion to determine the final fate of the victims—to be released, delivered to the legal prison system, or killed. The court's finding of discretion in the conduct of the repression undermined Alfonsín's strategy of limiting trials to the upper military ranks.

The court sentenced two members of the first junta (March 1976–March 1981), the primary architects and managers of the dirty war, to life imprisonment—the maximum penalty, since Alfonsín's government had abolished the death penalty. General Videla was convicted of 66 charges of homicide, 306 of illegal detention aggravated by threats and violence, 13 of torture followed by murder, and 26 of robbery. Admiral Massera was sentenced on 3 charges of homicide, 60 of illegal detention aggravated by threats and violence, 12 of torture, and 7 of robbery. Reflecting the air force's subordinate role in the repression, the third member of the first junta, Brigadier Orlando Ramón Agosti, received a sentence of four and a half years on charges of torture and robbery. The army and navy commanders of the second junta (March–December 1981) received sentences of seventeen and eight years, respectively, while their air force colleague and all three commanders of the third junta (December 1981–June 1982) were acquitted. Those sentenced were to spend their time in a military prison under the control of their former subordinates—not a small concession to the commanders.[31]

Public reaction to the verdict was mixed. Massive street protests denounced the court's leniency, and human rights spokespersons reacted negatively. The Madres protested inside the courtroom; their president, Hebe de Bonafini, said, "The trial has defrauded the people and the sentence is tragic." Emilio Mignone, president of CELS, said the result "does not meet expectations. The sentences are extremely short." Other Argentines, however, saw the verdict as the defeat of the military impunity that had underpinned the reign of state terrorism. For some, the trial represented a sharp break not only with the recent dictatorship but with the previous half century of Argentine history, during which the military had been unaccountable for its actions. The trial was a purgative, a new beginning for the country. The people and institutions of Argentina had investigated, judged, and sentenced former rulers for grave human rights violations. The government and courts had navigated uncharted waters and embarked on the perilous course of bringing to justice men who were not militarily vanquished foreign enemies but fellow citizens who still enjoyed the loyalty of the armed forces that they had until recently commanded, and who still possessed the power to overthrow the country's institutions and reimpose military rule.[32]

While *Nunca más* and the trial of the juntas addressed crimes of the past, the government also looked to the future by implementing measures designed to prevent a repetition of the recent human rights crisis. Alfonsín established a subsecretariat of human rights in the Ministry of the Interior, staffed by over twenty people, whose functions were to investigate new denunciations of disappearances that had not been submitted to CONADEP; to process claims of continuing human rights abuses; to provide educational material, teacher training, and public information on human rights; and to maintain CONADEP's files, which were closed to the public. A new division was created in the Ministry of Foreign Relations to insert human rights criteria into foreign policy formulation—a testimonial to the influence of Jimmy Carter's foreign policy innovation. Two government entities were established to address other legacies of the Proceso: a coordinating commission on missing children and a committee to promote exiles' return—both phased out after a few years. While these institutions did not perform to the satisfaction of some human rights groups, they did establish the legitimacy of the state's role as active promoter, rather than simply presumed guardian, of human rights.[33]

Pushing his balancing act to the limit, Alfonsín also attempted in several ways to reshape the armed forces. Among several important measures, he retired some two-thirds of the army's generals and one-third of the navy's admirals; slashed the military budget by approximately 40 percent during his administration, reducing it from 3.5 percent to 1.9 percent of gross domestic product; cut the number of conscripts by over half; removed units of the powerful First Army Corps from their strategic location outside Buenos Aires; and strengthened civilian authority within the Ministry of Defense. The administration also attempted to change the military culture that had driven the dirty war by reforming the extensive system of military education. It sought to break down the isolation of military schools and modify the curricula that inculcated national security doctrine, antileftism, extreme nationalism, and the superiority of the military caste over other Argentine citizens. This was a difficult challenge, however, given the tenacious resistance to civilian influence in what for decades had been an autonomous military domain, and relatively little was accomplished in this area. After three years of debate, Congress in 1988 passed a law limiting the military's role to external defense, but this proved difficult to enforce.[34]

The formation in 1984 of the Centro de Militares para la Democracia Argentina (Center of Military Personnel for Argentine Democracy, CEMIDA), by a group of several hundred retired officers, was a hopeful sign of change, but CEMIDA's clashes with the army officers' club, the Círculo Militar (Military Circle), and the military's subsequent behavior made it clear that military advocates of democracy were a minority. Moreover, the forced personnel changes, reductions in staffing and budgets, and attempted educational reforms were seen as unwarranted attacks on military institutions; rather than molding new attitudes and values, these measures tended to reinforce the existing military culture. Assessing military attitudes four years after the dictatorship's end, CELS drew a chilling conclusion: "The officers who today are gaining influence in the armed forces are more totalitarian and fanatical than the generation that took over the country in 1976."[35]

Human rights groups also looked to the future while seeking justice for the past. They sought to change the military by rooting out known repressors from the officer ranks by lobbying against the promotion of men implicated in abductions, torture, and murder. Such individuals routinely appeared on lists of officers up for promotion to the rank of colonel or above, which the military command presented periodically to the president, who recommended the promotions, and to the Senate, which approved them. If denied promotion, officers were automatically retired. The Senate, with a right-wing majority, was not normally sympathetic to the human rights movement's concerns. And since the commanders viewed any dissent from their judgment as unwarranted interference and forcefully conveyed this view to the executive and to the Senate, the human rights organizations scored many more failures than successes. The 1988 promotion of the notorious naval officer Alfredo Astiz was a particularly stinging defeat.[36]

With their own teams of lawyers and child psychologists, the Abuelas de Plaza de Mayo made some progress in the first years after the dictatorship in locating and identifying missing children, and in some cases restoring them to their biological families. Of some five hundred children that the Abuelas estimated to have been born in captivity or abducted with parents who subsequently disappeared, the group had located nearly fifty by 1989. When the children had been illegally adopted by families clearly implicated in the repression, judges normally granted custody to surviving biological family members; in cases of adoptive parents having adopted in good faith and not being tainted by the dirty war, the cases were more complicated and emotionally devastating. After some stalling, the government aided the Abuelas' quest by establishing a national genetic data bank in 1987 to facilitate the identification of children's biological relatives, and in 1988 by appointing a special prosecutor for cases of missing children.[37]

Meanwhile, in a clear reaction to the years of repression, the period of Alfonsín's administration witnessed a remarkable spread of human rights consciousness and culture throughout Argentine civil society. After their silence, the media, particularly new ones founded in the 1980s, provided extensive coverage of human rights issues. The film industry produced large numbers of documentary and feature films on human rights themes, the best known of which, *The Official Story*, explored the issue of stolen and subsequently adopted children. Between 1984 and 1986, a fourth of Argentina's substantial film production dealt with human rights themes. Human rights education became standard from primary to professional schools. Schools, unions, political parties, municipalities, and provincial governments established human rights commissions to investigate, commemorate, and educate. Unions, schools, and cities installed plaques listing the names of their disappeared. The anniversary of the Night of the Pencils was widely commemorated in schools—in Buenos Aires, for example, with a day of studying human rights. Citizens of several municipalities held unprecedented "ethical tribunals" to protest the presence among them of known repressors, including a medical doctor and a priest. These developments signaled that in the early post–dirty war years—under the impact of Nunca más, the trial of the juntas, and the work of the human rights movement—a broad segment of Argentine society identified and expressed solidarity with the cause of human rights and the quest for truth and justice.[38]

The Reassertion of Impunity, 1986–1995

Following the trial of the juntas, Argentines turned their attention to the more than three thousand criminal charges that had been filed by mid-1986 by victims' families, human rights organizations, and foreign governments against over 650 active and retired officers. Among the accused were some of the most notorious repressors from the highest military ranks who had been zone commanders under the juntas: Admiral Rubén Chamorro, head of ESMA; General Ramón Camps, chief of police of Buenos Aires Province; General Luciano Benjamín Menéndez, commander of the Third Army Corps based in Córdoba; General Carlos Guillermo Suárez Mason, commander of the First Army Corps based in greater Buenos Aires; and numerous others. Trials were also pending or under way for a large number of officers of lesser rank when events upset the balance between justice and governability.[39]

From the outset of Alfonsín's presidency, there had been intense military pressures against investigations and prosecutions. The military had used intimidation, warnings, bombings, and several outright threats of rebellion. The high command was particularly protective of the accused who remained on active duty, approximately a third of all cases before the courts. As investigations and prosecutions proceeded in their slow and erratic way, military resistance stiffened. In numerous instances, officers simply refused to obey the orders of civilian judges. Ranking officers frequently made public pronouncements defending the dirty war and directly challenging civilian authority. Military attitudes were reflected in practices such as the staging of ceremonies honoring military men fallen in the fight against "subversion" and active-duty officers visiting their jailed colleagues to show solidarity. Saber rattling intensified at times of particular tension, such as the release of *Nunca más* and the trial of the juntas. The military's attitudes and actions were backed by rightist politicians, some of the press that had supported the dirty war, and implicitly by the Catholic Church hierarchy, which essentially called for reconciliation through forgetting the past.[40]

Caught between a growing number of court actions against military men and police—an estimated six thousand charges had been filed by December 1986—and increasingly strident military challenges to its authority that threatened to undermine its credibility and legitimacy, even its survival, the Alfonsín administration revived its initiative to limit the trials, which Congress earlier had thwarted and the judiciary had ignored. Having annulled the military's self-amnesty, the president rejected calls for a new amnesty law but began to consider a law of *"punto final"* (final period or full stop), a statute of limitations which would set a deadline for the filing of new charges rather than allowing the judicial process to continue indefinitely, keeping the country and the military in a prolonged state of agitation.[41]

Human rights organizations and public opinion overwhelmingly opposed a *punto final*, as did many within Alfonsín's Radical Party. Nonetheless, the president ignored mass protests, brushed aside press criticism, and, citing "reasons of state" for his decision, invoked party discipline to secure the needed Radical votes in Congress. With rightist support, Congress enacted the *punto final* law on December 23, 1986, setting a sixty-day deadline for the filing of new charges. The law passed the day after the Consejo Supremo had dropped all charges against fifteen admirals in the high-profile case of human rights crimes at ESMA, provocatively declaring that there had been no detentions or torture conducted at the naval facility known as the Argentine Auschwitz. While human rights organizations reacted angrily to the *punto final* law, army commander General Héctor Ríos Ereñú opined that "the country will now be able to enter the long stage of profound reconciliation." Clearly, just a year after the juntas' trial had established a standard for justice, the tide had shifted toward impunity.[42]

With summer vacations beginning, the timing of the *punto final* law could not have been worse for advocates of justice. Nonetheless, human rights organizations, lawyers, and many judges suspended their holidays and worked feverishly, filing almost five hundred new cases against over three hundred military personnel, including numerous high-ranking officers, before the sixty-day deadline expired. While human rights advocates were deeply aggrieved that a large proportion of the repressors identified by CONADEP had their trials cancelled or escaped prosecution altogether, the unantici-pated outcome of the *punto final* stiffened the military's resolve to stop the ju-dicial process altogether.[43]

The next step in the retreat from justice followed the Holy Week crisis of April 1987, which grew out of the refusal of Ernesto Barreiro, a notorious tor-turer from La Perla detention center in Córdoba, to obey a civil court order to turn himself in for arraignment. While military defiance of civilian au-thority was not unusual, in this instance it escalated into a full revolt by spe-cial forces units, the *carapintadas* (painted faces) led by Colonel Aldo Rico at Buenos Aires' Campo de Mayo, the country's largest army base. In response to the high command's refusal to put down the rebellion, Alfonsín called on civil society to show its support for democracy and justice; hundreds of thou-sands of people took to the streets, and thousands more surrounded the base itself, directly challenging the soldiers. Alfonsín dramatically helicoptered into the base, conversed with Rico, and proclaimed victory. But the terms of the bargain were a further concession to impunity.[44]

Despite further mass protests, Alfonsín submitted a "due obedience" bill which passed Congress on June 4, 1987. In his introduction of the bill, Al-fonsín wrote, "I know perfectly well that as a result of this law individuals who may have been the material authors of extremely grave crimes may go free. And I don't like that." But, he argued, "the criminal responsibility for human rights violations belongs to those who conceived the plan, with its aberrant methodology, and ordered it carried out."[45] Modifying the definition of due obedience written into the 1984 law on military justice, this statute established the legality of following any and all orders by eliminating murder and torture from the list of "aberrant and atrocious acts" that Congress had added, leaving open the possibility of prosecution only for rape, theft, and baby stealing. Alfonsín's new bill applied the redefined due obedience prin-ciple to all personnel below the rank of colonel or its equivalent; however, bending to heightened military pressure, Congress reduced the pool of offi-cers subject to prosecution to only the chiefs of the security zones that the initial junta had set up, as well as the heads of security forces, leaving around fifty men susceptible to prosecution.[46]

Enactment of the due obedience law on the heels of the *punto final*, in the judgment of a country woman from the northeastern province of Corrientes, meant that "the genocide was legitimate."[47] Despite this capitulation, two additional *carapintada* revolts in 1988, both suppressed by the high com-mand, signaled that some military men would be satisfied with nothing less than complete absolution for everyone implicated in human rights crimes as well as the reversal of budget cuts and the restoration of military dignity.[48]

The deteriorating prospects for justice received a further blow in January 1989 when a previously unknown guerrilla group called Movimiento Todos por la Patria (All for the Fatherland Movement) attacked La Tablada army base, outside Buenos Aires, leaving over forty dead and at least one hundred injured. This stark reminder of 1970s guerrilla violence, combined with the revelation that the group's leader was a lawyer working for CELS, revived the military's and the right's old suspicions of links between human rights organizations and left terrorism. A *Buenos Aires Herald* editorial stated, "La Tablada proved what they [the right] had said [all] along: that the human rights movement was but a cover-up for obscure subversive conspiracies and their members were bloodthirsty terrorists in disguise. . . . It will now be much more difficult for those of us who believe no person under any circumstance can be justifiably tortured or murdered to make our point."[49] The La Tablada incident strengthened the military position, while the increasingly radical line of the most prominent human rights group, the original Madres de Plaza de Mayo, and the emotional drain of five years of tension over the course of transitional justice led much of the mainstream public to distance itself from the human rights movement, undercutting its ability to influence public opinion and policy.[50]

The dynamism of the first two years of democracy—CONADEP's work, the publication of *Nunca más*, and the trial of the juntas—which had appeared to set Argentina on a course of rebuilding its moral and institutional foundations, had slowly foundered before the resurgence of impunity. Human rights groups, victims, and families of victims, who had enjoyed the support of public opinion and government upon the return of democracy, now found themselves increasingly isolated, their protests reduced to unwelcome reminders of a past that the majority of Argentines apparently preferred to forget. The energy that had characterized the human rights movement in the early postdictatorship years, manifested in the spread of a culture of human rights and the vogue of memorialization, likewise waned. And the negative impact of La Tablada on the human rights movement opened the door to further setbacks.

By the end of Alfonsín's presidency in July 1989, the balance between justice and governability that the president sought had eluded Argentina.[51] While relatively small numbers of repressors remained in prison or subject to trial, the country's fragile new democratic institutions were clearly incapable of exercising authority over the military. An assessment made by two human rights NGOs in 1987 remained valid in 1989: "The principal obstacle in President Alfonsín's path continues being military resistance to the rule of law. Resistance to judicial authority has been sufficiently powerful to prevent any significant step toward an acceptance of democratic values."[52] Civilian attempts to control and reshape the military only made it more reactionary. Military men were not only unrepentant, but most were proud of the work they had done between 1976 and 1983 and were unable to understand why a significant portion of Argentine society did not appreciate having been saved from subversion and Marxism, even at the cost of some lives. Thus, rather than offering a sign of contrition, a gesture to foster reconciliation, the military sought to close the book on the dirty war on its own terms. It found a collaborator in President Carlos Saúl Menem (1989–1999).[53]

As a leader of the Peronist opposition in the late 1980s, Menem had been a vocal critic of Alfonsín's *punto final* and due obedience laws. During the 1989 presidential campaign, debate focused on the country's economy, which had entered one of its periodic crises, and little mention was made of the military and human rights. But Menem had a trade-off in mind: pardons for human rights crimes and the recent military uprisings in exchange for further reductions of military budgets and staff and a firm commitment by the military commanders to prevent further rebellions by their subordinates. Once elected, he unsuccessfully pressured outgoing President Alfonsín to use his powers of pardon on behalf of convicted and indicted officers. When Menem, shortly after his inauguration, announced his intention to issue pardons, he touched off massive protests at home and widespread criticism from abroad. Yet on October 8, 1989, he pardoned 213 military men, including those indicted but not convicted for dirty war crimes and those sentenced for misconduct in the Malvinas war and the three rebellions against the Alfonsín government. To make the case for reconciliation, he invoked the theory of the two devils, pardoning sixty-four guerrillas but not the Montoneros' Mario Firmenich.[54]

In late 1990, Menem announced his intention to pardon all remaining convicted officers, including the junta members, before year's end. Opinion polls found overwhelming opposition to the pardons, and massive protests again erupted. However, another orchestrated *carapintada* revolt broke out on December 3, countering pressure from the mobilized opposition against the pardons. Less than a month later, citing the need for reconciliation and claiming moral authority from his own five years' detention under the dictatorship, Menem pardoned former junta members Videla, Massera, Agosti, Viola, and Lambruschini, as well as former chiefs of the Buenos Aires provincial police Camps and Ricchieri, former general Suárez Mason, and others, thus emptying the Magdalena military prison of human rights violators. He also pardoned Montonero leader Firmenich and a few other civilians. In the contest between justice and impunity, the latter won a sweet victory on December 29, 1990.[55]

Public pronouncements following the pardons revealed the depth of the chasm still dividing Argentines and shed light on the ongoing struggle over truth, justice, and memory. Eight human rights organizations signed a manifesto declaring, "We denounce as absolutely fallacious the pretension of reaching peace and civilized coexistence by denying the values upon which peace and coexistence are built: Life, liberty, truth, justice—in sum, the complete respect for human rights." The pardon, it continued, "is an affront to the universal conscience."[56] The same day, Videla released a public letter confirming his unchanged view of what had transpired between 1976 and 1983: The pardoned officers, he said, "defended the nation against subversive aggression [and] prevented the establishment of a totalitarian regime." He demanded "the vindication of the army and the restoration of military honor" and expressed his solidarity "with those who mourn the dead, wounded, and mutilated fallen in defense of the fatherland." Videla's notion of reconciliation was evident in his expression of sympathy for those killed or wounded—but not disappeared—in defense of "mistaken ideas."[57]

Having dashed hopes for justice, the Menem government offered reparations for victims of human rights violations and their families. This resulted from pressure by the Inter-American Court of Human Rights to settle cases brought to it, as well as from Menem's view that reparations would help bury the past. Reparations in Argentina went first to former political prisoners and those who were released from prison on condition of going into exile. Some eleven thousand persons received the equivalent of seventy-four dollars per day of prison or exile, to a maximum of 220,000 dollars, in government bonds. Only in 1994 did the surviving family members of the disappeared or murdered receive an offer of reparations. Those who filed claims received the equivalent of 220,000 dollars in government bonds. The offer of reparations for the disappeared was very controversial. The original Madres group adamantly opposed financial compensation, claming that accepting an indemnity would be tantamount to recognizing their children's deaths, which they consistently denied on the principle that death required a body, and a body required punishment: "That which must be remedied with justice cannot be remedied with money. No one is going to put a price on the lives of our children." The government estimated that the reparations programs would cost between 2.5 and 3.5 billion dollars.[58]

During Menem's first term as president, the subject of justice for the crimes of the dirty war was virtually out of the news. Against the backdrop of an economic boom beginning in 1991, Menem's resulting popularity, the fallout of La Tablada, and the seemingly insurmountable legal obstacles to the pursuit of justice, the human rights movement was increasingly marginalized from visibility and influence. Nonetheless, a few developments after 1990 had positive implications for human rights. In June 1994, conscription ended, and Argentina's armed forces became volunteer institutions. By that time, after additional personnel and budget cuts, active duty forces numbered sixty-seven thousand, approximately half the size of the military in 1976 and one of the smallest armed forces on a per capita basis in Latin America. Military rebellions ceased, although at the cost of concessions that partially restored the armed forces' role in intelligence and internal security.[59]

Intent on running for a second term despite the constitution's one-term limit, Menem entered with the opposition Radicals into negotiations that led in 1994 to wide-ranging amendments to the 1853 constitution. In addition to allowing presidential reelection—while shortening the term from six to four years and weakening presidential powers—the negotiations led to provisions strengthening democracy and to inclusion of a section on human rights, absent in the original constitution, which the Radicals had advocated during Alfonsín's term. Reflecting the residual influence of the human rights movement, continuing revulsion at Menem's pardons, suspicions about his commitment to human rights, and the Radical Party's position, the constitutional revisions went further: section 75, article 22 established the primacy of international treaties and concordats over domestic law and gave "constitutional hierarchy" to nine international human rights instruments to which Argentina was a signatory, including the Universal Declaration of Human Rights and its empowering covenants, the American Declaration of the Rights and Duties of Man, and the UN conventions against genocide and torture. It also established that by a two-thirds vote, Congress could give constitutional status to human rights treaties and protocols ratified in the future, allowing one of the conventions inspired by the dirty war—the Inter-American Convention on Forced Disappearance of Persons—to become part of the constitution in 1997.[60]

When the 1994 constitutional revisions were approved, the international human rights regime was in the process of evolving from the stage of monitoring compliance with human rights norms to the stage of enforcement. The UN had established the International Criminal Tribunal for the former Yugoslavia in May 1993, and the International Criminal Tribunal for Rwanda would follow in November 1994; but other developments, including the Pinochet arrest and the establishment of the International Criminal Court, were still in the future. Thus the possibility that section 75, article 2, might be applied to crimes of the dirty war seemed remote. Nonetheless, the continuing evolution of international human rights jurisprudence would shortly reveal its significance.

Two additional constitution amendments had implications for human rights. The federal judiciary, which had been dominated by the presidency, was placed on an independent footing, allowing it more easily to respond to changes in international human rights jurisprudence. And the city of Buenos Aires, heretofore a federal district run by the national government, was granted autonomy. Given the concentration of human rights organizations and progressive political groups in the capital, the city government, with an elected legislature and mayor, would henceforth take a leading role in human rights issues.[61]

Revival of the Momentum for Justice

A series of developments in the mid-1990s again altered the course of transitional justice in Argentina. These events reopened society's wounds and memories and reenergized the human rights movement. They revived the stalled quest for justice and the momentum to commemorate victims and forge and preserve historical memory. The most dramatic development began with a March 2, 1995, television program in which Horacio Verbitsky, a prominent investigative journalist, revealed information on operations at ESMA that he had gathered in secret interviews with Adolfo Scilingo, a retired naval officer. Scilingo was not repentant for his involvement in the dirty war; rather, he had become resentful over his forced retirement from the navy. He appeared on television the week following Verbitsky's revelations to tell of his participation in the weekly death flights that dropped prisoners into the Atlantic, claiming, by his estimate, between 1,500 and 2,000 lives. At last, in a most dramatic way, the military's blood pact of silence was broken.[62]

Scilingo's detailed revelations riveted Argentines to their television sets and to Verbitsky's serialized story that appeared later in book form as *El vuelo* (The Flight). Scilingo confirmed, in a stunningly authoritative way, what testimony before CONADEP and the juntas' trial had earlier revealed: that the flights carried drugged prisoners who, selected to "fly," were told they were being "transferred" to rehabilitation camps; that they were pushed out alive; and that chaplains participated by salving the crews' consciences upon their return to ESMA. According to Scilingo, the death flights occurred weekly for two years. In order to seal the blood pact among officers, flight duty was rotated among all of them. He had participated in two flights and had shoved thirty prisoners out. His worst memory was of a prisoner who, as he was being launched, was sufficiently conscious to grab Scilingo, almost dragging him along.[63]

Families of the disappeared, particularly those whose loved ones had reportedly been held in ESMA, were devastated by the chilling details, calmly related in matter-of-fact fashion by an apparently normal, rational man. The human rights organizations renewed their demand for lists of the disappeared that they believed the military had kept. Now that the secret detention center at ESMA and the navy's methods of murder had been exposed from the inside, the military and their supporters had greater difficulty denying the horrors revealed in Nunca más and the trial of the juntas. For the large portion of the public that had paid little attention to the human rights issues, and for those who still refused to accept the revelations of Nunca más and the trial as reality, Scilingo's revelations were an unwelcome, jarring reminder that Argentina had accounts to settle before reconciliation could occur.[64]

Scilingo's testimony was the most important development that brought human rights issues back to the forefront following several years of marginalization. The "Scilingo effect" spurred other televised confessions, one by a former army sergeant, Víctor Ibáñez, who had served at the Campo de Mayo base. In April, he indicated that the army also had used death flights to dispose of some 2,300 persons, and he named some of the victims. In May, Julio Simón, aka el Turco Julián, a well-known torturer and inventor of the rectóscopo, came forward on television to discuss his specialty. He stated that "all the abducted were tortured" and that "the general norm was to kill everyone." He concluded, "I regret nothing."[65]

Following Ibáñez's implication of the army, army commander General Martín Balza went on television on April 26, 1995, to offer a critique of the army's role in the dirty war. Balza shocked the nation and his colleagues by first declaring that despite the turmoil of that time, the 1976 seizure of power had been illegitimate, and then admitting that the army had killed people. He did not embrace the 1985 judges' ruling that disappearance had been explicit policy; however, he assumed responsibility, on behalf of his institution, for "the errors in the struggle among Argentines"—not "the errors that 'might' have occurred"—the normal military discourse. To the thousands who lost family members, he said, "I can only offer them respect, silence before their pain and the commitment of all my efforts to a future that does not repeat the past." In a dramatic gesture, Balza dismissed the principle of due obedience that had saved so many of his colleagues from prosecution: "Without euphemisms, I state clearly: Anyone who violates the National Constitution commits a crime, anyone who gives immoral orders commits a crime, anyone who carries out immoral orders commits a crime, whoever employs unjust, immoral means to achieve just ends commits a crime."[66] Balza also ordered army personnel who had knowledge of disappearances to divulge it in a manner that protected their anonymity—an order that fell on deaf ears. Meanwhile, the navy, the air force, and the police remained silent.

Although falling short of a formal apology, Balza's speech was the first Latin American military acceptance of responsibility for human rights violations. Sixty-nine percent of persons polled in Buenos Aires thought that Balza's action would contribute to reconciliation, and only 17 percent thought it would not.[67] CELS founder and head Emilio Mignone called Balza's speech "extremely important"; while not entirely satisfactory, it "is a beginning and it opens a dialogue." Expressing a minority view, Hebe de Bonafini of the hard-line Madres called him a "killer" and his statement "hypocritical."[68] From across the Andes, General Pinochet, still commander of the Chilean army, said that "the only ones who ask for forgiveness are those who feel guilty."[69]

Balza's sentiments were not widely shared within the military. Massera, Suárez Mason, and other protagonists of terrorism denied that crimes had been committed. A few days after his speech, a group of seventy retired generals released a public letter rejecting Balza's main premises and repeating the standard military interpretation of the dirty war. The Círculo Militar, the army officers' association that occupies an opulent palace in the heart of Buenos Aires, began work on a two-volume homage to the military and police killed in the "war against subversion," designed to counter Balza's assertions as well as the "truth" put out by the "Marxist" human rights organizations. The book included biographies of all 495 killed between 1960 (the beginning of subversion, in the military view) and the 1989 La Tablada attack, newspaper clippings on the terrorist acts that killed them, and an introduction lauding their efforts in "a just and necessary war" against "terrorist aggression planned outside the country"—a war that "prevented the installation of an institutional regime . . . today advocated by Mrs. Bonafini [president of the hard-line Madres]." The army also established a "Museum of Subversion" at its Campo de Mayo base.[70]

In the spirit of the "Scilingo effect," the church also announced a self-criticism of its role during the dictatorship. Still governed by conservatives, the Council of Bishops was unable to agree on the text of a statement by its announced deadline of December 1995. Finally, in April 1996, it issued a tepid communiqué admitting no responsibility in the dirty war and asserting that it had periodically alerted the military authorities to abuses but had not been heeded. It made no mention of the active role that priests had played in the repression or of the religious hierarchy's public defenses of the military regime. Invoking a version of the two devils theory, it asked God's forgiveness for crimes committed by Catholics on both sides of the struggle. The statement concluded with language worthy of Videla or Massera: "We humbly ask forgiveness from God, our Lord, for the faults that might be attributed to us. For our part, we are disposed to pardon the offenses that might have been directed at the Church."[71]

Finally, following the lead of Pope John Paul II, who asked for forgiveness for the church's past errors in the 2000 "Jubilee Year," the Argentine bishops issued a mild statement of repentance in September 2000. They acknowledged mistakes made by Argentina's Catholics in the dirty war, and also asked for pardon for their own failings: "We have been indulgent with totalitarian postures, hurting democracy. We have discriminated against many brothers without committing ourselves to the defense of their rights."[72]

Anniversaries are junctures that activate memory. The Scilingo bombshell roughly coincided with the tenth anniversary of the trial of the juntas and was bracketed by two other important anniversaries: the tenth of the publication of *Nunca más* in 1994, and the twentieth of the military coup in 1996. These events, the passage of time, the aging of victims and victims' families, and the Scilingo effect generated a new wave of commemoration and the creation and preservation of memory. In 1994, the twentieth anniversary of the death of the first of many classmates killed by the AAA, two architecture graduates from the National University of La Plata in Buenos Aires Province decided to erect a memorial to their murdered and disappeared friends from the architecture school. Inaugurated in 1995, the monument was one of the earliest public spaces—other than walls holding plaques—dedicated to victims of state terrorism.[73]

During 1994, 1995, 1996, and beyond, the revelations and anniversaries unleashed a torrent of activity and reinvigorated the human rights movement and significant sectors of Argentine society. Many books, films, and videos appeared; human rights film festivals were held; and *Nunca más* was republished in weekly installments, selling two hundred thousand copies per week. The marches to the Plaza de Mayo drew the largest crowds in years. At the heart of the anniversary activities was the erection of memorials, both permanent sites and temporary venues such as art exhibits and drama and film presentations. Not infrequently, these endeavors led to the violent contestation of public spaces as police or rightist militants acted to block events or destroy plaques and other public displays.[74]

Families of the disappeared placed newspaper ads with photos of their relatives on the anniversary of their disappearance, events were named or renamed for victims of the dirty war, and sites of particular significance were declared public patrimony. High schools, university faculties, unions, neighborhoods, and cities and towns dedicated plaques to their disappeared and killed. Plazas and streets were named for victims of the repression such as journalist Rodolfo Walsh, killed in 1977, and Azucena de Villaflor de Vincente, the disappeared founding president of the Madres de Plaza de Mayo. Ceremonies were held and plaques dedicated on anniversaries of landmark events such as the Night of the Pencils and the abduction of the founding Madres and the French nuns. Human rights education in public schools was expanded and improved with the aid of human rights organizations, some of which established internships that allowed youth of the post–dirty war generation to gain close-up knowledge of state terrorism.[75]

In response to the groundswell of human rights activism, several provincial governments appointed commissions to establish museums of memory. The province of Buenos Aires, for example, formed a Provincial Commission for Memory in 1999 and planned a museum, which opened in La Plata in 2002. Plans for a major museum of memory in the city of Buenos Aires dated to the late 1980s, and the city legislature approved the concept in 1996. However, progress was frustrated by disagreements over its location: most human rights groups favored a former detention center such as El Olimpo or ESMA, but the military resisted giving up its facilities. In 1998, Menem decreed that ESMA be razed and replaced by a monument to "national unity." The human rights movement tenaciously opposed this initiative, considering it another attempt to bury the past and subvert memory; it successfully sued to thwart the presidential initiative. Meanwhile, construction began on a Parque de la Memoria (Park of Memory), located near ESMA.[76]

Of the organizations devoted to collecting, preserving, and disseminating documentation on state terrorism and human rights, the most important is Memoria Abierta (Open Memory), founded in 2000 and sponsored by a consortium of eight human rights organizations. Taking cues from the many organizations around the world that memorialize and educate about the Holocaust, it has collected hundreds of videotaped testimonies, created materials for use in schools, and held numerous educational workshops. In one of several acts designed to promote public awareness of the importance of memory, Memoria Abierta organized an event in which relatives of the disappeared who were dropped into the ocean from the death flights threw flowers into the Río de la Plata, symbolically claiming the river and the Atlantic Ocean into which it flows as a space for remembering.[77]

The Scilingo effect and the numerous anniversaries also reenergized the human rights organizations' quest for truth and justice. The Madres de Plaza de Mayo had split in 1986 over strategies for pushing their cause under civilian government, particularly over the issues of exhumations and reparations.

The new association, Madres de Plaza de Mayo—Línea Fundadora (Founding Line), took a more mainstream approach, while the original group became increasingly radicalized and eclectic in the causes it pursued. However, the dual presence produced even more activity. The Thursday afternoon marches in the Plaza de Mayo continued, featuring Madres in their signature white scarves, and each organization carried out an annual "march of resistance," which mobilized thousands of people. Each group maintained a large membership with provincial branches, operated with a substantial budget, and communicated through newsletters and websites. The original Madres established a bookstore and café near the national Congress and opened a popular university in 2001.[78]

The Abuelas de Plaza de Mayo intensified their primary mission of establishing the identities and locating the missing children of their disappeared children. By 2002, they had located seventy-three of the estimated five hundred missing children. The aging of the children, now in their mid- to late twenties, presented new challenges for the indomitable grandmothers and their volunteers.[79]

A new human rights organization, Hijos por la Identidad y la Justicia y contra el Olvido y el Silencio (Children for Identity and Justice and against Forgetting and Silence) appeared in 1995 and soon made an impact within the reinvigorated movement. Known by its acronym, HIJOS (children), the new organization consisted of children of the murdered and disappeared. These youth, in their teens and twenties, forged new approaches to publicizing human rights crimes and pushing for justice. They held periodic demonstrations, called *escraches* (from the slang term *escrachar*, to uncover), in which they targeted the homes and neighborhoods of repressors, from former junta leaders to known torturers, in order to publicly shame them and challenge their impunity. Marching with banners, drums, and whistles, a group of HIJOS would arrive noisily in the neighborhood; denounce the repressor's crimes; hand out flyers with the particulars, including the target's photograph; and sometimes paint sidewalks and walls. In February 1998, they shamed torturer Jorge Carlos Radice; in May, navy doctor Raúl Sánchez Ruiz, who delivered babies at ESMA; in June 1999, Admiral Massera. *Escraches* were often violently broken up, but they called attention to repressors' presence and their freedom in ways that could not be ignored—directly confronting impunity and showing that the demonstrators did not fear their parents' killers. While some neighbors acted as they had done during the dirty war, hiding behind closed shutters, others shed their fear or apathy and joined HIJOS in condemning and ostracizing the repressors. HIJOS' shaming drove some criminals essentially to give up their public lives.[80]

On December 5, 2002, in the Plaza de Mayo, the Madres de Plaza de Mayo—Línea Fundadora carried out an extremely emotional and very important act with HIJOS. A large number of the Madres, now aging and possibly unable to continue their work much longer, transferred their mission and their moral authority by taking off the diaper-inspired scarves they had worn for twenty-five years and placing them around the necks of HIJOS members, some of them their biological grandchildren, the rest in the same age cohort. The powerful message was that, if the HIJOS do not stumble along the way, the struggle for truth, justice, commemoration, and memory will continue well into the future.[81]

The human rights organizations specializing in legal work, CELS and APDH, redoubled their efforts and developed new legal strategies. One approach focused on a crime not covered by the 1987 due obedience law: "appropriation of minors and substitution of identity," or child kidnapping. Since the beneficiaries of Menem's pardons had been neither convicted of nor pardoned for child kidnapping, this approach offered the possibility of fruitful legal proceedings. Taking advantage of the Abuelas' extensive research on missing children, human rights organizations began bringing cases before the courts in 1996. In 1998, judges began ordering the detention of ranking officers, including Videla and Massera. By 2000, over a dozen retired and active-duty officers were in custody or, if over seventy, under house arrest, and over one hundred cases of baby kidnapping were under investigation.[82]

The international human rights lobby, having evolved and matured since the end of the dictatorship, was fully engaged and extremely helpful in the revival of the quest for justice in Argentina. In 1995, with the financial support of the Ford Foundation, CELS launched its "program for the application of international law to human rights in local courts," an initiative based on section 75, article 22, of the revised constitution and on recent developments in international human rights jurisprudence. This initiative involved educating and persuading judges to begin implementing the provision that international treaties supersede Argentine law—a new and untested legal approach. Amnesty International, the International Commission of Jurists, Human Rights Watch, the International Red Cross, and numerous other organizations monitored the Argentine situation, supplied research, and drafted briefs. A 1995 amicus curiae brief submitted by a coalition of international NGOs, for example, paved the way for the reopening of investigations of disappearances. The Inter-American Commission on Human Rights accepted numerous cases from Argentina, while the Inter-American Court of Human Rights pressed for the acceptance of its rulings in Argentine courts.[83]

Several foreign governments had previously demanded the extradition of repressors for the death or disappearance of their nationals. Some, such as Alfredo Astiz, had been tried and sentenced in absentia but continued enjoying their freedom in Argentina. Beginning in 1996, international judicial activism intensified as several countries escalated their demands for the extradition of Argentine military men to testify about or stand trial for the disappearances of their nationals. Spanish judge Baltasar Garzón ordered over one hundred military and police to testify in Madrid about some three hundred disappeared Spanish citizens, and an Italian court launched an investigation into the disappearances of over seventy Italians and Argentines of Italian origin; the Italian case culminated in 2000 with the trial and conviction in absentia of seven army officers. Other countries followed Spain and Italy in pursuing information about and justice for their disappeared or murdered nationals. While the Argentine government denied all extradition requests, foreign intervention encouraged the Argentine human rights movement and provided a new level of legitimacy for its quest.[84]

CELS's initiative, the accelerated change in international human rights jurisprudence, and heightened pressures from abroad opened new avenues for investigations and potential prosecutions. Basing itself on a recent ruling by the Inter-American Court of Human Rights that relatives of the disappeared have the "right to truth" about the fate of their family members, a federal court in La Plata in 1998 ordered investigations into all frozen cases of disappearance under its jurisdiction—some 1,800 in total. Other federal courts soon followed La Plata's lead, and hundreds of officers who had enjoyed a decade of complete impunity were called to testify regarding the whereabouts of the disappeared.[85]

While the "right to truth" cases reopened investigations, the *punto final* and due obedience laws, as well as Menem's pardons, still shielded repressors from prosecution. To overcome this barrier, human rights lawyers pushed the courts to embrace the international principle that crimes against humanity cannot be amnestied by any law or pardon. Among many precedents, they cited a recent Inter-American Court of Human Rights ruling that signatories to the various human rights covenants were obligated to investigate and, if appropriate, prosecute violators of the covenants' provisions regardless of amnesty laws in any form. Meanwhile, in 1998, Congress repealed the *punto final* and due obedience laws; however, since they were not annulled, the new laws were interpreted as not being retroactive, and thus human rights violators remained protected. Another 1998 law opened CONADEP's records to persons claiming human rights violations—a further aid to lawsuits.[86]

In March 2001, federal judge Gabriel Cavallo ruled the *punto final* and due obedience laws unconstitutional, null, and void. Basing himself on Argentine and international law and the Inter-American Commission on Human Rights' ruling against amnesty laws, he declared disappearances to be crimes against humanity, which could not be amnestied. Other courts followed Cavallo's groundbreaking decision, and the Buenos Aires Appeals Court upheld the rulings in November 2001. Principle became reality with the 2002 arrest of third junta leader General Galtieri and forty-two others on charges of abduction, torture, and execution of twenty persons in 1980. This breach of the shield of impunity would potentially subject hundreds of officers to prosecution. While Argentines awaited a Supreme Court ruling, international human rights NGOs intensified the pressure for a favorable ruling.[87]

Even before Judge Cavallo's ruling and General Galtieri's arrest, many of the repressors of the dirty war had suffered the consequences of the reinvigoration of the human rights movement. HIJOS's work in outing repressors, combined with the universal reach of the international human rights regime, demonstrated most dramatically in the arrest of General Pinochet in London, changed conditions for the dozens of active and retired officers who had been indicted in any of several countries, as well as others who feared indictment at any moment. Shamed out of public life and unable to travel abroad for fear of arrest under international warrants, a number of the military men who had run the apparatus of state terrorism became, in effect, prisoners in their own homes. Many more, however, still lived in freedom.[88]

Military reaction to the revival of investigations, arrests, and prosecutions, although forceful, was muted so long as General Balza remained army commander. Efforts to establish a new truth commission based on the "right to truth" principle, however, were dropped under intense military pressure. After Balza's retirement in 1999, military responses reverted to form. Balza's successor, General Ricardo Brinzoni, issued public statements denying systematic baby kidnapping, ranking officers visited jailed colleagues in shows of solidarity, and judges and human rights workers suffered threats, intimidation, and break-ins at their offices. These pressures re-created a less extreme version of the climate of military reaction between the 1985 trial of the juntas and Menem's 1990 pardons. Menem's successor, President Fernando de la Rúa (1999–2001) of the Radical Party, who had promised cooperation on human rights issues during his campaign, took a largely hands-off approach to the military backlash. In addition, he continued Menem's practices of promoting officers accused of being repressors and refusing to cooperate with extradition requests for human rights violators.[89]

The revival of military assertions of impunity underscored the wisdom of another post-Scilingo CELS initiative: the development of a legal culture of human rights in Argentina that would solidify and complement the rooting of a culture of rights in civil society. Since 1995, CELS has spent increasing amounts of its time and energy in addressing current human rights problems. It has used legal activism and has taken advantage of the increasingly independent judiciary and active support from the international human rights organizations to attack state abuses of power and lack of accountability—matters such as police excesses and corruption, denials of due process, and infringement of press freedom, all of which blossomed during Menem's presidency. CELS's purview also included economic, social, and cultural rights; in this vein, the organization has sued the government to provide education and health care for all, to live up to labor agreements, and to protect indigenous rights. In both areas of rights, CELS has scored sufficient victories to establish precedent for future cases. CELS members believe that creating a culture of human rights will strengthen the rule of law, fortify Argentina's fragile democracy, and by so doing prevent a recurrence of the 1976–1983 nightmare.[90]

The severe economic, social, and political crisis that shook Argentina in December 2001 jeopardized the revived momentum toward justice. The economic boom of the early 1990s had faded by the mid-1990s; by 2000, poverty and unemployment had become endemic, leading to protests around the country. The denouement came in December 2001, when the Argentine peso, pegged to the U.S. dollar since the early 1990s, suddenly lost two-thirds of its value. The government subsequently defaulted on both domestic and international debts and froze bank accounts, and unemployment mushroomed. Riots on December 20 and 21 killed over twenty-five people and led to President de la Rúa's resignation. Argentina then had three interim presidents in the following two weeks, until Peronist Eduardo Duhalde managed to form a relatively stable interim government on January 2, 2002. In the midst of the worst economic crisis since the Great Depression, interest in human rights violations of the past was temporarily eclipsed by very real, compelling concerns for day-to-day survival and for Argentina's political future.[91]

A notable aspect of the crisis was that the military did not step forward to save the patria. In the past, an economic, social, and political collapse of such proportions would undoubtedly have triggered a coup. Instead, each of the four presidents who followed de la Rúa took office by the constitutionally prescribed rules of succession. Observers wondered whether this reflected a rooting of democratic values in the military and the country or whether the crisis was so grave that the military leadership rejected the challenge of dealing with it. The army commander explained, "The military option was no longer possible . . . because both civilians and the military preferred it that way."[92]

The Collapse of Impunity in Argentina

Approaching the presidential election that had been called for April 2003, most Argentines were profoundly pessimistic about the range of candidates. Many were surprised when the little-known governor of the lightly populated Patagonian province of Santa Cruz, left Peronist Néstor Kirchner, emerged from the crowded field as president-elect. Yet, from the beginning of his term, Kirchner displayed dynamism and charisma that gave rise to the term "the K factor." Since both Kirchner and his wife, Cristina Fernández, had been persecuted under the military government, the human rights movement hoped for a sympathetic hearing from the new president.[93]

Despite the overwhelming challenges posed by the highest rates of unemployment and poverty ever recorded in Argentina and the pressing demands of foreign and domestic creditors, within days of his May 25 inauguration, Kirchner began addressing human rights, looking both to the past and to the future. He approached the presidency, he said, "without rancor but with memory." He invited the Madres to the presidential palace, where he told them he considered himself "a son of the Madres de Plaza de Mayo." Saying that he wanted military commanders "committed to the future, not to the past," Kirchner forced the retirement of dozens of generals and admirals, including the branch commanders. He also purged the federal police. Looking to the unresolved legacy of the dirty war, Kirchner pushed for the effective annulment of the *punto final* and due obedience laws in order for prosecutions to proceed. In August 2003, Congress complied, with language indicating retroactivity. Kirchner also rescinded de la Rúa's decree prohibiting the extradition of Argentines accused of violating the human rights of foreign nationals.[94]

Kirchner's bold and energetic actions created a climate for additional progress on truth and justice. More judges joined the few who earlier had looked to international human rights law for guidance, and they ruled with increasing frequency in favor of victims and their families, invoking the principle that amnesty does not apply to crimes against humanity to nullify the *punto final* and due obedience laws. Lower courts also began ruling that Menem's pardons were invalid. As a result, numerous officers previously spared prosecution or freed by the laws or the pardons found themselves again in jeopardy, and some found themselves in jail. Not since Alfonsín's first two years in office had the weight of the state been so visibly tilted toward justice and against impunity.[95]

Kirchner's most dramatic action regarding human rights came on the twenty-eighth anniversary of the coup, March 24, 2004. In a ceremony held at ESMA, he announced that the naval facility, the Argentina Auschwitz that Menem had tried to raze, would become a museum of memory. Referring to the human rights violations routinely carried out at ESMA, he said, "I come to ask for forgiveness on behalf of the state for the shame of having remained silent about these atrocities during twenty years of democracy. And to those who committed these macabre and sinister acts, now we can call you what you are by name: You are murderers who have been repudiated by the people." In tandem with Kirchner's announcement, navy commander Admiral Jorge Godoy publicly acknowledged what everyone knew but the navy had consistently denied: that ESMA had housed a secret detention center and had been a participant in state terrorism.[96]

On the same day, in the presence of Kirchner, his cabinet, and ranking officers, new army commander General Roberto Bendini removed the portraits of former junta leaders Videla and Bignone from the gallery of former directors of the Colegio Militar (Military Academy). Kirchner said, "The removal of the portraits marks a clear decision of the entire country, the armed forces, the army, to end a lamentable period for our country. March 24 should become the living conscience of that which must never again [nunca más] happen." CELS warmly approved the gesture, saying that "those ominous shadows will no longer preside over the formation of army officers."[97] In protest, four generals—but only four—submitted their retirement papers.

The long struggle to end impunity in Argentina triumphed on June 15, 2005, when the Supreme Court, by a vote of seven in favor, one opposed, and one abstention, upheld the appellate court's decision that the *punto final* and due obedience laws were unconstitutional, at the same time upholding the 2003 legislation that had annulled the 1986 and 1987 laws. This opened the way for the prosecution of hundreds of, and possibly over a thousand, individuals for human rights crimes committed during the dirty war. A joint statement issued by eleven Argentine human rights organizations said, "The years of struggle have not been in vain. We are convinced that if we continue to persevere, we will succeed in putting every *genocida* [practitioner of genocide] where he belongs: in jail."[98] The last shield for a few, Menem's pardons, immediately became the next target of the human rights movement. However, with precedents already set in the lower courts, the impunity of the pardoned may be ephemeral.

Notes

1. General Ramón Camps, quoted in the Buenos Aires magazine *Humor*, December 17, 1983.

2. Juan Méndez, quoted in Mark R. Amstutz, *The Healing of Nations: The Promise and Limits of Political Forgiveness* (Lanham, MD: Rowman & Littlefield, 2005), 114.

3. Note that the two Central American republics that employed state terrorism extensively, El Salvador and Guatemala, were ruled by civilians—in close alliance with the military—during most of the period when state terrorism was employed. In Peru as well, the most extensive use of state terrorism came under civilian government.

4. Raúl Alfonsín, *Memoria política: transición a la democracia y derechos humanos* (Buenos Aires: Fondo de Cultura Económica, 2004), 34.

5. Works on transitions and democratization are cited in chapter 2, notes 45 and 47. The following discussion of politics and civil-military relations in post-1983 Argentina draws heavily on Alison Brysk, *The Politics of Human Rights in Argentina: Protest, Change, and Democratization* (Stanford, CA: Stanford University Press, 1994); Edward C. Epstein, ed., *The New Argentine Democracy: The Search for a Successful Formula* (Westport, CT: Praeger, 1992); J. Patrice McSherry, *Incomplete Transition: Military Power and Democracy in Argentina* (New York: St Martin's Press, 1997); Horacio Verbitsky, *Civiles y militares: memoria secreta de la transición*, 2nd ed. (Buenos Aires: Editorial Contrapunto, 1987); Ignacio C. M. Massun, *Alfonsín: una difícil transición* (Buenos Aires: Editorial Métodos, 1999); Carlos Santiago Nino, *Radical Evil on Trial* (New Haven, CT: Yale University Press, 1996), 67–104, 108–17; and Alfonsín, *Memoria política*.

6. Alfonsín, *Memoria política*, 36.

7. The members of the fourth and last junta were excluded because their tenure, from July 1982 to December 1983, was dedicated primarily to arranging the transition to civilian government. Brysk, *Politics of Human Rights*, 63–68.

8. Centro de Estudios Legales y Sociales (CELS) and Americas Watch, *Verdad y justicia en la Argentina: actualización* (Buenos Aires: CELS and Americas Watch, 1991); McSherry, *Incomplete Transition*, 117–230; David Pion-Berlin, *Through Corridors of Power: Institutions and Civil-Military Relations in Argentina* (College Park: Pennsylvania State University Press, 1997), 75–78; Laura Tedesco, *Democracy in Argentina: Hope and Disillusion* (London: Frank Cass, 1999), 62–65.

9. Comisión Nacional sobre la Desaparición de Personas (CONADEP), *Nunca más: informe de la Comisión Nacional sobre la Desaparición de Personas*, 5th ed. (Buenos Aires: Editorial Universitaria de Buenos Aires, 1999), 443.

10. Salvador María Lozada, *Los derechos humanos y la impunidad en la Argentina (1974–1999)* (Buenos Aires: Nuevohacer, 1999), 135–218. The decree establishing CONADEP is published in Marcelo A. Sancinetti, *Derechos humanos en la Argentina postdictatorial* (Buenos Aires: Lerner Editores, 1988), 177–79.

11. Brysk, *Politics of Human Rights*, 68–72; CELS and Americas Watch, *Verdad y justicia*, 33–36; Priscilla B. Hayner, *Unspeakable Truths: Confronting State Terror and Atrocity* (New York: Routledge, 2001), 33–34.

12. CONADEP, *Nunca más*, 443–71; Brysk, *Politics of Human Rights*, 68–72.

13. CONADEP, *Nunca más*, 473.

14. CONADEP, *Nunca más*, 480; see chapter 4, 107, for Camps's and Saint Jean's visions of the application of state terror.

15. *Clarín*, November 30, 1984, gives the figure of 1,300 repressors; Brysk, *Politics of Human Rights*, 71–72, suggests approximately 1,500.

16. Hayner, *Unspeakable Truths*, 133–53, discusses the healing aspects of truth telling and the dangers of retraumatization from that experience.

17. Two truth commissions preceded Argentina's, but neither made a mark. Uganda established such a commission in 1974, but it served at the direction of dictator Idi Amin, who did not publish its report. Bolivia established a congressional commission to investigate past violations in 1982; however, after documenting 155 disappearances, the commission disbanded without publishing a final report. Thus Argentina's was the first truth commission to gain international recognition. The truth commissions in El Salvador and Guatemala were organized by the UN, and the Catholic Church investigated and reported on human rights violations in Brazil and did an independent report in Guatemala. Without forming a truth commission, the Mexican government of Vicente Fox launched an investigation into disappearances of leftists in the 1970s. On truth commissions, see Hayner, *Unspeakable Truths*; and Robert I. Rotberg and Dennis Thompson, eds., *Truth v. Justice: The Morality of Truth Commissions* (Princeton, NJ: Princeton University Press, 2000).

18. This and the following three paragraphs draw from Brysk, *Politics of Human Rights*, 72–73; Iain Guest, *Behind the Disappearances: Argentina's Dirty War against Human Rights and the United Nations* (Philadelphia: University of Pennsylvania Press, 1990), 494–507; Marguerite Guzmán Bouvard, *Revolutionizing Motherhood: The Mothers of the Plaza de Mayo* (Wilmington, DE: Scholarly Resources, 1994), 148–51.

19. Guest, *Behind the Disappearances*, 406.

20. Equipo Argentino de Antropología Forense, *Tumbas anónimas: informe sobre la identificación de restos de víctimas de la represión ilegal* (Buenos Aires: Equipo Argentino de Antropología Forense, 1992). See also the team's annual reports and its website, www.eaaf.org.

21. Alfonsín, *Memoria política*, 45.

22. Eduardo Luis Duhalde, *El estado terrorista argentino: quince años después, una mirada crítica* (Buenos Aires: Editorial Universitaria de Buenos Aires, 1998), 167–78; CELS and Americas Watch, *Verdad y justicia*, 27.

23. Pion-Berlin, *Through Corridors of Power*, 77–82; Tedesco, *Democracy in Argentina*, 64–68.

24. Sancinetti, *Derechos humanos*, 11–18, 185–93; Pion-Berlin, *Through Corridors of Power*, 77–82. Carlos Nino, a principal adviser to Alfonsín, indicated that the government planned to try a maximum of 150 officers, and possibly as few as 20. Brysk, *Politics of Human Rights*, 74–76.

25. Brysk, *Politics of Human Rights*, 76; Pion-Berlin, *Through Corridors of Power*, 80–82, 95.

26. So read the headline of the first edition of a weekly newspaper established exclusively to report on the trial: *El Diario del Juicio*, no. 1 (May 27, 1985). In addition to newspaper coverage, television showed images from the trial, but without sound.

27. El Diario del Juicio; Amnesty International, Argentina: The Military Juntas and Human Rights—Report of the Trial of the Former Junta Members, 1985 (London: Amnesty International, 1987); Jorge Camarasa, Rubén Felice, and Daniel González, El juicio: proceso al horror (Buenos Aires: Sudamericana/Planeta Editores, 1985); Sancinetti, Derechos humanos, 1–60, 221–28.

28. Camarasa, Felice, and González, El juicio, 203.

29. El Diario del Juicio, June 4, 1985; June 18, 1985; and June 11, 1985. See also María Seoane and Héctor Ruiz Núñez, La noche de los lápices, 2nd ed. (Buenos Aires: Planeta, 1992) and the 1986 film with the same title directed by Héctor Olivera.

30. Camarasa, Felice, and González, El juicio, 195, 197.

31. Amnesty International, Argentina: The Military Juntas, 53–81.

32. Clarín, December 10, 1985; El Tiempo Argentino, December 10, 1985; Brysk, Politics of Human Rights, 87, 225. The Argentines apparently paid little or no attention to the 1975 trials of Greek military men for human rights violations during the 1967–1974 military regime, which might have provided some guidance for the prosecution. See Terence Roehrig, The Prosecution of Former Military Leaders in Newly Democratic Nations: The Cases of Argentina, Greece, and South Korea (Jefferson, NC: McFarland, 2002).

33. Brysk, Politics of Human Rights, 115–18. Approximately 3,000 additional disappearances had been documented by 2000. Alexandra Barahona de Brito, "Truth, Justice, Memory, and Democratization in the Southern Cone," in The Politics of Memory: Transitional Justice in Democratizing Societies, ed. Alexandra Barahona de Brito, Carmen González-Enríquez, and Paloma Aguilar (Oxford: Oxford University Press, 2001), 121.

34. Deborah L. Norden, Military Rebellion in Argentina: Between Coups and Consolidation (Lincoln: University of Nebraska Press, 1996), 78–105; Pion-Berlin, Through Corridors of Power, 107–77; Brysk, Politics of Human Rights, 92–96; Peter G. Snow and Luigi Manzetti, Political Forces in Argentina, 3rd ed. (Westport, CT: Praeger, 1993), 112–14; Carlos H. Acuña and Catalina Smulovitz, "Adjusting the Armed Forces to Democracy: Successes, Failures, and Ambiguities in the Southern Cone," in Constructing Democracy: Human Rights, Citizenship, and Society in Latin America, ed. Elizabeth Jelin and Eric Hershberg (Boulder, CO: Westview Press, 1996), 14–21; Alfonsín, Memoria política, 251–64.

35. CELS and Americas Watch, Verdad y justicia, 76; Brysk, Politics of Human Rights, 97–98.

36. Brysk, Politics of Human Rights, 96–97.

37. Rita Arditti, Searching for Life: The Grandmothers of the Plaza de Mayo and the Disappeared Children of Argentina (Berkeley: University of California Press, 1999), 102–58; Abuelas de Plaza de Mayo, año III, no. 15 (July 2002), covers the Abuelas' twenty-five-year history; Alba Lanzillotto interview, Buenos Aires, December 10, 2002.

38. Brysk, Politics of Human Rights, 123–48; Luis Roniger and Mario Sznajder, The Legacy of Human-Rights Violations in the Southern Cone: Argentina, Chile, and Uruguay (Oxford: Oxford University Press, 1999), 190–206.

39. CELS and Americas Watch, *Verdad y justicia*, 47–61; *Argentina: Juicios a los militares. Documentos secretos, decretos-leyes, jurisprudencia. Cuadernos de la Asociación Americana de Juristas*, no. 4 (1988).

40. McSherry, *Incomplete Transition*, 117–47, 173–82; CELS and Americas Watch, *Verdad y justicia*, 71–73; *La Razón*, December 10, 1985; *La Prensa*, December 23, 1986.

41. Sancinetti, *Derechos humanos*, 61–90; Barahona de Brito, "Truth, Justice, Memory," 122.

42. *La Prensa*, December 24, 1986; Sancinetti, *Derechos humanos*, 233–42; CELS and Americas Watch, *Verdad y justicia*, 50–51.

43. Tedesco, *Democracy in Argentina*, 122–25. Brysk, *Politics of Human Rights*, 82, notes that in Entre Ríos Province, the number of officers liable to prosecution fell from around forty to six or seven.

44. Norden, *Military Rebellion*, 125–30; Alfonsín defends himself against the charge of negotiating with and capitulating to Rico in *Memoria política*, 55–75.

45. Sancinetti, *Derechos humanos*, 280–81 (entire speech 277–82).

46. Sancinetti, *Derechos humanos*, 91–152; Pion-Berlin, *Through Corridors of Power*, 99–101. Human rights groups estimated that the due obedience law reduced 450 pending cases to 50; by October 1988, only 17 officers remained on trial. Brysk, *Politics of Human Rights*, 83–84.

47. Marguerite Feitlowitz, *A Lexicon of Terror: Argentina and the Legacies of Torture* (New York: Oxford University Press, 1998), 142.

48. Norden, *Military Rebellion*, 130–35; CELS and Americas Watch, *Verdad y justicia*, 94–98.

49. Roberto Herrscher, "Reflections on Human Rights," *Buenos Aires Herald*, February 23, 1989. The military used the La Tablada incident successfully to press for the restoration of some of its internal security functions: Barahona de Brito, "Truth, Justice, Memory," 124.

50. Brysk, *Politics of Human Rights*, 118–21.

51. Faced with a severe economic crisis, Alfonsín resigned his office five months before his term expired, following his successor's election.

52. CELS and Americas Watch, *Verdad y justicia*, 76.

53. On Menem's presidency (1989–1999) see Rogelio Alaniz, *La década menemista* (Santa Fe, Argentina: Universidad Nacional del Litoral, 2000); Romero, *A History of Argentina*, 285–317.

54. CELS and Americas Watch, *Verdad y justicia*, 83–85; Roniger and Sznajder, *Legacy of Human-Rights Violations*, 77–78; Lozada, *Derechos humanos*, 215–18. Menem padded the list of pardoned "subversives" with several disappeared persons to make his action appear equitable.

55. CELS and Americas Watch, *Verdad y justicia*, 85–88.

56. *Página 12*, December 30, 1990.

57. *La Nación*, December 31, 1990.

58. Hayner, *Unspeakable Truths*, 170–72, 174–78, 316–17. The quotation is from Asociación Madres de Plaza de Mayo, "Nuestras consignas," pamphlet, n.d.

59. Martín Abregú, "Human Rights after the Dictatorship: Lessons from Argentina," *NACLA Report on the Americas* 34, no. 1 (July–August 2000): 12–18; McSherry, *Incomplete Transition*, 231–67; *The Europa World Year Book 1996* (London: Europa Publications, 1996), 1:385; Lucy Taylor, *Citizenship, Participation and Democracy: Changing Dynamics in Chile and Argentina* (New York: St. Martin's Press, 1998), 73–76.

60. Janet Koven Levit, "The Constitutionalization of Human Rights in Argentina: Problem or Promise?" *Columbia Journal of Transnational Law* 37 (1999): 281–356 (Westlaw); CELS, *Informe anual sobre la situación de los derechos humanos en la Argentina: 1995* (Buenos Aires: CELS, 1995), 2–3; Alfonsín, *Memoria política*, 193–240.

61. Constitution of Argentina, articles 108–20, 129 at www.georgetown.edu/pdba/ Constitutions/Argentina/argen94.html (accessed October 22, 2005).

62. See Horacio Verbitsky, *The Flight: Confessions of an Argentine Dirty Warrior*, trans. Esther Allen (New York: New Press, 1996).

63. Verbitsky, *The Flight*; Feitlowitz, *A Lexicon of Terror*, 193–201.

64. Feitlowitz, *A Lexicon of Terror*, 193–238; Marta Vásquez interview, Buenos Aires, December 10, 2002.

65. CELS, *Informe anual 1995*, viii, 123–45; Feitlowitz, *A Lexicon of Terror*, 58, 206–13.

66. *La Nación*, April 27, 1995.

67. *La Prensa*, April 28, 1995.

68. *La Prensa*, April 28, 1995.

69. *El periodista*, August 3, 2003 at www.elperiodista.cl/newtenberg/1428/article-35153.html (accessed October 17, 2003).

70. Círculo Militar, *In Memoriam* (Buenos Aires: Círculo Militar, 1998, 1999), 2:10–11; Roniger and Sznajder, *The Legacy of Human-Rights Violations*, 316n53.

71. *Página 12*, April 28, 1996.

72. World Watch—Catholic World Report, October 2000 at www.catholic.net.rcc/ Periodicals/Igpress/2000-10/wargentina.html (accessed August 17, 2004); CELS, *Informe anual 2000*, 35–41.

73. Feitlowitz, *A Lexicon of Terror*, 178–84.

74. Elizabeth Jelin, "The Minefields of Memory," *NACLA Report on the Americas* 32, no. 2 (September–October 1998): 23–29; Elizabeth Jelin and Susana G. Kaufman, "Layers of Memories: Twenty Years after in Argentina," in *Genocide, Collective Violence, and Popular Memory: The Politics of Remembrance in the Twentieth Century*, ed. David E. Lorey and William H. Beezley (Wilmington, DE: Scholarly Resources, 2002), 31–52.

75. Jelin and Kaufman, "Layers of Memories"; CELS, *Informe anual 1998*, 42–43; Feitlowitz, *A Lexicon of Terror*, 186–92. Examples of commemoration abound: On April 26, 1996, *Página 12* carried announcements on the anniversaries of the 1977 disappearance of Dr. Daniel Alberto Goldberg and Jorge Salvador Gullo, disappeared two years later. In 2001, athletic events in Buenos Aires and in Italy were named for dis-

appeared athlete Miguel Sánchez. The legislature of Buenos Aires Province claimed an abandoned house where four youths were killed by the military twenty-five years earlier as part of the province's cultural patrimony. *La Nación*, January 9, 2001.

76. CELS, *Informe anual 1998*, 39–42; CELS, *Informe anual 2000*, 28; announcement from Provincia de Buenos Aires, Comisión Provincial por la Memoria, December 4, 2002.

77. *Clarín*, March 26, 2001; Patricia Valdéz, director of Memoria Abierta, interviews, Buenos Aires, December 4 and 11, 2002.

78. Asociación Madres de Plaza de Mayo, *Historia de las Madres de Plaza de Mayo* (Buenos Aires: Ediciones Asociación Madres de Plaza de Mayo, 1999); Mercedes Colas de Meroño interview, Buenos Aires, December 5, 2002; Bouvard, *Revolutionizing Motherhood*, 162–64.

79. Alba Lancillotto interview, Buenos Aires, December 10, 2002.

80. Susana Kaiser, "Outing Torturers in Postdictatorship Argentina," *NACLA Report on the Americas* 34, no. 1 (July–August 2000): 14–15; CELS, *Informe anual 1998*, 48–52; CELS, *Informe anual 2000*, 62–64. Archbishop Desmond Tutu, who chaired South Africa's Truth and Reconciliation Commission, suggests that public "shaming" may serve as a partial substitute for criminal punishment. Amy Gutmann and Dennis Thompson, "The Moral Foundations of Truth Commissions," in *Truth v. Justice*, ed. Rotberg and Thompson, 22–44 (esp. 43). Note that HIJOS has a branch in Sweden, where many Argentines took exile. Naomi Roht-Arriaza, "The Role of International Actors in National Accountability Processes," in *The Politics of Memory*, ed. Barahona de Brito, González-Enríquez, and Aguilar, 54.

81. *Página 12*, December 6, 2002.

82. Martín Abregú, "Human Rights after the Dictatorship," 13–14; CELS, *Informe anual 1998*, 88–104.

83. CELS, *Informe anual 1995*, 2–3; CELS, *La aplicación de los tratados sobre derechos humanos por los tribunales locales* (Buenos Aires: Editores del Puerto, 1997); Naomi Roht-Arriaza, *The Pinochet Effect: Transnational Justice in the Age of Human Rights* (Philadelphia: University of Pennsylvania Press, 2005), 101–8; Barahona de Brito, "Truth, Justice, Memory," 138–39. CELS valued the international support, saying that "the international community has an important and very effective role to play in ending impunity in our region": CELS, *Informe anual 1998*, 21.

84. Eduardo Anguita, *Sano juicio: Baltasar Garzón, algunos sobrevivientes y la lucha contra la impunidad en Latinoamérica* (Buenos Aires: Editorial Sudamericana, 2001); Ernesto Ekaizer, *Yo, Augusto* (Buenos Aires: Aguilar, 2003), 363–472; Roht-Arriaza, *The Pinochet Effect*, 118–49. Roht-Arriaza, "The Role of International Actors," 53–54. Astiz was convicted in France in 1990. After going to Spain to testify in the trials of other alleged repressors, Adolfo Scilingo was tried in 2005 and sentenced to 640 years; he is currently in a Spanish prison.

85. Raquel Aldana, "Steps Closer to Justice for Past Crimes in Chile and Argentina: A Story of Judicial Boldness," The Frederick K. Cox International Law Center War

Crimes Research Portal, November 17, 2004 at http://law.case.edu/war-crimes-Research-Portal/instant_analysis.asp?id=12 (accessed November 5, 2005); Roht-Arriaza, *The Pinochet Effect*, 102–8; Barahona de Brito, "Truth, Justice, Memory," 138–39; María José Guembe interview, Buenos Aires, December 12, 2002.

86. Aldana, "Steps Closer"; Roht-Arriaza, *The Pinochet Effect*, 102–8.

87. See CELS, *Informe anual 2001*; CELS, *Informe anual 2002*; Roht-Arriaza, *The Pinochet Effect*, 113–16. For a summary, see Abregú, "Human Rights after the Dictatorship." Examples of international NGO aid to the Argentine human rights movement in this quest include: *Argentina: Amicus Curiae Brief on the Incompatibility with International Law of the Full Stop and Due Obedience Laws Presented by the International Commission of Jurists, Amnesty International and Human Rights Watch before the National Chamber for Federal Criminal and Correctional Matters of the Republic of Argentina* (June 2001); and Amnesty International, *Argentina: Legal Memorandum, the Full Stop and Due Obedience Laws: Submitted by Amnesty International and the International Commission of Jurists* (December 2003).

88. Kaiser, "Outing Torturers."

89. CELS, *Informe anual 1998*, 17–23; CELS, *Informe anual 2000*, 17–33; CELS, *Informe anual 2002*, 12–14; J. Patrice McSherry, "Military Rumblings in Argentina," *NACLA Report on the Americas* 34, no. 1 (July–August 2000): 16–17.

90. Abregú, "Human Rights after the Dictatorship." The CELS annual reports from 1996 to the present reflect the organization's emphasis on enforcement of human rights as defined in Argentine law.

91. The Argentine economy shrank by 20 percent between 1999 and 2002; the official unemployment rate was 24 percent at the end of 2002, although the real rate was considerably higher. *Buenos Aires Herald*, December 3, 2002; Romero, *A History of Argentina*, 333–49; Andrés Gaudin, "Thirteen Days That Shook Argentina—And What Now?" *NACLA Report on the Americas* 35, no. 5 (March–April 2002): 6–9.

92. Gaudin, "Thirteen Days," 5.

93. Andrés Gaudin, "The Kirchner Factor," *NACLA Report on the Americas* 38, no. 4 (January–February 2005): 16–18; Gaudin, "Thirteen Days." In November and December 2002, the author of this book spoke with dozens of Argentines, nearly all of whom expressed pessimism that the forthcoming election would yield positive results.

94. *NACLA Report on the Americas* 37, no. 1 (July–August 2003): 2–5; Gaudin, "The Kirchner Factor." Additional information on Kirchner's election and subsequent actions is gleaned from a variety of daily press and websites.

95. Roht-Arriaza, *The Pinochet Effect*, 116–17. A federal judge ruled in March 2004 that Menem's pardons were unconstitutional. *Los Angeles Times*, March 20, 2004.

96. *NACLA Report on the Americas* 37, no. 6 (May–June 2004): 44–45; *Los Angeles Times*, March 25, 2004.

97. CELS, "24 de marzo de 2004 Verdad, Justicia y Memoria," at www.cels.org.ar (accessed January 6, 2005); *Página 12*, June 16, 2005.

98. *La Nación*, June 16, 2005.

CHAPTER SIX

~

Chile: Impunity, Truth, and Justice in a Protected Democracy

The expression "human rights violations" is a euphemistic and soothing formulation. In reality they were extremely grave crimes, committed in the name of the State and with its authorization: arbitrary detentions, deportations and disappearances of persons, torture and murder ordered by the State.

—Helmut Frenz, Lutheran bishop of Chile[1]

What "human rights" were trampled during my government? None!

—General Augusto C. Pinochet[2]

Following Pinochet's defeat in the October 1988 plebiscite, when voters rejected an eight-year extension of his rule, the Chilean political process unfolded as dictated by the 1980 constitution's provisional articles. General elections were held in December 1989, fourteen months later. The Concertación de Partidos por la Democracia (Coalition of Parties for Democracy), the successor to the broad center-left coalition that defeated the dictator in the plebiscite, won the presidency and a majority in the Chamber of Deputies while losing the Senate. Christian Democratic President Patricio Aylwin and the new Congress were inaugurated on March 11, 1990, sixteen and a half years to the day after the overthrow of Chilean democracy.[3]

The Politics of Transitional Justice

As in Argentina and other countries undergoing transitions from repressive to democratic government, the constellation of national and international political forces shaped the course of transitional justice in postdictatorial Chile. One of the two main forces within the Chilean polity that favored uncovering the truth about human rights violations and bringing the perpetrators to justice was the Concertación. The coalition's primary components were the Christian Democrats, still Chile's largest party, and the Socialists, now divided between the original Socialist Party and the new Partido por la Democracia (Party for Democracy, PPD). As a result of the fierce persecution they had endured and the experience of exile in both socialist and social democratic countries, the Socialists of both parties had moderated their positions on redistributive issues and had made the consolidation of democracy their top priority; in the popular lexicon, they had been "renovated." The Concertación presented a united front on human rights issues where possible, but, given the extreme repression they had suffered following September 11, 1973, the Socialists and the PPD were firmer in their support of pursuing justice than were many Christian Democrats. Outside the Concertación, the Communist Party, its influence greatly diminished since 1973, also pushed to hold the military accountable for its actions.[4]

The other major force advocating truth and justice was the strong human rights movement that had developed during the dictatorship, supported by the international human rights lobby. As in Argentina, once the common enemy was out of office, the movement often split on strategy and tactics, with the groups composed of victims' families, particularly the Group of Families of the Detained Disappeared (AFDD) consistently taking a harder line than most other organizations. Nonetheless, the human rights movement proved very influential, and its close ties with the Concertación gave it more leverage in the politics of transitional justice than its Argentine counterpart was able to exercise.[5]

In addition to the domestic pressures for truth and justice, the international human rights organizations, both intergovernmental and NGOs, played a major role in shaping transitional justice in Chile. At the dictatorship's end, the international human rights regime had evolved well beyond what it had been when the military seized power in 1973. The Cold War was ending, and the U.S. government had no stake in supporting state terrorist governments in Latin America or in protecting their leaders from prosecution. New treaties had been adopted on torture and disappearance—both reflecting the impact of the Chilean and Argentine experience on the international community—and a number of other human rights had been enshrined in conventions. Both the UN and OAS monitoring systems had been strengthened and had become more active. The Inter-American Court of Human Rights had been functioning since 1980, and Human Rights Watch and its Americas Watch branch had enhanced the NGO human rights monitoring capability. Yet international human rights had not yet evolved to the stage of enforcement. This development would occur in the 1990s, when Chile and Argentina would be at the forefront of the process of addressing the legacies of state terrorism.[6]

The most potent opposition to investigations and prosecutions of human rights violators was the military, still led by Pinochet, who, before surrendering the presidency, extended his tenure as army commander for another eight years. Pinochet had articulated his formula for achieving reconciliation in a 1989 interview: "Do you know how to put out fires? It's never done piece by piece. You take a bucket of cold water, throw it on, and it's all over."[7] In addition, most of the political right favored burying the past. The hard right Unión Democrática Independiente (Independent Democratic Union, UDI) and the more moderate Renovación Nacional (National Renovation, RN) controlled the Senate by virtue of nine appointed senators and an electoral system that favored the right, giving them veto power over any legislation designed to promote a reckoning with past human rights violations. In addition to the power of the military and the right parties, the cause of impunity enjoyed the support of much of the sizable minority of Chile's population who remained loyal to Pinochet. Some within this bloc did not oppose dealing with human rights issues, but a vociferous element of the right shared the military's view that a few thousand casualties was a small price to pay for victory in the "war" against the Marxists.[8]

A Shield of Impunity

In charting a course through the multifaceted and complex questions of transitional justice, Aylwin and his allies had ample precedent on which to draw. In contrast to President Raúl Alfonsín and his administration, who six years earlier had had to invent the entire process, Aylwin had the benefit of the Argentine experience as well as the transitions in Brazil, Uruguay, and countries beyond Latin America. But the contrast with Argentina could hardly have been greater. Across the Andes, the armed forces had surrendered power in disgrace after losing legitimacy, both as a governing body and as a fighting force. After the Falklands fiasco and in the midst of an economic crisis, they had covered themselves with the fig leaf of a decreed amnesty and their "Final Document" justifying the dirty war and had retreated to the barracks, leaving the initiative to the Alfonsín government. In Chile, the challenge was to pursue justice within a political system that had been constructed to guarantee military impunity. Aylwin took office in the "protected democracy" that Pinochet had fashioned, with the ex-dictator continuing as commander of the army, and against the backdrop of a military proud of both saving Chile from Marxism and of constructing an economy widely considered the model for Latin America. Chile's pacted transition offered far fewer possibilities of achieving justice than had Argentina's early years of democracy.

Beginning with the March 1978 amnesty, Pinochet had been constructing a shield of impunity for the military, the police, and himself. His 1980 constitution and numerous laws added layers of protection against investigation and prosecution. The key elements in this suit of armor were a number of "authoritarian enclaves" in the constitution, laws, and the electoral code.[9] These provisions involved the military directly in governance, thus formalizing its tutelary role. They also gave important powers of appointment to the Supreme Court, whose members Pinochet had selected, and they overrepresented the right in Congress. The new political system, moreover, had been skillfully designed to prevent change in the constitution, the laws, and the institutions left by the dictatorship.

Among the authoritarian enclaves was the National Security Council. Its role was to advise the president on matters of security—an elastic definition that could include almost any issue. Its eight members included the three military commanders, the head of the Carabineros, and two others who by virtue of the appointment process were guaranteed to be pro-Pinochet. Another key authoritarian enclave was the Constitutional Tribunal, whose mandate was to assure the constitutionality of all bills introduced in Congress. It had the power to make binding and unappealable decisions on the constitutionality of bills at any stage of the legislative process. Consisting of three members appointed by the Supreme Court, two by the National Security Council, one by the Senate, and only one by the president, this body was certain to veto any legislation that might threaten the shield of impunity.[10]

The legislative branch of government was skewed in favor of the right, and hence impunity, by the composition of the Senate and by the electoral system devised by Pinochet's advisers. Nine of the Senate's forty-seven members were "designated," meaning appointed directly or indirectly by Pinochet for eight-year terms. These included former commanders of the army, navy, air force, and Carabineros and three named by the Supreme Court, whose members Pinochet had appointed.[11] The electoral code strongly overrepresented rural districts, where large landowners had regained control after restoration of the estates dismantled by Frei's and Allende's agrarian reforms. In addition, the d'Hondt electoral system of two-seat districts overrepresented the right and made it difficult for the Concertación to win both seats even in heavily working-class districts.[12]

Thus the protected democracy designed by Pinochet's advisers prevented the center-left coalition that elected Aylwin, the next three presidents of Chile, and consistent majorities in the Chamber of Deputies from undoing the key undemocratic features of the political system. The designated senators, the d'Hondt electoral method, and rural overrepresentation assured a right-wing majority in the Senate capable of vetoing any bill passed by the Chamber of Deputies. Rightist veto power was further anchored in the constitution's requirement of a two-thirds vote of the full membership of both houses for constitutional amendments and four-sevenths to modify "organic constitutional laws," which regulated key institutions such as the armed forces and the electoral system. The electoral system and the legislative structure bequeathed by Pinochet made it impossible to abolish the designated senators, reform the electoral or military code, dismantle the authoritarian security and press laws the regime had left in place, or enact any laws impinging on military impunity, including repeal of the 1978 amnesty law, without the unlikely collaboration of rightist legislators. Most of the authoritarian enclaves were finally eliminated through constitutional amendments in 2005, but the electoral code remained.[13]

Under the constitution and the Organic Constitutional Law of the Armed Forces, the Chilean military was virtually autonomous—a military state within the state. It was the guarantor of the "institutional order of the Republic." The only presidential leverage over the makeup of the military hierarchy was the power to appoint the army, navy, air force, and Carabineros commanders from a slate of the five most senior officers in each branch, and the power to approve or deny promotions. Having made the appointments, the president could not remove the commanders during their four-year terms until the constitutional reform of 2005. Over the years, selecting commanders with little or no "blood on their hands" and blocking promotions of some of the worst repressors would prove to be a useful tool for inducing gradual change in the military institutions. The military budget was only partially government controlled, and the inner workings of the military, such as education and training, promotions below the highest ranks, and justice, were well insulated against civilian intrusion. Overall, in the early years of the transition, the military appeared to exercise more control over government than government exercised over the military.[14]

After losing the October 1988 plebiscite, Pinochet continued as president, with full dictatorial powers intact, until Aylwin's inauguration in March 1990. Keenly aware of the fate of Argentina's military in the early Alfonsín years, Pinochet used these seventeen months to issue decree laws known as the *leyes de amarre* (tie-up laws), designed to further buttress his and the military's impunity and to restrict the powers of the civilian government that would succeed him. Among these was the Organic Constitutional Law of the Armed Forces, issued the month before Aylwin's inauguration. In addition, the dictator shuffled the corps of army generals to place die-hard loyalists in the most powerful positions.[15]

Pinochet also strengthened his hold on the Supreme Court by offering retirement bonuses to the eleven justices over seventy-five years of age; seven accepted and were replaced by "unconditionals" upon whom he could rely to uphold the amnesty law and to limit or block prosecutions for crimes committed after March 1978—the period not covered by the amnesty. He also incorporated at least two thousand CNI personnel into army intelligence, placing them directly under his command: this enhanced the powers of intimidation that he would constantly use and placed the operatives of state terrorism under the protection of military justice. In addition, the CNI's files were sanitized or destroyed and its detention sites remodeled or, in the case of Villa Grimaldi, bulldozed. Another *ley de amarre* prevented the removal of Pinochet's appointees in government service.[16]

Having fine-tuned the political system in his last months in office, Pinochet was satisfied that everything was "tied up." President Aylwin and the new Congress inherited a set of institutions that, from early in his dictatorship, Pinochet had deemed the appropriate model for Chile—a "protected democracy" designed to prevent the return of leftists to power, to protect the free market economy, and to guarantee military impunity. In the view of some, this amounted to "Pinochet without Pinochet."[17]

While tying up the loose ends, Pinochet also agreed to the demands of the center and left parties for some modifications of his extremely authoritarian 1980 constitution—changes that he believed would not affect his and the military's impunity. RN, the more moderate right wing party, likewise supported modification or elimination of some of the constitution's most antidemocratic features in order to make the political system more workable and, in a period of democratic renewal throughout Latin America, to end Chile's status as a pariah state. Moreover, since amendments would have to be approved in a plebiscite conducted under the new democratic rules, with an electoral registry and freedom to campaign, Pinochet's opposition, by the act of voting, would be conceding the constitution's legitimacy for a second time.[18] Thus, following multilateral negotiations, fifty-four constitutional amendments were approved in a July 1989 plebiscite. Most attention focused on political reforms such as reducing presidential power, easing restrictions on political parties, and defining the makeup of Congress and electoral districts. Little noticed at the time, an amendment to article 5 inserted international human rights instruments into the constitution by expanding the rights that the state was obligated to "respect and promote," from those guaranteed by the original 1980 constitution to those included in the international treaties ratified by Chile. This amendment would become important a few years later.[19]

Justice versus Impunity, 1990–1998

The president of the Chamber of Deputies' Human Rights Committee aptly described the context of transitional justice in Chile: "The great challenge that the government faces is to make [the quest for] truth, justice, and liberty compatible with democratic stability."[20] On one hand, the Concertación platform for the 1989 election had called for justice for victims of human rights violations, to be accomplished by repealing the 1978 amnesty law and prosecuting the repressors. On the other, in a speech to his military colleagues four months before the election, Pinochet issued a list of nine demands upon the government, whatever its makeup, that would succeed him. Two of these directly conflicted with the Concertación plan for justice: "respect the jurisdiction of military justice," and "maintain the amnesty law in full force."[21] So were drawn the battle lines over the legacies of state terrorism in Chile.

In his first speech to Congress, Aylwin made "clarifying the truth and doing justice in human rights matters" his top priorities.[22] The end of the dictatorship raised the expectations of surviving victims, families of the murdered and disappeared, and the human rights movement for achieving justice. Discoveries and exhumations of mass graves containing bodies of the disappeared, which began just after Aylwin's inauguration, triggered memory and spurred calls for action. Yet Aylwin was hemmed in by the amnesty law, Pinochet's political system, and the practical necessity of not overly provoking the military. Thus, in the same speech, the president recognized the need to balance the military's demands for impunity with expectations for justice: "The moral conscience of the nation requires that the truth be revealed [and] justice be done to the extent possible (*en la medida de lo posible*)—reconciling the virtue of justice with the virtue of prudence."[23]

In practical terms, the balance between justice and prudence meant a tacit recognition that the 1978 amnesty law was untouchable. Of all the initiatives capable of provoking a military reaction, a push to repeal the amnesty, with the attendant congressional debate, media coverage, and the possibility of popular mobilization that could spin out of control, would be the most dangerous to the survival of civilian government. Thus, despite the campaign pledge to attempt to repeal the amnesty law, the administration introduced no bill to do so and discouraged its congressional allies from raising the issue. None of the few amnesty repeal bills introduced in the Concertación-controlled Chamber of Deputies reached the Senate. Rightist pressure to extend the amnesty to Pinochet's last day in office, however, likewise failed.[24]

Having bowed to Pinochet's threats and to political reality, the Aylwin administration worked vigorously on human rights in several ways: reshaping Chileans' collective memory through symbolic actions and commemoration, establishing the truth about human rights violations during the dictatorship, offering reparations for victims and their families, ratifying additional international human rights treaties, pursuing measures to prevent future human rights violations, and prosecuting a few high-profile human rights crimes not covered by the amnesty. The president moved quickly on this agenda because, in his words, "the spiritual health of Chile requires us . . . to accomplish in a reasonable period these tasks of moral healing."[25]

Early in his term, Aylwin engaged heavily in symbolic acts, commemoration, and construction of memory to counter the dictatorship's version of the truth concerning sixteen and a half years of national history. He met with the human rights organizations to show his support. The day after his formal swearing in, he held a second, mass inauguration before seventy thousand people at the National Stadium, symbolically reclaiming the space where thousands had been held, and many tortured and executed, following the coup. Fifteen women performed the *cueca sola*, a version of the national dance done by the woman without her partner, which had developed during the dictatorship as a form of protest; each held a photograph of her absent loved one. The names of hundreds of disappeared persons appeared on the scoreboard. In June, Aylwin dispatched six of his cabinet ministers to the memorial service held for nineteen disappeared persons found in a mass grave near the former prison camp at Pisagua. Pisagua stood out among the many mass graves discovered because the desert climate had partially mummified the victims: the blindfolds and ropes used to bind their hands had survived since 1973, as had the expressions of horror on their faces that were clearly distinguishable in the images disseminated by the media.[26]

On September 4, 1990, exactly twenty years after his election as president, Salvador Allende was given the public funeral he had been denied in 1973. His body was exhumed from the family plot in Viña del Mar, where it had been hastily buried the day after his death, and taken to Santiago for the honors. Following mass in the Santiago Cathedral, it was interred in the capital's General Cemetery before a huge crowd. Because the military objected to rendering the honors required at state funerals, Allende's funeral was not officially designated as such; nonetheless, the level of protocol, Aylwin's speech, and the attendance of the entire cabinet made it clear that the ceremony was designed symbolically to give Allende his rightful place in national history alongside the country's other presidents, all of whom, with one exception, are buried in the venerable cemetery.[27] This gesture also proclaimed that the period of Allende's government was something other than the rule of extremists and criminals, as portrayed throughout the dictatorship.

Two other important projects of commemoration were initiated in 1990: a memorial wall inside the General Cemetery listing all known victims of murder and disappearance, finished in 1994, and a "peace park" on the site of the bulldozed Villa Grimaldi, which was not completed until 1997.[28]

Symbolic politics pitted Aylwin directly against Pinochet. In a 1990 speech on the birthday of independence leader Bernardo O'Higgins, Aylwin reminded the country that at a difficult point in the fledgling republic's history, O'Higgins had voluntarily relinquished his title and powers of "Supreme Director of the Nation" and had gone into exile in order to prevent further internal conflict—unsubtly suggesting that Pinochet emulate the independence hero's example at a similarly delicate point in Chile's history. At the same time, without the government's knowledge or authorization, Pinochet proclaimed the "Month of the Army" in order to further ingrain the message that the military had saved Chile in 1973. The Month of the Army extended from August 20, O'Higgins's birthday, through the September 18 anniversary of independence, and culminated on September 19, the traditional "Day of the Army." Pinochet clearly won this confrontation of symbolic politics.[29]

Six weeks after taking office, Aylwin created by decree the Comisión Nacional de Verdad y Reconciliación (National Commission on Truth and Reconciliation). Given the tense political climate and Pinochet's explicit warnings not to investigate the past, this was an audacious step. The course of transitional justice in neighboring countries, moreover, suggested that digging up the past might only result in frustration. In Brazil, where the military controlled the transition, no official truth commission was established, although a private church-supported study documented extensive use of torture under military rule. In Uruguay, the truth commission established to examine the

1973–1984 dictatorship documented 164 disappearances; however, succumbing to intense military and political pressure, the commission decided that it was unable to establish that disappearance was official policy—a great disappointment to human rights advocates. And as we have seen, the Argentine truth commission encountered strong military resistance. Moreover, by the time Aylwin created the Chilean commission, a resurgent military had forced the reversal of the justice that had been accomplished in Argentina.[30]

Conditions in Chile, nonetheless, demanded a truth commission. There was a large and vigorous human rights movement and a government dominated by enemies of the past regime, many of whom had experienced detention, torture, and/or exile. The Concertación campaign platform called for a truth commission, among its varied demands regarding human rights. The repression of the early postcoup months had been very public, and the work of the DINA and the CNI was well known, thanks largely to publications of the human rights organizations, even if details remained secret. Discoveries and exhumations of mass graves intensified the pressure to launch the search for truth. "Only on a foundation of truth," said Aylwin in his decree establishing the truth commission, "will it be possible to meet the basic demands of justice and create the necessary conditions for achieving true national reconciliation. Only the knowledge of the truth will restore the dignity of the victims in the public mind, allow their relatives and mourners to honor them fittingly, and in some measure make it possible to make amends for the damage done."[31]

Aylwin borrowed liberally from the Argentine model. However, given the different political situation in Chile, he had to carefully assemble a commission that would reflect the balance that he sought between justice and governability and would be credible to Chile's strong pro-Pinochet minority. To head the eight-person commission, he selected the distinguished jurist and former senator and ambassador Raúl Rettig, whose name is often used to identify the commission and its report. The remaining seven were divided between supporters and opponents of the former dictatorship: The two human rights activists were moderates within the movement, as were the Pinochet supporters, who included one member who had served the regime on the Supreme Court and another in the cabinet. The Chilean and Argentine truth commissions accurately reflected the differences between the transitions in the two countries. With the military in retreat in Argentina, President Alfonsín could and did appoint individuals committed a priori to holding the military accountable for its alleged crimes. In Chile, where the military was powerful and triumphant, the truth commission had to have the appearance of independence and detachment.[32]

Like Argentina's CONADEP, the Rettig Commission had a limited mandate. Its charge was to investigate deaths and disappearances but not arbitrary detention, torture not resulting in death, rape, and other violations. Like CONADEP, the Rettig Commission lacked subpoena power. It was to identify victims by name and, in a concession to the military, was to include victims of violence against the Pinochet government. It was not to divulge the names of perpetrators of the violations but was required to submit relevant information about crimes to the courts. Finally, the commission was charged with recommending measures of reparation and means of preventing human rights violations in the future.

The Rettig Commission operated under severe constraints of time and resources. Its investigative staff consisted of seventeen lawyers, each with a law student assistant, and six social workers. It was initially given six months to complete its task, and then a three-month extension. The commission received testimony at its Santiago headquarters, provincial government offices, and embassies and consulates abroad. The human rights organizations, particularly the Catholic Church's Vicaría de la Solidaridad, supplied voluminous information, but the commission reported minimal cooperation from the military, which routinely denied possessing requested material or claimed institutional privilege.[33]

The Rettig Commission submitted its report to President Aylwin on February 8, 1991. From the 3,877 testimonies received, the commission meticulously documented 1,068 deaths and 957 disappearances caused by government agents "or persons at their service." In addition, it established 164 deaths due to "political violence," which included military, police, and civilians killed by civilians in the postcoup violence; regime opponents killed in the 1982–1986 protests; and victims of left terrorism in the 1980s. It rejected 508 cases that did not fit within its mandate—for example, people tortured but not killed—and 449 in which only a name was provided. It left 641 other cases unresolved owing to lack of time or evidence. The report made it clear that, owing to limited time, resources, and cooperation, it had been unable to identify all mortal victims of human rights violations between 1973 and 1990.[34]

The Rettig Report established both global and individual truth: beyond enumerating victims of human rights violations, it offered a sober and evenhanded interpretation of the circumstances leading to the coup and the dictatorship. It argued, contrary to the military view, that Chile had not been at war after September 11, 1973, and that the vast majority of victims were unarmed civilians, not dangerous armed guerrillas. It explained how a military uprising designed to overthrow a president became a regime of state terrorism—without using that terminology. The report described the workings of the DINA and its secret detention centers and discussed torture, naming some of the common techniques used. In a section that contrasted with the report's general clinical tone, it reproduced emotional quotations from the testimonies it received.[35]

Signed by all eight commission members with their divergent political views, the Rettig Report established a compelling record of Chile's human rights crisis. Despite its limitations, the report produced, for the first time, substantive evidence of the breadth and depth of state terrorism and an alternate truth that contested the military version of Chilean history between 1973 and 1990. Aylwin made the report public in a March 4, 1991, televised address. He claimed that "no one, in good faith, can reject it" and asked victims and their families to forgive the repressors and for the military to "make some gesture of recognition of the pain caused and collaborate in lessening it."[36]

The military promptly rejected both the Rettig Report and Aylwin's call for reconciliation. The army, navy, air force, and Carabineros commanders delivered their separate responses on March 27 in a setting designed to intimidate: the National Security Council. While all denounced the commission's conclusions, Pinochet's response was particularly vitriolic. He labeled the report "unilateral truth," repeated the military's version of a real and legitimate war against Marxism, and refused to acknowledge any excesses, much less a deliberate policy of state terrorism. The armed forces and police, declared Pinochet, "completed their mission, defeating the totalitarian threat. . . . The Chilean army certainly sees no reason to ask pardon from anyone for having taken part in this patriotic effort." Finally, Pinochet repeated his threat against prosecutions of military personnel: "The army of Chile solemnly declares that it will not accept being placed before the citizenry in the seat of the accused for having saved the liberty and sovereignty of the fatherland."[37]

The Rettig Report also faulted the judiciary for failing to prevent human rights violations during the dictatorship: "The judiciary's inability to halt the grave human rights violations in Chile was partly due to serious shortcomings in the legal system as well as to the weakness and lack of vigor on the part of many judges in fully carrying out their obligation to assure that the essential rights of persons are truly respected."[38] The Supreme Court responded, enumerating its attempts to improve efficiency in the processing of writs of habeas corpus and explaining the limitations on its ability to influence the military government. The commission, argued the justices, exceeded its mandate and "made an impassioned, rash, and tendentious judgment of the judiciary, based on shoddy investigation and probable political prejudice, which ends up assigning the judges a degree of responsibility almost equal to that of the perpetrators of the human rights abuses themselves."³⁹

Rightist political groups uniformly criticized the report. While the human rights movement in general received it favorably, President Sola Sierra of the AFDD fired back at both Aylwin and Pinochet: "No one has asked us to pardon them, nor do we want them to ask us to pardon them." Hugo Cárcamo, president of the Group of Families of the Executed for Political Reasons (AFEP), labeled the report a "product of a negotiation with the right and military sectors."⁴⁰

After a month in which the Rettig Report dominated the news, Jaime Guzmán, the *gremialist* leader, architect of the 1980 constitution, icon of the Pinochet regime, and current senator, was assassinated by the Communist-affiliated Manuel Rodríguez Patriotic Front (FPMR). Following a series of attacks on military regime figures and bank robberies by leftist groups, this event abruptly altered the political dynamic and the course of transitional justice. The resurrected theme of leftist terrorism replaced human rights violations in the headlines and on television news, placing Aylwin and the human rights movement on the defensive before the undisguised rage of Pinochet and the right. In order to reduce the friction with his adversaries, the president canceled a national tour by cabinet ministers and Rettig Commission members that was designed to publicize the report. In the words of rightist politician Andrés Allamand, "The killing of Jaime Guzmán has buried the Rettig report."⁴¹ Allamand was correct: a poll conducted three months after the assassination found that only 3.4 percent of Chileans believed that resolving human rights issues should be the government's top priority.⁴² The report thus did not have the impact on Chilean society that *Nunca más* had made on Argentina; rather, the murder set back the cause of justice as the La Tablada attack had done in Argentina.

The Rettig Report made a number of recommendations for reparations and for preventing human rights violations in the future. Most of its proposals for prevention involved reforming the judiciary and bringing the military under civilian control. Given the right's veto power in the Senate and its heightened intransigence following the Guzmán assassination, the more ambitious proposals were doomed to failure. Some of the less controversial recommendations were implemented, however, particularly those that the right thought would contribute to closure of the human rights issue. These included ratification of the American Convention on Human Rights and recognition of the Inter-American Court of Human Rights' jurisdiction in cases originating in Chile. These international instruments would apply from the time of their ratification, not retroactively.⁴³

As recommended by the Rettig Commission, Congress established the Corporación Nacional para la Reparación y Reconciliación (National Corporation for Reparation and Reconciliation) in January 1992. The corporation was charged with a number of tasks, among them, devising educational policies to develop a culture of human rights in Chile. It also administered material compensation to surviving family members of the executed and detained disappeared. Pensions for sole survivors were set at approximately 380 U.S. dollars per month, slightly higher than the official minimum wage, while multiple survivors divided a larger check, and all received health benefits. Victims' children received generous educational benefits and exemption from mandatory military service. In 1997, nearly five thousand Chileans were receiving compensation at a cost to the state of nearly sixteen million dollars annually. To the recipients, this reparation was more than money; in the words of a victim's daughter, "Every time a check arrives, it's a recognition of the crime."[44]

The corporation also pursued the Rettig Commission's unfinished work. It examined the commission's 641 unresolved cases and received new testimony about deaths and disappearances under the dictatorship during a 180-day period. In its 1996 final report, the corporation added 776 individuals killed and 123 disappeared to the Rettig Report's figures, making the official toll 3,197, of whom 2,774 were victims of state terrorism.[45]

Exiles and public employees who were purged following the coup also received Aylwin's attention. Some exiles had already returned home, particularly after 1984 when the prohibition against return was relaxed, but the great majority of the two hundred thousand Chileans forced to flee the dictatorship were still abroad when Aylwin assumed the presidency. Congress quickly passed laws validating degrees and professional certificates earned abroad and exempting US$25,000 of returning exiles' property from customs duties. The Oficina Nacional de Retorno (National Return Office) opened in August 1990 and closed four years later after serving fifty-six thousand persons. It functioned primarily as a referral agency, matching returnees' needs with services offered by NGOs. By a 1993 law, the fifty-eight thousand former public employees fired by the dictatorship received pensions.[46]

Another form of redress for the past was the release of political prisoners held by the dictatorship under Pinochet's state security, weapons control, and antiterrorism laws. When Aylwin took office, there were some four hundred incarcerated political prisoners and over a thousand facing charges. Owing to provisions in the constitution and the antiterrorism laws, most were ineligible for pardons or were under the jurisdiction of military justice. Aylwin pardoned several prisoners the day after his inauguration, but a reaction from the right slowed this approach. The Concertación then negotiated an agreement with RN that broadened the president's authority to pardon and expedited processing of the cases. Nonetheless, it took over four years, into the next presidential term, for the prisons to be cleared of persons who had actively and sometimes violently fought against the dictatorship.[47]

From the outset, it was clear that the quest for justice in the courts would be difficult. Pinochet's last-minute packing of the Supreme Court with hardliners stiffened judicial resistance to hearing human rights cases. Most judges continued acting as they had under the dictatorship, dismissing cases or forwarding them to military courts where they were closed. Shortly after Aylwin's inauguration, the Supreme Court unanimously upheld the amnesty law and went further, ruling that the amnesty prevented not only prosecution but also investigation of cases brought to civilian courts.[48]

Despite this posture, Aylwin pressed for investigations based on his conviction that national reconciliation required, at a minimum, the complete truth—particularly given the obstacles to justice. Upon releasing the Rettig Report, he urged the Supreme Court, despite the amnesty law, to investigate the cases the commission had forwarded, as well as the hundreds of cases already brought by individuals and human rights organizations. The government argued that the amnesty did not bar investigations, because until the body is found the crime is ongoing. Only after the crime is resolved can the perpetrator be amnestied. "In my view," Aylwin wrote, expounding what came to be called the Aylwin Doctrine, "the amnesty in force, which the Government respects, cannot be an obstacle to the realization of a judicial investigation and the determination of responsibilities, especially in the cases of disappeared persons."[49] At the end of 1992, the Supreme Court accepted Aylwin's lawyers' arguments; within a year, several hundred investigations were under way, and the frequency with which officers were summoned to testify became a major source of tension between civil and military authorities.[50]

Aylwin did not hesitate to push the prosecution of two high-profile cases not covered by the amnesty and which were unlikely to cause a serious military reaction. One was the highly publicized 1985 *degollados* case in which fifteen Carabineros and a civilian were accused of slashing the throats of three Communists and leaving the bodies along a rural road near Santiago. All were found guilty and were sentenced in 1994, after the end of Aylwin's term. The courts also revived the long-dormant prosecution of former DINA commander Manuel Contreras and subcommander Pedro Espinoza for the 1976 murder of Orlando Letelier and Ronni Moffitt in Washington, D.C.—a case that Pinochet had specifically exempted from the amnesty law in order to minimize friction with President Jimmy Carter. Contreras and Espinoza were convicted in November 1993, and the Supreme Court upheld the conviction in May 1995; they drew light sentences of seven and six years, respectively.[51]

While Aylwin labored to bring out the truth, establish reparations, and pursue justice "to the extent possible," Pinochet and the military worked to minimize investigations and deflect prosecutions of nonamnestied crimes. The soft approach to preserving impunity involved keeping intact the version of history that the dictatorship had implanted through the power of its propaganda machine, absolute control of the media and school curricula, and fear. In this they were abetted by restrictive press laws carried over from the dictatorship and a degree of self-censorship within the mass media, a habit learned under Pinochet that proved difficult to break. The "burial" of the Rettig Report following the Guzmán assassination facilitated the military's task. It was not until 1993, the twentieth anniversary of the coup, that the electronic and print media for the first time explored September 11 in depth; the inquiry, however, did not extend beyond that fateful day to the dictatorship itself.[52]

Pinochet and the military constantly defended their legacy, reminding Chileans that they were the winners in a real war, that they had saved the country from Marxism, and that they were proud of their accomplishments. Any account of the military's role between 1973 and 1990 that differed from theirs was simply a plot to tarnish the prestige of the armed forces. Future army commander Ricardo Izurieta, for example, said in a speech, "Many of those who censure us . . . today can live peacefully in the country and fight for the perfection of democracy. This is thanks to the fact that those men at arms fought, exercised vigilance, ran risks, and suffered losses, which those that now benefit from our sacrifice never felt or suffered."[53]

The new "Month of the Army" was an integral part of the effort to preserve the military version of truth. September 11 was code for the country's salvation: plazas and streets carried that name, including a major section of the primary artery connecting downtown Santiago with the wealthy "barrio alto." September 11 was a national holiday celebrating Chile's "second national independence"—its liberation from the Marxists—replete with military ceremonies that far overshadowed the Socialist Party's annual pilgrimage to the tomb of their *compañero* Salvador Allende who died that day in 1973. Almost every September 11 produced casualties when protesters clashed with police. The Concertación's repeated legislative efforts to abolish the September 11 holiday failed.[54]

Another means of maintaining impunity was to constantly remind Chileans that Aylwin and the Concertación served at Pinochet's pleasure.

Beginning with Aylwin's inauguration, when a resplendently uniformed, glowering Pinochet draped the presidential sash over Aylwin's shoulders in a ceremony designed to humiliate the new president, the general constantly showed his contempt for civilian government. He ignored his nominal superior, the minister of defense, making decisions affecting the army—and hence the country—on his own. He snubbed Aylwin, usually sending the head of his Advisory Committee, composed of ranking hard-liners, to deliver his messages to the commander in chief. As a daily reminder of his power, Pinochet continued to travel from home to office to weekend retreat as he had as president—in a motorcade, much more impressive than Aylwin's, consisting of several armored Mercedes-Benzes escorted by military vehicles and a helicopter, accompanied by his medical doctor and police who stopped traffic with sirens and flashing lights so that he could traverse the capital at eighty kilometers per hour. This pattern of behavior sent the unsubtle message that the limited democracy he had bequeathed was a gift that he could take back at any time.[55]

Pinochet had broadcast his understanding of the unwritten terms of the transition in October 1989, prior to Aylwin's election: "The day they touch one of my men, the rule of law [*estado de derecho*] will be over."[56] He frequently reminded his foes of this position with public warnings and threats, sometimes delivered personally and often through retired officers. He publicly advised Aylwin against establishing a truth commission, and after its creation, he warned of its potential consequences on more than one occasion. On the coup anniversary in 1990, Pinochet declared that if the circumstances of 1973 should be repeated, the army "would have not a moment of doubt in acting as before."[57] Warnings also came in nonverbal form, including symbolic actions and photographs in the press showing a stern, threatening, uniformed Pinochet.

When the government crossed the behavioral line that Pinochet had drawn, he went further. On December 19, 1990, he showed his displeasure with the administration's insistence on resolving human rights issues and with a congressional investigation into a financial scandal involving his son by putting the army on a nationwide alert—without informing the minister of defense. Coming just sixteen days after the fourth *carapintada* revolt across the Andes, this maneuver, which the general called a readiness exercise, sparked rumors of a coup and quickly led Congress to drop the offending investigation.[58]

The tensest moment of Aylwin's administration occurred while the president was on a state visit to Europe. Civil-military relations had become tense over alleged government interference in military matters and over human rights issues. Then, on May 28, 1993, after newspaper headlines announced the reopening of the investigation into his son's financial dealings and the subpoenaing of eight generals to testify in human rights cases, Pinochet produced a graphic reminder of September 11, 1973. He assembled all but two of the army's generals at military headquarters across the street from the presidential palace, deployed heavily armed troops in battle camouflage around the building, and put the army on a state of alert. He demanded that the investigation of his son be dropped and that investigations of human rights violations be expedited and conducted discreetly—a de facto *punto final* or full stop law.[59]

This event, known as the *boinazo* for the black berets (*boínas*) of the deployed commandos, was the breaking point for the president. The most aggressive of Pinochet's continuing demonstrations of who held the real power in Chile, the *boinazo* finally convinced Aylwin that prolonging the ongoing human rights investigations posed a grave threat to the country's fragile transition. The fate of the nearly twelve hundred disappeared persons whose remains had not been found was a particularly thorny issue. Rather than a statute of limitations, as enacted in Argentina's *punto final* law, the president submitted a bill in August 1993 to expedite judicial investigations and guarantee the anonymity of those charged with human rights crimes; once the facts were established, the case would be closed and the perpetrators amnestied. The families of the disappeared would receive the knowledge of the circumstances of their loved ones' deaths, and perhaps some remains to bury. This, Aylwin said, would "aid in the process of national reconciliation and in strengthening our democracy."[60]

The bill offered no quid pro quo to those seeking justice, nor did it compel testimony. It met the vigorous opposition of the human rights movement, especially of AFDD, whose hopes for justice it would quash. The PPD and the Socialists, who together constituted a strong and indispensable minority within the governing Concertación, and whose members had been severely repressed, also strongly opposed the bill, along with some Christian Democrats. Faced with agitation in the streets and the potential breakup of his congressional coalition, Aylwin withdrew his initiative after a month.[61] For the remaining six months of his term, the president downplayed the human rights issue in order to reduce civil-military tensions.

After four years of civilian government, despite Aylwin's symbolic politics, the establishment of the essential truth except for the fate of the disappeared, and the enactment of reparation policies, Chile clearly had not "turned the page" on its past. While the majority of the families of victims of state terror had accepted the compensation offered and had perhaps made some accommodation with reality, the military's continuing triumphalism and rejection of dialogue prevented even the first step toward national reconciliation. Those most insistent on pushing for justice were the members of AFDD, whose persistent cry, "*¿dónde están?*" continued to ring out. But as in Argentina following Menem's pardons, the human rights movement became marginalized as the military drew the line on justice, the Chilean economy boomed, and time passed. Cristián Precht, former head of the Vicaría de la Solidaridad, summed up the situation near the end of Aylwin's term: "Today (December 1993) the situation has changed much in terms of knowledge of the truth and little in terms of justice. The wound is still open . . . and hundreds of families still retain the hope of learning about the final destiny of their loved ones and giving them a dignified burial."[62]

In contrast to Argentina, however, the outcome of military intimidation was not a *punto final* law, thanks to the coincidence of views between the human rights movement and the Socialist-PPD congressional bloc—a source of leverage that the Argentine human rights movement did not have when Alfonsín opted for the *punto final* and due obedience laws. While the authoritarian enclaves of the political system worked as planned to thwart legislation opposed by the military, particularly derogation of the amnesty law, Concertación control of the Chamber of Deputies likewise thwarted the right's efforts to strengthen or extend the amnesty. And despite constant intimidation and threats and the military's open disdain for the authority of Aylwin's government, Chile, unlike Argentina, had not experienced outright military rebellion that might have ruptured its perilous transition toward stable civilian governance.

At the end of Aylwin's term in March 1994, justice and impunity remained at loggerheads. The amnesty that sustained impunity remained intact, but, without a *punto final*, the possibility of justice remained open. Given the rapid evolution of international human rights jurisprudence in the 1990s and into the new century, as well as changing circumstances within Chile, the absence of a *punto final* law would eventually facilitate the quest for justice.

While stymied in his pursuit of justice, Aylwin did accomplish his other primary goal of assuring the continuity of civilian governance. He transferred the presidential sash in March 1994 to his elected successor, Christian Democrat Eduardo Frei Ruiz-Tagle. Son of the former president, Frei was an engineer and businessman who received 58 percent of the vote for a presidential term that had been extended from four to six years—the same as the pre-1973 presidential term. During the campaign, Frei had signaled that human rights would not be among his major concerns and had even opined that he believed the big issues had been resolved under Aylwin. The human rights movement, expecting little of Frei, was not disappointed by his lack of sensitivity to its concerns.[63] Nonetheless, in addition to further strengthening civilian authority, the president made some decisions that bore favorably on the quest for justice.

Early in Frei's term, the conclusions of the two high-profile cases prosecuted under Aylwin revealed the possibility of justice, but at the same time they laid bare the government's embarrassing inability to hold the military and police to civilian authority. In March 1994, the perpetrators of the *degollados* murder were sentenced. Because a court had finally issued a sentence "commensurate with the gravity of a human rights crime," Human Rights Watch Americas optimistically, and prematurely, pronounced that the *degollados* verdict "breached a wall of impunity which held intact for more than twenty years."[64] Yet Frei, his hands tied by the constitution, was unable to remove Carabinero commander Rodolfo Stange, on whose watch the crime had occurred and whose subordinates had been convicted, from office. Frei publicly asked Stange to resign, but the commander refused for eighteen months to do so, causing serious tensions and exposing the government's weakness.[65] After the Supreme Court in 1995 upheld the convictions of Contreras and Espinoza, the former DINA commander and his deputy refused to turn themselves in. Shielded by military forces, Espinoza defied the Supreme Court for a month, and Contreras for six; in a deal brokered by Pinochet, Contreras finally surrendered on condition that he be guarded in a civilian prison exclusively by army personnel. The military made it clear that it considered Espinoza and Contreras to be exceptions, and that other trials of military personnel would not be tolerated.[66]

Despite the military's warning, within six months of Frei's inauguration the courts were investigating over six hundred cases involving some one thousand military and police personnel. As tensions mounted, Frei saw an opportunity to offer a solution to the human rights cases in exchange for the Concertación's desired changes in the institutional order. Following negotiations with RN, a bill emerged to expedite investigations and trials; to guarantee the secrecy of proceedings; and, for those crimes committed before March 1978, to apply the amnesty law. In exchange, the designated senators would be abolished, and the National Security Council and the Constitutional Tribunal would be modified. Again, human rights organizations and the Socialist-PPD bloc opposed the trade-off, as did the military, the UDI, and some within RN, and this approach to closing the book on the past failed.[67]

The Spanish courts began legal proceedings against Chilean military officers in 1996. In attempting to extradite Argentine military leaders, Judge Baltasar Garzón had discovered Operation Condor and the case of Spaniard

Carmelo Soria, a UN functionary killed by the DINA in 1976. Soria's case had been reopened in Chile in 1995, but the following year the Supreme Court ruled that the amnesty prevented prosecution and closed the case. The following month, the Spanish judiciary brought charges against the former Chilean junta—a move little noticed at the time but which would later impact the course of human rights history.[68]

While failing to resolve the conundrum of transitional justice, Frei, at some peril, used his very limited authority over the military to attempt to instill more liberal values within the ranks. In November 1997, he rejected the promotion to brigadier general of Jaime Lepe, a Pinochet confidant and former DINA officer who had allegedly orchestrated the killing of Carmelo Soria. The army publicly objected to what it considered unwarranted interference in military affairs. Prior to the expiration of Pinochet's term as army commander, scheduled for March 1998, Frei took advantage of the other source of presidential leverage over the military: the appointment of commanders. Limited in his selection to a list of the five most senior officers, Frei passed over the top four army officers, including Pinochet's preferred successor, and appointed General Ricardo Izurieta, the one least directly associated with state terrorism. In another move that displeased the military, Frei in 1998 announced the opening of a DNA bank to aid in the identification of remains of the disappeared.[69]

During the first four years of Frei's term, the courts had shown little inclination to challenge the amnesty law. Some of the investigations they had initiated under the Aylwin Doctrine were still open, some had been closed, and others had passed to military justice. Human rights advocates had taken hope from two 1994 lower court decisions that applied international humanitarian law to Chile. These rulings were based on one of the 1989 constitutional amendments negotiated between the Concertación and Pinochet—the seemingly innocuous change in article 5 that obligated the government to "respect and promote" the human rights stipulated in international treaties to which Chile was signatory. While Pinochet's advisers had obviously discounted the possibility of retroactivity, the judges in 1994 argued that since the junta had declared the country at war on September 11, 1973, the military government was bound by the Geneva Conventions on the conduct of war, which Chile had ratified in 1951. Since the conventions prohibit execution, torture, and inhumane treatment of prisoners, the 1978 amnesty was invalid in such cases because those war crimes could not be amnestied. Over a year later, however, the Supreme Court overturned the lower court rulings by upholding the validity of the amnesty law. Pressures from the OAS, UN human rights organizations, and NGOs to conform to international law fell on deaf ears.[70]

In 1997, Frei introduced a judicial reform package that focused on the Supreme Court. Unlike Aylwin's judicial reform proposals, Frei's did not include major provisions opposed by the right; rather, it was presented as a measure to modernize the justice system by streamlining the widely recognized cumbersome procedures of the Supreme Court to bring it in line with the needs of Chile's new free market economy. The proposal was also touted as essential to combating a recent crime wave, with which the judiciary was ill equipped to deal. Its endorsement by the publisher of the influential *El Mercurio*, whose son had recently been kidnapped, helped secure the right's support.[71]

Exploiting a rare congressional consensus, Frei succeeded in getting the essentials of his reform package enacted. The legislation created a public prosecutor's office at the ministerial level, separating investigative from trial functions, both of which had been the domain of the Supreme Court. This eliminated the ability of the justices to slow down or bury investigations and gave the executive branch new leverage. It also expanded the Supreme Court from seventeen to twenty-one members and established a mandatory retirement age of seventy-five, which affected six judges immediately. The requirement that Supreme Court justices be confirmed by a two-thirds vote in the Senate eased doubts on the right; while this assured that human rights activists would not be confirmed, it also gave the Concertación senators the votes needed to reject supporters of impunity should they be nominated by a future rightist president. By 1998, after both voluntary and forced retirements and the addition of four new positions on the court, only four of the twenty-one members were Pinochet appointees. In tandem with the changes in international human rights jurisprudence, Frei's judicial reform accelerated the court's shift away from the hard-line views on human rights with which Pinochet had imbued it.[72]

The General/Senator's Fateful Trip

The year 1998 marked a quarter century since the military coup that overthrew the government of Salvador Allende. Major anniversaries of divisive and emotional events evoke memory, heighten tensions, provoke conflict, and promote commemoration, as seen in Argentina during the series of anniversaries between 1994 and 1996. In the period leading up to the Chilean anniversary, and particularly in 1998, the media and the publishing industry produced unprecedented numbers of memoirs, chronicles, and analyses of the UP years and the dictatorship. But in Chile, it was the trajectory of one man, Augusto C. Pinochet—more than memory, commemoration, celebration, or condemnation of September 11—that made the headlines, reopened deep wounds and the chasm separating the two Chiles, and reinvigorated the causes of truth and justice.[73]

On January 20, 1998, the Santiago Court of Appeals broke new ground by accepting for the first time a criminal complaint against Pinochet. Implicitly questioning the validity of the 1978 amnesty law, the court accepted a suit brought by Gladys Marín, head of the Communist Party, for the 1976 abduction and disappearance of her husband and four fellow party members. Seven weeks later, Pinochet completed his term as army commander, a position he had held since Salvador Allende appointed him in August 1973. Upon his retirement, the army, without consulting the minister of defense, honored him with the unprecedented title of commander in chief *benemérito* (distinguished, meritorious) in an elaborate ceremony attended by thousands of sympathizers.[74]

At this point, one of his advisers' most clever artifices for preserving the general's impunity came into play. By the terms of the constitution, former presidents who had served a minimum of six years would become senators for life. Pinochet had set Aylwin's term at four years, but having served some fifteen years with the title of president, newly minted Senator Pinochet would receive the same protection afforded his congressional colleagues: immunity from prosecution while serving his term. Only one legislative term, however, was defined as a lifetime. Pinochet, therefore, was unlikely to have lost sleep over the Supreme Court's recent acceptance of criminal charges against him.[75]

Pinochet's swearing in as a senator polarized the country like no event since the end of the dictatorship. It provoked mass demonstrations outside the congressional building and throughout the country that resulted in clashes with police and numerous injuries and arrests. Inside the chamber, some Concertación senators protested by displaying large photographs of detained and disappeared persons with the AFDD's emblematic slogan, "*¿dónde están?*" In a move that produced serious tensions between government and opposition and within the Concertación itself, a group of deputies launched an "*acusación constitucional*" or impeachment against Pinochet for "gravely compromising the honor and security of the nation" during his 1990–1998 term as army commander. If upheld by the Senate—an impossibility, given its composition—the impeachment would have stripped Pinochet of his congressional immunity from prosecution. President Frei opposed the move, viewing it as excessively provocative to the military, and pressured his congressional allies to reject it. With a number of Christian Democrats voting against it, the impeachment failed in the Chamber of Deputies, 62 to 55.[76] The senator's impunity continued intact.

Energized by the Pinochet controversy, the Concertación congressional bloc renewed the push to abolish the official September 11 holiday commemorating the coup. Encouraged by the more moderate right, Pinochet, assuming the unaccustomed role of conciliator, agreed to its replacement with a "day of national unity" to be observed in the first week of September beginning in 1999. This act of symbolic politics, hailed by some as a "historic accord," suggested a softening of the general's notorious toughness. However, with his still-intact powers of intimidation and the presence in the Senate of many of his former military colleagues and political appointees, Pinochet was expected to stiffen what was already a very hard and inflexible right in the Senate. By some calculations, the prospects for justice for human rights crimes committed during his regime suffered a serious reversal with his installation in the Senate.[77]

Pinochet's investiture as senator for life, the debates over his impeachment and the national holiday, and the observance of the twenty-fifth anniversary of September 11 elicited great outbreaks of memory, emotion, rancor, pride, and sadness. To many Chileans, Pinochet's installation mocked the very notion that they lived in a democracy, however protected. To victims and their families, it was painful to see the man they considered the commander of torture, death, and disappearance resume public office in the new congressional chamber that he had built in Valparaíso in order to dilute the power of government—rather than reopening the historic Congress in Santiago that he had shut down twenty-five years earlier. Memory had been churning, the past had been relived, the "nation of enemies" had been resurrected since the beginning of 1998. However, the last two and a half months of a memorable year would be even more intense.

Chilean transitional justice collided with the international human rights regime on October 16, 1998. Pinochet had traveled to London on September 21 to have back surgery and visit his friend Margaret Thatcher. In an event that shocked the world, Pinochet was arrested in London on warrants from Spanish National Court Judge Baltasar Garzón on charges of torture, genocide, and terrorism. Bound by an extradition treaty with Spain, British authorities held Pinochet—first in the clinic where he was recuperating from surgery, then under a comfortable house arrest—while sorting out the complexities of dealing with a former head of state who claimed immunity on several grounds.[78]

Pinochet's arrest and its aftermath abruptly introduced the world to the new trends in jurisprudence and the heightened activism that had been transforming international human rights. This has become known as the "Pinochet effect." More than any other single development, including the

Bosnia and Rwanda tribunals, the Pinochet drama woke the public, as well as current and former repressors around the world, to the new reality that universal jurisdiction and the invalidity of amnesties for crimes against humanity were not merely abstract principles, but enforceable law. This awakening led many human rights violators to forgo international travel.[79]

The senator's arrest convulsed Chile, placing human rights at the center of the national consciousness, pitting pro- and anti-Pinochet groups and individuals against each other in the media and in the streets, and severely straining civilian-military relations. For Pinochet's enemies, his arrest was a moral victory that was fully warranted by the refusal of Chilean courts to do justice. His supporters countered that the Chilean courts were perfectly competent to try him and that his arrest was an intrusion into purely Chilean matters and an affront to national sovereignty. A foreign observer reported, "Just two months ago, any talk of human rights, of political accountability for the dictatorship, was relegated to the margins of Chilean politics. . . . Now, there is no topic of national discussion except human rights and the past and future of Pinochet."[80] Pinochet's arrest peeled back another layer of the fear that state terrorism had instilled in many Chileans: in the words of the AFDD president, "With the arrest, people began to talk. The fear began to diminish."[81] Sociologist Tomás Moulián put it more elegantly: the arrest "brought Pinochet back to earth and caused the loss of that aura of invincibility—a sort of symbolic death."[82]

From the outset, Frei followed the course dictated by the continuing power of the military and his commitment to strengthening the still fragile civilian government. The administration argued for Pinochet's release on the grounds of his diplomatic immunity as a former head of state and as sitting senator on an alleged diplomatic mission in London. It rejected the Spanish claim of universal jurisdiction and proclaimed the Chilean courts capable of doing justice. Frei dispatched his foreign minister to London and Madrid and withdrew his ambassadors from both countries in protest. Despite these efforts, the government was unable to present a united front to the British and the Spanish. In November, several Socialist members of the Chamber of Deputies, including Allende's daughter, testified in London on behalf of the Spanish extradition request.[83]

For Chileans at home and abroad, the arrest tapped deep veins of memory, as the Scilingo confession had done in Argentina three years earlier. Much more than the discoveries of mass graves, the annual September 11 holiday, Pinochet's swearing in as senator for life, or even the Rettig Report, the London episode brought back memories that victims and their families had suppressed or learned to live with. For Marcela Prádenas, who took exile in

Madrid after multiple detentions and tortures, the arrest was positive because "the tyrant was universally exposed," and people gained some hope for justice. To cope with the psychological impact of memory reactivation, she formed a discussion group with six other Chilean victims of human rights violations; even so, she had to seek professional help for her chronic post-traumatic stress disorder. The worst, she said, was "having to think constantly about what happened to you, and some people go under."[84]

Villa Grimaldi survivor Ofelia Nistal's first response to the news of Pinochet's arrest was disbelief, then "a great feeling of happiness" and encouragement to pursue justice.[85] Pat Bennetts, an Anglo-Chilean woman whose priest brother had been tortured and killed on the naval ship *Esmeralda*, recalled that the news "filled my eyes with tears of joy. It was like a birthday party, but the one who was to blow out the candles was missing. It was sad."[86] Alicia Margarita Piña Allende, whose husband and two brothers-in-law were executed, experienced mixed emotions; while the arrest reopened all her painful memories, she also said that, "until the arrest, Chileans didn't believe the mothers and wives of the murdered and disappeared. That was the great thing about that event."[87] Looking back nearly five years later, Isabel Allende, the late president's daughter and newly elected president of the Chamber of Deputies, said that as a result of the arrest, "no one today doubts that the human rights violations [were] state policy, carried out by state agents, paid for by the state."[88] Pinochet's arrest and its fallout had such an impact on memories of torture that FASIC, which had offered therapy for torture victims since the 1970s, greatly expanded its service in Santiago and opened programs in Calama and Valdivia.[89]

As the disposition of Pinochet's case dragged on, Chile settled into a protracted political crisis. Students, workers, and Pinochet opponents in general rallied, marched, and went on strike. Human rights organizations and individuals initiated unprecedented numbers of suits against Pinochet and hundreds of officers. Pinochet supporters countered with their own demonstrations, and Patria y Libertad, the right-wing paramilitary group that had fought Allende's administration, issued dire threats to the media. On at least two occasions, the right parties abandoned Congress, once for two weeks, to protest Pinochet's continuing detention. In one of the lighter episodes, the right-wing mayor of the wealthy Santiago municipality of Providencia ordered his sanitation workers not to collect garbage from the Spanish embassy, located in his jurisdiction; shortly thereafter, the mayor of one of Santiago's poorest municipalities dispatched its trucks to collect the accumulating trash. She declared to the surprised Spaniards, "If you are willing to take our rubbish [Pinochet], then we will gladly take yours."[90]

While the two sides mobilized to protest or celebrate in Chile, they also confronted each other with placards and insults outside Pinochet's London "chalet" and the British courts. Recognizing that the Pinochet case was political as well as judicial, both sides sought to influence British public opinion as well as the judges. Thousands of exiles who had remained in Europe made the pilgrimage to support the Spanish extradition request. Hundreds of Pinochet supporters who could afford the passage, including General Izurieta, flew to London to support the senator. Others, referred to on the streets as the "rent-a-mob," were paid to go.[91]

General Ricardo Izurieta, who had sworn his allegiance to both his retired commander and to the constitutional president, orchestrated the military reaction. Although Frei had chosen him because of his "clean hands," Izurieta proved to be a dogged defender of Pinochet. He frequently met Frei in the setting of the National Security Council to stiffen the president's resolve to press for Pinochet's release. Generals and admirals, both active and retired, conferred frequently and issued public demands on the government to secure Pinochet's release. Threatened by the unraveling of its version of history as the accusations against Pinochet filled the world's media, the army held seminars on bases throughout the country to reinforce the "correct" understandings and attitudes and to close ranks against the alternate truth. However, as the streets of Chile filled with noisy demonstrators in scenes reminiscent of the turbulent UP days, the military experienced cracks in its blood pact of silence. Both the son of former DINA director Manuel Contreras and Pinochet's former personal pilot revealed that living people and exhumed bodies of executed prisoners had been thrown into the ocean and onto high Andean peaks in order to hide evidence of criminal actions.[92]

Adding to the turmoil and tension that reigned in Chile during Pinochet's confinement was the beginning of the 1999 presidential campaign. After supporting two successive Christian Democratic candidates, the left bloc in the Concertación pushed for one of its own, Public Works Minister Ricardo Lagos of the Socialist Party, to carry the coalition's banner. Conservative Christian Democrats worried about the prospect of a Socialist in the Moneda; others feared that by dredging up the UP years, the right would be able to wrest the presidency from the Concertación; and some wondered whether, despite the "renovation" of the Socialists and the "tied-up" political system that prevented significant change, the military would tolerate a Lagos presidency. Nonetheless, in an unprecedented intracoalition primary election in May, Lagos took 71 percent of the vote and was named the Concertación's candidate. The right coalition nominated Joaquín Lavín of the UDI, an economist and mayor of a wealthy Santiago suburb who had worked for the

Pinochet government. In a telling commentary on the times, Lavín took pains to distance himself from Pinochet just as Lagos emphasized his own transformation since 1973.[93]

Further roiling the waters was a landmark July 1999 decision by Judge Juan Guzmán that officers who led the October 1973 "Caravan of Death," which resulted in dozens of summary executions, were subject to prosecution for *secuestro calificado*—kidnapping of disappeared persons whose bodies had not been found. Guzmán reasoned that since the crime was ongoing until the bodies were produced, it was not covered by the amnesty. While this legal interpretation of the amnesty law had surfaced earlier, it had not been applied to such high-profile figures, who included five of Pinochet's direct subordinates. Izurieta assembled thirty-seven of the army's forty-one active-duty generals in a retreat to study the issue, and afterward publicly announced the army's apprehensions about the decision and the number of new prosecutions it would permit; again, the military demanded a *punto final*. Meanwhile, more evidence surfaced of the dictatorship's human rights violations and of Pinochet's involvement in them: the media provided more coverage of the exhumation of bodies and their disposal by incineration or by being thrown into the ocean, and a human rights attorney released what appeared to be official documentation of Pinochet's knowledge and approval of the DINA's repressive activities.[94]

In 1999, the Argentine practice of public shaming, the *escrache*, appeared in Chile, where it was known as the *funa*. On October 1, members of three human rights groups demonstrated loudly outside the Santiago clinic of cardiologist Alejandro Forero Alvarez, who allegedly had provided medical oversight of torture. Although not present at the clinic, the doctor reported to the press that he had been gravely affected by the shaming. The second *funa* occurred at the home of a known DINA torturer in suburban Santiago at the end of October, and others followed. A retired general sought a court injunction against further *funas*, attesting to their effectiveness.[95]

In London, Pinochet scored an initial legal victory when a court ruled that his immunity was valid. This was reversed on appeal to the House of Lords, which narrowed the extraditable charges to cases of torture committed after September 1988, when both Britain and Chile had ratified the UN Convention on Torture. Judge Garzón quickly submitted thirty-two additional torture complaints from Pinochet's last year and a half in office, including the cases of six persons who had died during or following torture. Meanwhile, several other countries, including France, Switzerland, and Sweden, joined Spain in demanding Pinochet's extradition as British and Spanish corporations with large investments in Chile pressured behind the scenes for Pinochet's release. Despite the extreme humiliation of his arrest, Pinochet in various statements revealed his continuing lack of repentance, his arrogance, and his scorn for the daily demonstrations outside his compound. He told the *Sunday Times*, "My compatriots have accepted our nation's past."[96]

The legal battles proceeded slowly in the context of mounting political and economic pressures. After many twists and turns, the British decision hinged not on substantive questions about the principles of universal jurisdiction or the validity of amnesties for crimes against humanity, but on medical examinations ordered to determine whether the senator, who turned eighty-four in August 1999, was fit to stand trial. On March 2, 2000, British authorities released Pinochet on humanitarian grounds owing to his age and failing health, after sixteen and a half months of house arrest. He flew home in a Chilean air force plane to an elaborate welcoming ceremony staged by the military commanders and hundreds of supporters. After being helped off the airplane in a wheelchair, he raised his cane in a triumphal gesture and walked slowly but steadily across the tarmac, saying in effect that he had fooled the British. He was taken to the military hospital in a convoy of four helicopters that flew over the Moneda Palace en route. The Frei administration vigorously protested the ceremony and the overflight.[97]

The "Pinochet Effect" in Chile

In the years following Pinochet's release from house arrest in London, Chile experienced substantial progress in bringing former repressors to justice. Nonetheless, the 1978 amnesty law remained in place despite the reform of the Supreme Court and mounting pressures from the domestic human rights movement and the international human rights lobby. Both the UN and the Inter-American Commission on Human Rights argued that the law violated Chile's international obligation to prosecute perpetrators of gross human rights violations—an obligation recognized in article 5 of the constitution as revised in 1989. Progress toward justice in the courts was not linear: Human rights organizations decried numerous setbacks while applauding the overall forward movement. Rather than a radical break with the past, such as Argentina experienced with the 2003 election of Néstor Kirchner, the pattern in Chile was the erosion of impunity on a case-by-case basis.[98]

A few days after Pinochet's return, Socialist Ricardo Lagos, who had narrowly won in a run-off election, was inaugurated as Chile's third president after Pinochet. Lagos inherited from Frei an ongoing effort to resolve the most contentious legacy of state terrorism, an issue that was consuming Chile: the fate of the nearly twelve hundred detained disappeared, whose remains had not been found. To defuse the intolerably tense political atmosphere of mid-1999, Frei's minister of defense, Edmundo Pérez Yoma, had convened a group of human rights, military, religious, professional, and political figures in a Mesa de Diálogo, or roundtable, to map a path toward a solution acceptable to all sides. Frei selected the Mesa de Diálogo approach because of the urgency of the situation and because previous attempts to legislate on core issues of transitional justice had failed.[99]

It took the twenty-three Mesa members from August 1999 to June 2000—three months into Lagos's presidency—to agree upon procedures and rules, which centered on encouraging active and retired military with knowledge of the disappeared to come forward by guaranteeing that information they divulged would be treated as a "professional secret": neither they nor anyone they implicated would be identified. Investigations to establish the fate of the disappeared would be expedited and the cases closed as quickly as possible without the establishment of criminal liability. In short, this was the same formula that both Aylwin and Frei had advanced in their proposed legislation. But, in the tense atmosphere of 1999 and 2000 created by Pinochet's arrest, for the first time military men and most human rights groups—the AFDD and a few others excepted—agreed that concrete steps were required to bring closure to the viscerally divisive issue of the disappeared and to promote national reconciliation. Both sides made major concessions to achieve these ends: the military for the first time admitted that crimes had occurred, and the human rights organizations, also for the first time, proved willing to give up the possibility of justice in exchange for truth.[100]

Following the Mesa de Diálogo's recommendations, Congress quickly enacted a law to establish the professional secret. The churches agreed to receive the information, in a discreet fashion, over a six-month period, thus avoiding the public venue of the courts, and the government agreed to provide special judicial staff to expedite investigations based on the information received. Since the perpetrators of the disappearances would remain anonymous by virtue of the professional secret, the military should not have to worry about the status of the amnesty law, which, as recent court decisions demonstrated, was under attack. Recovery of the remains, or at least knowledge of the final resting place of their loved ones, would presumably "give peace, in some measure, to the families."[101]

The military made a show of cooperating with the effort to locate the disappeared: ranking officers urged subordinates to come forward, and the retired army generals' association announced its collaboration in order to "heal the country's wounds and end the divisions that hurt us so much."[102] However, despite the promise of anonymity and absolution, the rapidly changing legal climate and the energized quest for justice were intimidating to officers who, as little as two years earlier, had expected to finish their careers and enjoy peaceful retirements basking in the satisfaction of a job well done. In addition, some officers undoubtedly rejected cooperation on principle. Although the Mesa de Diálogo was a failure, its unanimous report broke new ground in establishing responsibility for crimes and committing all parties to "the firm decision not to permit their repetition."[103]

Lagos announced on January 8, 2001, that the Mesa de Diálogo report clarified the fate of only 180 of the nearly 1,200 unresolved cases of the detained disappeared. Even worse than the small number identified was the confirmation of the sporadic stories about remains being dug up from their original mass graves, many of them in the final months of the dictatorship, and dropped into the ocean to hide evidence of orchestrated murders.

For most families of the disappeared, the result of the Mesa de Diálogo was the opposite of closure: it was the prolongation of the uncertainty with which they had lived for so many years. Other families received the horrifying knowledge that their loved one had been exhumed and dumped into the ocean, suffering in effect a second death; for these families, there would never be a body to mourn. The widow and seven children of disappeared labor leader Juan Luis Rivera Matus, whose remains were reported to have been thrown into the Pacific, suffered this double trauma with a different twist. Three months after gathering on the coast and casting flowers into the water in a symbolic funeral, they were informed that his remains had been identified during a judicial investigation after the roundtable had ended, in a common grave, thus launching a new period of grieving.[104]

In the report's aftermath, a frustrated President Lagos demanded more information, and a group of children of detained disappeared parents brought a suit against military commanders for obstruction of justice. Although embittered by the outcome, the AFDD acknowledged some accomplishment: "The military has recognized for the first time in twenty-seven years that it not only arrested, tortured, assassinated, but also that it disappeared using horrific practices of extermination."[105] For the military, the outcome of the Mesa de Diálogo was a lost opportunity to begin making amends and refurbishing its image—analogous to the Argentine military's rejection of Alfonsín's offer to cleanse itself by prosecuting the former junta leaders. And just as the Argentine military suffered consequences for its failure to cooperate—although later reversed by the *punto final* and due obedience laws and Menem's pardons—the Chilean military would also pay a price for its intransigence.

Despite its failure, the Mesa de Diálogo started a process of expedited investigations that soon assumed a dynamic of its own. As required by the roundtable agreement, the government expanded the staff for judicial investigations to handle the expected revelations about the disappeared. It appointed nine special judges dedicated exclusively to investigating cases of the disappeared and assigned them to the Ministry of the Interior's human rights division. Fifty-one other judges throughout the country were instructed to give priority to cases of the disappeared within their jurisdictions, and the government gave additional resources to the Medical Legal Service to speed forensic investigations on remains of the disappeared. The administration repeatedly extended the mandates of the special judges, who continued to discover remains well after the expiration of the designated six-month period for receiving information under the protection of the professional secret. Having lost their opportunity to provide information in exchange for confirmed impunity, both retired and active military officers called again for a *punto final* law. Lagos and the Concertación-controlled Chamber of Deputies, however, firmly rejected any new nonjudicial approach to the issue of the detained disappeared, and the president repeatedly affirmed that the courts would decide.[106]

In the twenty-seven months between Pinochet's arrest and the Mesa de Diálogo report, the dynamic of transitional justice shifted decisively in favor of victims and their families. By implementing the procedure recommended by the Mesa de Diálogo, extending it, and insisting on the jurisdiction of the courts, the government was able, for the first time in Chile, to seize the initiative in pursuit of justice. As the cases poured in and the international human rights lobby—the UN, the Inter-American human rights organizations, and the NGOs—applied pressure and provided encouragement and research, the courts became bolder in adopting new jurisprudence. The courts were driven, moreover, by a desire to redeem their tarnished reputation as collaborators with repression; in the words of a political analyst, "The justices . . . are trying to show they are no longer the pawns of Pinochet."[107]

In March 2001, the Supreme Court refused to rule on the validity of the 1978 amnesty law, in effect leaving its interpretation to the discretion of individual judges. Officers were prosecuted for *secuestro calificado* as well as previously unused categories of crime such as illicit association and illegal exhumation—the latter applied to the numerous cases in which remains were dug up and dumped into the ocean to avoid detection.[108] As the new jurisprudence spread throughout the courts, the 1978 amnesty law, in the opinion of one human rights lawyer, was "tacitly repealed." In August 2003, President Lagos asked rhetorically, "If I had the ability to revoke the amnesty, what would be the juridical effects? None."[109]

General/Senator Pinochet was among those affected by the new political and juridical realities. Emboldened by the arrest and legal proceedings in London and persuaded by the Chilean government's rhetoric about its willingness and ability to try him, the courts initiated proceedings that less than two years earlier would have been unthinkable. Seeking to indict Pinochet in the Caravan of Death case, Judge Juan Guzmán got the Santiago Court of Appeals to lift his congressional immunity from prosecution in June 2000; the following day, Izurieta and 120 retired generals visited Pinochet at his home to show solidarity. The Supreme Court confirmed the appellate court's decision two months later, removing the last apparent obstacle to a trial. This occurred at a time when polls showed that over 70 percent of Chileans wanted to see the ex-dictator tried.[110]

However, as the intricate dance proceeded, the moment of the ultimate confrontation between justice and impunity—the trial of Pinochet—began to recede. Despite his humiliation and the loss of much of the support that he had enjoyed before his legal problems began, Pinochet alternately obeyed and defied court orders regarding appearances, house arrest, medical exams, and fingerprinting, against the advice of the army leadership, which saw this obstructionist behavior as damaging to the institution's reputation. His lawyers focused on the London solution. As the two sides appeared headed for collision, on July 9, 2001, the Santiago Court of Appeals "temporarily and partially" suspended Pinochet's indictment in the Caravan of Death case, citing his mental incapacity to stand trial. On July 1, 2002, the Supreme Court definitively ended Pinochet's indictment, depriving victims of state terrorism and their families of their greatest possible satisfaction. Pinochet then resigned his Senate seat, but in his capacity as former president, he retained his immunity from prosecution—for what it was worth.[111]

Some Chileans celebrated; others wept. Critics of the court's decision argued that it was based on a deal between the government and the military to defuse tensions, rather than on sound jurisprudence.[112] The persistent Judge Guzmán indicted Pinochet twice more in 2004, for his complicity in Operation Condor and for the murder of his predecessor as army commander, General Carlos Prats. The same script played itself out again: After lifting his immunity from prosecution in both cases, the Supreme Court in early 2005 repeated its 2002 finding that Pinochet was unfit to stand trial. By mid-2005, Pinochet had been indicted and stripped of his immunity twice more, in the last case for stashing illicitly acquired dollars in secret accounts in U.S. banks.[113]

By this time, the eighty-nine-year-old ex-dictator had become almost irrelevant. The continuing news coverage of his London captivity and his legal travails at home made Chileans intimately familiar with the gruesome details of the crimes with which he was charged. While they valued the results of his sixteen and a half years in office, the political right, the business elites, and the military had concluded that he was a liability. His towering stature had shrunk, and his ability to instill fear had evaporated; he had become a pathetic figure and a virtual pariah in the country that he claimed to have saved from the Marxist hordes. The revelations about his secret bank accounts made him look more like an old-fashioned, corrupt Caribbean-style dictator than the savior of Chile.[114]

Pinochet's reprieves did nothing to stop the growing momentum for justice in Chile. The same day that the Supreme Court quashed the first Pinochet prosecution, Judge Guzmán indicted five retired officers for their activities at the Villa Grimaldi torture center. By mid-2004, over three hundred active and retired military men, including twenty-one army generals, had been indicted, tried, or convicted in Chile for crimes against human rights, most of them committed during the period covered by the 1978 amnesty law; some were involved in multiple cases, and several had received sentences of life imprisonment. Along with sensational headline cases involving the Caravan of Death, Operation Condor, and high-profile killings and disappearances were hundreds of cases involving *campesinos*, workers, and children. Some of the biggest names of the dictatorship had been on the docket, along with rank-and-file repressors with little name recognition. In addition to those officers processed by Chilean justice, dozens more who were indicted in foreign countries had abandoned any hope of travel abroad after Pinochet's encounter with universal jurisdiction.[115]

The military response to the mounting assault on impunity was surprisingly moderate. Army commander Juan Emilio Cheyre, who succeeded Izurieta in March 2002, frequently raised the institution's concern over the large number of officers who were called to testify and were subjected to indictments and trials, but without the bluster and threats Pinochet had used to keep justice at bay. He made a point to show respect for the courts, saying that the army would support its members in their legal battles "to the extent it should, but not beyond."[116] Following the August 2002 conviction and sentencing of twelve army men, including four generals, for the 1982 murder of labor leader Tucapel Jiménez, Cheyre said, "We are interested in the truth, although it is painful. I believe it liberates and brings peace to the spirits. These are individual responsibilities . . . for a crime that should never have been committed, that pains us and which we reject."[117] This followed a statement by the air force commander that his institution did not worry about trials, because it was necessary to turn the page.[118] Under Cheyre, army personnel on active duty, when convicted, were retired from service. Cheyre went so far as to use the evocative phrase "*nunca más*" from across the Andes in assuring the public that the army would never in the future commit "excesses, crimes, and human rights violations."[119]

Also telling was the equanimity with which the military commanders accepted Lagos's appointment of Michelle Bachelet as his second minister of defense in January 2002. Not only was she the first woman to hold the position and a member of the Socialist Party, but she was the daughter of Air Force General Alberto Bachelet, who died in detention following torture in the wake of the coup. Michelle Bachelet herself had been tortured at Villa Grimaldi and exiled.[120]

The military also began engaging in symbolic reparations. In September 2002, Cheyre sponsored a mass in honor of General Carlos Prats and his wife, assassinated twenty-eight years earlier by the DINA in Buenos Aires. Attended by the couple's daughters, the event symbolically restored Prats's place in the army's history. In March 2004, Cheyre paid tribute to General René Schneider, who had been killed in the CIA-inspired attempt to prevent Allende's assumption of office following the 1970 election, and hung his portrait in the gallery of former army commanders. Meanwhile, in June 2003, the army, navy, and air force announced the reincorporation into the ranks of those cashiered following the coup for being pro-Allende or too soft on the left; in addition to having their dignity and their pensions restored, they would receive indemnities for their severance.[121]

The post-1998 climate also encouraged additional efforts to forge memory, promote human rights education, and create a culture of human rights. The revision of school texts and curricula to promote civic education and reinterpret recent national history accelerated. The University of Chile's law school founded a Center for Human Rights in 2001. In November 2003, the minister of education decreed the obligation of all schools to exhibit the Universal Declaration of Human Rights. Human rights organizations pushed ahead with a project to create archives of documents from the period of the dictatorship as a means of preserving the memory of state terrorism.[122]

Stimulated by Pinochet's arrest, the Mesa de Diálogo, and the thirtieth anniversary of the coup, government, groups, and individuals engaged increasingly in commemoration. In June 2000, Lagos inaugurated a statue of Allende in the Plaza de la Constitución, adjacent to the Moneda Palace; funded by private donations, the statue was only the third memorial to a president in that historic locale. In March 2002, the government announced that a "house of culture for life and respect for the human being" would be built on the grounds of a demolished DINA detention center in Santiago. In the months surrounding the thirtieth anniversary, the Estadio Chile was renamed Víctor Jara

Stadium in honor of the folk singer killed there. The National Stadium was declared a national monument to highlight and preserve the memory of its role in the 1973 terror. A monument was begun to the seventy local people, mostly *campesinos*, killed or disappeared around the rural town of Paine, near Santiago. Cities and towns throughout the country held ceremonies and erected monuments, and several renamed streets and plazas in honor of Salvador Allende. On September 11, 2003, Lagos ceremonially opened a reconstructed door on the side of the Moneda Palace at Morandé 80, which the military had sealed after Allende's body had been carried through it out of the burning building. The following month, several of the high-profile UP figures imprisoned for a year on Dawson Island made a symbolic return to the frigid site.[123]

Two months after the thirtieth anniversary, Lagos appointed a Comisión Nacional sobre Prisión Política y Tortura (National Commission on Political Imprisonment and Torture) to investigate and recommend reparations for victims. The commission delivered its report a year later. In a six-month period, it gathered over 35,000 testimonies within Chile and in forty foreign countries. Of these, it determined that 27,255 persons fully established their status as political prisoners, and 94 percent of those had established that they had been tortured; most of the remaining 7,000 were rejected for incomplete testimonies but would be reconsidered. The commission recommended pensions, improved mental health care, and a variety of other benefits to the victims; Congress enacted these measures in December 2004. President Lagos made it clear that more was involved than material benefits: "Because we have been capable of examining the truth up close, we can begin to overcome the pain, heal the wounds."[124]

Upon publication of the report on political prisoners and torture in November 2004, army commander Cheyre issued the most comprehensive statement to date of responsibilities for the human rights violations committed during the dictatorship. He prefaced his remarks by announcing the elimination of the army's intelligence battalion, a step both substantive and symbolic. In language reminiscent of the Rettig Report, he recounted a number of steps the army had taken to rid itself of a Cold War mentality "which accepted as legitimate all processes and methods of fighting to take and maintain power." This Cold War vision "made enemies of those who were merely adversaries and led to the reduction of respect for persons, their dignity, and their rights." Human rights violations, he continued, "can never, for anyone, have an ethical justification." Reaching the heart of his statement, Cheyre said, "The army of Chile has made the difficult and irreversible decision to assume institutional responsibility for all the punishable and morally unacceptable actions of the past." He also promised the introduction of human rights courses in the curriculum of military education.[125] Clearly, out from under the shadow of Pinochet, the military had recast itself for the new times.

Over thirty years after September 11, 1973, Chile showed many faces. A member of Salvador Allende's Socialist Party held the presidency, and Allende's daughter, Isabel Allende, served as president of the Chamber of Deputies. Despite Pinochet's best efforts, the left had returned to power. It was a "renovated" left in a "tied-up" political system—but the constitutional reforms of September 2005 would soon end some of the "authoritarian enclaves," including the appointed senators and the president's inability to remove military commanders. The military stood by, not without complaining, while justice proceeded. The political right had marginalized Pinochet. At the same time, many Chileans still lived with intense pain. Some clung to the hope of finding their disappeared loved ones, alive or dead. Torture victims struggled with the nightmares of their ordeal. Transitional justice and national reconciliation in Chile were still works in progress.

Notes

1. Lutheran Bishop of Chile Helmut Frenz, "Porqué este era el único camino," in *Chile, la memoria prohibida: las violaciones a los derechos humanos, 1973–1983*, by Rodrigo Atria et al. (Santiago: Pehuén Editores, 1989), 1:xxvi–xxvii.

2. General Augusto C. Pinochet, quoted in Raquel Correa and Elizabeth Subercaseaux, *Ego sum* (Santiago: Planeta, 1996), 138.

3. Studies of the postdictatorial period in Chile include Ascanio Cavallo, *La historia oculta de la transición: Chile 1990–1998* (Santiago: Grijalbo, 1998); Paul Drake and Iván Jaksić, eds., *El modelo chileno: democracia y desarrollo en los noventa* (Santiago: LOM Ediciones, 1999); Gregory Weeks, *The Military and Politics in Postauthoritarian Chile* (Tuscaloosa: University of Alabama Press, 2003); and Silvia Borzutzky and Lois Hecht Oppenheim, eds., *After Pinochet: The Chilean Road to Democracy and the Market* (Gainesville: University of Florida Press, 2006).

4. Claudio Fuentes, "Partidos y coaliciones en el Chile de los '90: entre pactos y proyectos," in *El modelo chileno*, ed. Drake and Jaksić, 191–222; Peter M. Siavelis, "Continuidad y transformación del sistema de partidos en una transición 'Modelo,'" in *El modelo chileno*, ed. Drake and Jaksić, 223–59; Elizabeth Lira and Brian Loveman, "Derechos humanos en la transición 'Modelo': Chile 1988–1999," in *El modelo chileno*, ed. Drake and Jaksić, 339–74; Kenneth M. Roberts, *The Modern Left and Social Movements in Chile and Peru* (Stanford, CA: Stanford University Press, 1998), 81–117.

5. Alexandra Barahona de Brito, *Human Rights and Democratization in Latin America: Uruguay and Chile* (Oxford: Oxford University Press, 1997), 112–21; John B. Londregan, *Legislative Institutions and Ideology in Chile* (Cambridge: Cambridge University Press, 2000), 180–92. See the Agrupación de Familiares de Detenidos

Desaparecidos de Chile, *Veinte años de historia de la Agrupación de Familiares de Detenidos Desaparecidos de Chile: un camino de imágenes* (Santiago: Corporación de Familiares de Detenidos Desaparecidos, 1997) and the same organization's annual *Resumen de actividades*.

6. See chapter 1. Even Pinochet's government had signed the UN torture treaty, but with stated reservations designed to exempt him and his military from prosecution.

7. Correa and Subercaseaux, *Ego sum*, 124.

8. Fuentes, "Partidos y coaliciones"; Siavelis, "Continuidad y transformación." One may get a rough idea of Pinochet's support from the 43 percent he received in the 1988 plebiscite and the 45 percent that two right-wing candidates, one of them his tapped would-be successor, received in the 1989 presidential election. However, a 1989 poll indicated that 67.5 percent of Chileans favored prosecution of human rights violators: Barahona de Brito, *Human Rights and Democratization*, 121–22.

9. The term "authoritarian enclaves" is widely used to describe some of the elements of the Chilean political system discussed below. Tomás Moulian, *Chile actual: anatomía de un mito* (Santiago: LOM-ARCIS, 1997), 45–56, prefers the label "iron cage."

10. Constitution of Chile, articles 81, 95, 96; the constitution can be accessed at www.georgetown.edu/pdba/Constitutions/Chile/chile89.html (accessed June 20, 2005). Peter M. Siavelis, *The President and Congress in Postauthoritarian Chile: Institutional Constraints to Democratic Consolidation* (University Park: Pennsylvania State University Press, 2000), 37–39.

11. While the composition of the National Security Council, the Constitutional Tribunal, and the group of designated senators could and would be liberalized to a degree by future presidential appointments, these three authoritarian enclaves, along with the Supreme Court, were ironclad guarantees of military impunity for the first eight years of Chile's transition.

12. Constitution of Chile, article 81; Siavelis, *The President and Congress*, 31–40; Londregan, *Legislative Institutions*, 84–93.

13. Both Aylwin and his successor, Eduardo Frei Ruiz-Tagle, unsuccessfully introduced legislation to eliminate some of the authoritarian enclaves. Eventually the appointments made by Frei and by a liberalized Supreme Court weakened the right's veto power in the Senate, and after Pinochet's arrest in London (see 202–7), the right parties agreed to fundamental changes. Thus, in September 2005, the constitution was amended to eliminate the nine designated senators when their terms ended in March 2006, to eliminate senators for life (see below, 201), to reduce the power of the National Security Council to make it purely advisory, and to give the president the power to fire military commanders. *The Economist*, September 15, 2005 (Internet).

14. Constitution of Chile, chapter 10; Organic Constitutional Law of the Armed Forces.

15. Barahona de Brito, *Human Rights and Democratization*, 102–3. Pinochet may have been paraphrasing Spain's dictator Francisco Franco, who, upon designating Prince Juan Carlos de Borbón his successor, gloated that he was leaving Spain's future "atado y bien atado" ("tied up, well tied up.") Quoted in Francisco J. Romero

Salvadó, *Twentieth-Century Spain: Politics and Society in Spain, 1898–1998* (New York: St. Martin's Press, 1999), 150.

16. Barahona de Brito, *Human Rights and Democratization*, 98–106. The number of CNI operatives incorporated into the army is disputed. Barahona de Brito, *Human Rights and Democratization*, 106, places the number at 19,000; Cavallo, *Historia oculta*, 31, 37, indicates that the number was 2,016.

17. Londregan, *Legislative Institutions and Ideology*, 51.

18. The 1988 plebiscite was the first time that the opposition participated in an election under the rules of Pinochet's constitution—an act that was interpreted as legitimizing the constitution.

19. Carlos Andrade Geywitz, *Reforma de la Constitución política de la República de Chile de 1980*, 2nd ed. (Santiago: Editorial Jurídica de Chile, 2002), 199–202; Andrade Geywitz covers the entire package of 1989 reforms (1–331). One of the amendments raised the number of elected senators from twenty-six to thirty-eight, reducing the power of the nine appointed senators.

20. Quoted in Lois Hecht Oppenheim, *Politics in Chile: Democracy, Authoritarianism, and the Search for Development*, 2nd ed. (Boulder, CO: Westview Press, 1999), 216.

21. Lira and Loveman, "Derechos humanos en la transición," 344. See Brian Loveman and Elizabeth Lira, *El espejismo de la reconciliación política: Chile 1990–2002* (Santiago: LOM Ediciones, 2002) for an excellent analysis of the politics of transitional justice in Chile. See Mark Amstutz, *The Healing of Nations: The Promise and Limits of Political Forgiveness* (Lanham, MD: Rowman & Littlefield, 2005), 139–63.

22. Patricio Aylwin Azócar, *La transición chilena: discursos escogidos marzo 1990–1992* (Santiago: Editorial Andrés Bello, 1992), 30. Works on the Aylwin administration include Rafael Otano, *Crónica de la transición* (Santiago: Planeta, 1995); Cavallo, *Historia oculta*, 11–235; and Brian Loveman, "The Transition to Civilian Government in Chile, 1990–1994," in *The Struggle for Democracy in Chile*, ed. Paul W. Drake and Iván Jaksić, rev. ed. (Lincoln: University of Nebraska Press, 1995), 305–37.

23. Aylwin, *La transición*, 33. A few mass graves had been discovered earlier, but with the installation of civilian government, some people lost enough fear to report grave sites they had known of for some time. International Commission of Jurists, *Chile: A Time of Reckoning; Human Rights and the Judiciary* (Geneva: Centre for the Independence of Judges and Lawyers, 1992), 113–28.

24. Jorge Correa S., "Cenicienta se queda en la fiesta: el poder judicial chileno en la década de los 90," in *El modelo chileno*, ed. Drake and Jaksić, 300–303; International Commission of Jurists, *Chile: A Time of Reckoning*, 193–99.

25. Aylwin, *La transición*, 21.

26. Otano, *Crónica*, 111–12; Cynthia Brown, *Human Rights and the "Politics of Agreements": Chile during President Aylwin's First Year* (New York: Americas Watch, 1991), 13–16; Alexander Wilde, "Irruptions of Memory: Expressive Politics in Chile's Transition to Democracy," in *Genocide, Collective Violence, and Popular Memory: The Politics of Remembrance in the Twentieth Century*, ed. David E. Lorey and

William H. Beezley (Wilmington, DE: Scholarly Resources, 2002), 8–9. Marjorie Agosín, "The Dance of Life: Women and Human Rights in Chile," in Marjorie Agosín, *Ashes of Revolt* (Fredonia, NY: White Pine Press, 1996), 143–51, discusses the *cueca sola*: "A woman who dances alone evokes in the cueca's rhythm the memory of the man who is absent, and the dance changes from a pleasurable experience to a well of pain and memory" (146).

27. Luis Roniger and Mario Sznajder, *The Legacy of Human-Rights Violations in the Southern Cone: Argentina, Chile, and Uruguay* (Oxford: Oxford University Press, 1999), 213–20; Wilde, "Irruptions of Memory," 10–11. The only exception is Gabriel González Videla (president 1946–1952), buried in his native La Serena.

28. Wilde, "Irruptions of Memory," 10–11.

29. Cavallo, *Historia oculta*, 48–53; Otano, *Crónica*, 149.

30. Cavallo, *Historia oculta*, 19–28. *Brasil: Nunca mais* (1985) was published in English as *Torture in Brazil: A Shocking Report on the Pervasive Use of Torture by Brazilian Military Governments, 1964–1979*, trans. Jaime Wright (Austin: University of Texas Press, 1998). See also Robert K. Goldman and Cynthia G. Brown, *Challenging Impunity: The Ley de Caducidad and the Referendum Campaign in Uruguay* (New York: Americas Watch, 1989); Barahona de Brito, *Human Rights and Democratization*, 165.

31. Chile, *Report of the Chilean National Commission on Truth and Reconciliation*, trans. Phillip E. Berryman (Notre Dame, IN: University of Notre Dame Press, 1993), 1:5; Brown, *Human Rights*, 13–16.

32. Mark Ensalaco, *Chile under Pinochet: Recovering the Truth* (Philadelphia: University of Pennsylvania Press, 2000), 184–86; Priscilla B. Hayner, *Unspeakable Truths: Confronting State Terror and Atrocity* (New York: Routledge, 2001), 35–38.

33. *Report of the Chilean National Commission*, 1:18–22.

34. *Report of the Chilean National Commission*.

35. *Report of the Chilean National Commission*; Barahona de Brito, *Human Rights and Democratization*, 155.

36. Aylwin, *La transición*, 131, 132; *La Epoca*, March 5, 1991.

37. *El Mercurio*, March 8, 1991.

38. *Report of the Chilean National Commission*, 1:126.

39. Supreme Court, May 13, 1991, no title, p. 23. Photocopy of the report courtesy of human rights attorney Verónica Reyna.

40. Ensalaco, *Chile under Pinochet*, 13; Barahona de Brito, *Human Rights and Democratization*, 161.

41. *El Mercurio*, April 10, 1991. Otano, *Crónica*, 174–86. Eleven years later, human rights lawyer Verónica Reyna said that as a result of the assassination, "the commission's report sank." Verónica Reyna interview, Santiago, November 19, 2002.

42. Barahona de Brito, *Human Rights and Democratization*, 167.

43. Correa, "Cenicienta," 303–6. Also www.oas.org/juridico/english/Sigs/b-32.html (accessed April 26, 2004) for the 1990 ratification and acceptance of the jurisdiction of the Inter-American Court of Human Rights.

44. Hayner, *Unspeakable Truths*, 172–74, 314–15 (quotation, 173); Lira and Loveman, "Derechos humanos en la transición," 357–59.

45. Corporación Nacional de Reparación y Reconciliación, *Informe sobre calificación de víctimas de violaciones de derechos humanos y de la violencia política* (Santiago: Corporación Nacional de Reparación y Reconciliación, 1996), 576.

46. Oficina Nacional de Retorno, "Informe Final" (Santiago: Oficina Nacional de Retorno, 1995); Thomas C. Wright and Rody Oñate, *Flight from Chile: Voices of Exile* (Albuquerque: University of New Mexico Press, 1998), 198–225; Barahona de Brito, *Human Rights and Democratization*, 153. Brian Loveman and Elizabeth Lira, eds., *Leyes de reconciliación en Chile: amnistías, indultos y reparaciones, 1819–1999* (Santiago: Universidad Jesuita Alberto Hurtado, 2001), 260–76, reproduces the law. See this volume for other documents from the military government through the Frei Ruiz-Tagle administration.

47. Loveman and Lira, *El espejismo*, 57–71; Brown, *Human Rights*, 52–61.

48. International Commission of Jurists, *Chile: A Time of Reckoning*, 200–5; Lisa Hilbink, "Un estado de derecho no liberal: la actuación del poder judicial chileno en los años 90," in *El modelo chileno*, ed. Drake and Jaksić, 324–26; Jorge Correa Sutil, "'No Victorious Army Has Ever Been Prosecuted . . .': The Unsettled Story of Transitional Justice in Chile," in *Transitional Justice and the Rule of Law in New Democracies*, ed. A. James McAdams (Notre Dame, IN: University of Notre Dame Press, 1997), 131–54.

49. *El Mercurio*, March 5, 1991, quoted in Brown, *Human Rights*, 51.

50. International Commission of Jurists, *Chile: A Time of Reckoning*, 247–48; Hilbink, "Un estado de derecho," 326.

51. Alejandra Matus Acuña and Francisco Javier Artaza, *Crimen con castigo* (Santiago: La Nación Ediciones B, 1996), 218–26; Weeks, *The Military and Politics*, 101–3.

52. Human Rights Watch, *The Limits of Tolerance: Freedom of Expression and the Public Debate in Chile* (New York: Human Rights Watch, 1998); Brown, *Human Rights*, 94–97. See, for example, *La Nación*, "Cuando Chile ardió en el caos," September 5, 1993.

53. Weeks, *The Military and Politics*, 64.

54. The "second independence day" was the message on a flyer distributed in the streets by Pinochet supporters on September 11, 1993. See the coverage of the September 11 holiday every year in the press on September 12. Roniger and Sznajder, *The Legacy of Human-Rights Violations*, 215–18.

55. Cavallo, *Historia oculta*, 29–37, 52–53; Otano, *Crónica*, 106–9, 148–59. A critic of the Concertación wrote, "The de facto power of Pinochet revealed that the glitter of the presidential sash was little more than window dressing." Tomás Moulian, "The Time of Forgetting: The Myths of the Chilean Transition," *NACLA Report on the Americas* 32, no. 2 (September–October 1998): 17.

56. *Las Ultimas Noticias*, October 14, 1989, quoted in Correa Sutil, "'No Victorious Army Has Ever Been Prosecuted . . . ,'" 151n14.

57. *La Epoca*, September 12, 1990; Weeks, *The Military and Politics*, 62–65.

58. Cavallo, *Historia oculta*, 67–85; Otano, *Crónica*, 306–20; Weeks, *The Military and Politics*, 66–72. For a chronological list of civil-military points of tension and confrontations between 1990 and 2000, see Loveman, *Chile*, 331–35.

59. Cavallo, *Historia oculta*, 194–216; Weeks, *The Military and Politics*, 83–92.

60. Loveman and Lira, *El espejismo*, 109–26 (quotation 112); Cavallo, *Historia oculta*, 217–22.

61. Loveman and Lira, *El espejismo*, 109–26; Otano, *Crónica*, 321–29.

62. Arzobispado de Santiago, Fundación de Documentación y Archivo de la Vicaría de la Solidaridad, "Detenidos desaparecidos" (unpublished working document, 8 vols., 1994), vol. 1, n.p.

63. Miguel Antonio Garretón M., "La (in)conducción política del segundo gobierno democrático," in *El período del Presidente Frei Ruiz-Tagle: reflexiones sobre el segundo gobierno concertacionista*, ed. Oscar Muñoz and Carolina Stefoni (Santiago: FLACSO-Chile, Editorial Universitaria, 2002), 63–67. This volume serves as a good introduction to the Frei Ruiz-Tagle presidency.

64. Barahona de Brito, *Human Rights and Democratization*, 185.

65. Cavallo, *Historia oculta*, 245–53; Weeks, *The Military and Politics*, 98–101.

66. Matus Acuña and Artaza, *Crimen con castigo*, 271–95; Weeks, *The Military and Politics*, 101–7, 114–16.

67. On civil-military relations under Frei, see Rodrigo Atria, "La relación civil-militar entre 1994 y 2000: bases para el cambio," in *El período del Presidente Frei Ruiz-Tagle*, ed. Muñoz and Stefoni, 221–41; Loveman and Lira, *El espejismo*, 148–73; Weeks, *The Military and Politics*, 114–37.

68. Eduardo Martín de Pozuelo and Santiago Tarín, *España acusa* (Barcelona: Plaza Janés, 1999), 127–45; Ernesto Ekaizer, *Yo, Augusto* (Buenos Aires: Aguilar, 2003), 293–308, 363–472; Eduardo Anguita, *Sano juicio: Baltasar Garzón, algunos sobrevivientes y la lucha contra la impunidad en Latinoamérica* (Buenos Aires: Editorial Sudamericana, 2001), 162–69.

69. Frei paid for this by having to acquiesce to military pressures in other areas. Cavallo, *Historia oculta*, 349–55; Garretón, "La (in)conducción política," 67–68.

70. Hilbink, "Un estado de derecho," 326–27. One example of such pressure was the Inter-American Commission on Human Rights' 1997 demand that the Chilean government repeal the amnesty law as required by article 5 of the constitution. Roniger and Sznajder, *The Legacy of Human-Rights Violations*, 302n57.

71. Rafael Blanco, "El programa de justicia del gobierno de Eduardo Frei," in *El período del Presidente Frei Ruiz-Tagle*, ed. Muñoz and Stefoni, 187–220.

72. Blanco, "El programa de justicia," 187–220; Andrade Geywitz, *Reforma de la Constitución*, 359–67, 375–87; Correa, "Cenicienta," 306–15.

73. See Wilde, "Irruptions of Memory," for the big events of 1990–1998 that elicited these memory irruptions.

74. FASIC, *Derechos humanos en Chile: resumen mensual*, January 1998; Arzopispado de Santiago, Fundación de Documentación y Archivo de la Vicaría de la Solidaridad, *Informe de derechos humanos*, first semester 1998, 3. These detailed publica-

tions are valuable sources for human rights news from Chile. They are available at http://fasic.org and www.vicariadelasolidaridad.cl, respectively.

75. Constitution of Chile, article 45. Aylwin's presidential term had been set at four years in the "tie-up" laws Pinochet left in place. The six-year provision precluded Aylwin from receiving an automatic senate seat. The constitution was revised in 1994 to fix the term at six years.

76. Siavelis, *The President and Congress*, 30–31, 107; Weeks, *The Military and Politics*, 127–37.

77. *El Mercurio*, August 20 and 23, 1998; *NACLA Report on the Americas* 32, no. 2 (September–October 1998): 5; Roger Burbach, *The Pinochet Affair: State Terrorism and Global Justice* (London: Zed Books, 2003), 91–94.

78. There is a large bibliography on Pinochet in London. The following paragraphs draw on Carlos Castresana interview, Madrid, December 11, 2001; Diana Woodhouse, ed., *The Pinochet Case: A Legal and Constitutional Analysis* (Oxford: Hart, 2000); Naomi Roht-Arriaza, *The Pinochet Effect: Transnational Justice in the Age of Human Rights* (Philadelphia: University of Pennsylvania Press, 2005), 32–66; Ekaizer, *Yo, Augusto*, 215–37, 475–966; and Mónica Pérez, *Augusto Pinochet, 503 días atrapado en Londres* (Santiago: Editorial Los Andes, 2000). See also the 2001 film directed by Patricio Guzmán, *The Pinochet Case*.

79. Roht-Arriaza, *The Pinochet Effect*. Another author's title reflects the same impact: Jorge Mario Eastman, *Pinochet: el déspota que revolucionó el derecho internacional* (Bogotá: TM Editores, 2000). Veteran human rights official Aryeh Neier lumped the events of the ex-Yugoslavia with Pinochet's arrest as seminal developments: "Augusto Pinochet and Slobodan Milosevic are symbols of the cruelty and barbarity of the last third of the twentieth century, but they also inspired the most significant advances in international accountability for the authors of great crimes." Neier, *Taking Liberties: Four Decades in the Struggle for Rights* (New York: Public Affairs, 2003), 363. On universal jurisdiction, see Roht-Arriaza, *The Pinochet Effect*, 6–14.

80. Marc Cooper, "Payback Time for Pinochetistas," *The Nation*, December 21, 1998, 24; Loveman and Lira, *El espejismo*, 253–77.

81. Viviana Díaz interview, November 21, 2002.

82. Tomás Moulian, "The Arrest and Its Aftermath," *NACLA Report on the Americas* 32, no. 6 (May–June 1999): 13.

83. Burbach, *The Pinochet Affair*, 104–6; *La Tercera*, November 23, 1998 (Internet); BBC News, December 9, 1998 (Internet).

84. Marcela Prádenas interview, Madrid, October 5, 2001. See Steve J. Stern, *Remembering Pinochet's Chile: On the Eve of London, 1998* (Durham, NC: Duke University Press, 2004), the first of three projected volumes on memory in postdictatorial Chile. Ariel Dorfman, *Exorcising Terror: The Incredible Unending Trial of General Augusto Pinochet* (New York: Seven Stories Press, 2002) is a personal chronicle of the author's reactions to the arrest and trial as well as an analysis of the events.

85. Ofelia Nistal interview, Madrid, December 10, 2001.

86. Pat Bennetts interview, Madrid, November 13, 2001. The story of her brother, Miguel Woodward, is told in Edward Crouzet, *Sangre sobre La Esmeralda: Sacerdote Miguel Woodward, vida y martirio* (Santiago: CESOC, 2000).

87. Alicia Margarita Piña Allende interview, Santiago, November 20, 2002.

88. *El País Semanal* (Madrid), June 15, 2003, 14.

89. Sara Carrasco interview, Santiago, November 20, 2002; FASIC, "Programa de salud integral para víctimas de tortura" (pamphlet, n.d.). See Inger Agger and Søren Buus Jensen, *Trauma and Healing under State Terrorism* (London: Zed Books, 1996).

90. *La Tercera*, December 2, 1998 (Internet), CHIP News, November 3, 1998 (Internet); Loveman, *Chile*, 349; Burbach, *The Pinochet Affair*, 105; Mónica Hermosilla interview, Santiago, November 23, 2002.

91. Burbach, *The Pinochet Affair*, 113–16; Roht-Arriaza, *The Pinochet Effect*, 37–40.

92. Loveman and Lira, *El espejismo*, 320–25.

93. Loveman, *Chile*, 354–55.

94. Roht-Arriaza, *The Pinochet Effect*, 67–96; Loveman and Lira, *El espejismo*, 320–25; Loveman, *Chile*, 329–30; Raquel Aldana, "Steps Closer to Justice for Past Crimes in Chile and Argentina: A Story of Judicial Boldness," the Frederick K. Cox International Law Center War Crimes Research Portal, November 17, 2004, at http://law.case.edu/War-Crimes-Research-Portal/instant_analysis.asp?id=12 (accessed August 12, 2005).

95. FASIC, *Derechos humanos*, November 1999; Vicaría de la Solidaridad, *Informe de derechos humanos*, 2nd semester, 1999, 47.

96. *Sunday Times*, November 8, 1998 (Internet); Woodhouse, ed., *The Pinochet Case*; Burbach, *The Pinochet Affair*, 117–22.

97. Ekaizer, *Yo, Augusto*, 967–73; FASIC, *Derechos humanos*, April 2000, 94; Roht-Arriaza, *The Pinochet Effect*, 67–68.

98. Human Rights Watch, "Discreet Path to Justice? Chile, Thirty Years after the Military Coup," September 2001 at http://hrw.org/backgrounder/americas/chile (accessed November 18, 2005).

99. Loveman and Lira, *El espejismo*, 300–31; Gobierno de Chile, "Acuerdo de la Mesa de Diálogo: hacia el reencuentro de todos los chilenos" (Santiago: Gobierno de Chile, 2000) (pamphlet).

100. Roht-Arriaza, *The Pinochet Effect*, 86–91.

101. Gobierno de Chile, "Mesa de Diálogo," 6.

102. *La Tercera*, June 22, 2000 (Internet).

103. Loveman and Lira, *El espejismo*, 326–28.

104. FASIC, *Derechos humanos*, January, February, April 2001; Roht-Arriaza, *The Pinochet Effect*, 91; Ana Rojas Castañeda interview, Santiago, November 20, 2002.

105. AFDD, "Declaración Pública," December 12, 2001 (mimeo); FASIC, *Derechos humanos*, January, February 2001.

106. FASIC, *Derechos humanos*, May, June 2001; Roht-Arriaza, *The Pinochet Effect*, 93–94; María Raquel Mejías interview, Santiago, November 21, 2002; Loveman and Lira, *El espejismo*, 333–438.

107. José Bengoa, quoted in Burbach, *The Pinochet Affair*, 125; José Zalaquett interview, Santiago, November 22, 2002.

108. FASIC, *Derechos humanos*, March, December 2001, June 2003, January 2004; Aldana, "Steps Closer to Justice."

109. FASIC, *Derechos humanos*, August 18, 2003.

110. Burbach, *The Pinochet Affair*, 123–45; Weeks, *The Military in Politics*, 146–51.

111. FASIC, *Derechos humanos*, July 2001, July 2002; Loveman and Lira, *El espejismo*, 349–50.

112. Human rights lawyer Carmen Hertz said, "The entire political and social establishment in Chile wanted an end to the Pinochet case. The Lagos government also abandoned its pledge not to interfere in the counts in the Pinochet case." Burbach, *The Pinochet Affair*, 140.

113. *Los Angeles Times*, March 16, 2005; *La Nación*, March 18, 2005 (Internet); FASIC, *Derechos humanos*, June 2005, September 2005.

114. Loveman and Lira, *El espejismo*, 349–50.

115. Human Rights Watch, "Essential Background: Overview of Human Rights in Chile," December 31, 2004 (Internet); FASIC, *Derechos humanos*, July 2003, June 2004.

116. FASIC, *Derechos humanos*, August 2002.

117. FASIC, *Derechos humanos*, September 2002.

118. FASIC, *Derechos humanos*, May 2002.

119. FASIC, *Derechos humanos*, May 2003.

120. Tina Rosenberg, "Chile's Military Must Now Report to One of Its Past Victims," *New York Times*, May 11, 2004 (Internet). Michelle Bachelet was elected president of Chile in 2006.

121. FASIC, *Derechos humanos*, September 2002, June 2003, March, June 2004.

122. The Center for Human Rights' website is www.cdh.uchile.cl (accessed February 6, 2006); the center launched a new publication, the *Anuario de derechos humanos*. Also FASIC, *Derechos humanos*, November 2003; Louis S. Bickford, "The Archival Imperative," *Human Rights Quarterly* 21, no. 4 (1999): 1097–1122; Bickford, "Human Rights Archives and Research on Historical Memory: Argentina, Chile, and Uruguay," *Latin American Research Review* 35 (2000): 160–82. Released the year before Pinochet's arrest, Patricio Guzmán's film *Chile, Obstinate Memory* criticizes the continuing suppression of popular memory of the UP years. Marcial Godoy-Anativia, "On Patricio Guzmán's *Chile, Obstinate Memory*," *NACLA Report on the Americas* 32, no. 2 (September–October 1998): 21.

123. *La Tercera*, June 26, 2000 (Internet); FASIC, *Derechos humanos*, March 2002, August, September, October 2003; Katherine Hite, "Resurrecting Allende," *NACLA Report on the Americas* 37, no. 1 (July–August 2003): 19–24; Louis Bickford,

"Preserving Memory: The Past and the Human Rights Movement in Chile," in *Democracy and Human Rights in Latin America*, ed. Richard S. Hillman, John A. Peeler, and Elsa Cardozo da Silva (Westport, CT: Praeger, 2002), 13. The July–August 2003 issue (vol. 37, no. 1) of *NACLA Report on the Americas* is titled "Chile: Thirty Years Later."

124. See the commission's report and Lagos's remarks at http://gobiernodechile.cl/commission-vlach/index.asp (accessed August 30, 2006).

125. *La Tercera*, November 4, 2004 (Internet).

CONCLUSION

~

Chile, Argentina, and International Human Rights

This book has examined state terrorism and its legacies in Chile and Argentina, focusing on the relationship between the histories of these countries and the evolution of international human rights. It has argued that from the establishment of regimes of state terrorism in 1973 and 1976, respectively, to the present period of reckoning with crimes against human rights, Chile and Argentina have had a reciprocal relationship with the international human rights regime. Influence has flowed in both directions—from the international to the domestic, and vice versa.

When the militaries took power, neither Chile nor Argentina had effective human rights organizations, and the international human rights conventions and institutions were incomplete and virtually untested. Today, Argentina and Chile have large, vigorous human rights movements, and the international human rights regime has evolved and matured. One cannot fully comprehend the recent histories of Chile and Argentina, indeed the history of much of Latin America, without taking into account the changing international human rights regime; and those histories in turn elucidate the evolution of international human rights from the stage of monitoring to that of enforcement—to "the age of human rights."[1]

The Pinochet dictatorship sheds important light on the state of international human rights in the 1970s and 1980s. Established a quarter century after the articulation of both the American and universal standards for human rights and after a substantial part of the international monitoring apparatus had been established, the Pinochet regime demonstrates the weakness of the existing machinery for the protection of human rights. Despite continuous pressure, dozens of negative reports on the human rights situation in Chile, and repeated condemnations in international forums, the regime doggedly pursued its mission of eradicating the left by all available means. The Cold War context, strong U.S. support except during the Carter administration, and the spread of state terrorism and repression throughout Latin America aided the Chilean dictatorship in rebuffing international efforts to moderate its human rights policy. Pinochet even derived some advantage from international criticism by positioning himself as the defender of national sovereignty against what he called Marxist-inspired foreign intervention in domestic affairs, helping to solidify his regime.

Of the few concessions the regime made to the human rights advocates, most were cosmetic. When it agreed to let the churches and international refugee agencies arrange exile for the thousands of people who had taken asylum in embassies, it got rid of a substantial part of the medium- to high-profile left. Following the Letelier assassination in Washington, Pinochet responded to pressure from the Carter administration in 1977 by dismantling the DINA, lifting the state of siege, and greatly reducing killings by state agents. However, replacing the DINA with the CNI and the state of siege with a state of exception changed almost nothing, and the relaxation of repression was due to the regime's very success in eliminating the last of the underground resistance groups in 1976. The dictatorship occasionally released prisoners at the urging of Amnesty International or other groups, but since these were normally well-known persons, sending them into exile rather than killing them was good for the regime's image. The regime continued to repress as needed until its end.

The role of human rights activism, nonetheless, was very important in Chile from 1973 to 1990 and afterward. The key internal element during the dictatorship was the Catholic Church—the one institution that Pinochet was unable to neutralize. By providing support to other human rights organizations, the church helped build a human rights movement in Chile that complemented and worked with the international organizations. The domestic human rights movement focused on ameliorating the consequences of the repression that it could not prevent. The services offered to victims of human rights violations, families of those victims, the persecuted, and victims of the new economic model were crucial to the physical and emotional survival of many Chileans. And the paper trail of court documents filed by the Vicaría de la Solidaridad and other human rights lawyers would be invaluable to establishing the truth of what happened between 1973 and 1990 and to the eventual pursuit of justice. The human rights movement may also have been a deterrent to even more brutal repression than that which occurred—a proposition that eludes measurement.

International reaction to the Chilean coup and the following months of open, unvarnished state terrorism was the single greatest catalyst to strengthening human rights activism since the Holocaust. Chile brought into sharp focus the disparity between human rights theory and practice, between the idealism of international treaties and declarations and the brutal reality of state terrorism. The Chilean situation stimulated the formation of new international NGOs, created the U.S. human rights movement, changed the course of U.S. foreign policy, and transformed the UN into an activist voice for human rights. More than any other event, the Chilean coup and its aftermath introduced human rights into the lexicon. In sum, Chile was the catalyst to the strengthening of the international human rights regime, which began immediately after the coup and culminated in the opening of the International Criminal Court in 2003.

While state terrorism in Chile created the momentum for increased human rights activism, the dirty war in Argentina propelled the process along. The Argentine regime shared essential characteristics with the Chilean terrorist state: the mission of eradicating the left, the rejection of any limitations on the means employed to accomplish its goal, and the accumulation of a massive toll of grave human rights violations. Unlike the Pinochet dictatorship, where the Catholic Church remained a thorn in the regime's side, the Argentine junta enjoyed the support or acquiescence of the most important national institutions, including the church, and neutralized or destroyed the rest. Despite the lack of institutional support, a domestic human rights movement developed and attempted valiantly to publicize the human rights violations and aid victims and their families. However, using brute force, stealth, and the power of its propaganda machine, the dictatorship was able to minimize the impact of the Madres de Plaza de Mayo and other domestic human rights groups. They were simply incapable of challenging the power of the Argentine military regime or stopping the massive application of state terrorism during the first four years of the Proceso. Nonetheless, as in the Chilean case, the work of the domestic human rights movement, particularly the Center for Legal and Social Studies (CELS) and the Permanent Assembly for Human Rights (APDH), in filing court cases and documenting disappearances and other abuses would be crucial to the postdictatorship quest for truth and justice.

Despite the broad similarities between state terrorism in the two countries, the Argentine experience with the international human rights lobby was different owing to the heightened international activism caused by the

Chilean coup and its aftermath. When the Argentine military staged its coup in March 1976, Pinochet had been in power only two and a half years. Although Pinochet was secure in his control over the country, Chile had become a pariah state, and the regime had been inducted into the UN's gallery of bêtes noires, a distinction it shared with South Africa and Israel. The Argentine officers were undoubtedly as confident as their Chilean counterparts about impunity for the crimes they committed, which they considered patriotic acts. But having observed the activation of the international human rights lobby in response to the Chilean situation, the Argentine junta sought to avoid giving grounds for investigations, condemnations, and possible sanctions. Thus it selected its primary method of eliminating "subversion," the disappearance, with the consequences of human rights violations in mind.

The Argentine military operated sub rosa from the outset in order to establish plausible deniability. Unlike the Chilean case, there was no curfew, uniformed soldiers were not photographed rounding up or executing people, and most of the bodies were never seen. Until the Madres de Plaza de Mayo began their Thursday afternoon marches thirteen months after the coup—the thirteen deadliest months of the Proceso—visitors to Argentina would not have suspected the carnage going on around them. While international NGOs reported, Argentine exiles denounced, and foreign governments protested their citizens' disappearances, there was lingering doubt in world opinion that the rumors and allegations about disappearances were true. Thus the Argentine dictatorship was able to dodge damning reports by the OAS and UN human rights commissions and the condemnations by the UN General Assembly that Pinochet repeatedly faced.

In 1979, however, after state terrorism had taken a toll of thousands of victims, the international human rights lobby, with its powers enhanced, took aim at the Argentine junta. The visit of the Inter-American Commission on Human Rights, authorized by the dictatorship under pressure from the Carter administration, was a turning point. Precisely because the method of disappearance had worked so well, and many Argentines thus were still unsure of the state's role in human rights violations, the commission's report, complete with names and explanations, had a bombshell impact when translated and smuggled into the country in 1980. The report was the first major blow to the regime; it began to undermine the credibility and coherence of the military state. Disappearances virtually ceased, and, spurred by compelling evidence of the depth and breadth of the government's nefarious activities, an opposition movement began to form, leading to the regime's demise three years later.

Argentina reinforced the impact that Chile had made on the international human rights regime. It further energized human rights organizations, both

NGO and intergovernmental. Several concrete developments occurred during the Proceso: Human Rights Watch and *Human Rights Quarterly* were both founded in 1978, and the UN's Working Group on Enforced or Involuntary Disappearances was established in 1980. Along with the emergence of state terrorism in Central America, Argentina and Chile led to the creation of Human Rights Watch's first regional division, Americas Watch, in 1981 and contributed to the doubling of the number of international human rights NGOs between 1983 and 1993.[2] And the Argentine and Chilean influence on international human rights norms is clearly evident in the major treaties and declarations adopted in the 1980s and 1990s on torture and disappearance.

The reciprocal relationship between Argentina and Chile and the international human rights regime continued after the end of state terrorism in those countries, when the human rights movements that had developed during the dictatorships turned their attention to truth and justice. Just as it had aided the domestic human rights movements during military rule, the international human rights lobby consistently and vigorously supported the cause of justice following the return of civilian rule. At the same time, postdictatorial Argentina and Chile continued to influence international human rights.

Initially, it was Argentina that made a major impact on the international scene. After the installation of a democratic government in December 1983, Argentina faced the challenge of reckoning with past grave human rights violations with few precedents to follow. As the first Latin American country to emerge from a regime of severe state terrorism and the first to attempt to hold former rulers accountable for human rights violations, Argentina developed policies and practices on a trial-and-error basis. In doing so, the Alfonsín administration, in conjunction with the human rights movement, set precedents for transitional justice around the world.

One of Alfonsín's first acts was to establish a truth commission, the National Commission on the Disappearance of Persons (CONADEP). As the result of the scrupulousness of its investigations, the dramatic nature of its findings, and the evocative title of its report, *Nunca más*, the Argentine truth commission became a model that has been applied in over thirty countries since 1983, and Argentine personnel have served as advisers to several commissions. The forensic anthropology team was also adapted by Argentine authorities for the task of identifying victims' remains—the complement to the work of truth commissions. The Argentine Forensic Anthropology Team has worked in over thirty countries on five continents. Given the censorship and misinformation that characterize state terrorist governments and the lingering fear these regimes instill, the repressors' version of truth would likely remain uncontested, or at least largely intact, without the work of truth commissions and forensic investigators. The alternative truth that they provide forms the basis for memory contestation and formation, and with that the likely discrediting of repressive regimes and the foundation for avoiding them in the future. Alfonsín also adopted measures designed to prevent a repetition of state terrorism, such as building human rights components into government agencies, requiring human rights education, and, with the help of the human rights movement, attempting to build a culture of human rights.

The Argentine experience with justice has been more difficult to replicate. Although the trial of the juntas was a major step toward Alfonsín's goal of exemplary punishment, the subsequent limiting of trials through *punto final* and due obedience laws, followed by the reversal of justice through Menem's pardons, underscored the difficulty of holding repressors accountable in the 1980s. Nonetheless, the Argentine experiment with justice and its reversal helped to develop the consciousness that inspired the international human rights community to develop higher standards and the means for enforcing them—the hallmark of the changes of the 1980s and 1990s. It is not coincidental that the International Criminal Court's first chief prosecutor, Luis Moreno-Ocampo, is an Argentine who served as deputy prosecutor in the 1985 trial of the juntas.[3]

While thus contributing in very significant ways to practices of transitional justice that have become common in countries emerging from periods of repression, Argentina was also profoundly affected by developments on the international scene, particularly after the mid-1990s. When CELS launched its program for the application of international human rights law in Argentine courts in 1995, in accordance with the 1994 constitutional reform, it received the backing of the international human rights lobby. The 1995 Scilingo revelations and Pinochet's arrest three years later restored the momentum for accountability and justice that had been lost in the second half of the 1980s. The OAS human rights machinery, Amnesty International, Human Rights Watch, the Spanish government, and numerous other human rights organizations, governments, and foundations directly aided the quest for justice in Argentina—efforts that bore their greatest fruit to date in the landmark 2005 Supreme Court decision confirming the constitutionality of the 2003 law that revoked the *punto final* and due obedience laws and eliminated definitively the impunity of hundreds, possibly over a thousand, repressors.

The elected government in Chile faced a scenario in 1990 that was far different from the situation in Argentina following Alfonsín's inauguration. Rather than a discredited military initially unable to defend itself from prosecution, Chile had a triumphalist military that was proud of its political and economic record and was protected against prosecution by a carefully constructed shield of impunity. Based on the 1978 amnesty law, the protected democracy that Pinochet had left in place, and the continuing political power of the military, impunity remained intact during the early postdictatorial years. Nonetheless, following Argentine precedents, President Patricio Aylwin launched the process of transitional justice by establishing a truth commission and engaging in symbolic politics of solidarity with the cause of justice.

In 1998, a dramatic demonstration of the new power of the international human rights regime abruptly changed the course of transitional justice in Chile and reverberated around the world. More forcefully than the report of the truth commission, Pinochet's 1998 arrest and the subsequent court proceedings in London undermined the military's version of truth and history, energized the human rights movement, and emboldened the judiciary. The arrest and subsequent legal battles in London and Chile made Pinochet's arguably the highest-profile human rights case since the Nuremberg trials.

The extradition request from Spain and the legal proceedings in London clearly revealed the evolution of international human rights. The UN had adopted its Convention against Torture and Other Cruel, Inhuman, or Degrading Treatment or Punishment in 1984. Spain had enacted a law granting itself universal jurisdiction over human rights crimes in 1985. The British government ratified the UN Convention against Torture in 1988, the same year that the Chilean government ratified it—with stated reservations—by the signature of Pinochet himself. The new UN convention and the principle of universal jurisdiction snared Pinochet; the other key principle of the new human rights jurisprudence, the invalidity of amnesties for crimes against humanity, did not need to be invoked. The revelations brought out in the legal process in London fully acquainted the world with the changes in international human rights as well as the workings of institutionalized state terrorism.

Following Pinochet's arrest, the full power of both international and domestic human rights organizations was unleashed on Chile as well as Argentina. The indomitable domestic human rights movement redoubled its efforts to breach the amnesty law. International human rights NGOs submitted amicus curiae briefs and provided other resources to Chilean human rights groups. The Inter-American Commission on Human Rights and the Inter-American Court of Human Rights weighed in, and the Ford Foundation and other organizations joined the struggle for justice.

Pinochet has repeatedly escaped trial in Chile since his return in March 2000. But the fact that he could have his immunity from prosecution stripped and be indicted in multiple cases is something that was unthinkable prior to his arrest. The London arrest and the beginning of proceedings against Pinochet in Chile opened the country to the power of the strengthened global human rights lobby. In contrast to Argentina, where the repeal of the *punto final* and due process laws opened the way to mass prosecutions, the 1978 amnesty law still stands in Chile. But under the assault of domestic and international advocates of justice, the amnesty law no longer preserves impunity, making hundreds of alleged repressors liable to prosecution.

Chile and Argentina made human rights history in the 1970s and 1980s as extreme cases of state terrorism that were instrumental in changing the world's approach to human rights. Today they are again making history, this time for the systematic investigation, prosecution, and sentencing of human rights violators in their own courts, at the hands of Argentine and Chilean judges. The erosion of impunity may offer some solace to victims of state terrorism and their families, but it cannot undo the ravages of torture or bring back the dead. Yet the recent developments in Chile and Argentina may be more than ex post facto remedies for human rights violations: they might possibly influence would-be repressors in any part of the world before they act, and in that small way help nudge the international human rights regime toward another stage in its evolution—the stage of deterrence.

Notes

1. The quotation is from the title of Naomi Roht-Arriaza, *The Pinochet Effect: Transnational Justice in the Age of Human Rights* (Philadelphia: University of Pennsylvania Press, 2005).

2. Margaret E. Keck and Kathryn Sikkink, *Activists beyond Borders: Advocacy Networks in International Politics* (Ithaca, NY: Cornell University Press, 1998), 90.

3. www.hrw.org/press/2003/04/icc042103.htm (accessed October 12, 2005).

~

Selected Bibliography

Interviews

Pat Bennetts, Madrid, November 13, 2001.
Sara Carrasco, Santiago, November 20, 2002.
Carlos Castresana, Madrid, December 11, 2001.
Mercedes Colas de Meroño, Buenos Aires, December 5, 2002.
Deyanira Corvalán, Santiago, November 15, 2002.
Viviana Díaz, Santiago, November 21, 2002.
María José Guembe, Buenos Aires, December 12, 2002.
Nancy Guzmán, Santiago, November 15, 2002.
Mónica Hermosilla, Santiago, November 23, 2002.
Alba Lanzillotto, Buenos Aires, December 10, 2002.
Diego Masera Cerutti, Mexico City, September 12, 2003.
María Raquel Mejías, Santiago, November 21, 2002.
Ilda Micucci, Buenos Aires, December 9, 2002.
Ofelia Nistal, Madrid, December 10, 2001.
Alicia Margarita Piña Allende, Santiago, November 20, 2002.
Marcela Prádenas, Madrid, October 5, 2001.
Verónica Reyna, Santiago, November 19 and 22, 2002.
Patrick Rice, Buenos Aires, December 9, 2002.
Ana Rojas Castañeda, Santiago, November 20, 2002.
Juana Shanahan, Santiago, November 20, 2002.
Carlos Slepoy, Madrid, October 30, 2001.

Patricia Valdéz, Buenos Aires, December 4 and 11, 2002.
Marta Vásquez, Buenos Aires, December 10, 2002.
José Zalaquett, Santiago, November 22, 2002.

Books, Articles, and Serial Publications

Abós, Alvaro. *Las organizaciones sindicales y el poder militar (1976–1983)*. Buenos Aires: Centro Editor de América Latina, 1984.
———. *Delitos ejemplares: historias de la corrupción argentina, 1810–1997*. Buenos Aires: Grupo Editorial Norma, 1999.
Abregú, Martín. "Human Rights after the Dictatorship: Lessons from Argentina," *NACLA Report on the Americas* 34, no. 1 (July–August 2000): 12–18.
Abuelas de Plaza de Mayo. *Niños desaparecidos en Argentina desde 1976*. Buenos Aires: Madres de Plaza de Mayo, 1999.
Agger, Inger, and Søren Buus Jensen. *Trauma and Healing under State Terrorism*. London: Zed Books, 1996.
Agosín, Marjorie. *Circles of Madness: Mothers of the Plaza de Mayo*. [Círculos de locura: madres de la Plaza de Mayo.] Fredonia, NY: White Pine Press, 1992.
———. *Surviving beyond Fear: Women, Children and Human Rights in Latin America*. Fredonia, NY: White Pine Press, 1993.
———. *Ashes of Revolt*. Fredonia, NY: White Pine Press, 1996.
———. *Tapestries of Hope, Threads of Love: The Arpillera Movement in Chile, 1974–1994*. Albuquerque: University of New Mexico Press, 1996.
Agrupación de Familiares de Detenidos Desaparecidos de Chile. *Veinte años de historia de la Agrupación de Familiares de Detenidos Desaparecidos de Chile: un camino de imágines*. Santiago: Corporación de Familiares de Detenidos Desaparecidos, 1997.
———. *Resumen de actividades* (various years).
Ahumada Lillo, Manuel. *Cerro Chena testimonio*. Santiago: Ediciones Tierra Mía, 2003.
Alabarces, Pablo. *Fútbol y patria: el fútbol y las narrativas de la nación en la Argentina*. Buenos Aires: Prometeo, 2002.
Alaniz, Rogelio. *La década menemista*. Santa Fe, Argentina: Universidad Nacional del Litoral, 2000.
Aldana, Raquel. "Steps Closer to Justice for Past Crimes in Chile and Argentina: A Story of Judicial Boldness." The Frederick K. Cox International Law Center War Crimes Portal, November 17, 2004.
Alexander, Robert J. *Juan Domingo Perón*. Boulder, CO: Westview Press, 1979.
Alfonsín, Raúl. *Memoria política: transición a la democracia y derechos humanos*. Buenos Aires: Fondo de Cultura Económica, 2004.
Allende, Isabel. *Of Love and Shadows*. Translated by Margaret Sayers Peden. New York: Dial Press, 2005.
Almeyda, Clodomiro. *Reencuentro con mi vida*. Santiago: Ediciones del Ornitorrinco, 1987.

Americas Watch. *El Salvador's Decade of Terror: Human Rights since the Assassination of Archbishop Romero*. New Haven, CT: Yale University Press, 1991.

Amnesty International. *Testimonio sobre campos secretos de detención en Argentina*. n.d.

———. *Report on the Mission to Argentina, November 6–15, 1976*. London: Amnesty Publications, 1977.

———. *Informe sobre presos politicos retenidos en campos secretos de detención en Chile, marzo de 1977*. Barcelona: La Faya-Ciencia, 1977.

———. *The "Disappeared" of Argentina: List of Cases Reported to Amnesty International, March 1976–February 1979*. London: Amnesty International, 1979.

———. *"Disappearances," a Workbook*. New York: Amnesty International, 1982.

———. *Argentina: The Military Juntas and Human Rights—Report of the Trial of the Former Junta Members, 1985*. London: Amnesty International, 1987.

———. *Chile, Torture and the Naval Training Ship the "Esmeralda."* London: International Secretariat, 2003.

———. *Cuba, "Essential Measures": Human Rights Crackdown in the Name of Security*. London: Amnesty International, 2003.

Amstutz, Mark R. *The Healing of Nations: The Promise and Limits of Political Forgiveness*. Lanham, MD: Rowman & Littlefield, 2005.

Andersen, Martin Edwin. *Dossier Secreto: Argentina's Desaparecidos and the Myth of the "Dirty War."* Boulder, CO: Westview Press, 1993.

Anderson, Jon Lee. *Che Guevara: A Revolutionary Life*. New York: Grove Press, 1997.

Anderson, Thomas P. *Matanza: El Salvador's Communist Revolt of 1932*. Lincoln: University of Nebraska Press, 1971.

Andrade Geywitz, Carlos. *Reforma de la Constitución política de la República de Chile de 1980*. 2nd ed. Santiago: Editorial Jurídica de Chile, 2002.

Anguita, Eduardo. *Sano juicio: Baltasar Garzón, algunos sobrevivientes y la lucha contra la impunidad en Latinoamérica*. Buenos Aires: Editorial Sudamericana, 2001.

Arce, Luz. *The Inferno: A Story of Terror and Survival in Chile*. Translated by Stacey Alba Skar. Madison: University of Wisconsin Press, 2004.

Arditti, Rita. *Searching for Life: The Grandmothers of the Plaza de Mayo and the Disappeared Children of Argentina*. Berkeley: University of California Press, 1999.

Argentina: juicios a los militares. Documentos secretos, decretos-leyes, jurisprudencia. Cuadernos de la Asociación Americana de Juristas, no. 4. 1988.

Armomy, Ariel C. *Argentina, the United States, and the Anti-Communist Crusade in Central America, 1977–1984*. Athens: Ohio University Center for International Studies, 1997.

Arriagada Herrera, Genaro. *El pensamiento político de los militares: estudios sobre Chile, Argentina, Brasil y Uruguay*. Santiago: Centro de Investigaciones Socioeconómicos, 1981.

———. *Pinochet: The Politics of Power*. Translated by Nancy Morris. Boston: Unwin and Hyman, 1988.

———. *Por la razón o la fuerza: Chile bajo Pinochet*. Santiago: Editorial Sudamericana, 1998.

Arzobispado de Santiago. Fundación de Documentación y Archivo de la Vicaría de la Solidaridad. "Detenidos desaparecidos" (unpublished working document, 8 vols., 1994), vol. 1.

———. Fundación de Documentación y Archivo de la Vicaría de la Solidaridad. *Informe de derechos humanos* (various numbers).

Asociación Madres de Plaza de Mayo. *Historia de las Madres de Plaza de Mayo*. Buenos Aires: Ediciones Asociación Madres de Plaza de Mayo, 1999.

———. *Massera: el genocida*. Buenos Aires: Editorial La Página, 1999.

Atria, Rodrigo, et al. *Chile, la memoria prohibida: las violaciones a los dereches humanos, 1973–1983*. 3 vols. Santiago: Pehuén Editores, 1989.

Aylwin Azócar, Patricio. *La transición chilena: discursos escogidos marzo 1990–1992*. Santiago: Editorial Andrés Bello, 1992.

Bacchus, Wilfred A. *Mission in Mufti: Brazil's Military Regimes, 1964–1985*. Westport, CT: Greenwood Press, 1990.

Baker, Stuart A., ed. *Patriot Debates*. Chicago: American Bar Association, 2005.

Ball, Howard. *Prosecuting War Crimes and Genocide: The Twentieth-Century Experience*. Lawrence: University of Kansas Press, 1999.

Barahona de Brito, Alexandra. *Human Rights and Democratization in Latin America: Uruguay and Chile*. Oxford: Oxford University Press, 1997.

Barahona de Brito, Alexandra, Carmen González-Enríquez, and Paloma Aguilar, eds. *The Politics of Memory: Transitional Justice in Democratizing Societies*. Oxford: Oxford University Press, 2001.

Basso, Carlos. *El último secreto de Colonia Dignidad*. Santiago: Editorial Mare Nostrum, 2002.

Berry, Albert, ed. *Poverty, Economic Reform, and Income Distribution in Latin America*. Boulder, CO: Lynne Rienner, 1998.

Bethell, Leslie, ed. *Chile since Independence*. Cambridge: Cambridge University Press, 1993.

Bickford, Louis S. "The Archival Imperative," *Human Rights Quarterly* 21, no. 4 (1999): 1097–1122.

———. "Human Rights Archives and Research on Historical Memory: Argentina, Chile, and Uruguay," *Latin American Research Review* 35 (2000): 160–82.

Bitar, Sergio. *Chile, Experiment in Democracy*. Translated by Sam Sherman. Philadelphia: Institute for the Study of Human Issues, 1986.

Blasier, Cole. *The Hovering Giant: U.S. Responses to Revolutionary Change in Latin America, 1910–1985*. Rev. ed. Pittsburgh: University of Pittsburgh Press, 1985.

Bonachea, Rolando, and Marta San Martín. *The Cuban Insurrection, 1952–1958*. New Brunswick, NJ: Transaction Books, 1974.

Bonachea, Rolando, and Nelson P. Valdés, eds. *Cuba in Revolution*. Garden City, NY: Anchor Books, 1972.

———, eds. *Revolutionary Struggle 1947–1958: Volume I of the Selected Works of Fidel Castro.* Cambridge, MA: MIT Press, 1972.

Bonasso, Miguel. *Recuerdo de la muerte.* Mexico City: Ediciones Era, 1984.

Bonsal, Philip W. *Cuba, Castro, and the United States.* Pittsburgh: University of Pittsburgh Press, 1972.

Boorstein, Edward. *The Economic Transformation of Cuba.* New York: Monthly Review Press, 1968.

Booth, John A. *The End and the Beginning: The Nicaraguan Revolution.* 2nd ed. Boulder, CO: Westview Press, 1985.

Borzutzky, Silvia, and Lois Hecht Oppenheim, eds. *After Pinochet: The Chilean Road to Democracy and the Market.* Gainesville: University of Florida Press, 2006.

Branch, Taylor, and Eugene M. Proper. *Labyrinth.* New York: Viking Press, 1982.

Torture in Brazil: A Shocking Report on the Pervasive Use of Torture by Brazilian Military Governments, 1964–1979. Translated by Jaime Wright. Austin: University of Texas Press, 1998.

Braylan, Marisa. *Report on the Situation of the Jewish Detainees-Disappeared during the Genocide Perpetrated in Argentina.* Buenos Aires: Social Research Center of DAIA-Argentinean Jewish Community Centers Association, 2000.

Brennan, James. *El Cordobazo.* Buenos Aires: Sudamericana, 1996.

Brown, Cynthia G., ed. *With Friends Like These: The Americas Watch Report on Human Rights and U.S. Policy in Latin America.* New York: Pantheon, 1985.

Brown, Cynthia G. *The Vicaría de la Solidaridad in Chile.* Santiago: Americas Watch, 1987.

———. *Human Rights and the "Politics of Agreements": Chile during President Aylwin's First Year.* New York: Americas Watch, 1991.

Brown, Jonathan C. *A Brief History of Argentina.* New York: Facts on File, 2003.

Bruno Genta, Jordán. *Guerra contrarevolucionaria: doctrina política.* Buenos Aires: Nuevo Order, 1965.

Brysk, Alison. *The Politics of Human Rights in Argentina: Protest, Change, and Democratization.* Stanford, CA: Stanford University Press, 1994.

Burbach, Roger. *The Pinochet Affair: State Terrorism and Global Justice.* London: Zed Books, 2003.

Bushnell, Timothy, et al., eds. *State Organized Terror: The Case of Violent Internal Repression.* Boulder, CO: Westview Press, 1991.

Camarasa, Jorge, Rubén Felice, and Daniel González. *El juicio: proceso al horror.* Buenos Aires: Sudamericana/Planeta Editores, 1985.

Camp, Roderick Ai, ed. *Democracy in Latin America: Patterns and Cycles.* Wilmington, DE: Scholarly Resources, 1996.

Carey, Elaine. *Plaza of Sacrifices: Gender, Power, and Terror in 1968 Mexico.* Albuquerque: University of New Mexico Press, 2005.

Carrió, Alejandro. *Los Crímenes del Cóndor: el caso Prats y la trama de conspiraciones entre los servicios de inteligencia del Cono Sur.* Buenos Aires: Sudamericana, 2005.

Castañeda, Jorge G. *Compañero: The Life and Death of Che Guevara*. Translated by Marina Castañeda. New York: Knopf, 1997.

Cavallo Castro, Ascanio. *La historia oculta de la transición: Chile 1990–1998*. Santiago: Grijalbo, 1998.

Cavallo Castro, Ascanio, Manuel Salazar Salvo, and Oscar Sepúlveda Pacheco. *Chile, 1973–1988: la historia oculta del régimen militar*. Santiago: Editorial Antártica, 1989.

Cavarozzi, Marcelo. *Autoritarismo y democracia*. Buenos Aires: Ariel, 1997.

Cea Egaña, José Luis. *Tratado de la Constitución de 1980: características generales, garantías constitucionales*. Santiago: Editorial Jurídica de Chile, 1988.

Centro de Estudios Legales y Sociales (CELS). *Informe anual sobre la situación de los derechos humanos en la Argentina*. Buenos Aires: CELS, various years.

——. *Testimonio sobre el centro clandestino de detención de la Escuela de Mecánica de la Armada Argentina (ESMA)*. Buenos Aires: CELS, 1984.

——. *Terrorismo de estado: 692 responsables*. Buenos Aires: CELS, 1986.

——. *La aplicación de los tratados sobre derechos humanos por los tribunales locales*. Buenos Aires: Editores del Puerto, 1997.

——. *Patti: manual del buen torturador*. Buenos Aires: CELS, 1999.

Centro de Estudios Legales y Sociales (CELS) and Americas Watch. *Verdad y justicia en la Argentina: actualización*. Buenos Aires: CELS and Americas Watch, 1991.

Chalmers, Douglas A., et al., eds. *The New Politics of Inequality in Latin America: Rethinking Participation and Representation*. New York: Oxford University Press, 1997.

Child, John. *Unequal Alliance: The Inter-American Military System, 1938–1978*. Boulder, CO: Westview Press, 1980.

Chile. *Report of the National Commission on Truth and Reconciliation*. Translated by Phillip E. Berryman. Notre Dame, IN: University of Notre Dame Press, 1993.

Chossudovsky, Michel. *The Globalisation of Poverty: Impacts of IMF and World Bank Reforms*. London: Zed Books, 1997.

Círculo Militar. *In Memoriam*. 2 vols. Buenos Aires: Círculo Militar, 1998–1999.

Cleary, Edward L. *The Struggle for Human Rights in Latin America*. Westport, CT: Praeger, 1997.

Collier, David, ed. *The New Authoritarianism in Latin America*. Princeton, NJ: Princeton University Press, 1979.

Collier, Simon, and William F. Sater. *A History of Chile, 1808–2002*. 2nd ed. Cambridge: Cambridge University Press, 2004.

Collins, Joseph, and John Lear. *Chile's Free Market Miracle: A Second Look*. Oakland, CA: Institute for Food and Development Policy, 1994.

Coloquio de Buenos Aires. *La desaparición forzada como crimen de lesa humanidad: el "nunca más" y la comunidad internacional*. Buenos Aires: Coloquio de Buenos Aires, 1989.

Comisión Argentina de Derechos Humanos. *Ex-ayudante del General Harguindeguy acusa: testimonio del inspector de la Policía Federal Argentina (R.O.) Rodolfo Peregrino Fernández*. Buenos Aires: Comisión Argentina de Derechos Humanos, 1983.

Comisión Nacional sobre la Desaparición de Personas (CONADEP). *Nunca más: informe de la Comisión Nacional sobre la Desaparición de Personas.* 5th ed. Buenos Aires: Editorial Universitaria de Buenos Aires, 1999.

Comité de Defensa de los Derechos del Pueblo (CODEPU). *Todas íbamos a ser reinas: estudio sobre nueve mujeres embarazadas que fueron detenidas y desaparecidas en Chile.* Santiago: Quimo Impresores, 1990.

Constable, Pamela, and Arturo Valenzuela. *A Nation of Enemies: Chile under Pinochet.* New York: W. W. Norton, 1991.

Corporación Nacional de Reparación y Reconciliación. *Informe sobre calificación de víctimas de violaciones de derechos humanos y de la violencia política.* Santiago: Corporación Nacional de Reparación y Reconciliación, 1996.

Corradi, Juan E. *The Fitful Republic.* Boulder, CO: Westview Press, 1985.

Corradi, Juan E., Patricia Weiss Fagen, and Manuel Antonio Garretón, eds. *Fear at the Edge: State Terror and Resistance in Latin America.* Berkeley: University of California Press, 1992.

Correa, Raquel, and Elizabeth Subercaseaux. *Ego sum.* Santiago: Planeta, 1996.

Crouzet, Edward. *Sangre sobre La Esmeralda: Sacerdote Miguel Woodward, vida y martirio.* Santiago: CESOC, 2000.

Davidson, Scott. *The Inter-American Human Rights System.* Aldershot, Hants, U.K.: Dartmouth Publishing, 1997.

De la Maza, Gonzalo, and Mario Garcés. *La explosión de las mayorías: protesta nacional, 1983–1984.* Santiago: Editorial ECO, 1985.

De Riz, Liliana. *Retorno y derrumbe: el ultimo gobierno peronista.* Mexico City: Folios Ediciones, 1981.

Deutsch, Sandra McGee. *Las Derechas: The Extreme Right in Argentina, Brazil, and Chile, 1890–1939.* Stanford, CA: Stanford University Press, 1999.

Deutsch, Sandra McGee, and Ronald H. Dalkart, eds. *The Argentine Right: Its History and Intellectual Origins, 1910 to the Present.* Wilmington, DE: Scholarly Resources, 1993.

De Wylder, Stefan. *Allende's Chile: The Political Economy of the Rise and Fall of the Unidad Popular.* Cambridge: Cambridge University Press, 1976.

Dinges, John. *The Condor Years: How Pinochet and His Allies Brought Terrorism to Three Continents.* New York: New Press, 2004.

Dinges, John, and Saul Landau. *Assassination on Embassy Row.* New York: McGraw-Hill, 1980.

Domínguez, Jorge I. *Cuba: Order and Revolution.* Cambridge, MA: Harvard University Press, 1978.

———. *To Make the World Safe for Revolution: Cuba's Foreign Policy.* Cambridge, MA: Harvard University Press, 1989.

———., ed. *Constructing Democratic Governance: Latin America and the Caribbean in the 1990s.* Baltimore: Johns Hopkins University Press, 1996.

Donnelly, Jack. *International Human Rights.* 2nd ed. Boulder, CO: Westview Press, 1998.

———. *Universal Human Rights in Theory and Practice.* 2nd ed. Ithaca, NY: Cornell University Press, 2003.

Dorfman, Ariel. *Death and the Maiden.* New York: Penguin, 1992.

———. *Exorcising Terror: The Incredible Unending Trial of General Augusto Pinochet.* New York: Seven Stories Press, 2002.

Drake, Paul W., and Iván Jaksić, eds. *El modelo chileno: democracia y desarrollo en los noventa.* Santiago: LOM Ediciones, 1999.

———, eds. *The Struggle for Democracy in Chile.* Rev. ed. Lincoln: University of Nebraska Press, 1995.

Driscoll, William, et al. *The International Criminal Court: Global Politics and the Quest for Justice.* New York: International Debate Education Association, 2004.

Duhalde, Eduardo Luis. *El estado terrorista argentino.* Barcelona: Editorial Argos Vergara, 1983.

———. *El estado terrorista argentino: quince años después, una mirada crítica.* Buenos Aires: Editorial Universitaria de Buenos Aires, 1998.

Eagleson, John, and Philip Scharper, eds. *Puebla and Beyond: Documentation and Commentary.* Translated by John Drury. Maryknoll, NY: Orbis Books, 1979.

Eastman, Jorge Mario. *Pinochet: el déspota que revolucionó el derecho internacional.* Bogotá: TM Editores, 2000.

Ekaizer, Ernesto. *Yo, Augusto.* Buenos Aires: Aguilar, 2003.

Ensalaco, Mark. *Chile under Pinochet: Recovering the Truth.* Philadelphia: University of Pennsylvania Press, 2000.

Epstein, Edward C., ed. *The New Argentine Democracy: The Search for a Successful Formula.* Westport, CT: Praeger, 1992.

Equipo Argentino de Antropología Forense. *Tumbas anónimas: informe sobre la identificación de restos de víctimas de la represión ilegal.* Buenos Aires: Equipo Argentino de Antropología Forense, 1992.

Escalante, Jorge. *La misión era matar: el juicio a la caravana Pinochet-Arellano.* Santiago: LOM Ediciones, 2000.

Etzioni, Amitai. *How Patriotic Is the Patriot Act? Freedom versus Security in the Age of Terrorism.* New York: Routledge, 2004.

Fagen, Richard R. *The Transformation of Political Culture in Cuba.* Stanford, CA: Stanford University Press, 1969.

Falla, Ricardo. *Massacres in the Jungle: Ixcán, Guatemala, 1975–1982.* Translated by Julia Howland. Boulder, CO: Westview Press, 1994.

Farcau, Bruce W. *The Chaco War: Bolivia and Paraguay, 1932–1935.* Westport, CT: Praeger, 1996.

Feitlowitz, Marguerite. *A Lexicon of Terror: Argentina and the Legacies of Torture.* New York: Oxford University Press, 1998.

Fisher, Jo. *Mothers of the Disappeared.* Boston: South End Press, 1989.

Fleet, Michael. *The Rise and Fall of Chilean Christian Democracy.* Princeton, NJ: Princeton University Press, 1985.

Fraser, Nicholas, and Marysa Navarro. *Evita.* Rev. ed. New York: W. W. Norton, 1996.

Fried, J. L., et al., eds. *Guatemala in Rebellion: Unfinished Revolution.* New York: Grove Press, 1982.

Frühling E., Hugo, ed. *Represión política y defensa de los derechos humanos*. Santiago: Centro de Estudios Sociales-CESOC, 1986.

Fundación de Ayuda Social de las Iglesias Cristianas (FASIC). *Derechos humanos en Chile: resumen mensual* (various numbers).

Gabetta, Carlos. *Todos somos subversivos*. Buenos Aires: Bruguera, 1983.

Galeano, Eduardo. *Guatemala: Occupied Country*. Translated by Cedric Belfrage. New York: Monthly Review Press, 1969.

Garcés D., Mario, and Nancy Nicholls L. *Para una historia de los derechos humanos en Chile: historia institucional de la Fundación de Ayuda Social de las Iglesias Cristianas FASIC 1975–1991*. Santiago: LOM Ediciones, 2005.

Gareau, Frederick H. *State Terrorism and the United States: From Counterinsurgency War to the War on Terrorism*. London: Zed Books, 2004.

Garretón Merino, Manuel A. *The Chilean Political Process*. Translated by Sharon Kellum with Gilbert W. Merkx. Boston: Unwin and Hyman, 1989.

Gaudin, Andrés. "Thirteen Days That Shook Argentina—And What Now?" *NACLA Report on the Americas* 35, no. 5 (March–April 2002): 6–9.

———. "The Kirchner Factor." *NACLA Report on the Americas* 38, no. 4 (January–February 2005): 16–18.

Gazmuri, Cristián, et al. *Eduardo Frei Montalva y su época*. 2 vols. Santiago: Aguilar, 2000.

Gellately, Robert, and Ben Kiernan, eds. *The Specter of Genocide: Mass Murder in Historical Perspective*. Cambridge, UK: Cambridge University Press, 2003.

Germani, Gino. *Política y sociedad en una época de transición: de la sociedad tradicional a la sociedad de masas*. Buenos Aires: Paidós, 1971.

Getty, J. Arch, and Oleg V. Naumov. *The Road to Terror: Stalin and the Self-Destruction of the Bolsheviks, 1932–1939*. Translated by Benjamin Sher. New Haven, CT: Yale University Press, 1999.

Gilio, María Esther. *The Tupamaro Guerrillas*. Translated by Anne Edmondson. New York: Ballantine Books, 1973.

Gill, Lesley. *The School of the Americas: Military Training and Political Violence in the Americas*. Durham, NC: Duke University Press, 2004.

Gillespie, Richard. *Soldiers of Perón*. Oxford: Oxford University Press, 1982.

Glasius, Marlies. *The International Criminal Court: A Global Civil Society Achievement*. New York: Routledge, 2005.

Godoy-Anativia, Marcial. "On Patricio Guzmán's *Chile, Obstinate Memory*." *NACLA Report on the Americas* 32, no. 2 (September–October 1998): 21.

Goldenberg, Boris. *The Cuban Revolution and Latin America*. New York: Praeger, 1966.

Goldman, Robert K., and Cynthia G. Brown. *Challenging Impunity: The Ley de Caducidad and the Referendum Campaign in Uruguay*. New York: Americas Watch, 1989.

Gómez Araneda, León. *Tras la huella de los desaparecidos*. Santiago: Ediciones Caleuche, 1990.

González Janzen, Ignacio. *La Triple-A*. Buenos Aires: Editorial Contrapunto, 1986.

Graber, G. S. *Caravans to Oblivion: The Armenian Genocide, 1915*. New York: Wiley, 1996.

Graham-Yool, Andrew. *The Press in Argentina, 1973–78*. London: Writers and Scholars Educational Trust, 1979.

Graziano, Frank. *Divine Violence: Spectacle, Psychosexuality, and Radical Christianity in the Argentine "Dirty War."* Boulder, CO: Westview Press, 1992.

Groisman, Enrique. *La Corte Suprema de Justicia durante la dictadura (1976–1983)*. Buenos Aires: CISEA, 1989.

Guest, Iain. *Behind the Disappearances: Argentina's Dirty War against Human Rights and the United Nations*. Philadelphia: University of Pennsylvania Press, 1990.

Guevara, Che. *Reminiscences of the Cuban Revolutionary War*. Translated by Victoria Ortiz. New York: Grove Press, 1968.

———. *Guerrilla Warfare*. 3rd ed. Wilmington, DE: Scholarly Resources, 1997.

Guzmán, Nancy. *Romo: confesiones de un torturador*. Santiago: Editorial Planeta, 2000.

Guzmán Bouvard, Marguerite. *Revolutionizing Motherhood: The Mothers of the Plaza de Mayo*. Wilmington, DE: SR Books, 1994.

Harrington, Edwin, and Mónica González. *Bomba en una calle de Palermo*. Santiago: Editorial Emisión, 1987.

Harris, David J., and Stephen Livingstone, eds. *The Inter-American System of Human Rights*. New York: Oxford University Press, 1998.

Hartlyn, Jonathan, Lars Schoultz, and Augusto Varas, eds. *The United States and Latin America in the 1990s: Beyond the Cold War*. Chapel Hill: University of North Carolina Press, 1992.

Haslam, Jonathan. *The Nixon Administration and the Death of Allende's Chile: A Case of Assisted Suicide*. London: Verso, 2005.

Hawkins, Darren G. *International Human Rights and Authoritarian Rule in Chile*. Lincoln: University of Nebraska Press, 2002.

Hayner, Priscilla B. *Unspeakable Truths: Confronting State Terror and Atrocity*. New York: Routledge, 2001.

Hevener Kaufman, Natalie. *Human Rights Treaties and the Senate: A History of Opposition*. Chapel Hill: University of North Carolina Press, 1990.

Hilb, Claudia, and Daniel Lutzky, eds. *La nueva izquierda argentina: 1960–1980*. Buenos Aires: Centro Editor de América Latina, 1984.

Hillman, Richard S., John A. Peeler, and Elsa Cardozo da Silva, eds. *Democracy and Human Rights in Latin America*. Westport, CT: Praeger, 2002.

Hitchens, Christopher. *The Trial of Henry Kissinger*. London: Verso, 2001.

Hite, Katherine. "Resurrecting Allende." *NACLA Report on the Americas* 37, no. 1 (July–August 2003): 19–24.

Hodges, Donald C. *The Latin American Revolution: Politics and Strategy from Apro-Marxism to Guevarism*. New York: William Morrow, 1974.

———. *Argentina's "Dirty War": An Intellectual History*. Austin: University of Texas Press, 1991.

Hojman, Eugenio. *1973–1989 Memorial de la dictadura: cronología de 16 años de pesadilla.* Santiago: Editorial Emisión, 1990.

Horowitz, Irving Louis, Josué de Castro, and John Gerassi, eds. *Latin American Radicalism.* New York: Vintage Books, 1969.

Human Rights Watch. *The Limits of Tolerance: Freedom of Expression and the Public Debate in Chile.* New York: Human Rights Watch, 1998.

Huntington, Samuel P. *The Third Wave: Democratization in the Late Twentieth Century.* Norman: University of Oklahoma Press, 1991.

Immerman, Richard M. *The CIA in Guatemala: The Foreign Policy of Intervention.* Austin: University of Texas Press, 1982.

Inter-American Commission on Human Rights. *Report on the Status of Human Rights in Chile: Findings of "On the Spot" Observations in the Republic of Chile July 22–August 2, 1974.* Washington, DC: OAS, 1974.

———. *Second Report on the Situation of Human Rights in Chile.* Washington, DC: OAS, 1976.

———. *Third Report on the Situation of Human Rights in Chile.* Washington, DC: OAS, 1977.

———. *Report on the Situation of Human Rights in Argentina.* Washington, DC: Inter-American Commission on Human Rights, 1980.

International Commission of Jurists. *Chile: A Time of Reckoning; Human Rights and the Judiciary.* Geneva: Centre for the Independence of Judges and Lawyers, 1992.

International Review of the Red Cross, no. 845 (March 2002).

James, Daniel. *Resistance and Integration: Peronism and the Argentine Working Class, 1946–1976.* Cambridge: Cambridge University Press, 1988.

Jarvis, Lovell S. *Chilean Agriculture under Military Rule: From Reform to Reaction, 1973–1980.* Berkeley: Institute of International Studies, University of California, 1985.

Jelin, Elizabeth. "The Minefields of Memory." *NACLA Report on the Americas* 32, no. 2 (September–October 1998): 23–29.

Jelin, Elizabeth, and Eric Hershberg. *Constructing Democracy: Human Rights, Citizenship, and Society in Latin America.* Boulder, CO: Westview, 1996.

Jonas, Susanne. *Of Centaurs and Doves: Guatemala's Peace Process.* Boulder, CO: Westview Press, 2000.

Jonassohn, Kurt, with Karin Solveig Björnson. *Genocide and Gross Human Rights Violations in Comparative Perspective.* New Brunswick, NJ: Transaction Publishers, 1998.

Kaiser, Susana. "Outing Torturers in Postdictatorship Argentina." *NACLA Report on the Americas* 34, no. 1 (July–August 2000): 14–15.

Kantor, Harry. *The Ideology and Politics of the Peruvian Aprista Movement.* New York: Octagon Books, 1966.

Kay, Crístobal, and Patricio Silva, eds. *Development and Social Change in the Chilean Countryside: From the Pre-Land Reform Period to the Democratic Transition.* Amsterdam: Centre for Latin American Research and Documentation, 1992.

Keck, Margaret E., and Kathryn Sikkink. *Activists beyond Borders: Advocacy Networks in International Politics*. Ithaca, NY: Cornell University Press, 1998.

Kenner, Martin, and James Petras, eds. *Fidel Castro Speaks*. New York: Grove Press, 1969.

Kiernan, Ben. *The Pol Pot Regime: Race, Power, and Genocide in Cambodia under the Khmer Rouge, 1975–1979*. New Haven, CT: Yale University Press, 2002.

Klare, Michael T. *War without End: American Planning for the Next Vietnams*. New York: Vintage Books, 1972.

Klare, Michael T., and Cynthia Arnson. *Supplying Repression: U.S. Support for Authoritarian Regimes Abroad*. Washington, DC: Institute for Policy Studies, 1981.

Kohl, James, and John Litt, eds. *Urban Guerrilla Warfare in Latin America*. Cambridge, MA: MIT Press, 1974.

Kohut, David, Olga Vilella, and Beatrice Julian. *Historical Dictionary of the "Dirty Wars."* Lanham, MD: Scarecrow Press, 2003.

Koonings, Kees, and Dirk Kruijt. *Societies of Fear: The Legacy of Civil War, Violence and Terror in Latin America*. London: Zed Books, 1999.

Kornbluh, Peter, ed. *The Pinochet File: A Declassified Dossier on Atrocity and Accountability*. New York: New Press, 2003.

Koven Levit, Janet. "The Constitutionalization of Human Rights in Argentina: Problem or Promise?" *Columbia Journal of Transnational Law* 37 (1999): 281–356 (Westlaw).

Laikin Elkin, Judith. "Recoleta: Civilization and Barbarism in Argentina." *Michigan Quarterly Review* 27 (1988): 221–39.

Landsberger, Henry A., ed. *Latin American Peasant Movements*. Ithaca, NY: Cornell University Press, 1969.

Lauren, Paul Gordon. *The Evolution of International Human Rights: Visions Seen*. 2nd ed. Philadelphia: University of Pennsylvania Press, 2003.

Lewis, Daniel K. *The History of Argentina*. Westport, CT: Greenwood Press, 2001.

Lewis, Paul H. *Guerrillas and Generals: The "Dirty War" in Argentina*. Westport, CT: Praeger, 2002.

Londregan, John B. *Legislative Institutions and Ideology in Chile*. Cambridge: Cambridge University Press, 2000.

Lorey, David E., and William H. Beezley, eds. *Genocide, Collective Violence, and Popular Memory: The Politics of Remembrance in the Twentieth Century*. Wilmington, DE: SR Books, 2002.

Loveman, Brian. *The Constitution of Tyranny: Regimes of Exception in Spanish America*. Pittsburgh: University of Pittsburgh Press, 1993.

———. *Chile: The Legacy of Hispanic Capitalism*. 3rd ed. New York: Oxford University Press, 2001.

Loveman, Brian, and Thomas M. Davies Jr. *The Politics of Antipolitics: The Military in Latin America*. Revised and updated ed. Wilmington, DE: Scholarly Resources, 1997.

Loveman, Brian, and Elizabeth Lira. *Las ardientes cenizas del olvido: vía chilena de reconciliación política 1932–1994*. Santiago: LOM Ediciones, 2000.

———. *El espejismo de la reconciliación política: Chile 1990–2002.* Santiago: LOM Ediciones, 2002.

———, eds. *Leyes de reconciliación en Chile: amnistías, indultos y reparaciones, 1819–1999.* Santiago: Universidad Jesuita Alberto Hurtado, 2001.

Lowden, Pamela. *Moral Opposition to Authoritarian Rule in Chile, 1973–1990.* London: Macmillan Press, 1996.

Lowenthal, Abraham F., and J. Samuel Fitch, eds. *Armies and Politics in Latin America.* Rev. ed. New York: Holmes & Meier, 1986.

Lozada, Salvador María. *Los derechos humanos y la impunidad en la Argentina (1974–1999).* Buenos Aires: Nuevohacer, 1999.

Luna, Félix. *Argentina de Perón a Lanusse, 1943–1973.* Barcelona: Planeta, 1972.

———. *Perón y su tiempo.* Buenos Aires: Sudamericana, 1986.

Mainwaring, Scott. "Authoritarianism and Democracy in Argentina." *Journal of Interamerican Studies and World Affairs* 26, no. 3 (August 1984).

Malloy, James M., and Mitchell A. Seligson, eds. *Authoritarians and Democrats: Regime Transition in Latin America.* Pittsburgh: University of Pittsburgh Press, 1987.

Marchak, Patricia. *God's Assassins: State Terrorism in Argentina in the 1970s.* Montreal: McGill-Queen's University Press, 1999.

Marras, Sergio. *Palabra de soldado: entrevistas de Sergio Marras.* Santiago: Ornitorrinco, 1989.

Martí, Ana María, et al. *ESMA "Trasladados": testimonio de tres liberadas, octubre de 1979.* Buenos Aires: Abuelas de Plaza de Mayo, Familiares de Desaparecidos y Detenidos por Razones Políticas, and Madres de Plaza de Mayo, Línea Fundadora, 1995.

Martín de Pozuelo, Eduardo, and Santiago Tarín. *España acusa.* Barcelona: Plaza Janés, 1999.

Martyniuk, Claudio Eduardo. *ESMA: fenomenología de la desaparición.* Buenos Aires: Prometeo Libros, 2004.

Martz, John D. *Acción Democrática: Evolution of a Modern Political Party in Venezuela.* Princeton, NJ: Princeton University Press, 1966.

———, ed. *United States Policy in Latin America: A Quarter Century of Crisis and Challenge, 1961–1986.* Lincoln: University of Nebraska Press, 1988.

Martz, John D., and Lars Schoultz, eds. *Latin America, the United States, and the Inter-American System.* Boulder, CO: Westview Press, 1980.

Massun, Ignacio C. M. *Alfonsín: una difícil transición.* Buenos Aires: Editorial Métodos, 1999.

Mattelart, Armand. *La burguesía en la escuela de Lenín: el gremialismo y la línea de masas de la burguesía chilena.* Lima: Centro de Documentación MIEC-JECI, 1974.

Matthews, Herbert. *The Cuban Story.* New York: George Braziller, 1961.

Matta, Pedro Alejandro. "A Walk through a 20th-Century Torture Center: Villa Grimaldi, Santiago de Chile; A Visitor's Guide." 2000.

Matus Acuña, Alejandra. *El libro negro de la justicia chilena.* Santiago: Editorial Planeta, 1999.

Matus Acuña, Alejandra, and Francisco Javier Artaza. *Crimen con castigo*. Santiago: La Nación Ediciones B, 1996.

McAdams, A. James, ed. *Transitional Justice and the Rule of Law in New Democracies*. Notre Dame, IN: University of Notre Dame Press, 1997.

McClintock, Cynthia. *Revolutionary Movements in Latin America: El Salvador's FMLN and Peru's Shining Path*. Washington, DC: United States Institute of Peace Press, 1998.

McDonough, Peter. *Power and Ideology in Brazil*. Princeton, NJ: Princeton University Press, 1981.

McSherry, J. Patrice. *Incomplete Transition: Military Power and Democracy in Argentina*. New York: St. Martin's Press, 1997.

———. "Military Rumblings in Argentina." *NACLA Report on the Americas* 34, no. 1 (July–August 2000): 16–17.

———. *Predatory States: Operation Condor and Covert War in Latin America*. Lanham, MD: Rowman & Littlefield, 2005.

Mellibovsky, Matilde. *Circle of Love over Death: Testimonies of the Mothers of the Plaza de Mayo*. Translated by Maria and Matthew Proser. Willimantic, CT: Curbstone Press, 1997.

Menjívar, Cecilia, and Néstor Rodríguez. *When States Kill: Latin America, the U.S., and Technologies of Terror*. Austin: University of Texas Press, 2005.

Merino Vega, Marcia Alejandra. *Mi verdad: "más allá del horror, yo acuso . . . ."* Santiago: Printed at A.T.G., S.A., 1993.

Mertus, Julie A. *Bait and Switch: Human Rights and U.S. Foreign Policy*. New York: Routledge, 2004.

Middlebrook, Martin. *The Fight for the Malvinas: The Argentine Forces in the Falklands War*. New York: Viking, 1989.

Mignone, Emilio F. *Witness to the Truth: The Complicity of Church and Dictatorship in Argentina, 1976–1983*. Translated by Phillip Berryman. Maryknoll, NY: Orbis Books, 1988.

———. *Derechos humanos y sociedad: el caso argentino*. Buenos Aires: Centro de Estudios Legales y Sociales-CELS, 1991.

Montgomery, Tommie Sue. *Revolution in El Salvador: Origins and Evolution*. 2nd ed. Boulder, CO: Westview Press, 1989.

———. *Revolution in El Salvador: From Civil Strife to Civil Peace*. 2nd ed. Boulder, CO: Westview Press, 1995.

Moreira Alves, María Helena. *State and Opposition in Military Brazil*. Austin: University of Texas Press, 1985.

Moro, Rubén. *The History of the South Atlantic Conflict: The War of the Malvinas*. New York: Praeger, 1989.

Moulian, Tomás. *Chile actual: anatomía de un mito*. Santiago: LOM-ARCIS, 1997.

———. "The Time of Forgetting: The Myths of the Chilean Transition." *NACLA Report on the Americas* 32, no. 2 (September–October 1998): 17.

———. "The Arrest and Its Aftermath." *NACLA Report on the Americas* 32, no. 6 (May–June 1999): 13.

Moyano, José María. *Argentina's Lost Patrol: Armed Struggle, 1969–1979*. New Haven, CT: Yale University Press, 1995.

Muñoz, Heraldo. *Las relaciones exteriores del gobierno militar chileno*. Santiago: Ediciones del Ornitorrinco, 1986.

Muñoz, Oscar, and Carolina Stefoni, eds. *El período del Presidente Frei Ruiz-Tagle: reflexiones sobre el segundo gobierno concertacionista*. Santiago: FLASCO-Chile, Editorial Universitaria, 2002.

North American Congress on Latin America. *NACLA Report on the Americas* (various issues).

Neier, Aryeh. *Taking Liberties: Four Decades in the Struggle for Rights*. New York: Public Affairs, 2003.

Nelson-Pallmeyer, Jack. *School of Assassins: Guns, Greed, and Globalization*. Maryknoll, NY: Orbis Books, 2001.

Nino, Carlos Santiago. *Radical Evil on Trial*. New Haven, CT: Yale University Press, 1996.

Norden, Deborah L. *Military Rebellion in Argentina: Between Coups and Consolidation*. Lincoln: University of Nebraska Press, 1996.

Nosiglia, Julio. *Botín de guerra*. Buenos Aires: Abuelas de Plaza de Mayo, 1985.

Nunn, Frederick M. *The Military in Chilean History: Essays on Civil-Military Relations, 1810–1973*. Albuquerque: University of New Mexico Press, 1976.

———. *The Time of the Generals: Latin American Professional Militarism in World Perspective*. Lincoln: University of Nebraska Press, 1992.

O'Donnell, Guillermo. *Bureaucratic Authoritarianism: Argentina, 1966–1973, in Comparative Perspective*. Translated by James McGuire and Rae Flory. Berkeley: University of California Press, 1988.

O'Donnell, Guillermo, and Philippe Schmitter. *Transitions from Authoritarian Rule: Tentative Conclusions about Uncertain Democracies*. Baltimore: Johns Hopkins University Press, 1986.

O'Donnell, Guillermo, Philippe Schmitter, and Laurence Whitehead, eds. *Transitions from Authoritarian Rule: Latin America*. Berkeley: University of California Press, 1988.

Olavarría Bravo, Arturo. *Chile bajo la Democracia Cristiana*. 6 vols. Santiago: Editorial Nascimento, 1966–1971.

Oppenheim, Lois Hecht. *Politics in Chile: Democracy, Authoritarianism, and the Search for Development*. 2nd ed. Boulder, CO: Westview Press, 1999.

Orellana, Patricio, and Elizabeth Q. Hutchison. *El movimiento de derechos humanos en Chile, 1973–1990*. Santiago: Centro de Estudios Políticos Latinoamericanos Simón Bolívar (CEPLA), 1991.

Orsolini, Mario Horacio. *La crisis del ejército*. Buenos Aires: Ediciones Arayú, 1964.

Otano, Rafael. *Crónica de la transición*. Santiago: Planeta, 1995.

Palmer, David Scott, ed. *The Shining Path of Peru*. New York: St. Martin's Press, 1992.

Partnoy, Alicia. *The Little School: Tales of Disappearance and Survival in Argentina*. Translated by Alicia Partnoy with Lois Athey and Sandra Braunstein. Pittsburgh: Cleis Press, 1986.

Peeler, John. *Building Democracy in Latin America*. Boulder, CO: Lynne Rienner, 1998.

Pérez, Mónica. *Augusto Pinochet, 503 días atrapado en Londres*. Santiago: Editorial Los Andes, 2000.

Pinochet de la Barra, Oscar. *El Cardenal Silva Henríquez: luchador por la justicia*. Santiago: Editorial Salesiana, 1987.

Pinochet Ugarte, Augusto. *El día decisivo*. 5th ed. Santiago: Editorial Andrés Bello, 1984.

———. *Camino recorrido: biografía de un soldado*. 3 vols. Santiago: Instituto Geográfico Militar de Chile, 1990–1994.

Pion-Berlin, David. "National Security Doctrine, Military Threat Perception and the 'Dirty War.'" *Comparative Political Studies* 21 (October 1988): 382–407.

———. *The Ideology of State Terror: Economic Doctrine and Political Repression in Argentina and Peru*. Boulder, CO: Lynne Rienner, 1989.

———. *Through Corridors of Power: Institutions and Civil-Military Relations in Argentina*. College Park: Pennsylvania State University Press, 1997.

Politzer, Patricia. *Fear in Chile: Lives under Pinochet*. Translated by Diane Wachtell. New York: Pantheon, 1989.

Pontoriero, Gustavo. *Sacerdotes para el Tercer Mundo: "El fermento en la masa" (1967–1976)*. Buenos Aires: Centro Editor de América Latina, 1991.

Porzecanski, Arturo C. *Uruguay's Tupamaros: The Urban Guerrilla*. New York: Praeger, 1973.

Power, Jonathan. *Like Water on Stone: The Story of Amnesty International*. Boston: Northeastern University Press, 2001.

Power, Samantha, and Graham Allison. *Realizing Human Rights: Moving from Inspiration to Impact*. New York: St. Martin's Press, 2000.

Prunier, Gérard. *The Rwanda Crisis: History of a Genocide*. New York: Columbia University Press, 1995.

Pucciarelli, Alfredo, ed. *La primacía de la política: Lanusse, Perón, y la nueva izquierda en tiempos del GAN*. Buenos Aires: Eudeba, 1999.

Quijada, Aníbal. *Cerco de púas*. Santiago: Fuego y Tierra, 1990.

Ramos, Joseph. *Neoconservative Economics in the Southern Cone of Latin America, 1973–1983*. Baltimore: Johns Hopkins University Press, 1986.

Reinsch, Paul S. "Parliamentary Government in Chile." *American Political Science Review* 3 (1909): 507–38.

Remmer, Karen. *Military Rule in Latin America*. Boston: Unwin and Hyman, 1989.

República Argentina, Poder Ejecutivo Nacional. *Evolution of Terrorist Delinquency in Argentina*. Buenos Aires: Poder Ejecutivo Nacional, 1980.

Reszczynski, Katia, Paz Rojas, and Patricia Barceló. *Tortura y resistencia en Chile: estudio médico-político*. Santiago: Editorial Emisión, 1991.

Roberts, Kenneth M. *The Modern Left and Social Movements in Chile and Peru*. Stanford, CA: Stanford University Press, 1998.

Robertson, Geoffrey. *Crimes against Humanity: The Struggle for Global Justice*. New York: New Press, 2000.

Rock, David. *Argentina 1516–1987: From Spanish Colony to Alfonsín*. Berkeley: University of California Press, 1987.

———. *Authoritarian Argentina: The Nationalist Movement, Its History, and Its Impact*. Berkeley: University of California Press, 1993.

Rodríguez Molas, Ricardo. *Historia de la tortura y el orden represivo en la Argentina*. 2 vols. Buenos Aires: Editorial Universitaria de Buenos Aires (EUDEBA), 1984–1985.

Roehrig, Terence. *The Prosecution of Former Military Leaders in Newly Democratic Nations: The Cases of Argentina, Greece, and South Korea*. Jefferson, NC: McFarland, 2002.

Roht-Arriaza, Naomi. *The Pinochet Effect: Transnational Justice in the Age of Human Rights*. Philadelphia: University of Pennsylvania Press, 2005.

Rojas, Carmen. *Recuerdos de una MIRista*. Montevideo: Ediciones del Taller, 1988.

Rojas de Estudillo, Rosario, et al. *Memorias contra el olvido*. Santiago: Amerinda Ediciones, 1987.

Romero, Luis Alberto. *A History of Argentina in the Twentieth Century*. Translated by James P. Brennan. University Park: Pennsylvania State University Press, 2002.

Romero Salvadó, Francisco J. *Twentieth-Century Spain: Politics and Society in Spain, 1898–1998*. New York: St. Martin's Press, 1999.

Roniger, Luis, and Mario Sznajder. *The Legacy of Human-Rights Violations in the Southern Cone: Argentina, Chile and Uruguay*. Oxford: Oxford University Press, 1999.

Rotberg, Robert I., and Dennis Thompson, eds. *Truth v. Justice: The Morality of Truth Commissions*. Princeton, NJ: Princeton University Press, 2000.

Rouquié, Alain. *Poder militar y sociedad política en la Argentina*. 2 vols. Translated by Arturo Iglesias Echegaray. Buenos Aires: Emecé Editores, 1981–1982.

———. *The Military and the State in Latin America*. Translated by Paul Sigmund. Berkeley: University of California Press, 1987.

Salazar Salvo, Manuel. *Contreras: historia de un intocable*. Santiago: Grijalbo, 1995.

Sánchez Albornoz, Nicolás. *The Population of Latin America: A History*. Berkeley: University of California Press, 1974.

Sancinetti, Marcelo A. *Derechos humanos en la Argentina postdictatorial*. Buenos Aires: Lerner Editores, 1988.

Schlesinger, Stephen, and Stephen Kinzer. *Bitter Fruit: The Untold Story of the American Coup in Guatemala*. Garden City, NJ: Doubleday, 1982.

Schneider, Cathy Lisa. *Shantytown Protest in Pinochet's Chile*. Philadelphia: Temple University Press, 1995.

Schoultz, Lars. *Human Rights and United States Policy toward Latin America*. Princeton, NJ: Princeton University Press, 1981.

———. *National Security and United States Policy toward Latin America*. Princeton, NJ: Princeton University Press, 1987.

Sells, Michael Anthony. *The Bridge Betrayed: Religion and Genocide in Bosnia.* Berkeley: University of California Press, 1996.

Selser, Gregorio. *El onganiato.* 2 vols. Buenos Aires: C. Samonta, 1972–1973.

Seoane, María. *Todo o nada.* Buenos Aires: Planeta, 1991.

Seoane, María, and Vicente Muleiro. *El dictador: La historia secreta y pública de Jorge Rafael Videla.* Buenos Aires: Sudamericana, 2000.

Seoane, María, and Héctor Ruiz Núñez. *La noche de los lápices.* 2nd ed. Buenos Aires: Planeta, 1992.

Servicio Paz y Justicia, Uruguay. *Uruguay Nunca Más: Human Rights Violations, 1972–1985.* Translated by Elizabeth Hampsten. Philadelphia: Temple University Press, 1992.

Siavelis, Peter M. *The President and Congress in Postauthoritarian Chile: Institutional Constraints to Democratic Consolidation.* University Park: Pennsylvania State University Press, 2000.

Sieder, Rachel, ed. *Guatemala after the Peace Accords.* London: Institute of Latin American Studies, 1998.

Sigmund, Paul E. *The Overthrow of Allende and the Politics of Chile, 1964–1976.* Pittsburgh: University of Pittsburgh Press, 1977.

———. *The United States and Democracy in Chile.* Baltimore: Johns Hopkins University Press, 1993.

Silva, Patricio. *Estado, neoliberalismo y política agraria en Chile, 1973–1981.* Amsterdam: CEDLA, 1987.

Simons, Geoff. *Indonesia, the Long Oppression.* New York: St. Martin's Press, 2000.

Simpson, John, and Jana Bennett. *The Disappeared and the Mothers of the Plaza.* New York: St. Martin's Press, 1985.

Skidmore, Thomas E. *The Politics of Military Rule in Brazil.* New York: Oxford University Press, 1988.

Sluka, Jeffrey A., ed. *Death Squad: The Anthropology of State Terror.* Philadelphia: University of Pennsylvania Press, 2000.

Smith, Brian H. *The Church and Politics in Chile: Challenges to Modern Catholicism.* Princeton, NJ: Princeton University Press, 1982.

Smith, Peter H. *Talons of the Eagle: Dynamics of U.S.-Latin American Relations.* 2nd ed. New York: Oxford University Press, 2000.

Smith, William C. *Authoritarianism and the Crisis of the Argentine Political Economy.* Stanford, CA: Stanford University Press, 1989.

Snow, Peter G., and Luigi Manzetti. *Political Forces in Argentina,* 3rd ed. Westport, CT: Praeger, 1993.

Solberg, Carl E. *Immigration and Nationalism, Argentina and Chile, 1890–1914.* Austin: University of Texas Press, 1970.

Sosnowski, Saúl, and Louise B. Popkin, eds. *Repression, Exile, and Democracy: Uruguayan Culture.* Translated by Louise B. Popkin. Durham, NC: Duke University Press, 1993.

Spooner, Mary Helen. *Soldiers in a Narrow Land: The Pinochet Regime in Chile.* Updated ed. Berkeley: University of California Press, 1999.

Steiner, Henry J., ed. *Truth Commissions: A Comparative Assessment*. Cambridge, MA: Harvard Law School Human Rights Program, 1997.

Stern, Steve J. *Remembering Pinochet's Chile: On the Eve of London, 1998*. Durham, NC: Duke University Press, 2004.

Stern, Steve J., ed. *Shining and Other Paths: War and Society in Peru, 1980–1995*. Durham, NC: Duke University Press, 1998.

Stewart, Graham H., and James L. Tigner. *Latin America and the United States*. 6th ed. Englewood Cliffs, NJ: Prentice-Hall, 1975.

Stover, Eric. *The Open Secret: Torture and the Medical Profession in Chile*. Washington, DC: American Association for the Advancement of Science, 1987.

Szulc, Tad. *Twilight of the Tyrants*. New York: Holt, 1959.

———. *Fidel: A Critical Portrait*. New York: William Morrow, 1986.

Taylor, Lucy. *Citizenship, Participation and Democracy: Changing Dynamics in Chile and Argentina*. New York: St. Martin's Press, 1998.

Tedesco, Laura. *Democracy in Argentina: Hope and Disillusion*. London: Frank Cass, 1999.

Teitel, Ruti. *Transitional Justice*. New York: Oxford University Press, 1999.

Timerman, Jacobo. *Prisoner without a Name, Cell without a Number*. Translated by Tony Talbott. New York: Vintage Books, 1988.

Tiscornia, Eduardo. *El destino circular de la Argentina, 1810–1984*. Buenos Aires: Librería Sarmiento, 1983.

Tolley, Howard, Jr. *The U.N. Commission on Human Rights*. Boulder, CO: Westview Press, 1987.

Trinquier, Roger. *Guerre, subversion, révolution*. Paris: R. Laffont, 1968.

Tulchin, Joseph S. *Argentina and the United States: A Conflicted Relationship*. Boston: Twayne, 1990.

Uekert, Brenda K. *Rivers of Blood: A Comparative Study of Government Massacres*. Westport, CT: Praeger, 1995.

Urso, Norberto Pedro. *Mansión Seré: un vuelo hacia el horror*. Buenos Aires: Ediciones de la Memoria, 2002.

Vacs, Aldo César. *Discreet Partners: Argentina and the USSR since 1917*. Pittsburgh: University of Pittsburgh Press, 1984.

Valdés, Hernán. *Diary of a Chilean Concentration Camp*. Translated by Jo Labanyi. London: Gollancz, 1975.

Valdés, Juan Gabriel. *Pinochet's Economists: The Chicago School in Chile*. Cambridge: Cambridge University Press, 1995.

Valenzuela, Arturo. *The Breakdown of Democratic Regimes: Chile*. Baltimore: Johns Hopkins University Press, 1978.

Valenzuela, J. Samuel, and Arturo Valenzuela. *Military Rule in Chile: Dictatorship and Oppositions*. Baltimore: Johns Hopkins University Press, 1986.

Vargas V., Otilia. *La dictadura me arrebató cinco hijos*. Santiago: Editorial Mosquito Comunicaciones, 1991.

Vásquez, Enrique. *La última: origen, apogeo y caída de la dictadura militar*. Buenos Aires: Eudeba, 1985.

Veiga, Raúl. *Las organizaciones de derechos humanos*. Buenos Aires: Centro Editor de América Latina, 1985.

Verbitsky, Horacio. *Civiles y militares: memoria secreta de la transición*. 2nd ed. Buenos Aires: Editorial Contrapunto, 1987.

———. *The Flight: Confessions of an Argentine Dirty Warrior*. Translated by Esther Allen. New York: New Press, 1996.

———. *Malvinas: la última batalla de la tercera Guerra Mundial*. Rev. ed. Buenos Aires: Editorial Sudamericana, 2002.

———. *Rodolfo Walsh y la prensa clandestina, 1976-1978*. Buenos Aires: Ediciones de la Urraca, 1985.

Verdugo, Patricia. *Quemados vivos*. Santiago: Aconcagua, 1986.

———. *Interferencia secreta: 11 de septiembre de 1973*. Includes compact disc. Santiago: Editorial Sudamericana, 1998.

———. *Chile, Pinochet, and the Caravan of Death*. Translated by Marcelo Montecino. Coral Gables, FL: North-South Center Press, 2001.

Vicaría de la Solidaridad. *Informe sobre 384 casos de personas desaparecidas, Julio '76*. 5 vols. Santiago: Vícaria de la Solidaridad, 1975.

Vidal, Hernán. *Dar la vida por la vida: la Agrupación Chilena de Familiares de Detenidos Desaparecidos*. Minneapolis: Institute for the Study of Ideologies and Literature, 1982.

———. *Frente Patriótico Manuel Rodríguez: el tabú del conflicto armado en Chile*. Santiago: Editorial Mosquito, 1995.

Waldmann, Peter, and Ernesto Garzón Valdéz. *El poder militar en la Argentina, 1976–1981*. Buenos Aires: Editorial Galerna, 1983.

Walker, Thomas W., ed. *Nicaragua: The First Five Years*. New York: Praeger, 1985.

Ward, Chris. *Stalin's Russia*. 2nd ed. New York: Oxford University Press, 1999.

Weber, Henri. *Nicaragua: The Sandinista Revolution*. Translated by Patrick Camiller. London: Verso Editions, 1981.

Weeks, Gregory. *The Military and Politics in Postauthoritarian Chile*. Tuscaloosa: University of Alabama Press, 2003.

Weitz, Eric D. *A Century of Genocide: Utopias of Race and Nation*. Princeton, NJ: Princeton University Press, 2003.

Welch, Claude E., Jr. *NGOs and Human Rights: Promise and Performance*. Philadelphia: University of Pennsylvania Press, 2001.

Welch, Richard E., Jr. *Response to Revolution: The United States and the Cuban Revolution, 1959–1961*. Chapel Hill: University of North Carolina Press, 1985.

Weschler, Lawrence. *A Miracle, a Universe: Settling Accounts with Torturers*. New York: Pantheon Books, 1990.

The White Book of the Change of Government in Chile: 11th of September. Santiago: Empresa Editora Nacional Gabriela Mistral, n.d.

Wickham-Crowley, Timothy P. *Guerrillas and Revolution in Latin America: A Comparative Study of Insurgents and Regimes since 1956*. Princeton, NJ: Princeton University Press, 1992.

Wilkinson, Daniel. *Silence on the Mountain: Stories of Terror, Betrayal, and Forgetting in Guatemala*. Boston: Houghton Mifflin, 2002.

Wilson, Richard. "Prosecuting Pinochet: International Crimes in Spanish Domestic Law." *Human Rights Quarterly* 21, no. 4 (1999): 927–79.

Winn, Peter, ed. *Victims of the Chilean Miracle: Workers and Neoliberalism in the Pinochet Era, 1973–2002.* Durham, NC: Duke University Press, 2004.

Woetzel, Robert K. *The Nuremberg Trials in International Law.* New York: Praeger, 1962.

Woodhouse, Diana, ed. *The Pinochet Case: A Legal and Constitutional Analysis.* Oxford: Hart, 2000.

Wright, Thomas C. *Landowners and Reform in Chile: The Sociedad Nacional de Agricultura, 1919–1940.* Urbana: University of Illinois Press, 1982.

———. *Latin America in the Era of the Cuban Revolution.* Rev. ed. Westport, CT: Praeger, 2001.

Wright, Thomas C., and Rody Oñate. *Flight from Chile: Voices of Exile.* Albuquerque: University of New Mexico Press, 1998.

Wyden, Peter. *Bay of Pigs.* New York: Simon & Schuster, 1979.

Young, Kirsten A. *The Law and Process of the U.N. Human Rights Commission.* Ardsley, NY: Transnational Publishers, 2002.

~

Index

255

~

About the Author

Thomas C. Wright is professor of history at the University of Nevada, Las Vegas. His primary research interest is twentieth-century Latin American political history. His books include *Latin America in the Era of the Cuban Revolution*, revised edition (2001); *Flight from Chile: Voices of Exile* (coauthor Rody Oñate, 1998); *Food, Politics, and Society in Latin America* (coeditor John C. Super, 1985); and *Landowners and Reform in Chile: The Sociedad Nacional de Agricultura, 1919–1940* (1982). Two of these books have appeared in Spanish translation. He has published several chapters and proceedings as well as articles in *Hispanic American Historical Review*, *Journal of Latin American Studies*, *Journal of Church and State*, *Latin American Research Review*, and other journals.

LATIN AMERICAN SILHOUETTES

Editors: William H. Beezley and Judith Ewell

For la Patria: Politics and the Armed Forces in Latin America
    By Brian Loveman
The Politics of Antipolitics: The Military in Latin America, Third Edition
    Edited by Brian Loveman and Thomas M. Davies Jr.
Argentine Caudillo: Juan Manuel de Rosas
    By John Lynch
The Women's Revolution in Mexico, 1910–1953
    Edited by Stephanie E. Mitchell and Patience A. Schell
Gringolandia: Mexican Identity and Perceptions of the United States
    By Stephen D. Morris
Real Life in Castro's Cuba
    By Catherine Moses
Brazil in the Making: Facets of National Identity
    Edited by Carmen Nava and Ludwig Lauerhass Jr.
Mexico in the 1940s: Modernity, Politics, and Corruption
    By Stephen R. Niblo
Feeding Mexico: The Political Uses of Food since 1910
    By Enrique C. Ochoa
Impressions of Cuba in the Nineteenth Century: The Travel Diary of Joseph J. Dimock
    Edited by Louis A. Pérez Jr.
Cantinflas and the Chaos of Mexican Modernity
    By Jeffrey M. Pilcher
The Divine Charter: Constitutionalism and Liberalism in Nineteenth-Century Mexico
    Edited by Jaime E. Rodríguez O.
Myths, Misdeeds, and Misunderstandings: The Roots of Conflict in U.S.-Mexican Relations
    Edited by Jaime E. Rodríguez O. and Kathryn Vincent
The Origins of Mexican National Politics, 1808–1847
    Edited by Jaime E. Rodríguez O.
Integral Outsiders: The American Colony in Mexico City, 1876–1911
    By William Schell Jr.
The French in Central America: Culture and Commerce
    By Thomas D. Schoonover
The Tale of Healer Miguel Perdomo Neira: Medicine, Ideologies, and Power in the Nineteenth-Century Andes
    By David Sowell
Based on a True Story: Latin American History at the Movies
    Edited by Donald F. Stevens
Cuban and Cuban-American Women: An Annotated Bibliography
    Edited and Compiled by K. Lynn Stoner, with Luis Hipólito Serrano Pérez
Patriotism, Politics, and Popular Liberalism in Nineteenth-Century Mexico: Juan Francisco Luca and the Puebla Sierra
    By Guy P. C. Thomson with David G. LaFrance
A Parisian in Brazil: The Travel Account of a Frenchwoman in Nineteenth-Century Rio de Janeiro
    By Adèle Toussaint-Samson
    Edited and introduced by June E. Hahner
Argentina: The Challenges of Modernization
    Edited by Joseph S. Tulchin with Allison M. Garland
Cuba and the Caribbean: Regional Issues and Trends in the Post–Cold War Era
    Edited by Joseph S. Tulchin, Andrés Serbín, and Rafael Hernández
State and Society in Spanish America during the Age of Revolution
    Edited by Victor M. Uribe-Uran
Disorder and Progress: Bandits, Police, and Mexican Development
    By Paul J. Vanderwood
Hacienda and Market in Eighteenth-Century Mexico: The Rural Economy of the Guadalajara Region, 1675–1820
    By Eric Van Young
Latin America in the Middle Period, 1750–1929
    By Stuart F. Voss
Repression, Resistance, and Democratic Transition in Central America
    Edited by Thomas W. Walker and Ariel C. Armony
Vagrants and Citizens: Politics and the Masses in Mexico City from Colony to Republic
    By Richard A. Warren
On the Border: Society and Culture between the United States and Mexico
    Edited by Andrew Grant Wood
Revolution in the Street: Women, Workers, and Urban Protest in Veracruz
    By Andrew Grant Wood
State Terrorism in Latin America: Chile, Argentina, and International Human Rights
    By Thomas C. Wright